Everybody's Bishop

The Rt. Rev. Samuel Fallows, D.D.

Everybody's Bishop

Being the Life and Times of
The Right Reverend SAMUEL FALLOWS, D.D.
By his daughter ALICE KATHARINE FALLOWS

ILLUSTRATED

J. H. SEARS & COMPANY · INC · NEW YORK

COPYRIGHT, 1927, BY

J. H. SEARS & CO., INCORPORATED

MANUFACTURED COMPLETE BY THE

KINGSPORT PRESS

KINGSPORT, TENNESSEE

United States of America

TO

ALL THE FRIENDS

OF

EVERYBODY'S BISHOP

ACKNOWLEDGMENT

This is the story of a man. Neither in intention nor in literary form is it a conventional history loaded with names, dates, petty events and footnotes. It is an effort to portray to to-day's generation the picture of a powerful and vivid personality which profoundly influenced the Middle West for the greater part of a century. What spiritual forces converged in this personality, what extraordinary patterns they assumed, over what worlds of thought and action they played and how they became a dominant power for Liberalism, Open-mindedness and Justice—these are our themes.

To save the reader any break of thought where a daughter's research ends and her recollection begins, the narrative has been kept in the third person throughout. The back trail over father's long life could never have been traversed without the constant aid and guidance of his old friends. Thanks are therefore due to a host of them whose mere names, listed here, would make a tedious catalogue. His boyhood companions, his dentist, his baker, his shoemaker, the hundreds of boys he brought through to clean manhood, "Bathhouse John" and all the other delightful figures of the old Chicago days have chipped in precious items for this story. Where the contribution of each one begins and ends, I am unable to say; but I know that each has added a dash of flavor to these pages.

First of all I wish to express my profound gratitude to Professor Walter B. Pitkin of Columbia University, without whose constant aid and inspiration, this book could not have been written. I am deeply indebted to George I. and William H. Haight of Chicago, in whose office the book was first conceived and blocked in; to Dr. William A. Freemantle, of Philadelphia, for his untiring help in the

preparation of the Church section and for proof reading; to Bishop
Robert L. Rudolph of Philadelphia; Bishop Willard Brewing,
Bishop Robert W. Peach, Rev. William Tracy, Rev. Everett J. S.
Sonne, Dr. William R. Collins, the present Pastor of St. Pauls; to
the loyal members of that Church, one and all, to the other friends
who have freely given their time; and to Dr. William S. White,
whose substantial aid has carried me through many a month of
literary work.

In the long task of collecting and interpreting historical material
I have been most ably supported by Dr. Louise Phelps Kellogg, who
read and listed all of Father's correspondence, to Rev. Howard A.
Leeper, Mrs. Edward W. Bemis, County Commissioner, to my
niece Annette Richards Fallows, to my brother Edward whose careful revision has made the book what it is; and to the rest of my
family.

For the checking of assembled facts and general editorial reading
I owe much to Mr. M. A. De Wolfe Howe, Dean Lewis of Lewis
Institute, Professor William L. Bailey, of Northwestern University,
Professor Carl Russell Fish, Professor Julius A. Olson, Dr. E. A.
Birge, former President of the University of Wisconsin, Mrs.
Wilkinson Collins, Anne Higginson Spicer, Mrs. Edward Simmons,
Gen. James E. Stuart, Mrs. Dora L. North, Mrs. Inez J. Bender.
Hardly less valuable has been the encouragement of the editors of
all of the Chicago papers; of Harry Hansen, now of the *New York
World,* and Karl E. Harriman editor of *The Red Book.*

The Wisconsin State Historical Society of Madison, the Chicago Historical Society and the Chicago and New York Public
Libraries have given their aid at every turn. For the mass of Civil
War letters and documents, collected with much labor, I must thank
Hosea Rood, Patriotic Instructor of the Grand Army of the Re-
public, who devoted many weeks to this task. And for considerable
light on several periods in father's Chicago activities, I am under
obligation to United States Senators Charles S. Deneen and Richard
Yates, Melville E. Stone; Dr. Charles O. Brown and T. Hamilton
Lewis.

Then there are also the Hon. Frank Orren Lowden, Vice President Charles G. Dawes and his brother Rufus, Chief Justice Taft,

General Pershing, the late Fred B. Upham, Bishop W. F. Mc-
Dowell, Dr. Shailer Matthews. Dr. William E. Huntington, Frederick D. Underwood, Alexander Revell and many others who have
added, now a mite and now a monument, to the whole.

This book, is, I hope, the essence of those many friendships
which were, perhaps, the greatest single glory, as they were the
greatest joy, of my father's career.

A. K. F.

CONTENTS

PAGE

PRELUDE 1

PART I

SAMMY FALLOWS' ENGLAND

CHAPTER
   I. A Dye-ditch in Pendleton 5
  II. An Ebony Ruler in Warrington 15
 III. Topsy-turvy Forty-eight in Manchester 18
 IV. Exodus 26

PART II

PIONEERING

    I. Creaking Wheels 35
   II. England in Wisconsin 41
  III. A Breeze-shaken Soul 49
  IV. Lions in the Path 62
   V. More Lions 69
  VI. Pegging Away 81
 VII. A Dollar's Worth of Education 86

PART III

THE BATTLE GROUND OF YOUTH

    I. Chaos 99
   II. Lost—a Dauphin: Found—a Lady and a Cause .. 108
  III. The Great Discovery 113
  IV. The Lord Said "Samuel" 120
   V. The Merry-go-round 123
  VI. A Shaping Wheel 133
 VII. Lucy Plays the Seraphine 141
VIII. A Man Comes Forth 146

xi

CONTENTS

PART IV

HE ESTABLISHES HIMSELF

CHAPTER   PAGE

I. SAMUEL PLANTS GUNPOWDER 153

II. HE WINS A VICTORY 156

III. HANDY MAN OF A MUSHROOM UNIVERSITY 161

IV. WEDDING AND WAR 167

V. A HARVARD TRANSFER 170

VI. DRIED APPLES, A BUNDLE AND A HAPPY ENDING 174

PART V

FORTH TO WAR

I. BURYING AND MARRYING IN OSHKOSH 181

II. BATTLES OF THE LORD 185

III. THE CHAPLAIN LEARNS TO LEAD 194

IV. HE COMES SINGING OUT OF HELL 204

PART VI

THE BATTLES OF PEACE

I. A CURTAIN RAISER 213

II. A SUPERINTENDENT MAKES HIS OBJECTIVE 219

III. THE SEEDS OF CHANGE 232

IV. A METHODIST GOES HALFWAY 239

PART VII

BISHOP IN A CHURCH

I. COLLEGE PRESIDENT 249

II. DR. FALLOWS GETS A TOE HOLD 253

III. BEES, RAMS, LUCY FALLOWS AND THE APOSTOLIC SUC-
CESSION 257

IV. THE BIBLE, BERNHARDT AND A SHOE CLERK 264

V. THE BISHOP STARTS HIS BUSINESS GOING 272

VI. A WHIRLWIND CRUSADE 274

VII. KEEPING STEP 280

VIII. IN TRAINING FOR TROUBLE 290

IX. HE MEETS HIS VESTRY 299

CONTENTS xiii

PART VIII

THE PULPIT IN THE MARKET PLACE

CHAPTER PAGE

I. Joy in the Morning 305
II. The Cheerful Giver 307
III. The Conquest of the Boy 311
IV. He Takes Up the Cudgels for Labor 318
V. The People's Institute 321
VI. The World's Fair 323
VII. Bishop's Beer 327
VIII. The Journalist 336
IX. He Demonstrates Brotherhood 346
X. The Coal Strike 351

PART IX

THE VELVET YEARS

I. Seventy Years Young 357
II. The Clearing House of Sorrow 363
III. A Golden Wedding and a Vacation 379
IV. Santa Claus and Sandwiches 381
V. Lucy Fallows Goes 386
VI. The Old Order Changeth 389
VII. Militant and Triumphant 391
VIII. A Shift of Base 400
IX. Taft and the Empty House 403
X. We That Are Strong 405

PART X

HE GOES SINGING DOWN THE HILL

I. At the Top of the Hill 411
II. His Westminster 423

Appendix
    Chronology 431
    The Reformed Episcopal Church 439
    Index 445

LIST OF ILLUSTRATIONS

PAGE

The Rt. Rev. Samuel Fallows, D. D. ....*Frontispiece*

Market Place, Manchester, England 22

The Free Grammar School, Manchester, England 30

The Erie Canal, and the Little Falls on the Mohawk River 46

State University, Madison 62

Negro Hucksters in the Civil War 78

Camp Randall, Madison, Wisconsin 110

An old daguerreotype 126

State Capitol at Madison, Wisconsin 142

Gone! 158

Great railway station at Chicago 174

Bishop Fallows' church 190

At the Columbian Exposition 206

The Homestead strike 222

Two of Bishop Fallows' activities in social service 254

The Bishop and his beer 270

Every door a saloon 286

Bishop Fallows and the son of General Grant 318

In the Philippines 334

The golden wedding 358

Veterans of two wars 366

The unveiling of the Grant Memorial 382

One of his last sermons 398

Bishop Fallows' funeral 414

Everybody's Bishop

———

*"I should be contented if I could talk
patriotism as Bishop Fallows lives it."*
—THEODORE ROOSEVELT.

PRELUDE

This is the story of a little English boy from the most provincial town of provincial England, who adopted America, and loved her mightily. He was deposited in the wilderness, friendless, poor and chanceless. In the Civil War he dropped his prayer book for a sword and came out a Brigadier General. Then he turned to the schools and helped to make possible for every Wisconsin child a free college education. He entered a new church, and, like an Alexander, went to Chicago in its early days, seeking more worlds, not to conquer, but to serve. For forty-seven years in that most contemporaneous city on earth, what he did and thought was current news. "Town parson," Judge Olson called him when Chicago was a parish of almost three million souls.

He loved like a Bishop and fought like a General. He took his pulpit in his hand and went with it into the market place. He was a pioneer of the Social Gospel. He healed the sick, he wrote books and made societies, invented Bishop's beer and ran a temperance saloon. He was President of a college, a patriot always on duty and a champion of every under dog. Presidents and convicts, Jews and Gentiles, Negroes and Chinamen, prohibitionists and dipsomaniacs, cub reporters and stray cats—all were his friends.

How he lived and laughed, worked and loved—God first, Lucy next, then all humanity; how he was ferment in the great Western development, part of its yeast and part of its bread; how he battled for the Chicago not made with hands; how the fight of a happy warrior against provincialism made him Everybody's Bishop, is the tale of a triumph of a personality that used obstacles as hurdles and defeats as opportunities.

1

PART I

SAMMY FALLOWS' ENGLAND

CHAPTER I

A DYE DITCH IN PENDLETON

"Dare you, Sammy! Dare you! Dare you to jump it!"

Sammy Fallows stood at the edge of the "Black Ditch" and turned an ear to the united voices of his three classmates from Bow-legged Dicky's Parish School.

He was caged in provincial England, in provincial and delightful Pendleton, in a six-year-old body subject to the laws of gravitation. But he was as eager as Columbus to prove to himself and the boys that the world, bounded on four sides by the town limits and the cautions of his parents, was not flat but full of daily spice and adventure.

Sammy glanced into the Black Ditch carrying off the spotted waters of a dyehouse. He stole a look at the safe bridge a few feet off and at smoky Manchester an omnibus ride away, Manchester, whose modern history began with William the Conqueror. Bow-legged Dicky, his teacher, had said so, that very afternoon. Well, he might never see Manchester again. The other bank was a continent away, at the very least.

If one did not reach it—But William the Conqueror! Sammy squared his sturdy little shoulders, shook back his black hair, set his fighting Norman jaw, and turned on his companions the gay, vivid blue eyes which were the Irish fourth of him. He waved them a careless hand, tensed his six-year-old legs and jumped—short.

He landed over his head in the variegated water. His chastened comrades fished him out and stood about him

5

aghast. The dye waters had made him pink, green, blue and yellow.

"Looks like a flower garden," volunteered the first comforter.

"No, a rainbow," amended the second.

"Glad I ain't 'im," said the third, which was a small boy's Pendleton equivalent for "Gee," in 1841.

Samuel, poor little human Joseph's coat of many colors, dripped his mottled way homeward through the village street —past the Priory sacred to Sir Elkanah Armitage, past the mill on Douglas Green, the "White Slave Factory." They gobbled up children there, boys and girls, and turned them out years later "Douglas Greeners," deformed, stunted men and women, crippled by terrible work and bad food. What if they should think he was a charity child, reach out a giant hand from the door and catch him?

Perhaps Mr. Bradshaw, a nice, kind man who wrote railway guides, would protect him. He had ha' pennies for good boys. This was his corner. No sign of him or of the other three from Bow-legged Dicky's school, either. Sammy felt alone in the universe. He ran and ran until he reached his own back door. He burst in on Anne as if all the furies were after him.

Anne was his mother. She rubbed and she scrubbed him. She spanked him, clothed him in fresh garments and sent him forth, looking, in spite of her best efforts, like a badly decorated Easter egg.

"Sammy," she said with the wrath of the too greatly tried, "don't ever do that again."

"No, ma'am," said Sammy.

He did not. He had learned obedience under the rod. But trailed once more by his awe-struck comrades, he marched back to the scene of his Waterloo. He stood on the bank a moment, weighing the risk of being dyed for life. Then, with the faith of those to whom a handicap is anathema, he jumped the stream successfully, not merely once, but back again for luck, to the thrown-up caps of his gallery and the sweet sound of their admiring shouts.

Samuel always had a gallery. He drew the other children as a jam pot draws the bees, and the group he led was always a happy group. The small boy was predestined to fight provincialism, if provincialism can be defined as anything which impedes the free movement of body, mind or spirit.

Before he was a day old, Anne caught him beating at his mummy-like baby wrappings with impotent little fists. When she drew him close and stilled his first lusty cry for food, the twelve-inch bundle seemed to have a vitality and decisiveness which none of her other babies had had. Anne, big mother soul in a dynamic little body, was greatly experienced in babies. She had had ten. Six had been carried, with tears, to the churchyard. Two boys and a girl had survived the terrible ordeal which the accepted baby hygiene made of infancy in those days.

Samuel, the tenth, had come to stay. She realized that. She also had a conviction that he would keep her as busy as all the other nine together did. In this he never disappointed her from the time he could toddle.

Before he was two, a great storm swept over Pendleton, uprooting trees and blowing down houses. At the height of it the Fallows' chimney rained down bricks. Samuel's exploring urge drove him to the fireplace to investigate as fast as two-year-old feet could navigate. Anne's hand withdrew him just in time to save his head from being smashed like a cockleshell, as he thrust it up the chimney to see what was throwing down the bricks, anyway.

Anne kept a mental calendar of Sammy's life, based on events in the Royal family, which she admired very much. He was born, for instance, on the thirteenth of December,

1835. She dated that by the fact that Thomas, her husband, was always talking about something called the Municipal Corporations Act that year, but more picturesquely by the fact that Queen Victoria, a much-bemothered girl of sixteen, whom she adored afar off, was confirmed then, at the Chapel Royal, St. James, with much ceremony.

She kept track of the dye-ditch episode because Queen Victoria's second child, the Prince of Wales, was born at the same time.

But, dear me, no proper Royal family could furnish events enough to keep pace with the adventures which one small Pendleton Columbus could achieve. Anne gave up her calendar after a while and simply took things as they came. In an old England of ordered ways and social paths beaten out by the customs of centuries, Samuel turned every day of his childhood into a swift-moving colorful drama and made it his mother's chief occupation to guess what he would do next.

She was really a wonderful person for a little boy to have as his own. She knew the most beautiful stories. When she smiled, her face went all crinkly, like the water of the big ship canal as the sun struck it. She was half North of Ireland, with more than a touch of Scotch farther back. She had the blessed sense of humor which has saved more days than most armies. Her voice always held a crooning note from having sung to so many babies. It seemed to heal the wounds of a little boy's spirit, even when his body was smarting from a well-deserved punishment.

Anne was the dominant figure in Sammy's early childhood. Thomas, his father, helped to make her so. He was a respected man in the community. Authoritative and conventional, his opinion carried weight. But inside his own four walls, he liked to delegate authority. He was the kind of father who usually answered to his children's requests:

"Ask your mother." No special instinct for adventure drove him on. He liked things as they were—even toothaches.

That seemed to Sammy to be carrying it a little far. He was just beginning to read, and his father was pacing the floor when he spelled out an advertisement in a paper. A man had invented something new for toothache, something to use yourself. You put it in the hole soft and it hardened —a self-stopper. The ache went. The tooth was saved. Great!

Sammy rushed to his father with the advertisement. Thomas read it and delivered his ultimatum: "I'd sooner keep a toothache I'm acquainted with than try this new-fangled contraption."

If a father's attitude was like that, he could not be counted upon for adventures, of course. But Anne could.

Daniel, his brother, could too. The love of the sea was in him. The big brother used to thrill his little brother on their walks to Manchester with his idea of life on the briny deep.

The dye ditch was merely the beginning of Samuel's excitements. Before he had finished his seventh year, he had pulled the whiskers of death at least twice. His teacher, in an unguarded moment, had impressed upon him the motto: "A habit of moving quickly is another way of saving time."

He remembered it in season and out. Practicing this motto one day when he was fearing a tardy mark at school, he swung around a corner at terrific speed and found himself under the feet of a horse ridden by a jockey leading another horse. The small boy escaped with a mere break of the orbital bone. But it left as its mark a furrow between his eyes, which he very much disliked because it made him look stern when he felt kind.

The accident which so nearly finished his career also ended the privilege which jockeys of that time enjoyed of riding their horses on the broad sidewalks of the town, and saved future little schoolboys from being frightened out of their five senses.

His second escape from an untimely end followed soon. Rushing into the house one afternoon, he eased a great thirst, after a strenuous game, with what he supposed was milk, but which was, instead, sugar of lead, carelessly left on the kitchen table. A very large dose of mustard and water, promptly administered by his frantic mother, saved him from the logical consequences of the dose, but left him with an abiding distaste of mustard combined with water.

With death lurking around corners and sitting on kitchen tables, Samuel's inquisitive little mind turned quite naturally to the life to come. It seemed best to be prepared.

At seven he felt a strong desire to be a Christian, but not in the Church of England way. His parents, born, baptized, confirmed and married in that communion, had become possessed by a desire for more warmth and less formality in their religion. They had gone pioneering into the Wesleyan Methodist Church five years before Samuel was born, fixing thus the form of his first religious expression and providing an inherited reason also why the liturgy of the older church drew him later to itself again.

Christianity, the Methodist way, was a state of discipline well calculated to keep a seven-year-old from any undue introspection or religious priggishness.

The small boy joined a class which met at the home of the senior minister, Rev. Thomas Nightingale, on the Sabbath morning early—very early, for it met before breakfast. At nine o'clock he went to Sunday school, at half-past ten to the morning service, after that to another class, again to Sunday school at half-past two and then to the evening service at six o'clock.

No lazy boy could hope to be a Methodist Christian in the town of Pendleton!

Sunday was a day apart, with no likeness at all to other

days. Even Samuel's eager week-day pace had to be tamed
to sober slowness for the walk to the Brunswick Street
Chapel. The sermons, often with no apparent terminal
facilities, were a test of endurance. During one of these
endless discourses he turned and twisted and squirmed and
squirmed and twisted and turned so conspicuously that his
mother was obliged to lead him out of church and convince
him by "muscular Christianity," applied where it would do
the most good, that even seven-year-old Christians must seem
to listen to the preacher, whatever they might be thinking.

The lesson had two results. It gave Samuel ever afterward a lively sympathy with little folks in church. It also
gave him a childish ideal, made actual in mature practice,
of what a minister with a whole congregation at his mercy
ought to be:

"Wide-awake," he said long afterward, "very active, full
of gestures, and very short in his discourse, with the 'amen'
near enough the 'firstly' not to make his hearers feel that
eternity had slipped in between."

School was accorded by Samuel's parents the reverence of
the hungry who have not had as much as they wanted of
it. They fed him early into the educational hopper, which
was designed to turn out pattern Englishmen, cut on the
same lines, thinking the same stereotyped thoughts, as far
as conscientious professors could manage it.

The favorite procedure in all the first stages of school
life was to birch the pupils through reading and writing and
figuring into a decent conformity to unoriginal thought and
action. Samuel was birched according to several different
techniques.

The first was applied by Mr. Richard Maymon, "Bow-
legged Dicky," so called by his pupils for obvious reasons.
He taught the parish school of Pendleton (connected with
St. Thomas Church) which Samuel attended, though his

parents no longer belonged to the Church of England. "Bow-legged Dicky" was a good teacher, according to English standards, but a very severe one, with a sense of humor that broke through at unpredictable intervals.

His unspared rod on the hands and backs of his pupils beat in many useful things besides grammar and arithmetic —punctuality, for example. One noon, Samuel, who was like a colt in his love of swift movement, took a half-mile run from the schoolhouse, for the sheer love of it. He returned late, a little after one, and, though entering with the rest, was spotted by his teacher and ordered to hold out his hand. There was a firm belief, apparently never tested, among the pupils that a horsehair put on one's hand would split the cane as it came down. Samuel shared in this faith, but alas, he had no protective horsehair in his pocket, so he had to take his punishment unmitigated—but he kept his faith in magic.

Alertness of mind was another thing that "Bow-legged Dicky" encouraged, anticipating, perhaps, the alertness tests of the present, which farm hands pass and college professors fail in. Just before school closed, he gave out questions in mental arithmetic and rewarded the pupil who answered ten questions most promptly with a ha'penny. In these exercises, Samuel shone.

One day he answered thirty questions in succession and was taking home three ha'pennies, feeling immensely rich. Mr. Maymon, with one of his rare bursts of humor, called him back to suggest that he open a bank account with the amount. But so overpowered was Samuel by his sudden wealth that he never even recognized the suggestion as humorous.

During school hours Samuel trotted obediently along the appointed way and took his birchings as they came. But out of hours his initiative and his love of fun had their innings, usually with his brother Willie, Samuel's shadow.

The two had much business together. They played decorous games in front of the house. Back of it—back for strategic reasons—they ate veal and ham pies and gooseberry tarts, the last word in childish dainties, filched from sister Anne.

"Bell-horse Day," the first of May was a charming time. All the country vehicles were made beautiful with flowers. The horses, gayly caparisoned, had sweet-toned bells upon the harnesses which gave the day its name. It began a strenuous week for Willie.

Afterward he had to play horse for hours at a time covered with an old piece of red cloth, ringing the big dinner bell and wearing an ignominious wreath of English posies around his neck, while Samuel drove him up and down and up and down.

A troop of Hussars, passing along the street one day, left consequences of another kind in their wake. The left sleeves of their coats hung loose. Samuel was immensely interested to know that these soldiers, summoned suddenly to action in the Battle of Waterloo, had had only time to put their right arms into their sleeves and, fighting one-armed in the great battle, had chosen to perpetuate the incident in their uniforms. On the moment, he staged a one-armed fight. But Willie, playing Napoleon in a sad reversal of a miniature Waterloo, felled Samuel in the first round and left him with an aching head and a conviction that two-armed fighting was good enough for any man outside the army.

Samuel had to be an example to Willie, of course. Occasionally the small boy forgot, as on that sorrowful day when, returning late from school, he found he had missed the visit of an uncle with one leg, who had lost the other at Trafalgar fighting with Lord Nelson. This hero had spent the whole afternoon telling hair-raising tales of his eventful life.

Could an eight-year-old be blamed for weeping and weeping, until Willie yielded up a sweet little sticky wad of "hard mixture" he had been hoarding and offered it on the altar of brotherly comfort?

The Southport excursions were the red-letter days of all the rose-tinted days, rare because the trip to the little seaport was rather costly for a family of seven. Willie and Sammy were brought nearer together than ever by them in the close communion of the same thrills.

The greatest of these was donkey riding. The two boys would sit side by side on one of the uncertain little beasts, the game being to stick on as long as possible. It ended in delicious terror when the donkey's rear end rose and landed them both in the soft sand. They crawled out of it with a whoop and got at the sport all over again.

If the eighteen forties had had a psychologist to rate the traits of people, he would have given Samuel one hundred per cent on cheerfulness, after seeing him through a Southport excursion. These outings began before daylight, so early that it seemed like the night before, and they ended at midnight. The family spirits usually dropped to zero on the last lap of the journey, but, true to his later habit, Samuel was as happy and buoyant at the end of this endurance contest as at its beginning.

With such an attitude toward life, of course his first eight years were just one beautiful day after another.

CHAPTER II

AN EBONY RULER IN WARRINGTON

When Samuel was eight, his father's great moment occurred. Thomas accepted a proposal to operate a large manufacturing plant at Warrington, a city of ten thousand people, ten miles from Liverpool.

He therefore removed his family from the lovely rolling country of Pendleton to the outskirts of Warrington.

To Samuel, it was the exchange of one fairy tale for another. The mill, a large six-story building, not far from the river Mersey, which ambled gently along beside the town, was as good as any castle. It was full of delights all day long, from the moment its six o'clock bell called the operatives, several hundred of them, together in the morning. Sammy and Willie used to think it was calling the name of their older brother John, "John Fallow-e-s, John Fallow-e-s," with a rising inflection on the last syllable of the name.

Samuel flying home at noon, dragged his slower geared little brother by the hand, down the street so narrow that two vehicles could not pass in it. He was so full of life he had to have a steadying little prayer with his mother before she would let him go in to see the three hundred looms at work. This amusement never palled. He could have watched them spin the cotton yarn all day. The ginghams that they wove went mostly to America, and Samuel, standing so quietly watching yard after yard come out of the machine, went with them across the sea as if on a magic carpet.

As far as church went, the change to Warrington was ex-

15

hilarating. The "chapel" attended by the family had a full orchestra, instead of an organ, "including a trombone and big bass viol, violins and wind instruments." Moreover, adjoining the large square pew occupied by the family was another in which sat two lively girls, at whom Samuel, in spite of the Pendleton lesson, made eyes when they made eyes at him, but more discreetly, so that Anne did not catch him at it.

Except for school, Warrington would have been that impossible thing, an ointment without a fly. As it was, the fly almost swallowed the ointment! For poor little Samuel, school was just one kind of severity after another. "Bow-legged Dicky's" variety seemed kindness itself compared with the brand in use at the Warrington "Select" school. The teacher's ebony ruler, eighteen inches long, cutting through the peaceful air, was Nemesis to every shivering youngster.

"It was the teacher's custom," said Samuel in a fragment of autobiography he wrote at eighty, "to have the boys print on large pieces of cardboard, in old English, texts and verses of Scripture, with flourishes all around the letters." One day Samuel was working on the text: "The Lord is good to all and His tender mercies are over all His works." The drawing was first done in pencil and then in ink. In writing "tender mercies," Samuel had much trouble in getting the right slant and thickness to the letters. Having suited himself at last, he put on the ink. The teacher came to his desk and laid a condemning finger on "tender mercies."

"Rub out those letters," he commanded, "and do them better."

"Please, sir," faltered the culprit, "they are inked."

"Inked!" roared the teacher, like the ogre he was. "I'll teach you to ink such work as that," and down came the ruler with tremendous whacks on Samuel's shrinking back.

Out of the pain and the agonizing impotence of those cruel moments Samuel vowed that when he grew up he would pay his teacher back for that punishment, blow for wicked blow.

At least, he thought he was vowing that. What really happened was a connection made deep in his consciousness where the springs of action hide themselves, so that never again could he see or hear or even think of an under dog, four-footed, two-footed or merely an abstract cause, without rushing to its rescue.

CHAPTER III

TOPSY-TURVY FORTY-EIGHT IN MANCHESTER

After two years, Samuel, with the family, left the mercies of Warrington, tender and otherwise, for Manchester, where they spent another two years.

Manchester! Great city, forever spinning at the center of England, spinning cotton, spinning the ideas which England would think to-morrow. What a playground for a little boy who dreamed dreams and loved crowds!

Samuel stood on the bridge above the river Irwell. He lingered beside the great canal which made the city a Venice of trade. His mind went back a thousand years to Agricola commanding a Roman station, forward to his own future.

He was attending the Manchester Free Grammar School, which was not free at all, except to the children of the middle and upper classes. If he were fortunate enough to secure a scholarship, he was to go to Oxford University. He liked the looks of that future.

Very much, also, he liked the present, the games, the fun.

Any Saturday night in Manchester was almost too good to be true. Crowds and crowds on the streets. Every shop wide open. Butchers walking up and down in front of theirs, shouting: "Ladies, make your markets."

Anne was almost always persuaded into buying something. She had a fatal weakness, too, for stopping to look at the nightcaps and the day caps sold on the street, by women, who had spent all the week making them.

Her son liked the rich variegated vests better and the

18

fashionable topcoats. He would have one of them when he went to Oxford.

You could get anything in the world in Manchester on Saturday night. Old umbrellas, very cheap. The work-people stumping along in their clogs bought those. Oranges, "four a penny"—oranges enough for an empire, it seemed to Samuel. But everybody was always eating them every-where in Manchester, on the streets, in the stations and trains, on the boats, in the omnibuses. There were wheels of fortune. Boys twirled them for nuts. But not Samuel. Anne saw to that.

Smithfield Market was the place of a thousand joys. She let him linger there. Exhibitions of wild beasts. Jugglers. Waxwork museums. Bands of music. Color. Noise. People. Excitement. All the things a little boy loved. Yes, Manchester on Saturday night was as exciting as a trip to the moon.

Samuel was beginning to take Manchester birchings and veal pies and gooseberry tarts and Saturday nights and play-mates and the other important things making up a boy's world for granted, when the Fates decided to make an Ameri-can of him.

They took a roundabout way of doing it.

In the first place the small boy chose his ancestors well for the experiment. Martial instincts came to him legitimately, from his father's side, through the members of a Lancashire family, many of whom fought with Wellington on the land and with Nelson on the sea, in the line of the one-legged uncle. Long life, too, was his hereditary portion. His grandfather lived to be ninety-one, his great-grandfather, ninety-six. A canny Scotch caution from his mother's an-cestors put steering gear on an imagination ready for any ad-venture.

Such an imagination was not a usual family trait. Fearon Fallows, the astronomer, was the only one in Samuel's immediate ancestry who seems to resemble him at all. The rest of his relatives appeared, for the most part, perfectly willing to travel the usual road, with never a wistful glance around their blinders at the bypaths.

But Fearon was different.

Son of a weaver, born in 1789, he gained the friendship of the vicar of his town and later of a gentleman of fortune who sent him through Cambridge, from which he graduated as third wrangler, married the daughter of the vicar, and, with her, went off to build an observatory on the Cape of Good Hope with nothing much except a small transit, an altitude, azimuth instruments, a clock, and much determination.

He charted the southern heavens as they never had been charted before; discharged daily a blunderbuss which gave the time to the British ships from India and elsewhere, and enabled them to get their bearings; was made a Fellow of the Royal Society; passed through eleven years of terrible hardship shared by his wife and growing family.

Nothing daunted when stricken with a fatal illness, he was carried on a blanket to his observatory daily to wind his chronometers and clocks until he was too weak to lift his hand. Then he passed out, leaving his mark on the history of astronomy and commemorated by forty lines in the speech of the President of the Royal Society of London, the Duke of Sussex, K. G., as the most distinguished Fellow who had died during the year.

Samuel and Fearon were alike in more than name, pointing perhaps to some unverified Norman ancestor, in common, when their name was de la Falaise. He must have been one of the primitives, this ancestor, so instinct with vitality and the elemental pleasure of merely being, that his very ghost, with armored body and the eleventh-century wind lifting his unhelmeted hair and blowing his beard, could lay a mighty hand on a descendant's shoulder, and say: "Fearon,

Samuel, kin of my kin, I have traveled the starry skies and
the seven seas and tasted of the waters under the earth and
nowhere have I found a semblance of the joy there is in
the mere adventure of living. Drink of life, boys, drink to
the full, down to the sweet bitterness of the last lingering
drop. Drink. Drink. Drink."

Both boys had as sheer, exuberant gladness in the mere unfolding of each succeeding day as if that surcharged Norman
conqueror had stood at their cradles and signed them with
his own invincible joy of living.

But not even a Norman chieftain, dead, could make
Samuel an American. The Fates had another way of turning that trick.

They provided the year, 1848, to turn as many things as
possible topsy-turvy.

In continental Europe thrones tottered and crowns went
rolling in the dust. Great Britain was a caldron of unrest,
Ireland was finding relief for her feelings, at least, in the
Young Ireland Rebellion. England writhed in the throes of
a financial and industrial crisis.

Across the water the first Woman's Rights Convention
was held at Seneca Falls, New York. The first circus
marched into Madison, Wisconsin, and the legislature of the
brand new state, not to miss the procession, adjourned without the formality of a vote.

England's Nemesis took an hour off from the nation one
afternoon in May, focused itself on the affairs of Samuel's
father, still manufacturing and exporting cotton goods,
swept away his profits at a stroke and left him penniless, with
five children on his hands. Thomas dropped on a chair,
utterly crushed, and bowed his head to fate, with his wife,
his daughter and two of his sons as company.

Samuel, doing a double-quick from school, as usual, burst
into the solemn room.

His mother explained. Ruin! Even at twelve he knew what it meant. No work. No food. No Manchester Free Grammar School with Oxford as a goal. Nothing! Like the rest, he was speechless.

Thomas raised his head at last, to face the future from the bottom of the ladder. His glance fell upon a circular tucked half under the big family Bible. He rose heavily, pulled it out with fingers that trembled and, leaning for support on the marble-topped table, began to read aloud about a wonderful place in America called "Ouisconsin," a Paradise, it seemed, ahead of time, with its fertile soil, flower-spangled prairies, lakes as beautiful as the English lakes, and opportunities for making a living growing on every bush.

He had sold ginghams and yarns to America. It seemed a pleasant place. "Perhaps it would be easier to begin again over there?"

He turned his harassed eyes on Anne.

She gathered her daughter, Anne, sitting beside her, a little closer. She thought of venturesome Daniel, her seventeen-year-old, away at sea. She looked at her husband, aged ten years in an hour, at John, the oldest son, able but temperamentally discouraged, at Willie playing quietly in a corner, at Samuel, as eager to be at life as an arrow to speed to its mark.

What had poor racked England to offer the family of a penniless man! Yet how her soul clung to it! It was life of her life, with its friendly neighbors; the jolly little gatherings at the Public House; Chapel, beginning the long, reverent Sunday; the warm invigorating services of week-day nights—happy, commonplace, pious England of the middle class.

She made the momentous decision, as she did the little ones, with no flurry of emotion. "I think it should be America," she said quietly. "When could we start?"

THE MARKET PLACE, forty years ago.
The Building with the pillars was the Fish Market, pulled down 1873. The Coal Exchange occupies the site.
From a Photograph by Mr. W. Ellis.

MARKET PLACE, MANCHESTER, ENGLAND
Manchester as Sammy Fallows and his family knew it. [*See Page 18*]

Samuel drew a long breath, preserved a dignified pace to the door, the pace prescribed for English Sundays and suitable to ruin. Then the incorrigible young optimist burst through the door and fell with a whoop upon his best friend, perched waiting on the gatepost.

"America!" he shouted as if he had discovered it. "We're going to America!"

Through the days of preparation, Samuel spun about the streets of Manchester like a happy little dervish.

Something called the Chartist Movement was worrying his father dreadfully. The Chartists were to make a great demonstration in London, and nobody knew what would happen. Thomas felt the government of England might fall. He was even afraid of what might happen in Manchester. On the dreaded day when all the shops closed and barred their windows, he took Samuel out into streets as still as Sunday. Nothing happened. The next day he came into the house with the tears streaming down his face, holding the Manchester *Guardian* in his hand.

"England is safe," he cried. "The government has held. Let us pray."

They prayed, but Samuel's mind would keep running off to his own present. It was so exciting. He was having the busiest hours of his young life making tales for the other boys about America, facts being entirely unessential. It was a beautiful game!

And how he was capping climaxes! Daniel, his elder brother, was away at sea, on a sailing vessel that was to round perilous Cape Horn and visit mysterious, beautiful sounding Callao, Peru, for the guano that was worth its weight in gold. He posed as hero material in his little brother's dreams. Never did adventurer have more thrills or hair-breadth escapes than Samuel on his mental trip with Daniel on the merchant ship.

Pouf! What was Callao now, compared to America? He

was in the hero class himself, and all his companions brought offerings and worshiped at his shrine.

He tobogganed from emotion to emotion with a recklessness and enthusiasm that would have brought every schoolmaster's cane in conventional England down upon his back.

The last days came. The placid neighborhood was stirred to feverish excitement by the preposterous daring of this venture of the Fallows family. Wild beasts, wild Indians, everything wild was lying in wait for them in that wild new country. The air fairly rang with dire predictions.

The last Sunday dawned, clear and cool. Anne wept quietly all through the long sermon and Samuel squeezed her hand. In the afternoon his Sunday school teacher gave him a little red hymn book (Wesley's) with his name written in it and an inscription. He had to wipe the tears out of his own eyes with the back of his hand. England was his birthplace. He loved it.

The last day of all was upon them before they knew it. Prayers were offered for them when they started, as solemn as the prayers for those about to die. The whole neighborhood accompanied them down to the fifty-ton barge waiting to take Manchester passengers through the canal to Liverpool.

As many as could took the little water journey with them. Samuel's chum had saved up enough shillings to be of the number, and stood solemnly beside him on the deck while he and Willie said good-by to Pendleton and all the other towns they knew.

At Liverpool the boys forgot their grief, examining the boat for which the Fallows family was booked—the American clipper ship, *Ben Lomond,* with her pointed nose, sharp lines, raking masts and great spread of canvas. Starting with the *Rainbow,* built only five years before in Baltimore for the China trade, the clippers went much faster than the ordinary ships. Samuel, late weaver of tales for his friends about these swift Mercurys of the ocean, was curious to see how much like the stories the real ship was.

The family embarked to a choking chorus of tearful farewells.

Samuel stood on the deck and waved. Something had happened to his eyes, so that his chum was just a bleary blur of gray on the dock, dwindling to a point as the ship receded.

The little boy stood on the deck and waved until it was dark. The mother country had made him English as far as she had gone. But she turned him over to America at twelve years old all boy.

CHAPTER IV

EXODUS

The captain and crew of the *Ben Lomond,* which carried
Thomas Fallows and his family from Liverpool to New York,
had an unusually busy voyage. They had to answer
Samuel's questions. Neptune exacted of the small boy no
tribute of seasickness, so he had all his time to explore the
ship from hold to halyards and to gather information.

He did both thoroughly—after the night of terror in the
Irish Channel, when the ship tossed about like a cork in a
violent storm and a piece of the rigging fell with a terrific
crash on the deck, and Samuel with the rest of the family
cowered in the little cabin, hatches battened down, waiting
for the ship to sink. Thomas prayed and committed his
charges "to the Father of all spirits."

But for the third time in his short life, Samuel cheated
death and with the morning sun and quieter waves was ready
to continue his nautical education. He had been carefully
taught that children should be seen and not heard. But no
one could help making friends with American sailors. They
told him tales, and they sang him chanteys, and they
answered enough questions to fill the dictionary he was to
write later. Even at eighty he remembered that he had an
appetite so voracious that he was hungry for the next meal
before he had finished the one he was eating. The voyage
lasted five weeks and five days, before the sight of Sandy
Hook sent the little boy with all the other passengers, into a
transport of joy. But when the ship docked in New York,

the Captain, who was "a very kind man," and the crew and even the cook still loved Samuel—an acid test, if ever there was one—for the charm of his personality.

New York was seventy-four years younger and slimmer than she is now. Fourteenth Street marked the end of the fashionable residence district, beginning at Bleecker Street.

It was the New York of Lyman Abbott, five days younger than Samuel, with whose path his own was to cross so pleasantly in later years.

The Central Park section of to-day grew a population of untidy goats and untidier squatters, both on a par to the eyes of the fastidious. A few lines of lumbering stage-coaches, within the confines of the city proper, furnished the only means of transportation for the New Yorkers who did not possess their own horses and carriages. Barnum's Museum, Christy's Minstrels and Perham's Panorama were the amusements of the orthodox.

Different though New York was in 1848, with a hint of Dutch stolidity in her architecture and in her gayety, her immortal fascination was the same. Hungry-eyed little Samuel found it a terrible disappointment that the beautiful city should be for him merely a temporary island between two boats. But so far as Thomas and Anne Ashworth were concerned, by the time they had marshaled John and Anne Second and Samuel and William through New York and on to the Hudson River passenger boat bound for Albany, they felt as relieved as Noah when he had closed the Ark on the last animal.

Samuel was never to forget the beauty and majesty of the great river with its looming Palisades, which made his doorway into the new life. The Erie Canal, the next link in the journey, seemed a shining roadway into an enchanted land.

Waiting with the rest of the family at Albany to board the passenger boat for Buffalo, Samuel felt as if the whole world were having a moving day, with the Erie Canal as its destination. At the landing, groups of Germans, Norwegians, Irish, English, Scotch, Welsh and Americans made a mixture of tongues like another Tower of Babel. The vastness of this army of home seekers, who would take the great West and tame it, made him feel suddenly like a Viking of old.

He threaded his way carefully, to avoid the baggage and sprawling babies of the foreign groups usurping the deck of the canal boat, to a point at the rail where he could watch the life of the Canal. Not that canals were new in his experience. Had he not been born so near the famous Manchester ship canal, that his first unauthorized excursions from the Pendleton garden gate had led him to its banks? But this American variety was such a panorama of interesting differences that it kept his brain dizzy, and brother Willie's, too. They grudged every minute Anne made them spend in sleep in the crowded little cabin. Even meals were almost an intrusion.

The canal boats were all towed by horses driven along the bank. Boys no older than themselves managed the motive power like veterans. Samuel and Willie never tired of watching them.

There were eight thousand boys on the Canal, a statistical gentleman on the Hudson River boat had told them.

They rather felt that the eight thousand had a monopoly of bliss. They seemed to lead such exciting lives. Swearing, a forbidden luxury for the brothers, seemed to be one of the necessary accomplishments of canal boys. Their fights were especially enlivening, occurring usually because one boat wanted to get ahead of another at a lock.

Some boats carried freight—all sorts of farm products: wheat, oats, hides, wool, meat, salt, anything that needed to be transported. They took ten days to the trip, had their own horses, usually two of them under the exclusive charge of the tow boys.

The packet and passenger boats went much faster than

the freight, by having relays of fast horses at given points all along the line. An unwritten law gave them the right of way at the locks.

The way the slow boats replenished their larders seemed to the brothers most alluring. Some one on deck would put a piece of money into a potato or apple, throw it onto the bank to a person with food to sell and, flying back, would come bread or vegetables or a chicken.

Samuel turned his pockets inside out to see if he couldn't buy something in this delightful way, but he could not find even a ha'penny.

If he could have, the peddler at the lock selling liniments for man and beast would have disposed of at least one bottle of a much-urged Balsam, because it had the word "magic" before it, and there was something about magic, overt or implied, that Samuel could not resist.

The boat soon became a little world in itself, with the passengers growing friendlier each hour. Evenings, they sang in groups or all together, wordlessly, if they could find a tune familiar to enough of them.

The barrier of nationality was not so great after all. Samuel and Willie and some of the little foreign boys soon invented the game, which could be played in any language, of suspending themselves from the numerous bridges under which they passed, dropping down into the stern of the boat just in time to escape falling into the water—a hair-raising sport, pursued in peace only because the elders had to lie flat on the deck when they came to the low bridges, to avoid being swept into the water, and could not see what their offspring were doing.

The contrasts of Samuel's old and new experiences came home frequently in some occurrence that brought out sharply the difference between England and America. At one point on the way he saw a railroad train, already quite a familiar sight in England. But the engine, he discovered, was very different from the English model which burned coal. It had a chimney constructed to burn wood, very wide at the top. When the engineer and fireman stepped out of the engine cab, he thought he was seeing a couple of members of the House of Lords. They were in full dress regalia, frock coats, tile hats, white gloves and all.

A land agent in much the same impressive array, who had been dispensing information and options to the passengers on Samuel's boat, made merry at his amazement, and explained, with more truth than some of his statements carried, that theirs was the uniform required, and that in America the engineer and fireman of a locomotive were only a degree or two in importance below the President of the United States, himself.

At Cohoes, a good-sized town where the boat stopped awhile, past, present and future came together like a clap of the hand. Samuel had a surprise there.

As a hospitable mill owner showed Thomas and his family through his establishment, Samuel spied some of the goods manufactured in their own mill in Warrington and exported to America, and fell upon them with joy.

Some pretty girls dressed gayly in silk passed the window where their group was standing.

"My girls!" observed the mill owner.

"Your daughters?" asked Thomas politely.

"No, no, my working girls."

"In silk!" exclaimed Thomas, all his English traditions rising in revolt.

"Yes," said the mill owner. "We are prosperous here. We can pay our girls enough to buy silk dresses and other furbelows, too."

Samuel's listening ears pricked up. Working girls in Warrington and Manchester had drab lives and wore dull clothes. Here, in this land of magic, mill hands could have a good time. "Yes, and they deserve it. *Yes, and they deserve it.*" The

THE GRAMMAR SCHOOL AND COLLEGE GATEWAY, LONG MILLGATE.

(From "Manchester, Old, and New," by W. Shaw)

THE FREE GRAMMAR SCHOOL, MANCHESTER, ENGLAND

The famous School at Manchester, where Sammy Fallows dreamed of going, and would have gone, if America had not called him.

[*See Page 18*]

words repeated themselves in the boy's brain. Later, as a champion of labor, he was to express that idea in a variety of ways!

The mill owner did his best to persuade Thomas to settle at Cohoes and engage in business.

He halted awhile between two opinions. Samuel, whom the West was calling with a thousand voices, waited anxiously. The land agent, never very far away from his good prospects, strolled up at the critical moment and began his fluent patter about Wisconsin's advantages. Fertile prairies! Cheap land! Wonderful alien law which gave foreigners citizenship sooner than almost any other state! The unheard-of increase of its population—only 11,000 whites in 1836; 230,915 now. More pouring in, hundreds every day, by way of the Ohio River, or by land in an endless procession of covered wagons.

God's own country would be full before long. It was no time to be a laggard. Did he want to keep this fine boy out of such a place?

The agent put his hand on the place where Samuel's head had been a moment before, and looked blankly at the spectacle of the boy moving on to another sensation, because he knew by the look of his father's face that the argument was won.

Thomas, persuaded anew, said good-by to the cordial mill owner. By this act he turned his back on the thing he could do well, fled to farming, which he never mastered at all, and provided for Samuel an ideal opportunity to develop energy which, in life as well as in mechanics, may be defined as a capacity for moving against resistance.

The journey from New York to Buffalo occupied five days. At Buffalo, busy, heterogeneous and full of foreigners, the Fallows family went aboard the *Hendrick Hudson,* a side-wheeler bound for Milwaukee. In spite of a shift in the cargo, which for the second time since they had left

Manchester all but landed them in a watery grave, the boat arrived safely in the Cream City.

By a curious bit of prophetic coincidence, Samuel's stoutly shod little English feet landed on the Milwaukee dock on the Fourth of July, 1848, the day on which Wisconsin, admitted to statehood in May, had her star formally added to the American flag.

State and boy were to be associated in celebrating many a future Fourth of July, but none could ever quite match the thrill of the first, dedicated to exploring the upper part of Milwaukee, now a solid city, nothing then but a hopeful marsh where he and Willie jumped from hummock to hummock. It pleased them to think that fierce American bogies lived in the marsh. Samuel, still very tippy from the combined motion of all his boats, found all the excitement his soul craved keeping his equilibrium on the wobbly hummocks.

PART II

PIONEERING

"'Tis that man might wander in it
That the world was made so wide."

—WILHELM MEISTER

CHAPTER I

CREAKING WHEELS

After two or three days in Milwaukee, Thomas found a farmer who would transport the immigrants to Bird's Ruins, where the Fallows tribe were to settle. They piled into his wagon all the loose Lares and Penates without which any Englishman is miserable—boxes, bundles, bureaus, stoves, clothes, chairs, dishes, a hand loom, as well as all the invisible hopes and dreams a family was bringing into a new life.

No wonder the load seemed "mountain high" to Samuel, as he and Willie perched precariously on top and the horses started off with an initial flourish that seemed to promise nothing less than a chariot race. The burst of speed lasted only to the outskirts of the town, when both the condition of the roads and the inclination of the farm horses checked it.

Samuel, all agog with the land agent's stories, wished that he could turn into one large ear and one large eye so that no marvel of this new land might escape him. What was his disappointment, then, to find almost nothing to miss!

After England, Wisconsin seemed to him so full of emptiness and creaking wheels that he felt as if the land agent had been perpetrating a huge joke when he told him that he would increase by one lively boy a population of 230,915. One of every five might be a New Yorker, as he said, and one in every thirty a hard-headed Vermonter, and there might be others from every state in the Union. Perhaps the United Kingdom and Germany, in point of numbers, did lead the foreign contingent, but where in the world did they all keep

35

themselves? Did they have burrows under the earth and hide by day, or what?

Mile after mile without seeing a human soul, they bumped into ruts and jolted perilously over the "railroads," facetiously so called, where the swampy portions of the road were filled in with rails and long pieces of timber, and wondered whether their muscles would hold their English bones together on these American roads. Once the two front wheels mired, making the wagon into an unofficial toboggan slide. Sammy and Willie, on top of the load felt as if they were at Southport again on the up-ended donkey, but the horses pulled their burden clear before the topmost passengers quite lost their balance, and rolled with all the rest of the family treasures into the marsh.

Always they squeaked, oh, how they squeaked! Their wheels, like the other American wheels of the time, turning on hubs of solid wood, could be heard half a mile away. Samuel, with the ears of a faun for sensitiveness, rode with his fingers in them half the time, to shut the sound out. The caravan creaked, creaked its way through great stretches of virgin forest; lovely burr-oak openings, with scattering trees and thick underbrush; marshes edged with tamarack and prairies set thick with gay flowers. The Wisconsin scenery was quite up to the specifications of the steamship circular, which had started from Manchester. But, except for scattered farmhouses and a few settlements, there was no trace of human life. Where was that great army of home seekers anyway? Samuel began to feel as if the state were so gigantic that the whole of England would scarcely make it a decent pocket handkerchief.

At Aztalan, one of the small settlements—with the usual huddle of houses, mostly log with clay-plastered cracks but beautifully situated with a gleam of flowing water and curiously shaped hills which the driver said were Indian mounds—the romance of the great Northwest first laid its spell on Samuel.

He sensed that the farmer slapping his reins over the backs of the slow horses might be a mine of information, and climbed down beside him.

For the next hour, listening to his stories, Samuel did not know he was in the Wisconsin of 1848 at all.

He stole through the shadows of a great primeval forest receding step by step as civilization laid a devastating hand upon it. He lived in the day of gay French governors; he shared the primitive thrills of the fur traders under the British governors; he shrank from the Red Man or stalked him, opened the lead mines with him, bled for him when the Black Hawk War, only sixteen years back, dug once and for all the grave of Indian hopes in Wisconsin.

Something elemental in Samuel responded to the driver's story. He felt that he had been present at the dawn of a creation, as Adam might have felt when the world was new. Some primitive need of his soul was satisfied. His spirit was like a homing pigeon. Having no words for such an experience, he sat quiet for as much as five minutes in a trance of contentment after the driver had again given his whole attention to his horses and his blackjack.

Then, as emotion with him had always to have a swift vent in action, he jumped down from the driver's seat, pulling Willie with him, and played Indian, stalking his little brother from the wooded spaces with such realism that Willie's shrieks of pure terror made Anne banish them to the top of the load again.

After three days of this drastic traveling west over eighty miles of road, even the boys were glad to end their journey at Bird's Ruins, about twenty miles east of Madison. It was called Bird's Ruins, they soon found, from a log house, fallen into decay, built and abandoned by Colonel Bird. It was only a town by courtesy—just two or three houses, a store and a tavern, an attempt, not overly successful, to be a center of convenience for a few miles of undeveloped country. Some one with a sense of humor very soon changed its name to Howard City, some one else to Hanchettville, in honor of a public-spirited citizen who contributed a store and a hotel to the town. His geographical immortality was brief, and before long the town became Marshall for keeps, with expanding outlines and a pleasant society.

Sammy and Willie were ready to find any world at all their oyster. Children and dogs made an alluring possibility of Bird's Ruins in the first five minutes. But their mother shaken by the journey almost to jelly and sick for England, had no eyes of faith for the present or the future blessedness of the town. It seemed to her the most God-forsaken of all God-forsaken places. Her heart dropped to her toes to think that this was the goal to which her decision, made so hopefully in Manchester, had brought them.

She would gladly have sat down beside the road and wept. But she made a game of unloading, instead, engaged Sammy and Willie in it as if it were a holiday sport, and flung out her first challenge to the new land to daunt her if it could.

After exploring the beautiful solitude of field and forest about them, she and Thomas selected a spot two miles west of Bird's Ruins.

The eighty acres they appropriated out of Wisconsin's fifty-six thousand and sixty square miles of land were useful rather than beautiful. But they did include a pleasant, sociable little brook, a good companion for a boy, and a picturesque log house on the hill under an apple tree. Forty acres Thomas bought from the government at a dollar and a quarter an acre, the other forty acres from its original owner.

Like many another home seeker of the forties, he had exhausted almost every dollar of his capital getting to this land of supposed milk and honey, a pleasant diet which, from the representations made, he almost believed some attentive angel would feed him from a golden spoon. There was milk and honey, to be sure. But one procured the first, by the labor of his hands and the sweat of his brow, from reluctant cows, the other one took away from wild bees that stung the unwary.

Samuel, the first week after he arrived, could have told you how they stung—in forty-five places at once. Forty-five painful lumps rose on your anatomy and you put on forty-five mud plasters, because the American boy, your guide, so wise in the ways of bees that he never got a sting, told you it was the thing to do.

To pay for part of the land, Samuel's father had to borrow money at an interest rate of twenty-five per cent. It was a small amount he borrowed, but the fear of that interest was to ride the family back, Old Man of the Sea fashion, for a long time to come. It became one of the fixed trials in the small boy's calculations, like the Saturday night bath in the kitchen in the round wooden wash tub used for the family laundry work every Monday morning. Whatever he might want, from a peppermint lozenge to a Latin grammar, he always knew he couldn't have because that everlasting interest had to be paid.

Wisconsin was an earthquake for the Fallows family. Here they were tumbled, almost overnight, out of pleasant, organized, established England, into a raw, inconvenient country where nothing was familiar, not even the language; where nothing was older than the new-laid egg American chickens made such a terrible fuss about.

Frontier grandmothers told Anne that Wisconsin was a Paradise of convenience compared with that of the earlier days when they carried their water from streams, lit their cabins with pine knots, beat off wolves and lived like hermits in a solitude broken only at endless intervals by the Circuit Rider.

Perhaps Anne did bend her back a degree or two less carrying water from inconvenient wells than from streams and rivers and tax her eyes a fraction less sewing or weaving or knitting at night by the light of the tallow dips. But what did those little differences amount to when everything was upside down and wrong side to?

The effect of Wisconsin upon the Fallows family was as if layer after layer of civilization had been peeled off, leaving them stripped to the core; as if the clock of time had suddenly turned them back to a primeval stage. It might be all very well for a human rubber ball like Samuel, who would have bobbed up serenely if the world itself had sat upon him. But Thomas and poor Anne, were sadly battered by that rude frontier life.

CHAPTER II

ENGLAND IN WISCONSIN

The first Summer and Fall in Wisconsin were to Samuel an adventure of incredible freedoms. His first taste of the great out of doors made him heady. He twiddled his delighted little spatulate toes in the dew of Wisconsin dawns and feasted his eyes on golden sunsets and splashed the hours between with the gorgeous colors which only the joy of a surcharged boyhood could supply. He and Willie and Jock, the dog, knew how to make of any free hour out of doors a heaven that angels might envy.

But if his father and mother had had time to keep a diary, their account of those days would have read like the preface to the Day of Doom. The terrible fact was that Thomas was not a farmer, either by nature or the grace of God. He was middle-aged, inflexible by temperament and stunned still by the catastrophe which had pitched him into poverty. Not by hook or by crook could he put on that buccaneer spirit which would have compelled America to come his way. He went at farming faithfully, but without inspiration. The eye of his inclination looked elsewhere. Soils and seeds and plows and harrows spoke a foreign language to his weaver mind.

Fallows means a dweller at the fallow land. But apparently no amount of dwelling "at the fallow land" could make a dyed-in-the-wool farmer of anyone by the name of Fallows. The boys all did something different, when they could. Sister Anne saved the family reputation after a while, but even she did it by proxy. She married a farmer.

41

If Samuel's eyes had been open to heartbreak, as they were after a while, he would have known what it meant when he found his father out in the little shed one afternoon where rubbish was stored, picking at his hand loom with loving fingers, as a musician might touch a broken harp. "No one needs weaving here," ventured Samuel, proud of his knowledge. "Nor the weaver," assented Thomas, and blew his nose very hard, mistaking a bit of a dust cloth Anne had given him for his handkerchief.

No wonder his shoulders bent and his head sagged. Unequipped and uninclined as he was, he had to persuade a reluctant little tract of mother earth with a mortgage on it to yield enough to feed and clothe a group of six human beings and at least one dog. The land was all he had in the world. It was a case of farm or perish, so he and the rest of the family farmed.

Farm or starve meant grueling work for them all. For a little boy of twelve, it involved getting up at half-past five in the morning, or earlier, doing chores, fetching and carrying tools, gathering kindling, helping fell trees, split rails, make fences, grub out roots and lift tons of rock out of a field, stone by stone. After supper it was chores again, and a last fifteen minutes under the stars when a boy's eyes were so sleepy that he could not tell whether the wavering candle he was holding for John to milk by had two flames or one.

Yet this hand-to-hand conflict with nature, which puzzled and worried and baffled Thomas, was tremendously exciting to the growing boy. It was a stirring challenge to something within him which had no tongue. Migration had made him a little unit in that swirling army which a great contagion of enthusiasm had swept out of its usual ruts on a gust of desire for untamed things. The journey from the staid town of Manchester, the stories on the boats, the thrill of the great free West opened Homeric reservoirs in his soul. When he put his plow into the virgin earth, which had been left

untouched since the beginning of time, and saw its sharp
prow cut through the rich black earth as the *Ben Lomond*
had through the sea, his brain almost burst with the thoughts
that came singing into it.

Samuel's little world, with a small log cabin as its center and
the sky and the horizon as its limits, seemed the busiest place
in two continents. What a joy it was, too, with its bees and
rabbits and pigeon shooting and the things that lived in
brooks! Even the smells were delicious, the fragrance of the
hay, of wood when you chopped into it, of the ten-day-old
kittens in a nest of hay, of Bess when you laid your head
against her flank at the morning milking, of the earth after
sunset or in damp places. The moments allowed for play
were few and far between, but when Thomas did say, "Well,
boys, I'll give you an hour off now," how unutterably sweet
it was!

Of course, without Jock, it couldn't have been the same. He
was that paragon, an utterly satisfactory dog. From his
aggressive young nose to his pliant little tail, he embodied all
those traits which Wisconsin required and England did not
provide. He was courageous, aggressive and adaptable. It
was no time at all before he learned to bark his way through
the Lord's Prayer, giving two sharp barks for the "amen,"
with this God-fearing family which invariably began the long
day with morning prayers.

Who, in England, would ever let a dog attend family
prayers? But Anne allowed it here in this beautiful topsy-
turvy America where everybody did what he pleased—after
a ten-or-twelve-hour day of work, of course. Toys, naturally, there were none. Indian plays took the place of bell
horses and Hussars, as materials for amusement, when the
rare hours for play fell from the hands of Thomas. One of
these mock Indian affrays so burned itself into Samuel's
memory that, fifty years afterward, he walked without a mo-

ment's hesitation to the very spot where it had happened, and described the scene.

He and Willie were staging a real Indian drama, with improvised tomahawks, feathers from the family rooster and three little neighbors whose mother was spending the afternoon with the two Annes. Willie was actually having a chance to do some of the scalping himself, instead of presenting his own unwilling locks for the ordeal, when real tragedy crept up on them so stealthily it all but caught them napping. The two small girls and their still smaller brother, playing settlers, were flying over a marshy bit of ground, shrieking rapturously, with Sammy and Willie in full pursuit, when the shriek of the foremost little girl turned to a cry of fright.

In a sudden silence, Samuel heard the rattle he had already been taught to dread and saw in the grass, almost at the feet of the child, the beaded eyes and raised head of a coiled snake.

It was too bad he could not know about that old Norman ancestor of his, to bless him then. Quite automatically, he pulled the small girl, paralyzed with fright, out of danger, seized from the littlest settler the stick with which he had been playing gun, and barefooted and barelegged engaged in a battle royal with Mr. Rattler. Thanks to the God who watches over children, it was the rattler, not Samuel, which was in condition, a few minutes later, for the funeral the five of them thought might be more exciting even than an Indian massacre.

Perhaps the rattlesnake, sacrificed on the altar of its own venomosity, which had served to confirm a habit of bravery in a growing boy, deserved a funeral and even the epitaph written with a charred stick on the smooth side of a piece of hickory bark for headstone.

America's great appeal to a born trail maker like Samuel was that, no matter what you might do, it would be done differently from the way you had ever done it before. Precedents changed overnight, and customs were new every morning. Even going to the store was an event. You took eggs and apples and whatever else you could get from the farm, and traded them for rice and tea and yarn and clothes or any other treasure-trove the general store carried.

"Just like savages," was Anne's comment when, all excitement, her son rushed into the house to tell her about his first trading. His mother was still undetached as a personality, for the small boy, from the things one took for granted, like God and the sunshine and food and the walls of the house. Otherwise, he might have suspected, behind the merry front she turned to every circumstance, the sick longing of her soul for all the things to which life and her love had anchored her. The challenge of an uncharted land, which set Samuel champing at his bit like a mettlesome horse on the *qui vive* for a gallop, was to her a terror and a menace. There was not one single familiar post to tie to.

In little things or big, nothing was the same in this land of upside-downs. There was not even a friendly Public House where you might go when your day's work was done and chat casually with cordial neighbors. People who believed in what they called "Temperance," with a very big T, wanted to brand even a mug of ale as a wile of the devil. Wesley's religion and Wesley's temperance, modified by a previous experience of the Church of England, were good enough for her. No one believed more thoroughly in a devil than she did. She knew his dealings too well. But never had she seen even the tip of his horn dipping at her over the rim of her ale glass.

A queer world, surely. Even the English virtues in which she had trained herself and her family—patience, obedience to custom, cheerful acquiescence in what the upper class handed out, humility, faithfulness to things as they were —were merely handicaps in this new life, which demanded that a man stand alone, with no props of civilization, and, by the sheer audacity of his initiative, trick nature into giving him a living.

As for romantic, gracious, soul-inspiring Queen Victoria, core of some of her sweetest dreams, she was replaced by some one they called the "President." Polk, his name was, now.

How could anyone make a calendar to date by out of the life of a man named Polk? Not she. A President might be elected even from the plain farmers who tip-toed up and down the aisle of the log schoolhouse where service was held on Sunday. Any boy might be President. Samuel! Her mind played with the thought so long that the small boy, working in a corner, asked her what she was thinking about, to make sure she had not gone to sleep over the pan of bread dough she was mixing.

"Oh, about you and Polk and Queen Victoria," she returned, indifferently.

She shook herself together. That would never do. No, no, she had other hopes for that keen-minded little son of hers, who had the gift of speech, she believed—hopes that possessed her whenever she sat still of a Sunday and listened to the God appointed person on the platform who gave her instructions about her soul's salvation.

Sometimes Samuel suspected those hopes. But one had to be very good and very obedient to be a preacher, and he was a long way from either. He was always having little squabbles with Willie and "making up" into better friends than ever, and quite often he forgot his duties as chore boy in attending to more interesting and more personal missions. If he had been any less the objective, wholesome, take-things-as-they-come little youngster that he was, he must have read Anne's heartache between the lines, when she summed up for the family her opinion of America, after she came home from her first "quilting."

The Erie Canal, at Little Falls, on the Mohawk River

In 1848, Samuel Fallows made the trip from Albany to Milwaukee via the Erie Canal.

[*See Page 27*]

"Yes, dears," she concluded, "I know the histories of all those ladies from the cradle up. That's America! Some one you meet in the road for the first time tells you things we in England wouldn't whisper to our mothers on our deathbeds. They put up fences to keep the cows out, not to keep their houses in. Everything is so open. It's as if— as if you were living in a gypsy tent on the side of the road, with the flaps up."

Thomas nodded. He understood. Samuel didn't. He never penetrated below the surface of her humor. He did not realize that in that apparently light-hearted moment the fundamental differences of two civilizations were at grips, that Anne must scrap her very personality to attain that new-world gesture which invites the whole world to sit on its doorstep. He did like gypsying. He thought his mother was paying America a compliment.

He dashed out of the door and turned a somersault to show how much he, too, liked the new country. Then he rushed off to see how his hazelnuts in their green shucks were drying on the sunny sloping shed roof. For it was a specially busy time. Hickory nuts were almost ripe, and the butternuts were just aching to be gathered.

Even if he had missed the homesickness that lay behind his mother's joking words, at that time, he could not see, from the vantage of a grown-up understanding, how he could possibly have evaded the significance of another conversation with Anne, one hot Sunday morning when she stood at the door looking out at the pitiless glare of the raw sunshine and the crude newness of everything.

"Do you remember the Parish Church at Warrington?" she asked her son. It was a beautiful cool mellow place of stained-glass light, where her old allegiance to the Church of England had often drawn her. "The tomb that went back to Cromwell's time? You spelled out the letters in the stone. They'll just be going to our own Wesleyan Chapel,

now, too, sitting in the fine square pews, listening to the
music, that big bass viol, the trombone, the violin. How
you used to love them!"

Service, in Wisconsin, was held in a little log schoolhouse, with earthen floor, slabs of wood set on uprights for
benches, where they all huddled together in a crowded democracy of worship. The congregation raised its voice to
no accompaniment heartily enough, but often out of tune.

Anne dropped to her knees and drew her small son, all
starched up in his Sunday clothes, down beside her. "Would
you not, oh, would you not, Sammy lad, give all the world to
be in Warrington this minute?"

Sammy considered. "If I were there," he decided judi-
cially, "I couldn't hear John give the pitch to the choir with
his tuning fork, and I do like that, you know."

Not until the scene flashed before him out of nowhere, at
a supremely homesick moment of the Civil War, did Samuel
get the key to what Anne was suffering at that moment.
Then he felt that he would give up every hope of promotion
if he could only steal back through the years, catch her out
of her gulf of loneliness onto a familiar little island of love,
and put an understanding arm about her shoulders. But
by that time Anne was a citizen of another country, far, far
older than England, and with much more beautiful music.

CHAPTER III

A BREEZE-SHAKEN SOUL

The thing that pitched Samuel's trembling little soul to the nethermost depths and lifted it to highest heaven was his first camp meeting.

In the curious perspective of memory, he could never be quite sure whether this soul-shaking event occurred during his first or his second year in America. But he was still very new in the land, fumbling about among its strange customs as if he were blindfold, trying to catch its step with all the awkwardness of a very raw recruit.

The hay was in—the only thing the Fallows family had to gather in—so it must have been before Thomas did much planting. Other farmers, long enough in Wisconsin to have crops, had finished harvesting. Lovely September days lapped the countryside in a dream of blue and gold.

On one of these days, Sammy and Willie, coming back from an errand at the village, spied a handbill nailed to a big oak, announcing a camp meeting to be held the next week somewhere in the general direction of Madison. They couldn't stop to see just where, because each was trying to outrace the other home in the effort to score a "scoop."

Samuel won. By the time small Willie panted up, he had delivered the great tidings to the four grown-ups, just ready to sit down to the supper table.

No Methodists could have lived in Dane County even so long as the Fallows family and escaped knowing about the camp meeting—that blessed adventure of the whole year

49

when one waved a wand at the pinching hardships and poverty and repressions of the four seasons in semi-frontier Wisconsin, said begone! and mounted on a spiritual craft which carried its passenger over wastes of icy wrath and tropical vistas of heavenly love.

It was just this emotional aspect of the camp meeting, as Thomas and Anne had gathered reports of it, that gave them pause when their son exploded his torpedo of news.

"I don't know," said Thomas, shaking his head solemnly, "about this camp meeting for us Wesleyan Methodists. They tried it in England, Anne, you remember, not so many years ago, and the men who insisted on keeping it up were put out of the Church. Somehow," he pursed up his lips, "it smacks to me a little of the devil."

"But—but," spluttered Samuel, "it's just a service out of doors, and we had those in England. The women over there spoke and prayed. They do here sometimes at the meeting."

He had vivid memories of that. Many of his English playmates had been Church of England boys, who, making an exception of Samuel, considered all other Methodists heretics, because they had parted from the Church and would as soon worship out of doors as in their own unconsecrated chapels. In this ministry, often a woman's voice was raised to rare eloquence. Anne, herself, sometimes broke into speech.

"A camp meeting is quite all right, father," his son, out of his superior knowledge, went on, "quite——"

Thomas raised his hand. "That will do," he said with finality. "Your mother and I will decide this question."

He turned to Anne, who was looking at Samuel, with a smile of comprehension making lovely every line of her face. She held out her arm, as she sat at the table, and drew the little boy within the circle of it.

"Well, dear," she said to Thomas, smothering her own doubts, "this is America, you know. Everybody goes, even

the Baptists and Presbyterians. I think we might try it
once."

Samuel's noisy delight was soon tempered to practical
ends. The next few days were a delightful whirl of preparation. There was no end to the odd jobs an active boy
could do. He and Willie trotted over to the Knaptons, who
had come from England when they did and settled on the
next section—ten children and the father and mother. Some
of the seven sons and a daughter or two were going to the
meeting, but the stay-at-homes agreed to feed the chickens
and pig and milk Bess and have an eye to things generally.

The really acute problem before the Fallows family was
what they could take to eat. Nobody was living on much
those first hard days in Wisconsin. Fish caught from one's
own stream and cooked without lard or butter, bread made
from meal or flour mixed with a little salt and water, and a
few potatoes made up the usual bill of fare in most house-
holds. Anne and Thomas and sister Anne and John shed
many of their English pounds that first year, because they
knew that little boys could not go too hungry and thrive. So
when there was not enough food to go around comfortably,
the grown-ups suddenly lost their appetites.

Sammy and Willie did the best they could, as camp meeting providers. They brought in wild grapes and plums.
They picked and pared apples until they felt as if the world
was made of apple. Anne denied the family even its semi-
occasional eggs, so as to be able to take a few hard-boiled to
camp meeting.

Samuel knew, of course, that a camp meeting was something arranged for the good of your soul. Souls of those
days were things, not a state of mind nor a segregated bit of
the subconscious. In the household of Thomas, especially,
they were always reckoned with. Samuel was on speaking
terms with his. He heard it prayed for every morning, and

he prayed for it himself every night. It was as good manners to inquire about the state of your soul as of your body. Your body died and was buried after awhile, but your soul went on forever. If it was saved, you were happy. If it was damned, you wandered about in everlasting torment.

Camp meeting was intended to avert just such a misfortune. But the expedition started off on a crisp clear Saturday morning exactly like a picnic. The two Annes sat by Thomas on the wagon seat in front, Willie and John and he, ready to lend a hand with the oxen, perched on the tail of the wagon, with their feet hanging over. The bedding and all the amazing goodies Anne had been able to concoct out of nothing were in the body of the cart. And the souls were in the bodies of the travelers. Thus, all went marching on to grace—goodies, souls and bodies.

John, as happy as the rest that morning, sang a joyful rendering of the dolorous words:

> "Must I be carried to the skies
>   On flowery beds of ease,
> While others fought to win the prize
>   And sailed through bloody seas?"

Samuel, tingling to his finger tips, fell to thinking about the Circuit Rider who was to conduct the revival, a wonderful figure in his imagination. His horse was his home, his saddlebags his baggage. They held everything, from a Bible to linen for binding wounds, when he played Good Samaritan. Heroes they were, Circuit Riders, voices crying in the wilderness, braving incredible danger to carry the Gospel to the unsaved in lonely settlements.

He felt as if Circuit Riders must be a blend of Solomon and Samson. Theirs was the life, a life of thrilling adventure—for all its privations.

One of them, on his circuit, bursting out of the woods at Madison, had preached the first sermon ever preached there, to the men building the Capitol, the sole population of the town. Old Peter Cartwright had baited an audience of desperadoes to fury and, just as they were starting to throttle the life out of him, had overturned the candles and fought his way to safety in the dark. Another, pursued by wolves for twenty miles, had killed one with his bare hands. Another, who could not get the people of a settlement to listen to him because they were expecting Indians any minute and felt that temporal provisions for safety were more important than eternal, were saved because the Circuit Rider made an unscathed way through a forest alive with the red men and brought help, just as the savages were advancing with their tomahawks.

Heroes? Oh, yes! And masters of men. The earlier camp meetings farther south had been stupendous affairs. One of the older visiting preachers at the schoolhouse had been to one and described it to the children. The Circuit Rider summoned his flock to a central point from the area of his whole circuit, a great wheel, a hundred miles, two hundred miles in diameter. They mobilized like soldiers at a general's call, thousands of them. The Circuit Rider made a Christian army of them and sent them back to their scattered homes, no longer isolated units, but bound by common ties, better men and women and better Americans.

Samuel knew that their own camp meeting must be a little affair. They were in a more thickly settled country with camp meetings every twenty miles or so. But he did hope the Circuit Rider would look like a hero.

His thoughts trailed off into the alluring sunshine. It seemed a living thing, as it touched the reddening leaves of the oaks and the brilliant sumac and the goldenrod. The air seemed full of wings—crickets' wings that sang, the wings of a great eagle, motionless against the sky, whirring wings of little feathered things that Jock stirred up, wings of small birds fluttering in the trees. Then, suddenly, the air seemed all vibrant with invisible wings, drawing up his soul to join them on swift white wings of its own—quite up out of all the pleasant earthly region he had known all his life. Like his little seven-year-old self at Pendleton, he felt again the throbbing desire to be a better something than he had ever been before.

"Sammy!" It was sister Anne's horrified voice.

"Sammy Fallows, if you squirm one single inch farther back, you'll be in the deep apple pie!"

Her brother, blessed with the swift power of adjustment which made possible forty moods in forty minutes, grinned a flickery grin, pulled out of his pocket an apple and jumped down to keep Jock company awhile, glad to feel his feet on solid earth again after his strange experience of wings.

Camp meeting proved to be much more than his wildest fancy had painted it. It was a week of amazing days which he hoped might never end. He knew it would be so from the moment they creaked up to the grove reserved for the meeting and found it ringed about with wagons. Oh, the beautiful crowds of people! Samuel had not seen so many since that beatific trip on the Erie Canal.

The neighbors were there in force, the Philander Porters and the Knaptons and the Sardine Muzzys and the Harts and a small, black-haired English lass, who seemed as good at making eyes as the little girls in the Warrington pew next to theirs. Dozens and dozens of other humans all laughing and chattering and pulling lunch baskets about.

The grove was set with rude benches, bare boards on supports. One in front they called the Mourner's Bench. Commanding the seats, under the big spreading tree, was a platform with a sloping roof. There were two tents, one for the ministers, and one for the shelter of the Presiding Elder, the Circuit Rider who was to "run things." The rest of the people were going to sleep on the ground or in the wagons.

That first midday dinner under the trees was to Samuel like a Feast of the Passover and a liberal education, all in one. Twenty or more of the party—it seemed like fifty to him—sat down at a rustic table of boards. He managed to get at the end of his family line, next to a boy from Waterloo, who had a Sun Prairie boy on his other side. Across the table was a Watertown man, who immediately entered into details about the woolen factory there, the only one for miles around, details that made the voice of Thomas, still the weaver, shaky with excitement.

All the towns, Samuel concluded idly, must have been started no later than last month. The men fell to talking about how they ought to be organized and how they oughtn't and what they had found was good and what they hadn't. They talked about Oregon, where slavery was forbidden and about the railroad, soon to push its way out from Milwaukee. They groaned about the eighty miles of bad road they had to travel over to get a market for anything. They pulled Polk to pieces (which pleased Anne) and speculated on what kind of a President Taylor would make if they elected him.

When he was older and wiser, Samuel realized what Thomas might have understood then if anyone had pointed it out to him—what a clever Master Weaver this camp meeting was, catching all the different threads of a hundred different interests, weaving them back and forth into a pattern, merging the differences, standardizing the likenesses, making one fabric out of units as divergent as the poles, which in due time would be the state of Wisconsin.

But the small boy, being too delightfully young for moralizing, gave his tiny threads quite unconsciously into the weaving hand of evolution, by turning from men's dull subjects to good boy talk with his neighbors. He started by telling how much he enjoyed trading. His account of it was not entirely successful. The Sun Prairie boy was very puffy about their storekeeper, the Reverend Silas Smith, eking out a precarious living by storekeeping. The pathos of it was not apparent to the boys. That he had a mighty arm was. Some of the roughs around Sun Prairie were much addicted to whisky and a visit to the store afterward for some horseplay. But the Reverend Silas Smith could always "conquer a peace."

Any boy with half an eye could see that a boy trading at the Sun Prairie store was likely to get excitement any time. Still Samuel wanted to contribute something, so he told about seeing the whisky barrel in their own store, which during the first Winter, was the storekeeper's sole stock in trade. The cautious man was so afraid of having nothing at all to sell that every time he drew out a gallon of whisky he put in a gallon of water. But it froze, so his fear was realized, and he did have nothing after all to sell.

The story, for a camp meeting, compared with that of a ministerial son of trade seemed almost ribald to Samuel after he had told it. He hastened to add that they now had a lodge of the Sons of Temperance.

But the Waterloo boy rather took the wind out of both their sails with his story of the Indians who were accustomed to go through Waterloo with their dead strapped to a pony, to bury them in the Indian burying ground a little beyond Waterloo, and, returning, would take anything they could lay their hands on. Once they had walked off with his family's whole supply of provisions for a week.

When the people gathered on the benches that night for the first service, sensitive little Samuel soon realized that a camp meeting was not a picnic at all, but a very terrible Day of Judgment before the time appointed. The Circuit Rider looked insignificant for the first few minutes, as he stood before them in his shad-bellied coat, with his broad hat laid on a table at his side. None of the heroic deeds the small boy had wreathed about him seemed to fit. No man so slight could hope to strangle wolves or throw an Indian in combat. Then Samuel forgot all about what the Circuit Rider could not do, in what he did.

He held his audience in a vise. He preached the wrath of God until they shrieked for mercy. Repentant sinners flocked to the Mourner's Bench until its boards creaked in tune with their sobs. Samuel saw the hand of sister Anne, sitting in front of him, clasped convulsively in the hand of William Knapton beside her. A side glance showed him the tears coursing down his father's face. Mother Anne sat beside him, rigid. Suddenly, John leaped over a seat and rushed down to the Mourner's Bench to labor with the sinners. The torches tied to the trees for light threw wicked shadows which seemed to be evil things, stealing in from the forest after lost souls. The slender little rim of a moon, the only familiar landmark, seemed infinitely far away.

A farmer's wife who had sat opposite them at the dinner table, a hard-working self-contained mother of a big family, "caught by the power," leaped to her feet with an ear-splitting cry, ran grotesquely down the wooded aisle and beat her head against a tree until she fell to the ground. The whole audience under the Elder's words became a group of primitives, with their souls all ungirt, swinging and swaying and crying in an agony of emotion, as did their prototypes in the woods of Thrace.

Samuel's soul expanded like a giant and filled the whole horizon. Just as it seemed to weigh a ton and to be as big as the world, the preacher began reiterating a horrific phrase:

"You are hair-hung and breeze-shaken over the Pit that has no bottom. Hair-hung, breeze-shaken! Hair-hung, breeze-shaken!" With a soul the terrible weight of his, even the "Amens" and "Hallelujahs" and "Praise the Lords" of the audience, which vibrated the dangerous air in which that soul was swinging, and the light current of wind, coming in from the pungent fields, seemed absolutely unmerciful. He and his soul, with a hair between it and hell, sat there and shook and shook with cold fear.

Then came the blessed promise of mercy, like rain on the mown grass. It fell on the tortured audience and Samuel like a blessing. The voice of the exhorter pleaded with them to come into the kingdom, as a mother would plead with her child. Cries rose all over the grove again, wrapping Samuel in a ecstasy of relief:

"I'm saved! I'm saved! I'm saved!" It was a great meeting, and many were converted.

Samuel slept that night in the wagon on one side of his mother. Willie was on the other, sister Anne in a neighbor's wagon, and John and his father rolled up cocoon fashion in a quilt on the ground.

The little boy had nightmares all that night and for many weeks thereafter, in which he and his soul dropped endlessly into a lake of brimstone. But the morning was as sweet as a September morning could be. On an early tour of investigation, he discovered the "possessed" mother of the night before heating milk in a saucepan, over a tiny camp fire, for a whimpering little two-year-old, pulling at her skirt. The mother had pulled down her hair to hide the bruises from the rough bark, and she nodded at him as placidly as if she had never been the victim of religious hysteria. She was enjoying a little added deference from her husband and her companions, as the recipient of special favors from the Lord, but otherwise her demonstration of the night before left her just the same as usual.

Back again at his own wagon, Samuel heard his father, who was no pioneer and distrusted the unusual sensations of the night before, trying to engineer a homeward movement. Thomas was surer than ever that a camp meeting was no place for a Wesleyan Methodist from England, but his whole family was opposing him. At that, he might have won out, for Anne was English and had her belief in the autocracy of the dominant male. But the Watertown man strolled over from his wagon at this critical moment and saved the day for the Fallows family. He and Thomas talked woolen factory so fast that the thought of home was forgotten and not revived until its proper time.

Camp meeting was just one excitement after another. Following the afternoon meeting, Samuel and Thomas were over at their wagon, feeding Buck and Bess, the oxen, when a big man in a pepper-and-salt suit, having a very rotund middle over which hung a big gold chain with a lump of native lead for a fob, advanced upon them with elaborate casualness. He praised the oxen almost extravagantly, but wondered if Thomas wouldn't do better, after all, everything considered, with horses on a new farm. He had two over at his wagon, fine strong creatures, built for work. He was willing to let them go at a bargain, because he had too many for his own use. Perhaps Thomas would like to see them.

He would, and he did, and Samuel also. The horses appeared all that their owner had said. But father and son saw and went away. Thomas had no money for a trade, and the trader had no desire to trade even. He must have had a great many too many horses, Samuel felt in his inexperience, because he saw four different sets, one after another, replace the original ones, all feeding complacently out of the tail of the wagon, while the horse trader exploited their advantages to possible purchasers.

The horse trader was a legitimate by-product of the camp meeting, Samuel soon discovered. Though no Methodist might play cards or dance without Satan at his elbow, he found that a Methodist might trade horses to his heart's content and still occupy a front seat in the Kingdom of Heaven, an assurance that was to enlighten, for him, some very dull periods of the Civil War.

Alive at every pore, the small boy absorbed each new phase of the camp meeting beatifically. Even the moments of real terror, that first evening under the Elder's flail, had had their certain pleasure, like the purge of the Greek drama. The psychology of that early West was the psychology of childhood, emotional, unreasoning. There was none of the after-taste of horror which reflection brings. As soon as the meeting was finished, the denunciation over, life went on happily again, except for the poor obstinate sinners who could not surrender. Samuel looked at them with a great deal of pity.

The last sermon, terrible in its finality, dealt with the bitter truth that Summer was ended, the harvest past and some were not saved. Many new candidates went scurrying up to the Mourner's Bench. The laboring of some of the "saints" with these sisters and brethren could be heard a mile away. But some would not and some could not be saved. The little boy's heart wept with those who turned away sorrowful.

But it leaped up, light as thistledown again, for the parting ceremony, which was pleasant enough to cheer any boy whose spirits were prone to rise.

It was a musical, rhythmic kind of function, symbolizing the joy of friendship and the sorrow of parting, dating, perhaps, back to the woods of Thrace. The whole company formed into a great ring in a clear space of the grove, and, while laughter sounded and tears flowed in a "melting time," each one in turn swung everyone else about by the hand, round the whole circle. It was a heart-warming exercise, which, under the guise of a religious observance, gave to its Methodist participants exactly the same kind of innocent enjoyment that Money Musk and the Virginia Reel did to their more worldly neighbors.

When all the good-bys to the new friends had been said, and mother Anne was emptying out the breakfast tea leaves, and Willie was carefully burying them, and John was lifting the last basket into the waiting wagon, Samuel, with the wisdom God gives to fools and children, told Anne the contribution the camp meeting had made to his growing mind. He gazed at the platform from which the Evangelist had thundered forth his diatribes.

"I'd like to stand up there," he said, "and see if I couldn't make them feel things, too."

At first, Anne looked upon this remark as a sign of grace. Then she wasn't so sure. If she had been a modern mother who brought up her babies on Holt and her growing boys on educational psychology, she would have known that by this casual remark her son was proclaiming himself of the artist class, one of those who, throughout this thing we call Life, would always be on the lookout to see how the great Presiding Elder produced His effects and to try to get the same effects himself.

CHAPTER IV

LIONS IN THE PATH

The limitations of the new life hit Samuel hard as soon
as school opened in the late Fall. In the little log schoolhouse,
with its floor of earth and benches made of slabs of wood
set on uprights, the eager boy met the first lions in his path.

Anne started off her two youngest, the first day of school,
with a lunch of bread and cheese and the admonition to be
good boys. They returned toward dusk in the afternoon,
with lagging steps and hanging heads. For once, the sparkle
was out of Samuel's blue eyes, and the discouraged sag of
his shoulders made her think of Thomas's.

"Did you like your teacher, Sammy?" she asked quickly.

The little boy turned his head away to hide the tremble
of his lips. "He—he doesn't know any more than I do," he
choked. "Not quite so much, perhaps," he added in an attempt to be strictly accurate.

Anne yielded to a sudden weakness in her knees and sat
down on the big flat stone which made the doorstep of the
little log house. Here she was, fresh from ordered England
where one bore children and let the wise civilization of a
dozen centuries rear them into men and women—workers
after their kind, lords and ladies after theirs. Never had
she imagined such a dilemma. What was the proper procedure in this land of upside downs, when your offspring
came home with the news that he knew more than his teacher?
No one had told her. She said to her little boy, between her
teeth:

"You must have your schooling."

STATE UNIVERSITY, MADISON.

Seifert & Lawton, Milwaukee.

Where Bishop Fallows graduated in 1859 as class valedictorian.

[See Page 159]

It sounded cheering for the moment. But her son soon found there was very little she could do about it. She could not make over conditions single-handed. He looked around the whole wide horizon and saw no help anywhere. There was really nothing in the world for him to do except to pull himself up by his own bootstraps, so, with all the strength he had, he proceeded to pull.

That Fall and Winter he taught himself and lent a hand to Willie, who still knew little enough to learn something from the teacher.

Studying at home has a luxurious sound of unforced schedule and ample leisures. But alas! it seemed quite otherwise to Samuel, in his corner of the little kitchen, which he shared with the rest of the family as the only comfortable space in a cold world.

He studied, usually, to the accompaniment of five voices; sister Anne's planning a new dress, perhaps, for the next husking, and wondering secretly if a certain young farmer would like it; Thomas's deliberate voice debating what crops to put in next spring; Willie's treble bewailing a finger hammered instead of a butternut, mother Anne's dear voice consoling him; John's planning the songs for singing school on Wednesday night, ending with the hopelessly fascinating suggestion that the male members of the family spear fish that evening.

If you were a conscientious student determined to get on, you rose at that point, took from its nail on the wall your long scarf knitted by Anne, wound it all about yourself in place of the overcoat nobody wore, clapped on a woolen cap and retired to the top of the kindling pile in the woodshed with your conjugations and declensions, till Jock rooted you out with an uproarious bark.

Then you went up to your own loft, pulled off your heavy shoes, wrapped all the bedclothes around you and pitched into Latin again, until your teeth chattered and your nose was so cold you hopped downstairs and peered at it in the wavy family mirror, to make sure it was not frozen.

By that time, plans for the spearing would be in full blast, and study would go glimmering.

If, under a régime of this kind, you, being thirteen and interested in any human fact at all, managed to get some Latin and Greek, "algebra and other mathematics," and even a little French and German into your head, you were guaranteed able to find concentration in a boiler factory easy.

For diversion, Samuel helped split rails for farm fences and went fishing. "The fishing was not of the apostolic kind," he said in a later moment of recollection, "with a net, but with a hook and line. The hook was sometimes a bent pin, with a small fat worm for bait," dropped from the log bridge which spanned the little farm stream. Just often enough to keep the fisherman's patience alive, a redhorse or a tiny perch made the one mistake of an impeccable life and bit.

Night spearing through the thick ice was a much more gorgeous and dramatic performance. It gave a small boy a feeling of being kin to trappers and hunters. When the night was darkest the fishermen stumbled through the woods to the stream, chopped a hole in the ice, and then, with lighted torches, enticed the fish to come to the opening to breathe and promptly impaled them with a three-pronged spear.

Not for a long time was Samuel to learn "that fishers of men must not impale their catch and toss them bleeding and wounded into the Kingdom, but must have the art and skill of the fishers for trout, or if they use the net must throw it on 'the right side of the ship.'" But even though the speared fish tasted very good out of the frying pan, especially when food was scarce and a boy's appetite sharp, an innate love of fair play made him cringe at this barbarous way of killing them. He was always glad when the stream was open again, and a fish could have, at least, a little run for its fatal worm.

What with out-of-door work and sports and an occasional indulgence in the simple grown-up amusements of the Methodists, Samuel could have marched through that Winter with his spiritual trumpets blowing, except for one thing. He could manage on starvation diet. All the family had to, at times. He could even look upon the fierce cold and relentless toil as minor blessings. But the fear of ignorance bit into each leisure moment like an acid.

In some corner of his boyish brain was the nagging conviction that the future without an education would be a worthless thing. Yet, getting an education in Dane County in 1848 seemed about as easy as being a frog at the bottom of a smooth-sided well with a foolish ambition to get to the top. Academies existed. But they were far away and cost money; so what good in the world could they be to a boy whose family had barely pennies enough to keep body and soul together that first Winter?

His neighbors, moreover, tried to poke down his ambition every time it lifted its head. Migration seemed to have worked a strange change in the farmers about, even the educated ones. The farm filled their earthly horizon, just as the Kingdom of Heaven did their unearthly. Love of the land was one reason for the change in their scale of values. Another was that any farm, with any spirit at all, could, with a round of unremitting tasks for every member of the family, limit the vision to what they could see when their noses were to the grindstone.

Samuel, anxious for knowledge, felt like a very small atom arrayed against a very large universe. The Pilgrim Fathers may have landed with the Bible in one hand and the primer in the other. He had no wish to dispute it. His grief was that the Wisconsin Fathers seemed still to be offering him the same old primer. Their idea of education included the three R's to fit one to read the almanac and compute the price of crops. But that was all—at least as far as free education was concerned. If anyone wished more, let him pay for it. The masculine pronoun was not an oversight, either, nor one of those generous symbols meant to stand for both sexes. Ladies were not encouraged to be learned.

A college education for a farmer boy, with no other prospects in sight, seemed nonsense. Spoil a good farmer to make a poor A.B.? Foolishness! A mild form of lunacy to be treated with camomile tea or a strait-jacket.

Small Sammy, just at that most sensitive moment, was an odd little figure. He was outgrowing the clumsy English clothes Anne's loving fingers made for him. His soft speech, with its broad a's and unexpected emphases and accents, was strange in Wisconsin ears. He knew it, and suffered agonies of shyness when he had to talk to people at the store or after church. When he would almost rather have been dead than different, here he was thrust into prominence in a skeptical neighborhood, as the boy who knew more than the schoolmaster and was teaching himself at home.

The Providence which tempers the wind to the shorn lamb was not totally unmindful, however, of the poor little frog in the Wisconsin well. Just when prospects seemed darkest, down dropped consolation in the shape of a friend, Azariah Hall, a boy of about his own age, as handicapped and as ambitious as he was himself.

They were good foils for each other. Azariah naturally shied away from people and had a touch of Saturn in his view toward life, while Samuel was exuberant and responsive to human beings in any shape. His enthusiasm acted like wine on his less volatile friend, while Azariah's native-born wisdom and common sense were invaluable in rubbing off his own Old World corners.

The two formed an offensive and defensive alliance against

Things-As-They-Were. Even two atoms did not make much splash in an unfriendly universe, but a common misery removed, at least, the curse of loneliness. The two pored together over the Latin dictionary purchased by incredible economies. They made headway of a kind, but it was not rapid.

Azariah eventually found a way out for both of them, but not until after three self-taught Winters and three laborious Summers in the fields, working at sixteen and two-thirds cents a day and board. Each Summer they had to run the gauntlet of the disapproving farmers, as they rested and drank the refreshing ginger and water brought by the women to help them through the grilling heat, as they swung the scythe or guided the plow. But they kept doggedly to their course, pulled their Latin grammars out of their jeans and studied the lists of verbs while they rested the horses, which they did at the end of each furrow.

Two fundamental traits were battling for possession of the little Sammy of those early Wisconsin years—a hunger for friendliness and approval, as utter as a Newfoundland puppy's and an instinct for mental trail making, which was as uncomfortable as a thorn in the side.

When a kindly farmer fixed him with his wise eyes in the hayfield and spluttered out, "Pshaw! Sammy, you've got the makings of a first-rate farmer. Why in time do you want to spoil it all with a college education? The farm's the place. Land, boy, stick to the land," the puppy part of him was longing with all its might to come to heel and obey this benign master. Moreover, he had a strong romantic love of the land to tempt him still further—a love so enduring that, after years and years of city life, it burgeoned out in vegetable gardens tucked away in side streets; morning glories trained over unsightly fences; a little oasis of green set with flowers in a Chicago back yard; in the wish, sometimes wrung out of the deep stress of unending activity, for a little place in the country with a cow and a horse and chickens, a dog like Jock, a very superior cat and a row of string beans.

He tried to figure out how he could stay basking in the pleasant area of this influential farmer's approval and at the same time see what lay beyond the next hill. Failing, he said a polite "Thank you, sir. I know, sir, but I think I'd like to go to college," picked up his scythe again and swung it all the afternoon to the tune of "Arma virumque cano," pronounced according to Webster.

The craving for friendship gave a doggish sigh, accepted defeat and a second place. For in that small moment of involuntary choice, he had allied himself with the trail blazers who never can stay put.

If Samuel's intellectual curiosity had been mortal, it must have died that Winter of starvation. Nowhere in Bird's Ruins or its environs was there anything to feed it. There were no libraries, public or private; one farmer had a set of Shakespeare, but it was much too precious to borrow; in the Fallows family there was not even the *New York Tribune*. What would a family with that terrible interest to pay be doing with a newspaper? Very few families were able to afford one, anyway. Samuel, famished for reading matter, heard from Azariah that he had heard that a man in a town ten miles away had a paper that he might be willing to spare. Samuel walked the ten miles on the chance of getting it. But the paper was gone and he walked the ten miles back with a heart that weighed a ton.

He took off his shoes and carried them to rest his feet and stubbed his toe fearfully against a hidden stone in the road. As he sat on a stump and rocked to and fro with the agony of it, he felt "cribbed, cabined, and confined" in the darkest depths of the blackest despair a boy had ever known. Finally, as he had been taught, he made a little prayer, to the effect that if God couldn't do anything about it, didn't He think He'd just better let him die!

CHAPTER V

MORE LIONS

What happened that evening tended to confirm the small boy's belief that Something, somewhere, heard the prayers you made and attended to them.

He limped home to Anne, feeling like an outcast from the world of joy, forever. After one look at his pitiful little face, she put on the supper table the wild strawberry jam contributed by an English neighbor, which she had been saving for a special occasion. But even after the second heaping teaspoonful from her lavish hand, Samuel still felt limp and helpless. Then the Answer to Prayer burst through the door with a whoop. Daniel, the adventurer, had come home. Such pandemonium was let loose in the little kitchen that Jock, inured by the boys to every noise there was, slunk out of the room with his tail between his legs.

Everybody wanted to know everything at once; whether Daniel had received their messages left for him in Manchester; how he had found the voyage, and whether he was hungry, and forty other things, until Thomas at last raised his rarely authoritative finger and declared that questions must be asked one at a time and in turn. Daniel held Willie on his knee with one hand and ate with the other. He talked so fast that Anne declared he shouldn't be asked another question till he had finished supper. Then, straightway, she asked one, because it was her turn and she simply couldn't wait to know how the old house looked, and what had happened to the next-door neighbor's rheumatism, and what they were wearing in Man-

69

chester, and the text of the preacher the Sabbath Daniel had spent there.

Again, from her questions and his father's, Samuel might have divined that their hearts were living in England while their bodies were in Dane County, Wisconsin; that the new country still held them by just a thread. But psychological analysis was not for him.

Perched on the edge of his chair with his heels hooked onto the round, his eyes popping out, he was waiting to explode his questions when his turn came—the first about his devoted Sunday-school teacher, because it was proper; the second about his chum, because it was vital. His cup of satisfaction was brimming over. In a dreary waste of self-teaching, once more he had been given a hero to trail. The world was as bright as a five-dollar gold piece.

Samuel's Answer to Prayer could not conjure up teachers and schools for him, but in every other respect in that Winter of handicaps Daniel was a perfectly satisfactory magician. The small brother went with him to singing school each Wednesday, the one important fixed event in the Methodist social calendar. John was its director, a kindly musical czar, pitching each song properly with his little tuning fork. Samuel had a clear strong voice which behaved like a docile little sheep in concert singing, but could never be trusted by John or its owner in a solo, because it had a trick of wandering up and down at will with no reference at all to the original tune.

He even slipped in with Daniel sometimes to candy pulls. While his brother, who had a gift that way, maneuvered the prettiest young lady in the room into position at the other end of the sticky rope of taffy he was pulling, his shadow followed suit by capturing the prettiest little girl, a spicy, snappy, dark-haired English lass who lived near them. Huskings, of course, were the really thrilling events, with the swift laughing contest between two teams, one of them cap-tained often by Daniel, who very soon became expert in husking the corn and just as expert in claiming the special privileges of the red ears.

But Daniel's stories were the best, dozens of them, and all as true as true. One of them, about Callao, gave the attentive brother a belief in miracles, all signed, sealed and witnessed. At the same moment, it transformed him into a Spanish grandee wearing a plumed hat and a velvet coat, posing elegantly on a street of that enchanted city.

The street of Callao, to be sure, on which Samuel stood in an attitude of careless ease, looked to anyone else like the cow shed. He, himself, appeared to be twirling a nonexistent something at the spot where mustaches grew and looking intently at the distant apple tree, which was all that any normal eyes could see from the cow-shed door.

But, in reality, he was looking across a sweep of water under which the original Callao had been buried, seeing in its clear depths broken walls and dead men's bones strewed on stone floors, and the glimmer of the golden temple gates which it was death to try to raise. It was expected that the good Lord would raise them Himself when He wanted to use them. What seemed to be an apple tree was really a mountain top rising from the waters of Callao Bay, the mountain top of the miracle.

A hundred years or so before, a simple fisherman, named Lorenzo, had been sitting quietly on that topmost top, fishing. Yes, fishing! The pinnacle was at sea level then. He was catching food for his family's dinner when zing! zish! whish! crash! boom! there he was sitting on a peak a thousand feet high, trying to catch his equilibrium after a tidal wave and an earthquake, wondering if a temperate man like himself could possibly have drunk enough at the Inn the night before to make him see things like that.

This fisherman was the only one saved out of the whole city, so they made him a saint and called him "San Lorenzo," instead of plain "Lorenzo." When he died, they built him a beautiful tomb.

So, if you were Samuel, you went on to your next chore supplied with a perfectly beautiful story and a comfortable belief that any miracle you read about was true, of course. For had not Daniel seen that tomb himself with his very own eyes? And there he was now! that hero brother of his, carrying out to the squealing pigs a bucket of scraps Anne had given him, though when one had lived through adventures like this, one walked in fancy over cloth of gold even to a Wisconsin pigpen!

The stories which sent wild shivers of delight racing up and down small Samuel's barometric spine gave Daniel's mother shivers of a very different character. They opened frightful vistas before her of the dangers to which Daniel's soul had been exposed. The unusual always had terrors for her, but when it was an unusual which she suspected of being a menace to her son's chances of eternal salvation, it became a kind of sword of Damocles over her head.

She could not let well enough alone. One day she put the little that was left of her security to the test. Daniel was sitting near her, greasing his high boots to go hunting, while she was paring the potatoes for dinner, and Samuel was struggling with some Greek roots. Anne reached over to pat her big boy's knee.

Out of a clear sky came the question she had been brooding over for months, carrying it with her all day, hearing it at night when every wind waked her out of a nightmare in which she saw Daniel's ship rocked and broken in the waves and Daniel lying unsaved at the bottom of the sea. After she had studied the sailors on the *Ben Lomond* as well as she could at long distance, the question goaded her more constantly than ever.

"Were the sailors on your ship good men?" she asked.

"Did they say their prayers before they went to bed?" The question was in the open at last.

Daniel's eyes held a swift vision of his companions, true to the core, but rough as any chestnut burr and with a Billingsgate command of language, fighting a gale to a finish and dropping into their bunks with their boots on, to be sleeping the sleep of utter exhaustion before their heads touched the pillow. "Surely they were good men," he answered heartily.

"I know, Danny," said Anne, pressing on to her undoing, "but did they say their prayers at night?"

"They couldn't always, the ship pitched so," explained Daniel tonelessly, as if he knew how vain it was to try to make Anne understand a religion that was of the open sea, and not of a night-robed figure at a decorous bedside between peaceful days.

The sword had dropped and her contentment was dead under it. Never again could she know a peaceful moment with Daniel wandering. But comfort still remained. She had him under her eye.

She finished the last of the potatoes, washed them on the table, with water dipped from the tin pail, dropped the parings into the pig bucket, wiped her hands, walked over to Daniel and ruffled his hair tenderly.

"Danny lad," she said softly, "you don't know how thankful I am to have you here, how completely thankful. It's so safe. You won't be wanting to go away again, will you?"

Samuel's whole small body was tense with listening for the answer.

"Mother," protested Daniel against the yearning and the longing in her voice, "you couldn't expect me to bury myself on a farm. I'd die of the dullness of it, die."

Even Anne's little morsel of comfort was ashes in her mouth. Daniel might be away at any time. But Samuel wished he were a cannon, so he could go off with a tremendous noise. He had made up his mind to go if Daniel went, even if it had to be as a stowaway.

Then a madcap spirit of adventure, out of a pagan past, caught the whole practical United States into its whirlwind arms, and the sea and Callao and Spanish galleons suddenly paled to insignificance for Samuel and Daniel. Gold had been discovered in California. Polk announced it in his December message to Congress. Thomas brought the news home, after trading at the store one afternoon.

Anne hoped it wasn't true. She didn't like Polk anyway. She didn't care for anything he said. He had taken Oregon away from poor little crowded England. That and this California place where the gold glittered had added five hundred thousand square miles to the United States. All the men seemed to think it was a great feather in Polk's cap. For her part, she couldn't see what the government needed of any more land. Wisconsin was as empty as a sieve, now. Armies and armies and armies of settlers could never fill it up. An odious creature, this Polk, she was sure. Daniel had seemed to be settling down just a little to the peaceful life of Wisconsin. Then along comes Polk with this bombshell.

She told them all what she thought about it, that first night, after Thomas came bristling in with the news—that gold was a temptation of the devil, and no good Methodist had any business to touch it with a forty-foot pole. But Daniel's face was flushed, and his fingers were twitching, as they always did when he was planning something wild and startling.

She and Samuel watched him through the weeks that followed, as a doctor might a fever patient, the little boy gaspingly afraid that he might not break out in some grand delirium of action, Anne equally afraid that he would.

By Spring, the gold rush was a riotous scramble. High and low, rich and poor, bankers, artists, women, laborers, doctors, lawyers, everybody dropped life where the craze caught them and started for California. Even a few Dane County farmers, the sanest men in the world, threw down their tools and went.

Samuel, seized by the madness, fairly seethed and boiled with the desire to take part in this glorious adventure. After a prairie schooner, a little off its beat, came through, with a whole family in the first happy stages of their great undertaking, he ventured to tell Daniel the burning wish of his heart.

Daniel shook his head with an emphasis that was final and clinched the matter with the deadly words:

"Never, Sammy, never. The gold field is no place for little boys."

"Little boys!" The damning phrase rang through that Summer of suppressions like a knell. Not to anyone, even to Willie, did Samuel dare to say a word again of the longing that was consuming him. Anne, with anxious eye on Daniel, was totally unsuspicious. When she finally did notice her small boy's restlessness, she felt of his wrist and looked at his tongue, then brought out molasses and sulphur as a cure.

She and Samuel both kept an eye on him. Each day the small brother poked around under his big brother's bed and in all the corners where he kept things, to make sure he had no bundle ready for a secret get-away which would not include him. Of course it wasn't like Daniel to work under cover. He was open and straightforward and ready to take consequences. But you never could tell!

The climax did not occur in any one of the hundred ways Samuel had imagined.

It followed a trip to Milwaukee made, in the late Fall, by him and Daniel, to sell a load of wheat. That journey would have been excitement enough to last a Dane County boy a year, if the gold field had not been in the offing. For Samuel was a small boy still, in spite of his precocity, a bundle of boyish superstitions, half-grown impulses and large capacity for amusement from small things. He could get a splendid thrill out of being trusted to drive Buck and Bright, the oxen. "Little boy." Pooh! That was a grown-up job, if ever there was one. Buck and Bright were a frisky team. No little boy had the skill and muscle and discretion it took to "gee" and "haw" them.

The brothers were seven days and seven nights making the round trip; days teeming with interest as they creaked off mile after mile; nights spent in farmhouses or simple taverns, where the stream of talk soon veered from politics and slavery to the wonder spot of all the world where men walked along a field and stooped down to pick up an unpromising dark lump of something and found it pure gold. One of the men, like themselves, traveling to Milwaukee, had read a letter from his wife's cousin which told about seventy people working in a little ravine, each taking out an ounce of gold a day. A woman who had worked with pan and shovel in dry diggings for forty days had cleaned up over two thousand dollars. Those were the very modest successes. The cousin, himself, was sitting on a stone one day, discouraged and about ready to give up, because he had found nothing at all. Just for something to do, he turned the stone over— and found a fortune under it. He saw two men working up to their waists in water, getting fifteen or twenty dollars out of every pan they washed, making a thousand dollars out of every day's work.

It made Crœsus seem like a piker. Women were out there getting rich, and *boys*. Samuel was all eyes and ears and attention. The man with the wife's cousin was going as soon as he could get his affairs in order. So were ever so many more of their fellow travelers.

Very little was made of the terrific journey—the Indians, the desert, the thirst, the bones of the unfortunates all along the way. It meant nothing to a man gripped by the gold hunger, either, that flour was four hundred dollars a barrel, sugar four dollars a pound, coffee, almost undrinkable, the same price; that a dollar shovel sold for ten, and rowboats had jumped from fifty dollars to five hundred. Clothes cost a small fortune.

Such details as these were very lightly passed over in the excited discussions, after supper at their overnight stops, sitting in the stuffy little tavern sitting room, blue with strong tobacco smoke, Samuel felt like a powder keg ready to blow up.

What was one Indian, or even two? Give him his own medicine. Scalp him!

Who couldn't stand a little thirst for the sake of gold? The unspeakable fun of finding it! Then think what it would mean! Schooling, all one wanted of it in one of those impossibly expensive Methodist academies that charged as much, perhaps, as three dollars a term for tuition! College! . . .

His mother! She would hate their going, of course. It might even make her cry a little. But when they brought her back that new black silk dress she wanted so much, she would just throw her arms around them both and say: "Oh, boys, I *am* so glad you went." Women were like that. Being at home so much, they couldn't understand things as a man did who could get out and hear things. Azariah felt that, too. Perhaps he would go. His mother, afflicted with ill health and a perfect plague of relatives, needed a new dress terribly.

Samuel knew that Daniel likewise on this trip was getting his brain chock full of dreams. Sometimes, after his big brother had fallen asleep, the little boy would lie awake stretched out very stiff and still in the hard narrow tavern bed, beside him. He heard the things Daniel muttered and knew he was on the long trail in his sleep.

Family finances were very low at this time. The brothers

were hoping to find this venture a little gold mine of their own. Alas, for their hopes! In Milwaukee they were paid only sixty-four cents a bushel for the wheat, which left so small a profit, after road expenses were paid, that it wasn't worth the counting.

The night the brothers reached home after this trip, the storm which had been gathering so long in Daniel's mind broke loose at last. He ate supper silently. When the meal was over, he stood up and pounded the table heavily. He declared that never again would he do another day's work on that farm if he died for it. It was the gold fields for him.

But Anne, the calm, the quiet, the invincible, the merry, stay and comfort of them all, took the matter in hand. She had reached the breaking point.

"I can't stand it! I can't stand it! I can't stand it!" she stormed.

She threw her arms around Daniel's neck, laid her cheek against his rough shirt, and in a perfect tempest of sobs loosed the long tension of her homesick days. The whole family stood about aghast. Daniel patted her, and Samuel hugged her from the rear.

"Danny, Danny!" she choked. "The long nights not knowing where you were! Not again, oh, not again! Your father needs you! And, oh, Danny lad, your soul. Stay with us, dear, stay with us."

Her big son put her away gently and strode out of the kitchen door, shadowed by Samuel. In the darkness of the starless night, he paced a little length of road at the foot of the slope in front of the house, up and down, up and down, like a wild free thing in a cage at the end of a chain. He clenched his hands and wrung them and groaned like something in mortal distress. Samuel, at his heels, noiseless and invisible in the darkness, shared his misery. His was the same battle. The instincts and desires of primordial man,

SCENE AT BEAUFORT, S. C.—NEGRO HUCKSTERS DISPOSING OF THEIR PRODUCE TO THE SOLDIERS.—FROM A SKETCH BY W. T. CRANE

NEGRO HUCKSTERS IN THE CIVIL WAR

It was in a scene very much like this that Bishop Fallows met little Walker, the tiny pickaninny huckster who brought him food to the camp near Memphis, Tennessee during the Civil War. [See Page 1891.

near the surface with them both, for forging out into the
unknown, for fighting bare handed what their hands found
to fight, grappling with so frail a thing as the Fifth Com-
mandment and the love of a soft little woman-thing like
Anne.

Samuel still felt that the black silk dress would set everything straight, but he dared not interrupt Daniel to tell him
so. At the end of what seemed to the small boy a thousand
years, Daniel gave one last great sigh, as if he waved a
heartsick good-by to the God of the open road, and went
back into the kitchen, Samuel trailing him in the shadow.

"I'm not going," he announced to Anne, who was calm
again outwardly, but whose fingers were too shaky to hold
her knitting needles. Her son even managed a small twisted
smile for which the Recording Angel must have wiped out all
the small misdeeds of all his other years. He accepted chains
for both himself and Samuel, though he never realized that
he had anchored, also, to a conventional life the little brother.

Anne, changing the destinies of her family that night, did
not realize it either. Nor that, passing the chance of two millionaires to lift the family out of all its troubles and put
it on the financial map of the world, she lost a new black
silk dress. The chances were equal that two broken tramps
might have come trailing home after a year or two. But
Anne's mind was on the eternals. She felt that she had
saved Daniel's soul alive. If she had known that she was
saving Samuel's, as well, no doxology yet written could have
expressed her thankfulness.

Daniel took up the trade of wagon making. A pathetic
compromise, that! To create the things that would travel
where he could not!

Years later, in the second story of a big Chicago church,
Samuel set up a little assaying kit in one corner of his ample
study and, with flame and pestle and mortar, found ease for
that thwarted boyish desire in testing specimens from a gold

mine in which he owned a share or two—a greedy mine, swallowing much more gold than it ever dreamed of returning.

After that night, when, for a moment, the road of release and adventure had unrolled before him, Samuel resumed his job of fighting the lions in his path to an education, and it did seem as if the miserable beasts roared louder than ever.

CHAPTER VI

PEGGING AWAY

The schoolboy turned from dreams of gold to peg away again at his Latin and mathematics. During the summers, he was tied to the work of the farm. When he was fifteen, fate once more offered him a way out of his difficulties.

The Porter school, the little log building where he had found the teacher who knew less than he did, was vacant. Its directors wanted John to take charge of the school and manage the unruly boys. John had come to be an important man in the community, teaching singing school and preaching, quite often, very acceptable sermons. But, wonder of wonders, the directors wished Samuel to assist John in teaching the school. Samuel's hope, never tethered very close to the ground, rose to the skies. His days of unsatisfactory self-teaching would be over. He would earn the money to go away and be taught. And how well he would teach! . . . Those fine directors should never be ashamed of their choice.

He needed a certificate from the Town Superintendent, Elder Green, a Baptist minister. To get it, he had to be examined by this minister—, a mere formality, he was assured. But the worthy gentleman, alas, found him not quite up on parsing. The Elder's conscience was an inelastic quantity. He was minus the charity that covers even a fraction of deficiency. He declined to grant the certificate, and Samuel's happy bubble burst.

He went home heartsick. Anne was melting tallow to run

81

into the candle molds beside her. When she had heard the sad story, her tears dropped into it, one by one.

"My son," she murmured, "my little son. You *must* have your chance."

Then, suddenly, she realized that the level of his eyes was above the level of her own, that in his home-made Sunday suit of American cloth, donned in honor of the Elder, he looked even taller than he was. She dropped more tears into the hot tallow and inadvertently made of that batch of candles the transient light before the shrine which every mother sets up in her heart to pray before, at the moment when her son leaves the safety of little boyhood for the temptations of the big world.

Not long after that, Anne averted disaster at a crucial moment. Twice, in the secrecy of his own loft, Samuel had shaved himself serially in a two-and-a-half-by-three-inch fragment of a broken mirror. On this day, he proceeded boldly to the kitchen and heated water in a little tin pan on the stove. Finding mother Anne knitting a sock in the corner, apparently heedless, though in reality attentive to the point of tremulousness, he brazenly borrowed John's razor and brush and soap and, carrying his hot water over to the mirror, began to lather himself in true professional style.

Willie, who was still getting some sustenance from the district school, was scheduled to speak a piece the next week. The whole family had communal interest in its preparation. As Samuel looked at his lathered face in the glass, an inspiration struck him. He began to mutter words and to gesticulate with the razor held at a wildly dangerous angle.

Sister Anne, coming in at this moment a trifle flustered from trying to unset a maternally minded hen, caught him at it.

"Why, Sammy Fallows," she exclaimed, "what in the world are you doing? With John's razor and his soap and everything?"

Samuel stuttered out a half truth, which was much more important than the whole.

"I was thinking how I would speak Willie's piece if I was Willie," he explained with another sweep of the razor.

"Perfectly silly, I call it," began sister Anne. Then she saw the warning look in the eyes of mother Anne, who had eased two other boys through their first shaves and their first long pants, and the finger on her motherly lips. She stopped abruptly.

Sister Anne did not understand, but she was feeling very kind and tender, because she was to be married in a few weeks to William Knapton who lived next door (not more than a mile away). As she had a very soft spot in her heart for Samuel, anyway, she went over and dropped a kiss on the top of his head and said no more. Thus began his best dramatic creating. And so, ever after, continued, whenever he soaped his face and lifted his razor and saw himself in the mirror—even down to the last shave he gave his happy, ruddy, eighty-six-year-old cheeks.

That Fall and Winter brought the schoolboy to the very edge of despair. The crops, never the prize crops of the neighborhood, had all failed the season before: Wheat had turned into or was superseded by chess, a kind of brome grass which was a devil's plague to the farmer. Many a discussion was carried on, as to whether or not wheat could really degenerate into chess. Samuel believed it could, because he saw an ear that was half wheat and half chess. But much more pointed than any botanical curiosity was the fact that had it not been for the chickens and the cow, Bess, they must all have faced starvation that Winter.

Never had he felt so acutely that he was getting nowhere with his studying. The stab at his pride given by Elder Green was one of the things that kept his ambition alive that Winter; the other was his friend Azariah. Such a pitiless crucible of living as Samuel knew either crushes out a boy's capacity for joy completely or makes it so strong that nothing else can ever down it.

Mrs. Hall, watching him in the kitchen where he and her boy were studying, even during that most arid period of his life felt as if he were a clear streak of sunshine across a gray day.   Out of dry Latin and rigid mathematics and hunger and discouragement, Samuel's laughter bubbled up like a happy little fountain.   Frank, Azariah's small blue-eyed scrap of a brother, for whom Samuel played hero as Daniel did for Samuel, would steal up holding the little box of pennies he was hoarding, and out of some pocket Samuel would conjure up a penny, as precious then as a five-dollar gold piece later, and slip it in when Azariah, made of the sterner stuff that would have banished Frank, was looking the other way.

"He'll make friends wherever he goes," was Mrs. Hall's verdict to Azariah, one day when Samuel had just lilted out the door with a joyous burst of song, "and I have a feeling that he may go quite a ways."   The little sentence dropped into Frank's mind and there it lay, only to come to speech again when Samuel's long life was all behind him and he had taken the far step into eternity.

One day, when the Hall kitchen was a Waterloo and the two boys were entirely overcome by the enemy, which happened to be an untranslatable passage of Latin, Azariah had the inspiration which was to give them victory.

Jumping up, knocking over his chair and scaring the kitten out of an inch's growth, Azariah shouted at the top of his lungs.

"Why don't we go to Aztalan?"

Now Aztalan was a kind of backwoods Athens where Mr. Harvey dwelt, a teacher with a reputation all through the region.   He was one of those early blessed ones who gave everything to keep the torch of learning alight and expected nothing. He cheerfully took what that gigantic polyglot migration to the West offered him—little German cubs, Bavarian, Scandinavian, English, Irish, Scotch, sprawling formless youngsters committed to the prejudices of their parents. He birched them and taught them and cajoled them into something that was neither German nor Irish nor English, nor Vermont nor Massachusetts, but that sturdy composite thing that comes out of a Mr. Harvey's melting pot—an American. If Wisconsin is proud of any of its part in the making of a nation or of anything in its own life as a state, it must take off a reverent hat to Mr. Harvey and the dozens like him who made its raw material into finished citizens.

As the Circuit Rider with his camp meetings was obeying a law of evolution, just so Mr. Harvey, thinking himself to be teaching only Latin and Greek, was really instilling citizenship.

Mr. Harvey! Aztalan! Samuel gasped at the utter audacity of Azariah's suggestion. "But the money," he ventured rather hopelessly, having none at all just then.

"Easy," Azariah assured him. "We'll find places to do chores for our board."

Eager, starved, adventurous Samuel jumped at the chance. He tore home, converted Anne, Thomas, John, Daniel, sister Anne, Willie and Jock to his way of thinking by a great burst of eloquence, and started off with Azariah the next week.

Ever so little, the lions on the path pulled apart. Samuel, at sixteen, walked through them to conquer the world, like Dick Whittington, with his bundle over his shoulder, without Dick's lucky cat, but with a single silver dollar in his pocket instead—Mexican at that—to buy an education.

CHAPTER VII

A DOLLAR'S WORTH OF EDUCATION

Samuel's capital of one silver dollar brought him so much more education, outside of books, than he had bargained for, that to an ambition a whit less eager it would have proved an overdose.

He and Azariah marched into Aztalan with wet feet, in an icy snowstorm. The Indian mounds were the merest little lumps in the snow line. The huddled houses looked bleak and uninviting. But to Samuel it was Aztalan, town of romance, where even their phlegmatic driver from Milwaukee had broken into eloquence that set the saga of the great Northwest, like a living fire, in his imagination. Now Aztalan was his own first great adventure, his open door.

As Azariah had prophesied, it was no trouble at all to find a place to work for his board. Mr. Brayton, who ran the general store and the post office, seemed fairly to snatch at his services. After the first week of work for him, Samuel could easily guess why.

Half-past five on the farm had seemed a very early waking hour, even with Anne's call bringing him over the edge of consciousness into a cheery atmosphere of mother love. Breaking ice in the basin for a sketchy morning wash could not be counted a pastime, it is true. But "two jerks of a lamb's tail" was quite long enough to jump himself into his clothes and out of the freezing little loft down into the kitchen where a steaming hot breakfast was always ready, close to

86

the snapping fire, and a greeting from Anne with a smile behind it.

A boy earning his board at Aztalan from Mr. Brayton waked to a very different morning. He was required to get up at four o'clock in the freezing weather, build two fires in the house and set water heating, so it would be warm for Mr. Brayton to use. He crawled into bed again until six, then turned out for good, tramped over to the store and kindled the fire there. He had to chop wood, both for the house and the store. That was merely the beginning of his day.

He was sworn in as assistant postmaster and had to help sort the mail brought each day by the stagecoach, drawn by four horses and driven with a great flourish up to the door. Aztalan was one of the important stops on the route, a mail distributing point for several towns around. The mail had to be sorted with lightning-like rapidity in the few minutes allowed. Complaints kept coming in about it. The wrong towns and the wrong people got the letters. All sorts of irregularities occurred with Uncle Sam's property.

The anxious assistant postmaster was quite at a loss to understand it until, coming into the store one day, he found his employer totally unconscious, standing holding out tape in his extended hands, like a wax figure, until he fell back against the shelves behind him. Samuel discovered then that he was subject to epileptic fits, with sudden lapses of consciousness. The mail tangle was explained. The mix-ups had always occurred when Samuel was out.

But the boy's relief was short lived. He found that Mr. Brayton was laying the blame for his own mistakes on the youth and inexperience of his young assistant. His anger flamed high until he reflected that Mr. Brayton probably believed what he said. The upshot of the matter was that he assumed the entire handling of the mail, in addition to all his other duties, and took his payment for the extra work in being glad that no fault was found with the mail service during his régime.

Every alternate Saturday the boy had the joy of a few hours at home, with Jock barking circles around him, Willie pulling him away to tell him secrets, Daniel smiling tolerantly at him, and all of them loving him. But he had to earn his little respite by walking eleven miles to get it, and walking back the eleven miles in the afternoon in time to do the evening chores. How many city boys of this soft twentieth century would care to do that?

To find any space for school and studying in such a program of work as Mr. Brayton laid out for Samuel would seem to have required the services of a professional wizard. But the boy accomplished it.

Mr. Harvey, his teacher, and one of the uncanonized saints of his time had not a grain of self-seeking in his make-up. He was a fine, athletic, unorthodox saint, one of those severe disciplinarians who would work his head off to help his promising pupils and larrup them within an inch of their lives, if he had the slightest suspicion they needed it.

To a boy who had struggled through three bare dreadful years of teaching himself, goaded on the whole time by the sharpest kind of a desire for knowledge, Mr. Harvey seemed like a miracle that happens just once in a lifetime. This indefatigable man had the true teacher's excitement in helping a determined, ambitious mind to unfold. After beating the elements of knowledge into farmer boys' heads all day, he would tramp over to Mr. Brayton's store night after night to help Samuel. Between his pupil's sales of butter and eggs and nails and tobacco, tea and woolen caps and postage stamps, he taught him Greek and the beginnings of mental science.

When he was sure the boy was out of hearing, he predicted a career for any youngster who could keep as many things going around in his head as a circus ringmaster. He delighted in recalling that prophecy when, as Superintendent of Schools himself, at Beaver Dam, he made obeisance to Samuel as his State Superintendent of Public Instruction. Still later in his sunset days, at Evanston, when Samuel, in Chicago, had enough interests to fill a card catalogue, it was his pet belief that his chastening rod had seasoned his pupil for Bishop timber.

Samuel went from Aztalan with the fervent hope that he would never again have to render so much service for so small a return as board at Mr. Brayton's! But the price was cheap, after all. For proud as any young knight who has won his accolade, he carried with him his first recommendation to teach, written in Mr. Harvey's beautiful hand.

Samuel's lucky star, at last, seemed inclined to take a hand in the game. The next year he attended a "select school" at Sun Prairie, though what the basis of selection was he would have been hard put to it to say. Again he had an excellent teacher, but as usual heavy-handed with the rod. The important thing was that he made excellent progress in his studies.

Then a barn near the Porter school became a landmark in the boy's development, and an address by the Reverend Jabez Brooks a turning point. The speaker was an agent of Lawrence University, recently established at Appleton, Wisconsin. He was selling perpetual scholarships for tuition for fifty dollars each.

By some necromancy of mathematics, impossible for a twentieth-century mind to comprehend, only the interest on fifty dollars at seven per cent would be required, making the instruction cost only three dollars and fifty cents a year at Lawrence, outside of incidental expenses.

The Reverend Jabez Brooks had been chosen for his eloquence. He told a story of the beginning of the university that made Samuel's blood run through his veins like fire. The boy could scarcely believe his ears.

He had no money and no prospect of any, but with the faith of an Abraham about to sacrifice an Isaac, he walked up to the rough, improvised little table under the loft full of sweet-smelling hay, and by the flickering light of the tallow dip, put down his name for a scholarship.

His rosy dreams lit the dark road home like a lantern, but when he reached the farm, cold black logic met him in the person of his older brother, John, always ready to furnish ballast for any new idea.

"How in the world are you going to raise the interest?" he asked when he heard the story.

Samuel's eyes glowed like a blue flame, as they did in moments of great excitement, and the glorious audacity of youth spoke in his ringing voice. "I made that investment in faith," he declared, "and I am going to college if I die for it."

It was his valiant challenge to the God of miracles to give him his chance. It came, of course. Such faith could not go unsatisfied. But it came with conditions which greatly increased his already hard-worked capacity for hurdling obstacles.

The school at Gravel Church, in Fountain Prairie near Columbus, Wisconsin, was without a teacher. Samuel applied for it. Again he had to be examined by a Town Superintendent who held the destiny of the township teachers in his hands. He lived thirteen miles away from the Fallows' farm. With the memory of Elder Green fresh in his mind, Samuel had no second sensation of walking on bubbles, light as air, as he tramped along to see his second Town Superintendent.

But it was a very cozy homelike affair after all. The dreaded dignitary proved to be a pleasant young man living with his father and mother on a farm near the school. They

chatted away merrily all evening, and at the end of it the
Superintendent invited Samuel to share his bed.

In the morning he merely asked the would-be teacher his
name and where he had gone to school, signed his certificate
and presented him with the school.

Samuel had looked forward to his first school as a kind
of little heaven on earth, the opening round in the glorious
battle of being grown-up. He could not have been quite
so blithe about it if he had known that he was to tackle
one of the most difficult schools in the whole state of Wisconsin. No former teacher had been able to last out the
Winter. This one was barely eighteen, rather slight in his
physique and with no previous experience to guide him.

The ringleaders in the school warfare did enough in
Samuel's first week to keep a reformatory staff occupied.
There were three of them—two cousins, boys, over-age and
with no business in school at all, under the law of the state
which made the school age from four to twenty-one years;
and the sister of one, a girl of sixteen, known by the school
rule of opposites as the "Prairie Infant," though she could
easily have qualified as the Fat Lady in any Dime Museum.

They were a precious trio, in school and out. Samuel was
left to deal with them alone. The three school trustees were
broken reeds, so afraid of them and of the rest of the family
that they gave their teacher no support, muscular or moral.
He did his best to keep a stiff upper lip, but sometimes he
was in a state of utter desperation, "the most homesick boy
that ever walked the earth," he confessed, in a fragment of
autobiography at eighty.

The climax of the school mutiny came the day after one
of the spelling bees held at the church, in which classes from
all of the neighboring districts were represented. The
teachers at these spelling bees were on exhibition, as well as
their pupils. The two men cousins had been insufferable on

this occasion, and Samuel, even the next day after school, was still smarting with mortification. A friend, three or four years older than he, who had obtained the consent of the directors to receive extra instruction in school, was with him. The two insurgents were hanging about the door.

"Let's settle things with these fellows," said Samuel's friend, whose ideas, at least, were heroic. "Let's cut some strong canes in the woods and tell them if they don't behave, they'll suffer."

It sounded good. Samuel put his trust in his ally. They went for the canes. The cousins were at the door as they came back.

"What are you going to do with those things?" jeered the two, feared by three trustees and the whole population of the town.

"Use them on you, if you don't behave in the future," returned Samuel, as valiant and as slender as David of old with his sling.

The crisis was on. The cousins followed them into the schoolhouse, indulging in a Wisconsin brand of Goliath language, so evil that Samuel tackled the larger of the two giants forthwith, pinned him against the wall and held him there. Here the resemblance to the Bible story ends. His friend, of course, should have throttled the other, and the course of true teaching have run smooth the rest of the Winter. The issue was different, but none the less interesting. The other cousin shouted at Samuel's friend:

"I'll settle you!"

"I've no quarrel with you," said this knock-kneed ally.

Samuel's heart dropped to his toes. The game was up. With one foe in front and another behind, there was no hope, outside of fiction, for the hero. The second beefy cousin fell upon Samuel and forced him against the seat. Then a curious thing happened. Something in the gameness of the youngster under his heavy hand must have appealed to the bully's better nature and saved him a little of the future punishment reserved for tormentors of teachers. He made no move whatever to strike, but instantly let go his hold. The two cousins marched out together, made no further trouble and soon afterwards left the school.

Samuel conquered the "Prairie Infant," also, but by other methods. When she had been particularly provoking one day, he touched her shoulders very lightly with a switch, something he had never done before and "never would do again to a woman"—he made up his mind then and there. He spoke very sharply, also, to the "Prairie Infant." He expected her, as a matter of course, to square off for a fight and braced himself to meet the catapulting two hundred pounds. But, to his utter amazement, she hung her head, instead, and burst into tears.

To his surprise, he found his own eyes were wet. He told Anne about it the next time he went home. She nodded her head wisely. It was the appeal of tears from which his family would always have to protect him, if they were to have any clothes in their wardrobes or food in their larders.

Unversed in the wiles of women and missing the point, he amplified the story. "Naughty as she had been, you see, she respected her teacher," he said. Again Anne nodded wisely and let it go at that. Samuel was a personable youngster, and even "Prairie Infants" are susceptible.

Though the brothers left, the girl remained in school and became a docile, tractable and adoring pupil, if a portly one, from that time on, a credit to any teacher.

For managing this arduous school, Samuel received the sum of fourteen dollars a month and "boarded round." He was learning as much in the school of human nature as he was teaching in his little log schoolhouse.

As a rule, the families with whom he boarded put on their company manners for "teacher," and, what was most delightful, generally killed the fatted chicken for him, as they did for the preacher. He never did quite master the psychology of "Prairie Infants," but he had an amused and kindly understanding of the foibles of some of the masculine members of the community.

One good old Methodist, with whom he became acquainted at close range, was noted for his gift of continuance in prayer. He loved him in his home, but squirmed in agony when he prayed at meeting for forty-five minutes on end.

He found food for much quiet amusement in another resident of the district, who would fall down often after praying and lie in a kind of trance for an hour at a time. Once Samuel saw him open his eyes just before it was time for the climax, look all around to be sure that there was no obstruction, and then proceed to drop spontaneously and dramatically.

In Samuel there dwelt a delicious little imp, with faun ears and a Puck squint to its eyes, that was always confounding those Queen Victoria virtues, so highly commended by his mother.

It was due to this doughty little imp that neither farm toil nor Elder Green nor homesickness nor the cousin and brother of a "Prairie Infant" could quite quench his pleasure in being alive.

Out of school hours it made him just a happy boy himself, jumping and wrestling and playing games with his pupils, with the zest of the youngest of them. Once, when the snow was so deep that the boys and girls could not get through the drifts to the schoolhouse and were huddled in the road, a soggy discouraged group, it gave him the inspiration to pile them all on oxen and turn the occasion into a perfect riot of joy. It was a half-hour of such pure ecstasy stored in the memory of one of the company, Azariah's little sister, that it kept fresh there when she was an old, old lady.

It was a priceless talisman, that little Puck. It gave Samuel the power of making commonplace days delightful, of getting a glory even in hardships—of "putting wings on sandals." It made him the best proof that the joy of life was not in its setting. Other boys, without his imp, might have been as happy, temporarily, as he was. A young king perhaps, with a crown for a plaything, a boy millionaire with a bagful of dollars for counters, a slum urchin, the freest and saddest thing in boydom. Crowns, however, have a trick of going out of fashion. Dollars get lost in the financial shuffle, and the freedom of the slum urchin too often terminates behind prison bars. But Samuel's happiness was of the indestructible variety. It was independent of poverty or riches, failure or success or anything else external. It came from a source within, and it lasted as long as he did. For it was the man himself.

The term ended, he went back to work on his father's farm, cap tilted, feet dancing, half his hard-earned fortune in his pocket. Now, at last, the way to Lawrence was clear.

PART III

THE BATTLE GROUND OF YOUTH

CHAPTER I

CHAOS

But poverty, the grim monitor of the pioneer boy's dreams, turned the cap-tilted teacher to the University of Wisconsin, not Lawrence, that Fall of '54.

The common sense of the whole family battered his reason into accepting the substitute. Wisconsin was near and cheap, they said. His twenty dollars would not last a month at Lawrence.

So he and John drove to Madison in the oxcart and climbed halfway up College Hill to the University of Wisconsin. A four-story rectangular box, called North Hall, housed all the institution there was, except its hopes.

The bundle of impulses and urges and instincts which was Samuel, at eighteen, jumped over the wheel into a new field of training.

He seemed merely a slight lad in homespun and clumsy shoes, with blue eyes that glowed and blazed under black brows. Grim little furrows, cut by the fight for schooling, ran from a strong nose to a tender mouth that set at times like a steel trap. But he was, in fact, the chaos nature makes of her strong sons growing up. He was swayed this way and that to the call of his mind, the strange new cries of his body, the clamor of his breeze-shaken soul. He was out of focus, the play of great forces, potential for good or evil. As a self, he was, as yet, unfound.

The boy from Hanchettville took a swift look at the Uni-

versity. His goal in Manchester, five years before, had been
first the Manchester Free Grammar School. After the grammar school, he was hoping for stately Oxford and the education of a scholar.

He flashed another glance at the rectangular box.

The free grammar school could swallow this whole backwoods university at one gulp and never wink. As for Oxford—Oxford would not have that building about the place,
even for a stable.

But it offered his only chance for an education.

Never at any crisis of his life did Samuel fail to apply the
philosophy of life which Josh Billings formulated later:

"When you must, you better."

Nor did he now.

He and John piled behind North Hall the farm wood out
of the oxcart for Samuel's stove. The new student shouldered his English leather trunk. John followed with the
week's supply of provisions. Then Samuel waved his free
hand toward the horizon—Madison, a jewel ringed in the
cobalt of her lakes, the Capitol dome, evanescent as a celestial
bubble in the rainbow haze of heat. Not Oxford, itself, could
produce a lovelier ensemble.

"Beautiful view," he said safely.

"Too bad," said John, the practical, adjusting his load for
a third-story climb, "too bad you can't *eat* the view."

Make hunger fierce enough, and fodder will seem a feast.
Through five long thwarted years of piecemeal schooling,
Samuel had starved for knowledge. Here, such as it was,
he had a larder full.

John clattered down the stairs. The new boy swept out
his room, inches thick with dust after the last occupant. He
sneezed and sang. "Oh, for a thousand tongues to sing,"
and sneezed and sang again till the senior down the hall asked
him what his name was, in the hope of stopping him.

But Samuel, rising to a fresh experience like a spring released, was too happy for silence. The barnlike room had a bedstead with a husk mattress, a chair and wooden table for Samuel; the same layout for his roommate. Like the university, it was rather a promise than a fulfillment. Still, in comparison with the dirt floors of a district school, North Hall was a palace. After a kitchen corner or a store, a room to oneself becomes a place of magic.

However much in externals this crude backwoods university might fall below the par of his English ideals, it provided for a boy at sixes and sevens with himself what no Oxford or Cambridge could have bettered. This was "Prof. John," a Princeton graduate, cultured, charming, with an authoritative voice and the delicate hand of a watchmaker.

Professor John Sterling was head of the preparatory department, where Samuel eked out his district school learning for a while before entering the regular course. He was also Professor of Mathematics and of Mental Science, janitor when the janitor failed, purchasing agent, librarian or acting chancellor at need.

Month after month, this "Father of the College," its first professor, held it together by the sheer force of his will, feeding himself on his devotion to an ideal, and not much more.

He was Samuel's "center of attraction and gravitation."

Later Prof. John shared honors and responsibility with the immortal Pat. Listed as janitor, Pat was a Wisconsin edition of Solomon, who managed the boys, passed judgment on the prospective wives of professors, advised chancellors and, in their absence, could have conducted the University in an Irish brogue, with perfect dignity.

Years later, when the daughter of Pat and the daughter of Professor Sterling had to be torn apart, because each was insisting with small fat-handed blows that *her* father owned this seat of learning, Samuel had become a regent of the University.

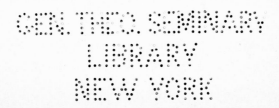

As a boy, Samuel thrilled to the hope of a future crammed with action. Prof. John showed him that a man may have his finger in forty pies at once and still be a credit to society.

One day, out of his tumult of desires and emotion, Samuel summoned courage to confide to this Professor his vague desire to be a preacher.

Prof. John, himself a graduate of Princeton Theological Seminary, threw an affectionate arm across his shoulders and said things that were anchors to a boy struggling to find himself in chaos.

"You will need to read," he said. "Take this. Use it whenever you wish," and he put the key of the college library in his hands.

Books! Arsenal of weapons for life! Books—denied him for five years! Books! And a boy so famished for print he had walked twenty miles again and again on the off chance of finding a newspaper!

One case of books on an upper floor! That was the library! Samuel knelt before it, breathless.

He read the titles through the glass—Washington Irving's "Tales of a Traveler," Scott's "Black Dwarf," "Old Mortality," Rollin's "Ancient History," "Legends of Hispaniola," Cooper's "Prairie" and the rest.

One by one, he took the precious volumes out and handled them reverently till the pain of his longing was a little appeased. At last he pounced on one, raced away with it to his own room, curled down on the floor under the window and was lost to time and space until the stars pricked through the twilight and he could no longer see the words on the page.

Samuel remained about a month at Wisconsin that first Fall, was taken into Athenæan, "Ath." for short, one of the two debating societies—the best thing in the curriculum to put a boy's individuality into the saddle and bid it get some-

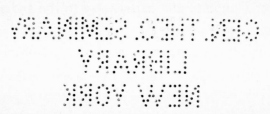

where—and to tuck Prof. John away in his mind as an inspiration for life.

Then the Lawrence perpetual scholarship began to burn a hole in his pocket. It might not be so perpetual, said Samuel to himself. Lawrence was the best in Wisconsin just then. Only six years old, dropped into the empty woods one day in 1848—the year of his own arrival; surrounded almost the next by the prosperous town of Appleton; now, in 1854, heading Wisconsin's educational aristocracy, it was one of the best-manned, best-financed, best-attended institutions in the state.

Oh, yes, in this new country, with your own eyes you could see a college growing out of the soil of devotion, watered with the showers of sacrifice.

Didn't he know the grip of it!

Why, merely hearing the story of Lawrence had drawn this modern Abraham to his altar—the schoolhouse desk—on the night that his life turned a corner. The patriarch about to slay his son performed no greater act of faith than Samuel when he said to the Lawrence agent:

"If you please, sir, put me down for a perpetual scholarship."

It was the cry of a small boy, starved for learning, to a bountiful God.

God had brought him that perpetual scholarship, not a doubt about it. Yet here it was doing no one a bit of good, merely getting worn out at the creases, because he had a prudent family.

Again and again he went over the story of Lawrence in his mind. Perhaps Wisconsin's story was interesting, too. But it had no distance to give enchantment. Lawrence? That was a romance!

The Honorable Amos Lawrence, mill owner of Boston, stanch Episcopalian, father of an embryo bishop, dreamed a dream of putting a college in an uninhabited Wisconsin forest. He did it on land he had bought from Eleazar Williams, supposed Lost Dauphin, and Missionary to the Indians.

Mr. Lawrence, longing to make his college Episcopal, realized that only Mid-West Methodists had the energy and push to make it go. Believing that some denomination must be behind any literary institution that was not to have its usefulness blighted, he lifted up his pen and wrote:

"I will give ten thousand dollars to found a college in the wilderness if the Methodists of the region will raise ten thousand more."

So the Methodists, a handful at the most, who traded eggs and apples for the very clothes they wore and saw a dollar once or twice in a blue moon, replied:

"Oh, yes, certainly, Mr. Lawrence. It will be no trouble at all."

Before a tree had been cut in Appleton, or a foot of ground cleared, a little group of them, missionary preachers, met at Oshkosh. The Reverend S. M. Stone, a preacher in charge of the Winnebago Circuit, offered his ten-by-twelve log cabin parsonage for the meeting.

"Well," said Brother Stone, "I'll start the ball rolling with a hundred dollars."

It was a fifth of all he had or ever expected to have. The rest of the brethren gave in proportion. The other Methodists, ministers and laymen, squeezed money out of the very stones themselves, and the ten thousand was raised.

Brother William Sampson, afterward, when building funds gave out, sold everything he had—a dwelling in Fond du Lac, two lots, thirty acres of land, one hundred and twenty acres of timber land, staked the price of it and all the reputation he had on the success of Lawrence University.

What a combination! A university founded by the Episcopal dollars of a Boston mill owner, dropped into a Wisconsin wilderness on the land of a Lost Dauphin, Missionary to the Indians, and run by Methodists.

Just before the end of Samuel's first month at the State University, rummaging in the cupboard of Prof. John, he found an article in an old magazine on Eleazar Williams, supposed Lost Dauphin. The man was the most precious saint and rascal, in one skin, yet unhung.

Mr. Williams had been brought up by Indians, was Catholic, Congregationalist and, at last, Episcopal missionary to the Red Men, according to the demands of the occasion. He had been offered a king's ransom, according to his story, by the Prince de Joinville to abdicate his right to the throne of France and had magnificently refused. He had married a charming fourteen-year-old girl, also with some claims to royal French blood. She had an ovation in New York society which put that of Pocahontas to the blush. That she loved some one else when her father ordered her one day to marry Eleazar troubled him neither in his rôle of Lost Dauphin nor of missionary. The fact that with her came some four thousand acres of land may have confused his sense of might and right.

Eleazar also had a magnificent dream of establishing a kind of Indian empire in the great Northwest. Shrewd John C. Calhoun backed him in that scheme with all the powerful backing he could command. Calhoun cared not at all for the drama of the thing, nor had he compassion for the poor Indian. He helped because nothing on earth would have given him greater joy than to commit that dangerous Northwest to a program which would make impossible the formation of any more anti-slave states within its boundaries.

As to Eleazar's pretensions to the throne of France, volumes were written about it. Affidavits were made by the score. The brutal shoemaker who took care of the little stolen Prince had struck him with a towel torn from the wall, nail and all. The nail had made a scar on the Prince's forehead. Behold the mark on Eleazar's! The little prince had some kind of hereditary marks on his knees. On Eleazar's clerical knees were the same marks! The crescent-shaped vaccination scar, identifying mark of the little Bourbon, appeared, likewise, on Eleazar's arm, for any doubting Thomas to see.

Hundreds of people were impressed by his claims, among them even the astute Honorable Amos Lawrence, of Boston, who was very difficult to hoodwink. He bought land out of the great tract that Eleazar owned, as rumor had it, to help him prosecute his claims. If it was part of the dowry of the unwilling little wife, its final use must have afforded her some consolation for an unhappy life.

Denied every other claim, Eleazar was, at the very least, a child stolen by the Indians after the terrible Deerfield Massacre. When his Lost Dauphin claims seemed to be collapsing, he could still command the excitement of trying to prove that some of the best blood of America ran in his veins.

After Samuel had devoured that article, the fat was in the fire. When he saw an actual picture of old Eleazar in the magazine—Bourbon oval obscured by the portly contours of hearty living, the two little white tabs of his Episcopal office beneath his rather thick chin—he realized what a mixture of demigod and rascal this was.

What boy, with a grain of imagination and a perpetual scholarship in his pocket, could stay away from a place where any day he might meet France face to face? Not Samuel!

Last flick to an insatiable curiosity, Lawrence had lady students, young ladies admitted by the charter, though Mr. Lawrence did not care for them at all. Lawrence was a co-educational university, the second in the whole United States.

The Lost Dauphin *and* the ladies!
Wisconsin's case was hopelessly lost.

On the next Saturday visit, Samuel burst into his home kitchen with an entirely new batch of Lawrence arguments which he had run the last half-mile to deliver.

He brazenly flaunted his diminished capital. He said he could walk the ninety miles to Lawrence. He dwelt on its many excellencies and on the fact that Anne was always bidding him to seek the best.

But he mentioned neither the Lost Dauphin nor the ladies. . . .

The family went down before his onslaught like prudent soldiers who know that defeat is inevitable.

Anne tested a loose button on his coat and looked at his shoes. Much of the way he would have to walk barefoot, she knew, to save them.

"Sammy, Sammy," she said, "it's a long, long walk, that ninety miles."

"Only four times and a half as far as Madison," said he, out of the undaunted glee of a boy getting his own way.

CHAPTER II

LOST—A DAUPHIN: FOUND—A LADY AND A CAUSE

Samuel went rainbow chasing up to Lawrence the next week.

He carried his belongings in a little valise that felt like lead before he was five miles out of Madison. He set it down often, partly to rest his arm, partly to bow gracefully to any stately tree he saw and keep in practice for the Dauphin.

A farmer with a load of apples caught him at it, once. Samuel tried to look casual, as if bowing were his usual form of roadside gymnastics. The farmer gave him a lift and apples to eat, so the episode closed pleasantly.

Limping into Appleton on feet that felt like cushions full of red-hot needles, the seeker after romance looked right and left for the Dauphin. What figure of fable he expected to see, he scarcely knew. Something princely in doublet and hose was his best hope, holding out a beringed hand from crimson cuff and saying—in French—"Advance, my son."

At the least, he hoped to gaze upon the priestly original of the magazine picture—Bourbon jowl over Episcopal tabs.

Not a sign of it to be seen! Not the ghost of a smell of France or Lost Dauphins hung about the town of the university. Lawrence was disinfected to the last inch of space by Methodism—which left all other orthodox Christians feeling at home, however, owing to its saving Episcopalian mixture.

How Samuel blessed his reticence about the Dauphin, when he learned, by guarded inquiries, that poor Eleazar the year

108

before had come to a sad, inglorious end all by himself, with the wife who did not love him far away. He had died in a horrid litter of uneaten food and unwashed dishes, in a poor little cabin—even that the charity of friends.

A shattered romance is easier to bear, unshared. Samuel's interest was volatile, but just at first, Lawrence, as a rainbow end, seemed as tame as the family woodpile.

Preparatory departments of the fifties differed not at all from one another in subjects or in drudgery. The new student studied just what he did at Wisconsin. Chapel had even an added touch of rigor, according to Samuel's friend and fellow sufferer, the Reverend Henry Colman, who later rose to ecclesiastical glory, proportioned perhaps, to the severity of his early discipline.

"I rang the bell," he writes, "made the fire for morning prayers at six when Professor Kellogg came down with his tallow dip, read and shivered and prayed, while the students sat around wrapped in long shawls or big overcoats which covered a multitude of negligences."

Nevertheless, it was Samuel's experience of education *de luxe*. He recited in the most beautiful building in the state, and he had his meals served to him on a table three times a day. The library had a room, instead of a bookcase. And Philalethean, which took the place of "Ath.", had quarters of its own.

Failing France, our traveler did at least meet Boston— Boston walking in the wilderness.

Dr. Cook, President of Lawrence, was this paradox. He had learning so highly polished that it shone like his gold-headed cane, his shoe tips and his silk hat. This he lifted with a Dauphin's grace, even to preparatory lads and to the ladies—young ladies, God bless them!

Granted everything else a duplicate of Wisconsin, the ladies made for Samuel a different world of Lawrence. Interesting creatures! They kept a man on tiptoes in his classes. He had waked to girls when that poor mountainous "Prairie Infant" had wept at his touch. Some girls might be more disturbing in class than others. That rosy-cheeked English one who lived near them now. Anne, his mother, rather liked her, because she was English. Thought she might have a temper of her own, though. Yes, she would *be* disturbing, not because of her temper, though . . .

One charming little blue-eyed creature in his Latin class at Lawrence had a dimple and a tiny curl that escaped engagingly from her smooth hair at the back. She told him all sorts of things he had scarcely dreamed of before; how downtrodden women were, for instance, and how they needed men as well as women to fight for their rights.

The Seneca Falls convention for Women's Rights, in 1848, and some of the later ones had been dreadfully misunderstood in Dane County, he discovered, even by Anne, his mother. He was sure that if this pink-cheeked, dimpled girl could talk to her, she would see it all in a minute, just as he did. Women and black folks, whose plight roused Anne almost to a fury, were all in the same boat.

Strange Anne had never seen it. He would tell her.

The boy from Hanchettville maneuvered the little suffragist to the river bank on an off afternoon and showed her a joke in a *Sartain's Magazine* two years old. The picture displayed a lady with three long curls dangling on each side of her classic head. Her knees were boldly crossed under her voluminous skirts, a slippered toe uplifted brazenly. In her tapering fingers was a fat cigar, on the table beside her, a stein. From her innocent lips the editor drew this gross sentiment:

"For my part I can't imagine what ladies find so attractive in that ridiculous bloomer dress. If we *must* imitate men, why then let it be in something sensible."

"Fancy," said the blue-eyed one, radical in view but not

CAMP RANDALL, MADISON, WISCONSIN.—Sketched by A. L. Rawson.

Where Bishop Fallows trained in the Civil War (1864) and received his Colonelcy in the 49th Regiment.

[See Page 204]

in garment, studying the lady. "Fancy," echoed Samuel, studying the living little anti-Bloomer, with the soft little curl at the back of her neck.

Young ladies were supposed to be admitted to Lawrence on an equality with men. The course was the same for both, except that French was substituted for Greek for the "ladies," with the privilege of taking Greek if they wished. Exercises and declamations and compositions were required weekly of the gentlemen, but composition only was required of the ladies. As a concession also to their femininity, Painting, Wax Flowers, Wax Fruit and Ornamental Hair Work were included among the extras.

Dr. Colman, Samuel's "Henry," speaking of those days in the warm afterglow of Lawrence's Fiftieth Anniversary, said with pardonable hyperbole:

"Here women as well as men have boasted with Emerson,

" 'I am the owner of the sphere,
    Of the seven stars and the solar year,
    Of Cæsar's hand, and Plato's brain,
    Of Lord Christ's heart and Shakespeare's strain.' "

The quotation would have infuriated the lady with the dimples greatly. Owner of the sphere? Oh, no! Not in Lawrence! Young ladies recited with the young gentlemen and held their own with them, but at graduation they had separate "Exhibitions," their name for Commencement.

Dr. Cook was the reason. Exiled in the wilderness, and Bostonian, he did not want it known in his East where co-education was anathema, that he was President of an institution which admitted both sexes on an equality!

At the end of a month, the pleasures of Lawrence, the conferences with the little Woman's Righter and Samuel's funds came to an end all at once.

He went away delightfully exhilarated by the thought that

armies of dimpled ladies needed a man to defend them.

The old darky, in the well-known story, could resist everything except temptation. Samuel was finding that he could resist everything except rainbows and causes.

A few weeks more the next year were all he ever had of the University. But so deep was his affection for Lawrence and that of Lawrence for him that he was treated like an alumnus all his days and received an LL.D. at her hands.

The tale of Samuel and the dimpled suffragist with the engaging curl? That was transient.

In a brief by and by she slipped into the limbo of forgotten loves.

Not for a king's ransom, not to save his life could he have told you whether her eyes were blue or brown.

But the cause of Suffrage, which she gave him—the first of his many causes—he fought for until it was won.

CHAPTER III

THE GREAT DISCOVERY

But on Samuel, back in Wisconsin, sweeping out his North Hall room, rested no ash of forgetfulness—at first.

His thoughts dwelt happily and often on that excursion up to Lawrence and on the wild-rose pink of a lady's cheek. The championship of her cause seemed doubly sweet in memory.

The moods of his mind, his body and his spirit were not so gusty for a while. But still he was a ship that had not found itself; its bolts and timbers were creaking, not ready yet to drive for a port at its Captain's will.

Then he forgot curls and causes and Lawrence for a while, because the mighty thing happened which set his very stars in their courses going a different way and flung him the purpose of his life from the opened hand of destiny.

It was advertised in that December of '54, on the spot of the college wall reserved for notices, as a joint meeting of Ath. and Hesperian. But it had quite another name among the immortals, the hem of whose garments the boy felt he was touching that evening.

Samuel was one of the two speakers at that meeting. His subject was the "Nineteenth Century." William F. Vilas, a slip of a boy with big ears, a good nose and a rounded forehead, spoke for Hesperian, the other debating society, on the subject, "Territorial Expansion."

William's father, a Judge from Vermont and an ardent Democrat, sat on a front seat, holding the bulgy umbrella he always carried to political and other public meetings. The students who likewise attended the meetings used it as a cue. When "Old Man Vilas" thumped, they clapped. When he didn't, they were silent. That night, after his son's maiden speech, he thumped thumps of paternal pride. The students clapped.

Samuel rose to speak, and his miracle happened. He caught the audience between his hands and he moved it this way and that. It was as docile and obedient as his own mind. It was his mind for the moment.

The Samuel within Samuel of these early college days was a tumult of ideas and thoughts and instincts and emotions, clothed like the figures in an Oriental market place. They surged against a background that was never black nor white nor merely gray, never duller than the veiled glory of an old Persian rug. Put in too small a space, they hammered and beat against an English intellect, cool, appraising, buttressed by the inherited traditions of centuries. Speech was their open door.

Whatever that particular line along which the artist gets his glimpse of the infinite which is genius, seems to him the most alluring and enchanting art of them all. At the crest of his enthusiasm, Samuel had no wish to change places with any other artist.

Painter! Tied to his canvas! What need has eloquence of a studio or a north light or an oblong of cloth or paper? Humanity your canvas, your personality your brush, your words the colors.

Sculptor! Who would wish marble with an audience to shape, cold as any block of stone, at first? Touched with a word here, a word there, dexterously, masterfully, lo, it comes to life. You are Pygmalion twenty times a day.

Actor! On boards, bounded by back sets, wings, drop curtain. Any orator can make a desert his stage.

Author! Slave of his pen and ink. The orator writes himself on the hearts of men and women and children, and the message flashes out over a lifetime.

Simplest, yet most mysterious, of all the arts is this of eloquence, sublime enough to stir a nation or a world, yet so tuned to little things that you could practice it, even sitting on a haycock in a Dane County field, with the blue sky overhead and Jock beside you. A few sounds on the air, a gesture, an inflection—your audience of one has his paws on your knees, and the heart in his eyes is yours for the asking.

Oh, yes, it is the rarest alchemy in all the world. You do something. Your audience does something. A new thing is born, so exquisitely evanescent it melts as you reach for it, so mighty that it may shape a life for all time and what lies beyond time, because it is not of time but of that fourth dimension where, at given moments, God touches human tongues.

Of course, Samuel did not indulge in all this rhapsody about the great joys and the small joys of eloquence that night after he had spoken at Ath. Such enthusiasm from such a novice would have seemed almost blasphemous.

Moreover, neither then nor at any other time was he greatly interested in acting as Boswell to his own feelings and emotions. It was much more fascinating to set them going and watch the results.

One touches Pisgah seldom in a space of eighteen years. After those gloriously hearty thumps of "Old Man Vilas," Prof. Sterling's "well done, my boy," the little broken phrases of approval from his college mates, Samuel found that the fierce excitement of the evening would not die, even when he had crawled in between his cold homespun sheets, with Anne's comforters a young mountain atop. His mind would not wind down from those high ethers where it was sailing.

At last, he plumped out of bed, lit his quarter of a tallow

dip, fumbled for the bookcase key in the left-hand side of his top bureau drawer, where he kept all his treasures, sped bare-footed into the hall and took from the case the most thrilling book he could find—"Old Mortality."

It was an insignificant little custom to establish on an evening when the most tremendous thing in his life had happened.

But again and again in later years, keyed up and restless after an intense speech, he would steal away to his study, with a detective or mystery story under his coat tails, like a guilty little urchin going fishing, because his helpmeet distrusted that form of diversion so late at night. He would be a boy once more, after his first speech, racing against the waning candle. When the final wifely call, symbol of later years and maturity, floated up the stairs in the middle of the hero's most villainous plot, he was back again in that North Hall room in the heyday of youth, with a guttering candle leaving him and his hero to blackness.

There was no school of elocution yet in the Western wilds. So he took to the woods.

Again and again, with the trees as auditors, he drove his voice up and down the scale to a-e-i-o-u-, a-e-i-o-u, staccato and lente, piano, forte, fortissimo, until he could make the high notes sing like birds, the middle ones resound like a bell and the low ones boom like organ tones.

He recited poems for the oaks and the maples and the beech trees.

He began to play at putting words of his own together.

Words to him, anyway, were never merely combinations of straight and curved lines, or of sounds made by certain fixed arrangements of the vocal machinery.

Sometimes they were jewels from which one rubbed the film of English to find Greece and Rome at the heart of them.

Sometimes they were a great army moving along the trodden ways, doing the simple bidding of men who worked much with their hands and talked little.

Sometimes they had pinions and lifted his spirit up, up, past all the other winged creatures, into the great spaces where morning stars sing together and forgotten worlds speak across infinities of time.

From his first model, the Circuit Rider, he caught the secret of vivid imagery.

But the molding of his talent was given by circumstances into other hands.

Madison, only six years away from the legislature which had bolted to see the first circus come into town, had awakened out of the comfortable crudity of its village stage to the necessities of culture.

It had inaugurated a Lecture Course, which brought together, in its raw little frontier self, almost the beginnings of time and space, by a method perfectly invaluable to a mind in the making.

For the most eminent men of the time in literature and oratory took the trip to Madison and delivered wisdom in their own persons.

Samuel watched the technique of the speakers as a cat does a mouse, ready to pounce on any point that could help him. The things he gathered from the gentlemen, besides technique, were a delicious revelation of the ragtag boy he was, below his attempted attitude of dignity and serious purpose.

John G. Saxe gave him a poem, quotable, ever afterward, with a playful finger upraised, on all sorts of occasions when some one was getting puffed up with the pride of birth that seemed to Samuel little occasion for pride, because the individual had nothing at all to do with it. The poem ended with the warning that you might, if you tried to ascend your family line, find it ending in a noose of stronger twine which troubled some worthy relation, and a final chuckle from Samuel which robbed his reproof of any sting.

Horace Mann, "the very Nestor of American education," lecturing for two hours on "Education and Virtue the Foundation of the Republic," wound the boy up to such a pitch of intellectual excitement that he found himself at the end "standing breathless, gripping the back of the pew in front."

Bayard Taylor startled his Methodist soul by saying that on the walls of an Egyptian temple, undisturbed for six thousand years, he had seen the inscription, "I am that I am," the name to be given to Pharaoh by Moses, who had heard it announced at the burning bush.

Wendell Phillips, clean shaven, granite chinned, Roman nosed, hair swirled in a beguiling scallop in front of each ear, came with the glamour upon him of having ascended a platform some years before, a beautiful young Apollo, a member of one of the first families of Boston; of having spoken against the murder of Lovejoy at this meeting, presided over by William Ellery Channing; of having descended the platform to be recognized as one of the foremost orators of the world. It was a fact to catch in the memory of a boy interested in oratory.

But a stray sentence out of his lecture on the "Lost Arts" proved a veritable dynamo.

"Those ancient Egyptians," the speaker said, "knew enough to ventilate their tombs. We moderns don't know enough to ventilate even our houses and our churches."

It was dangerous to drop any interesting suggestion into Samuel's mind and expect it to lie dead. It never did. Fortunately this one was good. If all the many hundreds of places that he insisted on ventilating from that time on could have been tabulated and the audiences who benefited been listed, he might have been awarded a place in a National Sanitary Commission's Hall of Fame!

Nor deep nor high, nor far nor near, were beyond the range of Samuel's eloquence—the fish of the sea; the God of the universe! Egypt; big bear boos for Professor John's first baby. His mind played host to every impression.

Azariah, rooming with Samuel, found it more fascinating than a game to watch him, half lathered, gesticulating with both hands, bursting out with fragments of speeches for Ath. or bits of pretty speeches for the girls at the next Deansville quilting party. He always expected to see the shaver slash his cheek with the razor, instead of the air. But Samuel never did.

CHAPTER IV

THE LORD SAID "SAMUEL"

Things happened so fast to the Hanchettville boy, in that first emancipating year of his preparatory course, that he felt like the man trying to stake out the shadow of the oak. Every time he pegged himself down, he found he had moved ahead.

First, his mind broke loose into freedom, then his soul.

Souls, in the Fallows family, were the most important things in the world. On the state of their health hung everlasting bliss or everlasting torment.

Samuel went to college clad in Methodist garments, subject to the hopes and fears of fervent Wisconsin Methodism, modified by the cooler, more ritualistic variety he had known in England.

His soul was more or less troublesome to him and to his mother. The Methodist dictum was that it should be, until certain salutary changes had taken place.

But he was such a wholesome-minded lad that, through his boyhood, even the terrible hair-raising damnation sermons which he continued to hear at camp meetings disturbed his happy relations with his Creator merely temporarily, and his soul suffered only the minor ailments of a growing child.

But after Lawrence and a coy little ringlet had awakened him to other fundamental things besides Latin and Greek, after the memorable conjunction of Ath. and Hesperian hitched his mental wagon to a star, he found himself subject to unexpected spiritual stirrings.

He and Azariah and H. Gardner, another Methodist student, took long walks and spent serious hours discussing the

120

symptoms of their souls. In the accepted Methodist phrase-ology, they talked about conversion and salvation, redeeming love and dying grace.

Up to a certain point, Samuel walked the given way and spoke the given words and thought the given thoughts.

But he could usually be trusted to add a touch of originality to any routine.

This touch he added on one memorable walk with Azariah and H. Gardner, which led their steps to a schoolhouse near Madison, where a revivalist of the true fire and brimstone sort was holding services.

Samuel stood with the others, a reed shaken in the wind of the exhorter's eloquent appeal to sinners. Finally, an idea, deep in his subconsciousness, flamed up to its first expression.

"Let us," he whispered to Azariah, "go and get converted, and then we can preach!"

He meant no irreverence. Religion was as natural to him and as unstrained as breathing itself.

He desired to preach. His mind flew to that goal, like a carrier pigeon. If conversion was necessary to that end, then converted he would be. Nor did he ever pause to consider that the conventional "call" to preach in Methodist circles followed conversion, but never preceded it.

He made his way to the Mourner's Bench, never realizing that he was breaking traditions at every step. Not that it would have made any special difference if he had.

It was characteristic of him, even in his 'teens, to obey the spirit and let the letter go where it would. The thing that counted was to preach the faith that was in him, and this was the way to take.

All that Summer, working on the farm, Samuel's soul seemed tossed about at battledore and shuttlecock.

His friend, H. Gardner, who was caught with Samuel in this whirlpool of emotion, was a merry youth, capable of entertaining the quilting party Azariah's sister gave, for a whole afternoon, with "his superfluous gas." But so powerfully did the Methodist spirit work within him that he recalled the experiences of their last unregenerate Summer, to Samuel in a letter, in words like these:

"The deep yearnings for some nobler, truer, holier life, that came to manifest themselves at times, and scare the silence of our loneliness; the awful consternation that finally seized us, as we were roused to the truth that we were without an interest in Christ; the earnest pleading for reconciliation to a holy God; the gradual dawning of the light of hope; the all-engaging beauty of the day star from on high, revealed to us; the still, small voice which bore the witness of the Spirit; the half-felt melody of seraphim, fit ushers of so glorious a morn; the spreading glories of the perfect day, enlightened by the Sun of Righteousness . . ."

H. Gardner, animated by a warm and loving spirit, used the accepted phraseology of his circle.

Samuel could never have couched his feelings in the same terms. Even his mysticism was pragmatic, charged not so much with contemplation as with the mission of bringing something to humanity.

Before the Summer was over, in the beautiful quaintness of the Methodist phrase, Samuel "had crept into the heart of God." There he dwelt very contentedly, with little self-flagellation, until the end of his life.

The pleasant outward recognition of his change of heart was a license to exhort bestowed upon him, one Sunday, at Porter's schoolhouse. The rest of the family and Anne were present. She wore her best and only black silk dress (the one Samuel had hoped to supersede, if he could have gone to the gold fields), with her English bonnet tied under her chin and her English heart as overflowing with thankfulness as if her gracious Victoria had stepped across the sea to make her boy a belted earl.

CHAPTER V

THE MERRY-GO-ROUND

The swift financial pace of Lawrence was its knell for Samuel. Board there cost two or three dollars a week.

So after swinging pendulum-like, for two preparatory years, between Lawrence and Wisconsin, he settled down to finish his course at the latter, and became a member of the sophomore class in 1856, with no freshman growing pains. "Settled," though, is a ridiculous word to describe his brief pauses at the University, when he had to earn even the pauses.

Expenses he reduced to a minimum. His room in North Hall cost him three dollars a term, his tuition four. Washing, according to the catalogue, was forty-seven cents a dozen. Too much. So he carried it home or did it himself.

For food he paid next to nothing—in cash. Each Saturday he walked out to the farm, twenty miles away, and returned before chapel Monday morning with his week's supply on his back, raw or ready to eat.

The raw food he cooked on a camphene stove, temperamental forefather of the alcohol lamp. Once it exploded when he was trying to recall what his latest divinity, gray eyed this time, had said about the Pleiades. That incident almost terminated his connection with divinities and everything else, except eternity.

With the urge for food as powerful as any of his other urges, and hollow to the toes, the daily allowance that only half filled him made daily discipline.

On one trip home, Anne, as a very special treat, put into his food knapsack a fresh-baked juicy berry pie.

"Sammy, Sammy," she warned, "do be careful of it."

He was, for a while. But halfway to Madison, weariness overcame him. He dropped his bag at the foot of a tree and relaxed comfortably against it. Never once did he think of the pie until he felt its juice warm against his skin. He pulled off his coat. There was a great pink spot as big as a saucer. That coat was the only one he had. It would be months before he could afford another. The spot was a tragedy. He washed it out as well as he could in a brook near by and hung the sorry garment on a bush.

He sat down while it dried and devoured at a sitting the damaged pie, planned to last a week. Then he put on his coat, shouldered his provision bag and went on his way with a whistle.

The whistle was symptomatic with Samuel, then, and to the end of his life.

Never was it braver than during the hunger fight of his college days. Sometimes home supplies ran low or it was impossible to make the weekly trip to the farm. During one of these times of famine, he and his roommate, Mr. Smith, who afterward went as a missionary somewhere, found a simple solution of the problem.

They bought a barrel of crackers, and they lived on nothing but crackers and milk for days at a time. During the open season they relieved the monotony by wild gooseberries and strawberries from the back campus, an addition to their diet which was decorative but not filling.

Samuel whistled hardest when empty as a drum, he marched past the students' dining room assailed by the appetizing odors of a hot meal in full swing, up to that lonely bowl of crackers and milk.

Meals, in the dining room cost only a dollar fifty to a dollar eighty cents a week, but it might have been a million as far as the boy from Hanchettville was concerned. It was not simply the food that made him feel, when he passed the dining room windows, a Lazarus looking on at a feast of Dives. He mourned quite as much the drill he was missing in foreign languages. At three tables the students spoke, respectively, Greek, Latin and French. French was spoken strictly according to the rules of English pronunciation, "Honi soit qui mal y pense," for instance, becoming "Honey swat kwee mally pence."

Whatever the ambitious student missed, he was spared the pain of the French conversationalists, who discovered that a real Frenchman was so dull he could not even recognize as his own tongue, French spoken à la Wisconsin.

The class of '59 was a different kind of test from the district school, which Samuel had led hands down, or preparatory departments, which were mere fill-ins.

In his class of eight, each lad had a distinctive quality which would raise him a little or a good deal above the average.

Boys of the fifties were not dragged by an ear between an ambitious parental thumb and forefinger to the college table and made to eat. Few sat there because their mothers thought it was the correct thing, or because their muscular systems might bring glory to their college. They were in college because they were gripped by an overwhelming desire for knowledge itself.

Like Samuel, the other seven were a survival of the fittest. They were picked material—the few boys in a community with originality enough to brave opposition and get out of a rut, the few in a generation who could be relied upon to carry the flag of progress a few yards farther.

Judged as companions or antagonists, they were highly interesting material. Phil Slaughter was to be respected as already a wizard of finance. Alexander Botkin's legal mind was a whetstone. As for Elbert Hand, no one supposed he had judge material under that carrot thatch of his.

He was an adventure story just as he stood in his big freshman shoes.

Drawn by the lure of gold, had he not accomplished the feat denied to Samuel of going to the gold fields in an oxcart at eighteen?

Had he not dug out a fortune after incredible hardships, returned home and, in the best Sanford and Merton style, paid off the debts of his parents and built them a house with gold that he had taken to Philadelphia, himself, and had minted?

A thrilling experience that, to sit in the Greek class with a boy whose exploits made even Homer's seem a little shopworn and out of date.

The courses offered could be taught in a few rooms left over in North Hall, after the students, the faculty, the dining room and the chapel had been assigned space. They included Greek, Latin, Moral Philosophy, Christian Evidences and a smattering of Natural Philosophy and Chemistry.

But then no college in the United States had more to offer. None, either, had a group of cultured professors thinking higher or living on less. Surely none were more honest.

"What *is* an imponderable fluid?" Samuel's beloved Prof. John was asked in class one day.

"I don't know," admitted the frank professor. "I don't know."

Professor Carr, about to do an experiment before the students, began with his usual formula:

"Young gentlemen, if the laws of nature operate as they ordinarily do, and I have reason to believe they will, this steel spring will burn in oxygen." Something went wrong that day and the experiment failed. "They didn't," he observed, referring to the laws of nature; and went on imperturbably with his lecture. One learned composure, as well as Chemistry, from Professor Carr.

AN OLD DAGUERREOTYPE

Brigadier General Samuel Fallows, Mrs. Fallows, and their son, Edward, at the close of the
Civil War in 1865.

[See Page 210]

The future governors, judges, United States senators, military generals, postmaster generals and bishops jogging Samuel's elbow every school day emerged to fame and glory on a list of subjects too short to fill the first page of a college catalogue to-day.

In spite of it or because of it was a question that concerned the boys of 1856 very little.

To master the curriculum they had and thrash a way to a degree was a feat for an acrobat and a pugilist. Patient Azariah Hall, with only backwoods preparation, needed nine self-supporting years to make the grade, his brother Frank, seven.

Samuel, thanks to Bow-legged Dicky and Warrington's ebony ruler, took his A.B. in five. That, too, when it was a case of "earn not, learn not," with chances for picking up ready money almost as scarce as hens' teeth. He would wrestle with college for a few weeks, then tackle a district school on the side until he could save enough to get back to the main show.

The kind fates, in one of his earning bouts, made him superintendent in his own township of Medina, at a "dollar a day while actually engaged in service." There, only three or four years before, had Elder Green, the conscientious, tripped him up for a tiny slip in parsing and blasted his hope of teaching. It was pleasant to be sharing the same rung of the ladder as the Elder. Samuel confessed to feeling both the honor and the humor of it.

Another source of income was preaching Sunday afternoons in country churches.

Samuel's preaching would never have qualified with the old Scotchman, betrayed into profanity by his very zeal of righteousness.

"Religion," he said, "without a hell isn't worth a damn."

In spite of hunger or hardship, Samuel's youth and his

joy of living so brimmed over that to those congregations of overworked farmers and their careworn families he always forgot to preach anything except the love of God, the hope of salvation and the glory of man—a habit of his which time never cured.

Because of his freshness and vitality and friendliness, Samuel was rather the fashion in student preachers. He became known, his friend the Reverend John Taylor remembers, throughout the region as the "Boy Preacher."

One of his assignments was to dedicate the church at Black Earth, a very little town, according to Mr. Taylor, only to be found on a very large map of Wisconsin, but big enough to be the birthplace and stepping-stone of himself and James L. High, one of Samuel's college discoveries with whom he never lost touch.

Word went about that Samuel Fallows, the tall slender student with shining eyes and quick smile, whose words glowed or scorched or blessed at his will, was to be the preacher. The whole countryside turned out to hear him.

After the dedication, lunch was served out of doors near the church. Johnny Taylor, waiting for the second table, was conscious that the preacher had made a good impression.

"They couldn't seem to get enough of him," he said. When lunch was over and famished Johnny Taylor about to have his innings at last—dear me, if the master of ceremonies didn't ask Mr. Fallows to make another speech! Good—but when a boy is starving!

Then Samuel sat down again—by John's own father, too, and they talked intently as if time and Johnny's patience had no limit. But the young preacher, also a natural journalist, was deftly extracting information from Johnny's father, a mining man, about tin mines in Cornwall, from which he hailed, and about lead mining in Wisconsin, which was his specialty. The information was Samuel's to use tellingly about forty-five years later, when he was investigating the great coal strike in Pennsylvania.

This journalistic instinct brought him the editorship of the *Student Miscellany* in his Sophomore year.

He contributed at least two initialed pieces—one on "The Few," pleading for the aristocracy of learning, the first and perhaps the last time that he defended any aristocracy, except that of goodness.

The second was a fervid plea for the black man. It was the day of the fugitive slave law. Benammi Garland, a great hulking brute of a slave owner had reached up into Wisconsin for what he called his runaway property—a negro, Joshua Glover, living peacefully and profitably at Fond du Lac. Benammi, with a warrant, retook his slave, while the fugitive was playing cards with three others in a shack. He threw him, tied, bleeding, half dead, into an open wagon and kicked him all the way to Milwaukee, through the long hours of a freezing night.

Samuel, brooding over the outrage, on the twenty-mile walk home from Madison, faced Anne in the doorway.

He told her about Joshua. He told her what he felt for Joshua's race. "I'll help them if I ever can," said Samuel.

"You must," his mother agreed.

The dramatic sequence of events following Joshua's capture threw all Samuel's former standards of law and order into confusion worst confounded. A mob battered down the door of Joshua's cell and rescued him. The local justice was courageous enough to stand up and say the law was wrong. Before long, Samuel beheld his state, a child in pinafores among the sisterhood of states, refusing to obey the law, daring to defy the United States Government.

It was like a monkey wrench thrown into his mental works, already in confusion. Was there a law above the law of country? Was there a higher law of God? Puzzling questions to a boy bred to an Englishman's respect for law.

The farmer politicians, spitting tobacco, and the statesmen who sat on judges' benches and swivel chairs, down in the Capitol, discussed the situation—that and the other problems tearing at Wisconsin. A band of crooked politicians known as the Forty Thieves thieved by night to a sound of revelry in the dovecotes, where they served champagne so potent that homeward going guests mistook the lamp posts for ropes by which to climb to heaven. By day, the precious forty delivered orders at the Capitol.

Samuel and his companions, in any spare moment, hurried down to the Capitol to watch the process of government conducted raw and unashamed in backwoods Wisconsin. They heard debates on various vital subjects.

Then they raced back up the Hill and debated them in Hesperian or Ath.

Courses might be as set as the laws of the Medes and Persians. Professors might whip their students along the same old round of Greek, Latin, Mathematics and Logic to their heart's content. But, lo! in Ath. the intellectual slave became a despot.

He settled the affairs of the world, debating such questions as these:

Ought women to be allowed the right of suffrage? Is free trade consistent with the principles of the United States Government? Has the discovery of the gold mines benefited the United States more than the rest of the world? Do the signs of the times indicate a subversion of our Republic? Has ill treatment at home brought more people to the United States than the prospects for the future? Should the student direct his studies in college with reference to a particular pursuit? Would a new translation of the Bible be a benefit to the world? If the boys overlooked any subject which would have floored the world's wisest, it was not intentional.

Samuel debated on everything with everybody. Charles

G. Dawes' father was one of the contestants against whom he tried a lance.

The minutes of Ath. written in the secretary's most careful hand, seem to bear out the judgment that Samuel was one of the best debaters in college. His side won four times out of five. He was also more than once President of Ath. with the attendant train of society politics, which were nuts to him.

Those faded Ath. minutes make plain another thing—what a perfectly haphazard merry-go-round, Samuel's college course had to be.

After the records showed him attending the society meetings for a few weeks, the next entry would be: "Samuel Fallows, of Hanchettville, excused for absence"—teaching school, what not.

To conjure a whole education out of anything so broken as his time in college seems much more of a trick than getting six rabbits out of a derby.

The Celtic in him was always turning duty into joy. No one since the owner of Pegasus had so much fun as did Samuel merely driving his mind through a Greek translation or getting it around a knotty problem before his guttering tallow dip closed the race.

Not that Samuel was a grind or a high-brow. Heaven save the mark! His body was like iron, from the farm work which hardened muscles like a pugilist's trainer. He kept fit in the Wisconsin gymnasium on the upper campus, left over from the days of Pan—a great white oak tree with hanging ropes. Each year he assisted in the terrific fight between the classes, over the lengths of those ropes—embryo of all future tugs of war. Sometimes he swam. Sometimes he fished, oftener a pursuit of food for him than an amusement.

But most congenial of all the sports to his high-geared physique was wrestling. He loved to tussle with the other boys. "There were very few of them he could not stand on their heads," wrote one of them, who retained to his ninetieth year a vivid memory of seeing the campus upside down under Samuel's hand.

Pranks even found their way into the crevices of those strenuous days—nights, to speak correctly. He and a future judge, a district attorney, a reviser of the criminal code, and other potential pillars of society, according to rumor, did the joke with the calf which was probably old when Moses, going to school in Egypt, must have put a sacred cow where it was never intended to be. The Wisconsin variety was propelled up three flights of narrow North Hall stairs and made to attend compulsory chapel.

The compulsory feature of chapel, even in the fifties, raised the protesting hair along the student spine and started a growl in its throat.

The next stunt to which unverified tradition attaches the name of Samuel also increased chapel attendance by unnatural means. The "Cabinet," joy of the professors, pride of the regents, "unsurpassed in the West for scientific purposes," containing, with specimens in Mineralogy and other branches of Natural History, a collection of the sorriest stuffed animals extant, was raided by a small group of students.

They gave each faculty chair an occupant, the chancellor's, the black bear, best preserved and a little pompous; Prof. John's, the kindest looking animal; the geologist, the raccoon, because they both dug; and the most unpopular professor's, a mangy rat.

Memorable, in the annals of this company, was a Robin Hood excursion. In a thrifty attempt to utilize nature's ice box, the butchers of Madison hung the turkeys outside of their shops to keep them frozen. One Winter night these birds were all appropriated and fastened like Midwinter May baskets to the professors' door knobs. Whereupon, these poorly paid gentlemen, feeling that Providence itself had had a watchful eye on their depleted larders, published a joint card of thanks to their unknown friends.

CHAPTER VI

A SHAPING WHEEL

Samuel, young, enthusiastic and crude, was given over by chance to the most anomalous shaping wheel in backwoods Wisconsin, Mr. William P. Huntington, farmer, descendant of a certain Richard Warren, "gentleman," of the *Mayflower*.

Mr. Huntington was Eastern born and Harvard bred, an A.B. and M.D. both, and a Unitarian minister, whose mother, an exquisitely saintly creature, had been read out of the Hadley Church because she believed in universal peace and read Channing's sermons. Before Gerrit Smith and Wendell Phillips made the practice conspicuous, he had been "egged" in the East for talking against slavery. This forced him to change his clothes, but not his opinions. He could sketch and model in clay and write Latin poetry. French, German, Italian were his pastime reading; the stars were his open book. He could pick up any flower of the field and give his children its impossibly long botanical name. He had carried on a successful boys' school in Wisconsin and conducted two government surveying expeditions in the northern woods, which involved elaborate mathematical calculations and some hardships. Deeply but unconventionally spiritual, he had a sense of beauty like Raphael's. He invented a device to keep grain bags open, which some way failed to work, and a foot warmer for cold country rides, that failed to warm.

With these perfect qualifications for living a scholar's life on an income provided by Providence, he embarked on an enterprise which might have staggered the most practical and expert pioneer in the whole state of Wisconsin. He bought an almost untilled farm of one hundred and sixty acres in the heart of Dane County, and named it Cedar Bluffs.

Truly, it was an exquisite little unit of beauty, about a half mile along a lovely curving bit of road. This road led from the house where Samuel's friend Azariah lived. The farm had red cedars—the only ones for miles around—bluffs and slopes, a winding creek, friendly trees in which the wild pigeons loved to roost. It boasted hollows where the lady slippers grew and charming spots which lent themselves to pleasant names in the family directory—Twin Meadows and Plum Thicket, Timothy Lot, the Copse and a dozen others. Mr. Huntington had moved out to the farm from Milwaukee about two years before, in the dead of Winter. With five children to educate, he had come to a region where good schools were as scarce as blackberries in January. Having only his own two hands and the eleven-year-old hands of his oldest son, Willie, he had set about the task of clearing, grubbing, sowing, reaping and reducing to submission one hundred and sixty acres of uncleared land, grown to white oak and bar oak and all the other oaks, and with enough stone in its soil, poor Willie used to think, to build a city.

Mr. Huntington was a farmer by accident; a sad accident for him, perhaps, a happy one for the community. For he became a center of culture where there was little, a poet in thought where there was none in conditions, a school of manners, even in the hayfield, in an old straw hat, a hickory shirt and blue denim trousers held up by homemade galluses of cloth.

The connection between the two was made one Fall when Samuel, quite out of funds and needing to teach again before he could hope to learn again, swung happily along the road skirting the Huntington farm. All his senses were on the alert to catch the beauty of a November day, touched with

the warmth and graciousness of Indian Summer. His errand
was to ask Mr. Huntington for a school he thought he had
at his disposal. A little thing—but a revolution hung on as
small an object as a chest of tea; and Samuel's fortune was
to be an entirely different affair because he crossed Mr. Huntington's path that morning.

He found Mr. Huntington beyond the South Meadow with
Willie, a slight blue-eyed lad, with longish hair quite ready
for a home-done hair cut. The two were just at the critical
stage of lifting the rider to the top of a length of a zigzag
snake fence, and Samuel sprang to help, before he made
known his request.

With the rider safely in place, Mr. Huntington, in his oldest clothes, with tufts of hair sticking through the breaks in
his hat, bestowed upon Samuel the bow of a courtier. The
boy felt as if he had stepped out of the Wisconsin landscape
into the pages of a novel.

No, Mr. Huntington told him, he was not Town Superintendent just then, but Justice of the Peace. If Samuel wished
to have a dispute settled or to get married, he would gladly
serve him, but he was sorry to say he would be unable to
accommodate him with a school.

When the bell from the farmhouse door announced dinner,
Mr. Huntington insisted that Samuel join them.

His mother had given him a motto once which was so
congenial that he had chosen it almost unconsciously to live
by—the best is none too good. It had kept up his standard
along the lines of his activities, but after that first memorable
dinner in the Huntington kitchen, his best had an entirely new
definition. The dinner would have been natural enough in
Boston or New York, but in the midst of frontier farming
country, where dinner was merely a stoking process for the
next piece of work, it had the effect to Samuel of a court
function.

Mrs. Huntington was as much the cause of it as her husband. When she greeted Samuel graciously, she looked so little and valiant and so pretty, with her big blue eyes and pink cheeks, that it seemed as if it would be quite in the picture for him to lift her little work-roughened hand to his lips and kiss it. When he found out later what a five-foot dynamo of energy she was, how she had been picked off a Massachusetts hillside, when she was only nineteen, by a man nineteen years her senior, to do all the things a scholar with his head in the clouds must needs leave undone—he felt rather that he should salute her as one of the unsung generals of history.

When he came to know her very well, it seemed as if she achieved the impossible every day. She cooked and she scrubbed, she spun and she churned and she gardened. She made the family's clothes, their soap, their candles and their sausages. When a sheep was killed, she fashioned sheep-skin mittens and wee kid shoes for the babies. She had eleven children in all; a rigid casing of Puritanism which her Unitarian husband never even dented; the warmest kind of a heart; a faith which made her say with superb confidence, when want was trying to stare her down, "You know the Lord always hears when you scrape the bottom of the flour barrel." Her fastidiousness kept the family standards of living true and well-bred in that crude Western country where there was every temptation of example and utter weariness to let them slip and run down at the heel.

In that noon hour which introduced Samuel to the Huntington family, she rounded up the hired man—a rare luxury in the Huntington household, collected the children, sent them to the basin on the bench outside to wash their hands, dished up the dinner, put it on the table and seated the nine members of the household with a whirl of quick orders and swift motions that roused the boy's instant admiration.

"General Washington couldn't have done it better," he told his mother afterward.

"The dear overworked lassie," said Anne out of her unerring sympathy.

"Grown up and married a long time, mother," reminded Samuel.

"But dear and overworked and a lassie at heart still," persisted Anne stubbornly, knowing the surface of capability the helpmeet of a visionary man must assume. "And see to it, Sammie, when you have a wife of your own, that you do not work all the lassie out of her."

Dinner was eaten in the Huntington kitchen that day, from a plain table spread with a coarse cloth and set with ironstone ware. But such was the power of personality and atmosphere that the effect on Samuel would not have been different if they had been sitting upon the ancestral mahogany and eating with polished silver from eggshell china.

They talked of books and poetry and music, encouraged by Mr. Huntington, who sent Willie away from the table for five minutes because he mispronounced the same word twice. Kittie had to take her elbows from the table several times. Little Flora had a quiet lesson from Helen, sitting next, on the proper way to hold her spoon.

All through the wonderful hour, the hired man, seated next to Willie, glowered at the rest of them. He shoveled in his food with his knife and gulped it as if he were a python. He drank his coffee out of his saucer with great noises. "Sounds just like the piggy," contributed five-year-old Freddie gleefully, and was hushed by his mother.

After Helen and Kittie had cleared off the table and brought on a delicious apple pie for desert, culture and crudity met in a combat. Mrs. Huntington asked the hired man politely if he would have a piece of pie. He held out his great horny half-washed hand across the table for his triangle.

Mr. Huntington, champion of the colored race and believer in democracy, gave Samuel one of the strongest lessons possible in the triumph of instinct over acquired ideals. He rose in his wrath, and the tufts of hair on each side of his bald head shook in sympathetic excitement. Then and there, in pioneer Wisconsin, he read the hired man a blistering lecture on his table manners. The hired man rose in his wrath and retorted that his work might be Mr. Huntington's but his manners were his own, and he'd be hanged if he'd change them for any schoolmaster who didn't know any more about farming than a turtle did about Greek.

Valorous little Mrs. Huntington's voice rose on a tone of command, though her words were mild. "The girls and I have the dishes to do. Will you *please* sit down, both of you, and eat your pie?"

They both sat down. The junior from Wisconsin University, fairly choking with the mirth he dared not display, concluded that the honors were even, since the hired man ate his pie from a plate but with a very ostentatious spoon.

Samuel spent the afternoon helping Willie and Mr. Huntington build snake fences in the meadow. The older man was as unruffled by the pie incident as if he had merely corrected an erring schoolboy.

Mr. Huntington did all these things for Samuel, beginning that afternoon in the meadow, at the period when youth was most plastic, and impressions stamped the pattern of his future life. Setting the rails one by one, he took the boy here and there through the whole field of knowledge until he was breathless. He drew him an alluring picture of his Harvard alma mater. With hair-trigger quickness, Samuel decided to go there, an ambition that he never relinquished until he went.

In the cool ironic Huntington way, he provided Samuel's ardent soul the shock of a dip in ice water by declaring that a camp meeting was no better than an Indian powwow. Afterward, he gave Samuel a book of the gentle Channing's to read. He presented him with a copy of the great Chalmers' sermon on the "Expulsive Power of a New Affection"—Chalmers, of Edinburgh, who stirred a seaman attending his service to such excitement, by his portrayal of the plight of a sinner, that the man cried out from the gallery, "For God's sake throw out the life line. Throw out the life line."

Samuel, reading Chalmers by a candle, was so gripped by the grandeur and sweep of thought in even the printed words that he could not finish the sermon in one night. "I could well understand," he said afterward, "why Robert Hall, one of England's greatest preachers, when he heard Dr. Chalmers preach, rose up in the middle of the service and said, "Well done, Chalmers." Thirty or forty years afterward, when Samuel produced a temperance beer to fight intemperance, to the great joy of the workingmen and the newspapers, it was on the text of that same expulsive power of a "new affection" that he based his experiment.

These three liberal men opened Samuel's eyes to the fact that an idea is an idea and not the Scotch or English or Wisconsin expression of it, that religion is religion and not the particular creed which happens to be its channel. It was the kind of understanding that made him see all men as brothers and made him, when the time came, one of the founders of the Church Federation and an advocate of any movement that led to church unity.

Perhaps no man polished and shaped Samuel more than Mr. Huntington. Still, since one emotion can work more revolutions than a regiment of brains, his most important contribution to Samuel's development, after all, was being Lucy's father. Lucy was his oldest daughter, away in Milwaukee, having a term of schooling at the Milwaukee Female College. The family spoke of her often, lovingly, but quite casually, taking her for granted like the flower beds or the well or the sunshine or anything else refreshing in the daily routine. Samuel listened as casually. But before long he was to wonder how anyone who knew her could even think casually of the wonder that was Lucy.

CHAPTER VII

LUCY PLAYS THE SERAPHINE

Like his other revolutionary experiences, love came to
Samuel with no warning. One day, fancy free, he looked
in at the door of the Huntington woodshed, which had been
converted into a temporary schoolroom. There stood Mr.
Huntington teaching his son, William, Azariah Hall and a
young girl sitting on the chopping block with her head bent
over a book—Lucy Huntington, of course, just back from
school and set in her time and her family like a star in the
firmament! Samuel knew it after his first glance. She lifted
her eyes to his. For an instant, the eternal woman in hers
met the eternal man in his. She dropped her lids in a panic
of shyness. But the miracle was already worked.

Lucy, living pastel with her softly parted hair, brown
eyes full of dreams, her sweet mouth and changing color,
became, on the instant, the quest of Samuel's dreams.

The dimpled little suffragist of Lawrence; the black-haired
English lass; gray eyes of Madison and all the nebulous girls
he could scarcely remember focused to one sitting with a
Latin book on her knee in her father's woodshed.

After that first meeting, life became an alternating rhythm
of college and vists to the Huntington farm. It was nothing
to walk out twenty miles from the university, to join the
horseback parties where Lucy and the other girls rode side,
saddle, in long skirts almost touching the ground.

What if he did have to study all night to make up for it?

141

He liked to ride beside her at the fastest pace dear old lame Tom, her mount, could manage. The strap of the decrepit sidesaddle slipped every rod or two, and Lucy might have fallen to her death in the tangling skirt, if he had not been there to watch.

Often he stayed for supper and listened to Mr. Huntington's words of wisdom and watched Lucy while he ate cornmeal mush and delicious light soda biscuits that might have been made of saleratus, for all he knew.

In the front room of the farmhouse, where company sat, while she finished her duties in the kitchen he liked to look at the artificial flowers she had made at the Milwaukee Female College with Kittie and Helen asking him in chorus if he had ever seen anything half so beautiful.

But, best of all, he liked to watch Lucy's fingers and her profile as she played and sang at the seraphine—a vest-pocket edition of the modern organ, the only instrument of its kind for miles around. She set its soul and Samuel's at liberty.

In May 13, 1858, Samuel, at the university, wrote her his first letter. It was a careful composition to which clung the earth in which his mind was growing—English masterpieces, the classics, the current vocabulary of correct professors.

But, through its formality, here and there broke the eager heart of a young man very much in love. It began:

MISS HUNTINGTON,
   DEAR FRIEND:
With feelings of peculiar pleasure I throw aside musty Latin and Greek, and the puzzling Mathematics, in order to have a cozy chat with you. Cadmus when he invented *letters* never dreamed that in after ages, friends who were miles apart, could converse through their medium, as though they were face to face. Now don't suppose Miss Huntington that I would convey the idea that Cadmus invented epistolary correspondence. I don't mean that. You would convict me of

STATE CAPITOL AT MADISON, WISCONSIN

In 1871, Samuel Fallows took the position as the Wisconsin State Superintendent of Public Instruction.

[*See Page 219*]

an anachronism if I did.   Some of my intimate friends accuse me of using big words sometimes.   You, I know, will pardon me if I do.

But I do think that the one who invented letters or epistles, ought to be handed down to posterity, with Cadmus the inventor of that which forms the medium of thought.

I understand you have entered upon your work.   I am proud to have you enrolled among the band of the teachers of Medina.   I am also proud and highly gratified, that you are instructing in the school, where my own poor humble efforts were expended.

Believe me the associations of that retired place will be more dear than ever, since you have gone to educate.   I hope you will have eminent success, and be richly rewarded for all your anxiety and toil, in the marked progress of your pupils.

Our term has opened with signal tokens of prosperity. There has been however much agitation in the Legislature respecting our University.   It is proposed to change the organic law of the Institution, making it more completely a University than it now is.

I have three classes this term to hear and four recitations. I shall not have much time to come home and visit.   I hope through the medium of Miss Huntington (if I dare be so presumptuous) to be informed of the events in my beloved town, for Medina is as dear to me as Mecca is to the followers of Mohammed.

I have a very pleasant room and a very pleasant roommate (Mr. Smith) this term.   I enjoy more and more the pleasures of college life, and have an increasing desire to progress in knowledge.   I do not keep myself as much isolated as formerly, but indulge in occasional visiting among acquaintances in the City.

But I must conclude this hastily written missive, and awaiting a thrice welcome letter from you,

I remain,

Yours truly,

Samuel Fallows

Should Lucy correspond with a young gentleman?

Her father and mother held a council after the younger

children were in bed. Seventeen! Entirely too young, was
the decree.

When Samuel next dropped his musty Latin and fled to
Lucy, her obedient mouth said properly:

"No, I think we should not correspond."

But her rebel eyes were crying out: "How I wish we
could!"

That night Samuel listened to her play a new piece from
Milwaukee on the seraphine, and sing a new song, his heart
pounding at his eardrums. He carried black torment of
jealousy back to Madison. Others liked to hear her sweet
contralto voice and catch the little elf of mischief glint-
ing behind her demureness as she played. Other youths
of the neighborhood, not tied to a university, could walk
across the fields any Saturday night, knock at the door and
say:

"Good evening, Miss Huntington."

And he, he was not to have even the cold consolation of
a letter! The denial was fuel to the flame that possessed
him.

But with a new altar on which to heap up gifts, he worked
the harder that he might have good reports for Lucy when
they met.

She, also, knew the pangs of jealousy. "Occasional visiting in the city." Just what did that phrase in his letter mean?
How often was "occasional"? Was he visiting the young
ladies?

The courtship, with him in Madison, had all the zest of
competition and uncertainty.

After the Midsummer ending of the college term, the
student was back again on his father's farm. The days were
full of out-of-door toil, but the twilights and the evenings
belonged to Lucy.

The Summer was not without its ups and downs for the
two. But a September day filled with early Autumn sun-

shine brought the climax.   Samuel, finishing his farm work early, hurried over to the Huntington farm.

Lucy, her mother told him, was down by the creek.   Swinging through the fields of yellowing corn, edged with milkweed and goldenrod, the eager young man reached the winding stream where "asters by the brookside make asters in the brook."   He followed its lovely curves to the mill pond where the wild ducks swam and thousands of wild pigeons cooed in the trees overhead.

Beyond the marsh, which on his last walk beside Lucy had been beautiful with lady slippers, pink and white and yellow, he found her—arms full of goldenrod, leading her troop of happy brothers and sisters.

After supper, Samuel maneuvered her skillfully into the solitude of the front room.   It was a feat in the modest fifties.   She played on the seraphine and sang to him softly, "There's Music in the Air" and "Believe Me If All Those Endearing Young Charms."

Beyond the closed parlor door, the house was all full of the noise of merry children.   Inside, quite close together, sat Samuel and Lucy—equal and opposite, two race tendencies, the trail-blazing one that pulls the world along new paths, the race-mother tendency that says:

"Be still, my child, and let your roots grow down."

Outside, the early crickets sang their friendly song and a belated quail sounded its last "Bob White."

Samuel laid his hand on Lucy's and led her gently through the open door, beyond the sound of the children's voices, into the orchard.   The trees hung thick with snow apples and Tolman sweets.   The moonlight haloed Lucy's head.

And Samuel's next letter began: "My dearest Lucy."

CHAPTER VIII

A MAN COMES FORTH

Samuel went back to Madison for his senior year, with Lucy as talisman. Wherever he went he saw her. She was with him in the library, before him on Sundays, in the pew in the Methodist church where he was pastor for the year.

On "surpassingly beautiful walks, amid groves of native trees, along the bank of the lake, thoughts of Lucy, of Metaphysics, of Moral Philosophy," mingled together.

When he opened his book, there was the thought of her. "I am always nerved by thy love. It is the greatest stimulus to mental endeavor I have." Haunting the post office for letters, it was only Lucy's "thrice precious ones" that he craved —Lucy his dearest love, "the greater half of his soul." And would she pardon the paradox?

These first letters of his and Lucy's are an antiphonal of devotion. Couched in the elaborate language of that Victorian time, they hold the essence of eternal Spring. They twist the heart of age and make anything but sweet and twenty bitterly homesick for the high swinging days of youth.

The two had a quaint little Quaker way of underlining affection by the use of "thee" and "thou." In the midst of perfectly humdrum information, too, each stops often to weave a crown of the dearest words in the language for the other's head. They are letters so athrill with devotion that, if the words had tripping feet and tongues they would march through time into eternity itself, singing their hymn of love.

When the letters had been written for a while and it was

146

no longer necessary to spell out the language of love, because they could speak it, Lucy gathered the letters into two packages, hers and Samuel's, tied them with pink ribbon and, in her careful script, marked them, "Engagement Letters." Where the two went, there the letters went.

Twice a year, at house-cleaning time, Lucy took them out and dusted them. By and by, when there were children in the household, they watched the little semi-annual rite with interested eyes. Curiosity waxed stronger with the years. They begged to read them. Their mother shook her head. Finally, one day wearied by too much pleading, she yielded.

The children, three of them, then, flew to the closet in the Chicago house, where the letters were kept in a little square green bandbox, on a high shelf. But when the older girl stood with the box in her arms, ready to lift off the cover, she stopped as a priest might stop, about to commit sacrilege. "We—we couldn't read them," she faltered, surprised to find it so. "They're—why, they're sacred!"

So, twice each year, for the fifty-seven years the love story lasted, Lucy's fingers were the only ones to touch the little packages of letters. When the world was seeming strangely empty without the living presence of the two who had been lovers to the end, the letters were lifted out of the little old green box by other hands.

Again, it seemed like invading a Holy of Holies to read what was written there, unforgivable except for the one reason which would have overcome the inborn reticence of them both—hers, because only so was it possible to bring to life again that splendid youthful figure, ambitious, eloquent, masterful, tender, which was her Samuel of engagement days; his, because only so might others know the utter sweetness and unselfishness and charm of Lucy at eighteen.

She was teaching school then; "thirty-one different scholars and a good share of them roguish little ones." She felt in one letter, that she "had failed to maintain that composure of mind amid the irritations and excitements of the school-room" that she should have. Again, in a coy mood, with her quaint little brand of worldly wiseness which could usually be trusted to give Samuel a Roland for his Oliver, she asked him who hungered for every crumb she gave him:

"Shall I tell you all the little items of news or are they dry to you? I have an idea that gentlemen regard ladies' gossip-ing with disgust, although they are sometimes compelled for politeness sake to *endure* it. As you were forced to submit to the company of that beautiful companion in your walk on the eve of your departure from Madison, I hope you may be spared another such infliction." Then she turned a gentle knife in the little wound she had made. "Mr. A. Hall and Mr. Tibbles were here the night after I received your letter giving an account of your walk."

With the engagement still a secret, Samuel knew that Mr. A. Hall and Mr. Tibbles were free to call on Lucy in any capacity they saw fit. He saw very plainly, too, that they did not intend to leave her pining. He could take from it comfort or disturbance as he pleased.

All the while that Samuel seemed completely engrossed with Lucy and the thousand and one interests of his senior year, the doer and the dreamer within him were having their sharpest and most decisive struggle.

For the first half of his senior year, he was in doubt about his life work. One afternoon, he flung out across the fields, deep into the heart of the woods. Not until dusk was on him and the shielding trees a blur did he stumble through them to the open space, across the campus and up to his own room.

He had made his decision. He announced it to Lucy.

"I have tried," he wrote her, "to shake off the conviction
of duty relative to preaching, but cannot, and have now fully
determined to give myself up fully to the work of the ministry."

And so youth brought forth a man.

PART IV

HE ESTABLISHES HIMSELF

CHAPTER I

SAMUEL PLANTS GUNPOWDER

Samuel had made his decision to enter the ministry. But Lucy, with a genius for goodness, was nevertheless a Unitarian. That fact threatened the future of them both, though any young person of to-day needs a diagram to understand why.

The religion of 1859, in Wisconsin and elsewhere, was an institution as essential to the community as the stock market is now. A prudent Christian, reflecting the spirit of the times, kept the daily record of his soul under his eye like a ticker tape.

People worshiped in denominations set off very sharply from each other by differences of creed and belief which influenced not only their thoughts, but their amusements. Congregationalists were the most tolerant about dancing, theaters and the like; Presbyterians, less so; while Methodists classed all worldly amusements as works of the Evil One.

Congregationalists bothered themselves least about the hereafter. Presbyterians were only at ease after they knew themselves of the elect and predestined to be saved. The Methodists, even after they were saved, felt that they must keep on earning their way to heaven by character and good works.

Divided as the orthodox denominations were on so many important points in the middle of the century, they united in damning Unitarians. Unitarians, in their opinion, were next to infidels, and infidels were one step removed from the devil.

For Unitarians rejected the Trinity. That led to the belief that Christ was essentially human and not the Son of God.

In this liberal day, when Christians hunger for unity, the denominational exclusiveness of the fifties seems like a relic of barbarism. Then, with Protestant antagonism toward Unitarianism at its strongest, behold Samuel engaged to Lucy.

If the two had expected to spend their lives on a Deansville farm, the situation might not have been so serious. Pioneering tended to level differences of belief. Where people were so few that denominations must join in a union service or go without, they joined. The Huntingtons, moreover, were too much of an asset in the community to be banned for their beliefs. But Samuel had no desire to hide his light under a Deansville bushel. He hoped to make it shine in the Methodist Church at large. Love laughs at locksmiths. But neither love nor laughter conquers prejudice. Not even one called of the Lord could summon faith in the Fifties to believe that he could make his living and his future in that church with Lucy, a Unitarian, as his wife.

Samuel recognized her spirituality as something rare and exquisite. What name it bore made no difference to him, personally. He knew that her Unitarianism was the gentle Channing kind that loves the Lord its God with all its heart and its neighbor as itself.

But he was faced with the necessity of earning a living for them both in a church where Unitarianism was anathema. With their future at stake, he wrote Lucy a letter and asked her a question.

"My church, shall I not say *our* church, love, is expecting much from me. I cannot be egotistical. My dear Lucy will not consider me such. But it is looking for good results from my connection with it.

"Catholic in its views—adapted in its flexible policy for rich and poor, learned and unlearned, I think I can accomplish more good than in any other. My friends, and I have warm ones in it, are looking on—shall I say with pride—at my progress? I feel at home perfectly in it. Does my dear Lucy think she can? Tell me frankly, love. I look for God's blessing, engaged in His work, and with thee blessings and joys and efficiency will be complete."

CHAPTER II

HE WINS A VICTORY

The young Methodist made his plea. Manlike, then, he went about his work; studied, debated, tutored and left the God of love to fight his battle for him. That question of his asked so easily: "Shall I not say *our* church, love?" threw Lucy into an agony of indecision.

Unitarianism was part of her New England inheritance from her parents—from the grandfather who had preached it and the grandmother who had been a martyr to it, years before, when for many months she had been denied the privileges of the Hadley Congregational Church because she worked for universal peace and read Channing's sermons. The judges put wounds in Grandmother Huntington's soul But they did not keep her from working for peace, and she kept on reading Channing.

Lucy was like her grandmother, gentle but inflexible on matters of principle. Intellectually, she was largely the product of her father's training. She had his instinctive fastidiousness of choice. She wanted the best in education and religion. The irony which made him call a Methodist camp meeting no better than an Indian powwow tempered her thought.

To add to her perplexities, his question acted, as well, like a high explosive in the Huntington family's religious consciousness. The crisis was due. The Methodism all around them had begun to shake the Unitarianism of the group. Propinquity was stronger than heredity. The young people sat next to Methodism in the district school and at singing

156

school. They husked corn next to it and, caught with the penalizing red ear, kissed it at husking bees. They pulled candy opposite it at candy pulls and listened to it from the schoolhouse platform on Sundays. What chance could a cool religion of intellect, like Unitarianism, have against a religion of feeling, expressing itself in hearty "Amens" and "Hallelujahs," warm handclasps and friendly "brothers" and "sisters," especially when it was applied seven days a week by the whole neighborhood!

Lucy Huntington realized all this. She knew that the other children of her family looked to her as an example. What she did might tip the scales for Methodism or the faith of her fathers, in the minds of all of them.

Religious decisions were no novelty in the family history. Quite recently, to Lucy senior's great distress, her husband's brother, Frederic Dan, a Unitarian minister, had become an Episcopalian.

Tradition said that two ancestors, some years before, had spent the cold evenings of an entire Massachusetts Winter fighting for their religious beliefs. One was a Unitarian, the other an Episcopalian. With the battle still a draw at the end of the Winter, they parted, agreeing to read the Bible from cover to cover for proof of their respective positions. This they did and met in the Fall again, each gnawed by the secret fear that he had forever ended the savor of discussion and life as well. For lo and behold! the Unitarian had turned Episcopalian, and the Episcopalian, Unitarian. They were so delighted to find themselves in opposite camps and fighting still, that they fell on each other's linsey-woolsey shoulders and wept for joy.

But Lucy Huntington was not her doughty old ancestors who loved conflict better than a square meal. Merely a faithful daughter, sister and sweetheart, she was trying to find her tortuous way out of a maze that has confronted the wisest heads in Christendom.

The outward conflict focused in discussions with her mother who was still nine-tenths Unitarian, as her daughter was nine-tenths Methodist. How the house rocked with the debate!

Mrs. Huntington fought for her church principle with the clever sense which makes her homemade aphorisms current in the vocabulary of her great-granddaughters to-day.

Lucy fought with her heart.

The whole family gave heed as it could to the argument between mother and daughter. Willie, pail in hand, not to miss a closing round, kept the overdue meal a little longer from the pigs.

Freddy forgot to get his pan of chips. Busy-handed Kittie and Helen swayed this way and that in mind, as they listened.

Mr. Huntington, entering with foaming milk pails, dropped bantering words into the controversy. But it was like trying to put out an active volcano with snowflakes.

When the battered young warrior could get away without seeming to show the white feather, she would fly upstairs to the sloping-roofed room shared with her sisters. There she would pour out her heart in a letter to Samuel, or with his latest letter tucked into her dress, steal out of doors to Plum Thicket or Pleasant Meadow, where Samuel's God and the Son of Samuel's God seemed nearer and tenderer and mightier to save than in the contracted little house.

In the meantime, Samuel went to try out the vice presidency of Galesville University, an institution just opened in Trempealeau County, up in the northwest corner of the state.

Holding down a strenuous new job, keeping up with his senior work, writing his valedictory, preaching on Sundays, he found plenty of time to write his Lucy, teaching at Medina

GONE!

Bishop Fallows believed in temperance and was strongly against the old type of saloon. [*See Page* 253]

near her home and struggling to change her religion.

Knowing that her decision meant his immediate success or failure he still could say:

"I would not, darling, warp thy mind from truth. I would not for my life lead thee into error. I would not have thee do violence to the convictions of thy soul."

With the endearments in his letters, the young Vice President mingled encouragement and instruction.

Lucy, still storm-tossed, wrote in one of hers:

"Your blessed words in your last have given me new hope and life. I will live nearer to Christ. I have been taught, dearest, that it was wrong to pray to Jesus. But I do not know that we are forbidden to. Is it right, love? I have often longed to lay my heart and its desires open before Him, but I dared only to the Father and then I felt less earnest because God seemed almost unapproachable."

Finally, Lucy's soul found rest. She was put on probation in Samuel's church, and at length she made her declaration of faith.

Only then did her husband-to-be tell her the truth.

"It would have been a detriment to me, if I may not say a curse, to have loved one irreligious, having no sympathy with me on the dearest most vital subjects."

He returned from Galesville to Madison and graduated, one of eight, with pomp enough for an army.

From his merry-go-round college course he carried off the highest honors. His valedictory followed the speech of the great Carl Schurz, on the program.

On that day he said an official good-by to Chancellor Lathrop and a system of education as old as the Middle Ages. He also welcomed a new chancellor and a new system.

After interminable exercises, he said farewell for his class to his alma mater with such feeling that he swayed his whole audience with enthusiasm, although it was seven o'clock in a town where six was the ritualistic hour for supper.

He had won his two great fights—an A.B. and a Methodist Lucy, and he was content.

CHAPTER III

HANDY MAN OF A MUSHROOM UNIVERSITY

Samuel Fallows was appointed Vice President of Galesville University, his first year out of college. After a Summer of doubt, Lucy Huntington, at the last moment, was appointed preceptress, and their path became the primrose path of joy.

Lucy had suffered misery beforehand over her unfitness to teach in a real university where five professors divided among them practically the whole field of human knowledge, with extras thrown in by Chancellor Barnard, of Wisconsin University, and Professor Daniels, State Geologist. Every name in the catalogue bristled with A.B.'s, A.M.'s and LL.D.'s.

Her fears vanished when she found the awesome University a raw wooden building, barely furnished, in a town so sparsely settled that it seemed to have no past at all.

She had not sat fifteen minutes with Samuel in the front room of the three-dollar-a-week boarding place he had found for her, before she was convinced that he was the handy man about the University. She had a shrewd suspicion that she would be the handy woman. In this she was not disappointed.

Samuel, under his high-sounding title of "Vice President," was also "Principal of the Preparatory and Normal Department; Professor of Ancient Languages and Mental Science; Lecturer on the Theory and Practice of Teaching;" also business adviser, physical director and keeper of the student morals—not so listed. He was, in short, everything that no one else could or would be.

161

When he wished to accept a more profitable position in Madison, Judge Gale, Galesville's President threw up his hands:

"We would have to close the University if you left," he cried. There was also the contract written in the Vice President's own firm bold hand, which bound him for two years.

By the terms of this contract, Samuel, for serving in all the capacities just mentioned, was to be paid four hundred and fifty dollars for half his time, to the end of 1860; six hundred dollars to the end of 1861, after that a little more. He also agreed, when his health would permit, "to lecture and assist in increasing the funds of the University," and to "devote his zeal and influence to the building up of the institution."

Lucy was disposed of in the same document for a salary of two hundred and fifty dollars a year.

A canny clause of the contract provided that neither Samuel nor Lucy could engage in "any other occupation or business without leave of the Board, and if either of them failed to teach during term time because of sickness or absence on their own account, a pro-rata amount should be deducted from their salary." Any modern pedagogue who would draw and enforce a contract like that would be run out of the educational field on a rail. But it was usual enough in the fifties.

Judge Gale, who held the destinies of the young people in his hand for the next two years, was a most estimable man.

Half starved for an education in his own youth, working up to a very influential position in Wisconsin by his own merits, he had an obsessing wish to provide for other denied children the college education that he himself lacked.

As an important citizen of La Crosse, he had tried, a short time before, to make his townspeople establish a college or a university, there. Failing entirely, he said to himself:

"Go to! I'll have my own university and a town and a county thrown in."

So he bought two thousand acres of land and set the town of Galesville in the midst of it. He cajoled the State Legislature into organizing the new county of Trempealeau with Galesville as its county seat, obtained a charter for a university to be located at the same place, and in 1859 opened his institution to the world. He, himself, was its President, its Professor of Ethics, Civil Policy and Political Economy, and very soon afterward, he made Samuel its Vice President.

Filled with the splendor of his vision, Judge Gale would have walked over burning plowshares for his university. What was a grand mood for the vision would have been very hard on Samuel and Lucy, if they had not been so lost, just then, in a dream of their own.

Judge Gale made willing packhorses of the youngsters. Lucy taught for all her life was worth. She loaded herself with extras. The extras were numerous enough for any taste.

Music on Pianoforte, Melodeon or guitar, $10 per term.
Perspective drawing, $5.
Embroidery, $5.
Oil Painting, $7.
Vocal Music, $1.

Ornamental hair work had to be omitted, but Lucy could teach her pupils to make lovely wax flowers.

Outside of extras, all the knowledge of the five professors, the Chancellor, the State Geologist and the Preceptress were available to preparatory and normal students for $4.50 per term, including languages; to collegiate students for $10. Both sexes were admitted to all departments. Both sexes graduated together.

Doing the work of three each, the pair found the days bubbling with fun.

One morning the Preceptress sat before the whole school on the platform, looking too dignified to be human. Samuel bent over, as if to give her directions for the day. With a perfectly sober face, he whispered a story about a woodchuck, which threw her into an agony of suppressed mirth—a story so funny that the mere mention of the word, woodchuck, when they had grandchildren, would send Lucy and Samuel into gales of laughter.

Evenings, when they could squeeze in time, they occupied the slippery haircloth sofa in the front room, just tinged with warmth from the decrepit stove.

A favorite diversion was reading each other their letters. One from a Methodist elder to Samuel provided a joke which capped even the humor of the woodchuck story.

The elder wrote to offer the minister-school teacher a charge. The only objection to Samuel in the minds of the people was his unmarried state. The elder suggested that it would be a very easy thing to remedy as a man could pick a sensible and suitable wife almost anywhere.

"Like a gooseberry, I suppose," sniffed Lucy, highly indignant.

A scrawly missive from Helen to her sister described a memorable family trip to Watertown. Helen was so stirred, even by the memory of the five-hour journey begun at half-past five in the morning, that she told the story in one breath, without a stroke of punctuation.

"We bought all of us a pair of shoes or boots Flora Kittie and 1½ yards of calico for dresses I will send you a piece in this letter 2 hoods and a belt for Kittie and me and some orange colored flannel with a little sprig in it for the babies some nightgowns."

All at once, remembering that there were such things as periods, she gave Lucy, who liked them, a double dose.

"Willie a black plush cap. and a vest. and Father a pair of black pants. and a hat. he wanted to get Willie a shawl. but they did not have any. Groceries. cotton cloth and Demens. Good bie dear Lucy."

Invincibly young, Lucy and Samuel made subduing difficulties a fine and delightful art. They could have gone on enjoying the game forever. But the imp of perversity, the attendant spirit of that whole Galesville chapter, put his miserable hand into the spokes of their delight. Of all things in the world, the last they expected, the Vice President was taken sick and ordered home.

He began his invalid journey shortly after the break of a sunless Wintry dawn. Arriving at La Crosse after a devious and toilsome course, around twelve at night, he left at a quarter-past two in the morning, for Minnesota Junction. There he took a train which arrived in Watertown about eleven the next morning. At that place he called upon the Principal of the High School Department, a Mr. Reed, who had attended Samuel's Commencement and remembered his valedictory address with great pleasure.

Samuel tried to make good a promise to Lucy, to "have an artist at La Crosse take his likeness" but the day was too cloudy, and in Watertown he could find no artist at all. "I will have myself transferred to paper, metal, or glass, for thy sweet eyes to rest upon, when I go to Madison," he promised. He arrived at the Fallows farm, about eight o'clock at night.

His first letter to Lucy confessed to a slight fatigue, though even that was tempered by the expectation of "being as good as new" in next to no time.

Thomas rejoiced in his son. But Anne received him like an angel's visit—unexpected and undeserved.

She was wearing the cap of an old lady now. Was she not over fifty? This postscript to his boyhood was almost too good to be true. She fussed over him and cooked things he liked to eat. She was not so strong as she used to be. The little kitchen seemed huge, sometimes, when she measured it with tired steps. But she never let Samuel know.

She shared his new joy in Lucy, as she had his old hopes. Her heart went out to the dear young lassie spending her first Christmas among strangers.

"She says," quoted Samuel in one of the many letters which helped to stiffen Lucy's courage: "I must tell you she feels very much for you in your isolation and sends all her love to you. She talks a great deal about Lucy. She says you must wrap warmly up when you go out and take care of yourself. I say so, too."

It was eight weeks before the Vice President could go back to Galesville.

They seemed a year to Lucy, lonely among all the Galesville friends, lacking Samuel.

To Anne, they seemed as transient as the sun in a day of shadows, touching the blossomed rose outside her kitchen window.

She made her boy a rice pudding full of raisins, the dessert he liked best, for his last dinner. She pushed him gently out of the door with a last message of greeting to Lucy.

All her wishes for her Benjamin were coming true. He was the Vice President of a University and good and a minister. He was engaged to a charming girl—a Methodist, too.

She waved and waved at the door and smiled when he looked back, but when he was out of sight she had to wipe the cobwebs out of her eyes.

CHAPTER IV

WEDDING AND WAR

The imp of perversity was still attending the affairs of the young couple.

Scarcely had the Vice President reached Galesville before the Preceptress was summoned home by the illness of her mother.

Judge Gale must have blessed the shrewd no-stay-no-pay clause in the contract, which made any burden of absence theirs entirely. He was having a hard enough time, as it was, trying to make ends meet around his budget. He did not succeed by acres and acres, so he eked out salaries with town lots—"worthless," Mr. Huntington called them. But Samuel amused himself in Lucy's absence by planning to build on one of them.

"I am having a bill of lumber for *our* house made out," he wrote her, "and have engaged $150 worth of work to be done upon it so we can occupy it in the Fall and have the rest finished at leisure. . . . It will make a very beautiful residence indeed."

With Galesville finances what they were, it seemed as if this servant of the Lord must be depending upon a special variety of colossal raven to bring timber and workmen, instead of food. Not by any natural means did a house seem even decently probable. He endured his loneliness much less patiently than Lucy had hers. Submissive at first to the decree of a Fall marriage, he felt his resignation go down like a house of cards.

"It must be earlier," he wrote to her.

"Impossible," replied the family.

But nothing was impossible with Lucy the stake. He and she together applied some method of meeting objections which crushed them like eggshells.

April ninth, 1860, at Cedar Bluffs was set for the wedding day.

On the afternoon of that day, the ceremony over, congratulations received, a little maid, rosy and quaint in her gray bonnet trimmed with blue, stepped out from her home with the man she loved, to conquer the world on a salary that nowadays would not support a quarter of a man in poverty.

Nobody was troubled by the fact. So far as ultimate values went, no one needed to be.

The Galesville contract, with more than a year to run, had to be fulfilled. Although those honeymoon days were full of hard work, shared together, they held a rapture one would like to keep in memory and will to one's children.

And then, across those happy hours, the Civil War came storming.

Lucy's heart stood still when Samuel tried to go as chaplain at the first call. It only began to beat again when he found the posts were all filled.

With what patience he could muster, he settled down to finish the last months of his Galesville contract. It was tortoise tactics for a hare. Released at last from his obligation to the University, he was free to try to realize a long-cherished hope. Harvard!

Never once had he abandoned his dream of going there, since Lucy's father had put the thought of it into his head, the first day they met over the snake fence.

His wife encouraged his dream. He must have the finest

possible equipment for his career. Harvard was the finest thing in the country. Harvard it must be.

"I can go back to the farm," said the bride of a few months, with no betrayal of the pain it cost.

They sold one of Judge Gale's despised town lots, given the Vice President in lieu of salary, for four hundred dollars. These they put securely in a leather belt. Banks were breaking every day.

The war was on, of course. But that would be over in three months, said everybody. Samuel could not halt his education for a three-months war which refused to let him in. So Lucy buckled the leather belt around his waist, and away he went on his educational quest.

CHAPTER V

A HARVARD TRANSFER

But breaking into Harvard was no pastime in 1861.

Boston was a trifle disappointing as the Athens of America. In spite of its atmosphere, its historic buildings, its associations, Samuel had to admit that compared with England it seemed unfinished. As he trudged along with two heavy valises, hunting a room, the streets of this city of his dreams seemed painfully like the streets of Madison and Milwaukee, only narrower and more crooked. Of Harvard, though, cradle of American education, started in 1636, he had better hopes.

The picture in his mind of the University was a blend of his own idea of stately, gracious Oxford, and the wonder spot his father-in-law's memory made of the Harvard of his youth. Reaching Cambridge, the traveler seemed again to hear Mr. Huntington, leaning on the snake fence, singing the glories of Harvard.

Of one and another he reverently asked the way to the University. At last, he came upon it, paused, and looked again. He saw a yard, not even turfed, and in it a few buildings, only beautiful to the eye of the imagination. The Pump was the one thing he recognized out of his father-in-law's vision.

This was Harvard! This the cradle of American education!

He swallowed down his disappointment. One did not judge Boston by the clothes she wore, nor Harvard by externals.

Knowledge was what he asked of the University, after all, not æsthetics.

Skirmishing about for information, he discovered some things that were useful and some that were not. The University had 896 students in all branches, taught by forty professors. Harvard boys learned what Samuel had learned in his eastern-manned Wisconsin, not any less, but certainly not much more. Graduates of that day, looking back in after years from peaks of achievement, said the courses were very dull and were dry as dust.

The ex-Vice President of Galesville, truly democratic, very limited in cash, was relieved to find that the scions of the first families lived almost as plainly as the farmer lads of his backwoods University. The coal that warmed them, they shoveled themselves into their own stoves, out of a closet in their rooms. They also carried their own wash water from the college pump. It was considered better form, just then, for a student to tug it up two or three flights himself, even if he had the price for a college scout in his well-lined wallet. A number of the boys were working their way. Very much like the lads of Wisconsin were these Harvard undergraduates, Samuel concluded, except that they seemed to have mislaid their r's among the family treasures.

The graduate department was, of course, his goal—the end of this particular rainbow. Philosophy, Philology, Theology, Mental Science—into these he wished to dig, deep and hard, the eager fingers of his mind. But the Graduate Department had an elusive quality. No one seemed to be able to pin it down to a local habitation and a name. After much wandering about, he found an authority on the subject at last, and put his questions. Graduate courses? "Oh, yes," he was told, "there were courses in Law, Medicine and Engineering." These were about as important to a prospective minister as skates to a South African. He said that in politer language and asked about Theology.

"Yes," if he wished to take a three-year's course.

The student said that he would like to take four hundred dollars' worth—say, one year of it.

"No, that is not allowed."

English? Philosophy? Philology? Mental Science? Were there no courses in these for an avid student with a little money and a few months to spare?

"Nothing, nothing whatsover."

Down went Samuel's spear arm. Out through the door of Harvard trailed he and his sad Crusade of Hopes.

If any seventh daughter of a seventh daughter had stopped the traveler on his way to his Boston room that afternoon and said: "Young sir, sixty years from now, grandmothers who never even had a high-school certificate to frame will sit beside their granddaughters in college classes; sixty years from now a farmer boy will get his college course over the radio while he milks his cow—"if any seventh daughter had dared to accost a young Methodist with any such preposterous nonsense, he would have called a policeman to commit her to an asylum where they deal with hashish dreams.

In his cheap hotel room that night Samuel faced the blackest despair he had known since, as a little hungry-minded boy, he had waked to the harsh fact that he knew more than his teacher. A dream of all his life was going into the discard. Eager scholar, he found every pathway to knowledge closed before him. Harvard had been his last hope. No other American university had more to offer. Not Princeton, Yale, Columbia, nor any of the others gave graduate courses in the subjects that he wanted.

He had in his pocket a well-creased letter from a Columbia professor of whom he had made inquiries, who wished very much, he said, that he might have this ambitious student in his classes. He explained why he could not:

"The President, in whose room I am now writing, informs me that the statutes of the college expressly prohibit the attendance of any but regularly matriculated students who must follow the stated curriculum—unless in the post-graduate branches of Law, Medicine and Engineering."

Not content with keeping a graduate from entering college, in 1860, they even put spikes on the walls, for fear he might crawl over and steal a bit of knowledge from their abundant tree.

So much for American education. Thus it was to remain a few years longer, until a young man by the name of Eliot breathed new life into the "dry bones of Harvard" and sent a new idea of education pulsing through the country. But that did not help a young man, in 1860, aching for more knowledge.

Then the good angel who watches over the ambitious led Samuel to the kind and wise Professor Bowen, of Harvard.

"Books, my dear young man, buy books," he ordered. "You can get no better teachers. Study them. Study people. Use your head. You need no other equipment for life."

CHAPTER VI

DRIED APPLES, A BUNDLE AND A HAPPY ENDING

The traveler divided his four hundred dollars into two equal piles. One he devoted to buying books—all the books on Professor Bowen's excellent list first, then more and more and more. A book or two at a time was all he had ever before dared to buy. Now extravagance was made a virtue. His very education depended upon books.

He bought books in first-hand shops. Then he discovered that money would go three or four times as far in a second-hand shop, and he uncovered in his psychology the special sense which makes a real book buyer able to go into the dingiest basement and, with his eyes shut, pick out treasures. This revelation was a by-product of Professor Bowen's advice, which forced members of Samuel's household, ever afterward, to participate with dust cloths, at least, in his life-long education. His appetite for books fed with what it grew on until it seemed as if a storage warehouse would be the only adequate space for his study.

With the other half of his four hundred dollars, he bought something for his wife, and ordered it shipped to Cedar Bluffs. Afterward, he took the train to visit her relatives at old Hadley, beautiful, historic old Hadley, on the Connecticut, between Northampton and Amherst. All the way there, the secret of what he had done with the other two hundred sang itself, like a tune, to the rhythm of the car wheels.

This visit to the Hadley relatives presented itself as an ordeal.

174

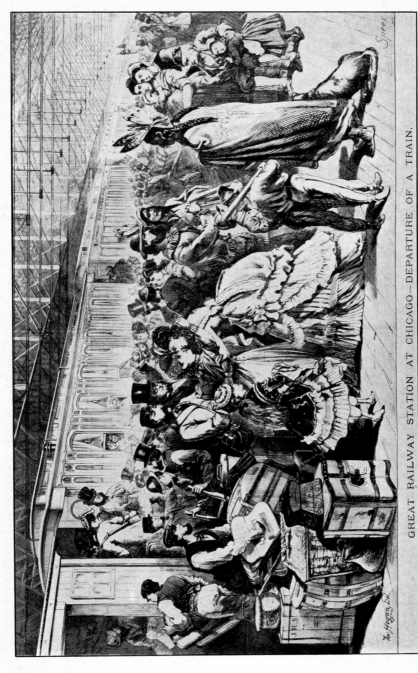

GREAT RAILWAY STATION AT CHICAGO—DEPARTURE OF A TRAIN.

The scene that greeted Samuel Fallows when he first visited Chicago, in 1860.

"Will Lucy be ashamed of her Samuel among such grand people?" he had asked her in the modesty of his first engagement days.

With smiling face and knees that quaked, he went in through the door of the old Colonial house. His wife had described it well. He could have gone blindfold to the very corner in the attic where Lucy Huntington had been sent by her father to get her spelling perfect.

In the house were his bride's grandfather and her uncle Frederic Huntington, the "bishop-timber" one. Stately Aunt Bethia was there, and so many more uncles and aunts-in-law and cousins-in-law that the visitor felt as if he were seeing them double.

Old silver! Old traditions! Old courtesy! The touch of New England formality in intimate relations was just a trifle chilling, at first, to Samuel. But it was gone after fifteen minutes' talk, like a film of ice before a May sun.

Grandfather Huntington, Lucy's husband found, was as interested in Western farming as if he were going to move out there the next day. Uncle Frederic, who had recently turned from Unitarian to Episcopalian and was filled with the joy of it, could pitch a load of hay as fast as Samuel, himself. The ladies of the family, he discovered, knew as much about the inner workings of household matters as his own mother.

They talked of the South. One of the uncles was away recruiting. Would the threads of union, of nationality, be strong enough to draw back the departing sisters without slavery? They all discussed the question gravely, by candle-light, over the orderly shining table. But no one ventured hopeful prophecies.

Samuel, in a letter, confided to Lucy his wish "to conduct himself among her relatives so that she should not be ashamed of him." He had his wish.

Even fastidious, reserved Aunt Bethia succumbed to his charm. In tiny, spidery script she wrote a letter to her niece, Lucy Bethia, named for her, about her husband. Moved out of her usual calm, she exclaimed: "We could not tell how he managed to make us all feel so well acquainted with him and like him so much upon so short an acquaintance."

Back in Boston again, the traveler found he had barely enough money to get him West. On the way to the train, he saw in a second-hand bookstore window a volume he coveted. Then and there, he proved himself of the dyed-in-the-wool book-lover tribe. He spent his last dollar for the treasure and lived on crackers and a handful of dried apples all the way home.

A very hungry young man burst into the farmhouse door two or three nights later, carrying, beside the two valises, an ungainly package which he handled as if it were eggs. The family brought him everything in the pantry, and, as he ate, he told them the odyssey of his wanderings.

No Harvard! Kittie remembered for fifty years Lucy's look of disappointment and the brightening of her face when Samuel told about Professor Bowen's advice and the two hundred dollars' worth of books.

The traveler opened the valises and brought out little trifles for them all, except his wife.

"No present for Lucy?" asked warm-hearted little Fred.

"It's on the way. It's on the way," said Samuel. His happy secret was bursting to get out. "It's a—P-I-A-N-O!"

Pandemonium broke loose. A piano for Lucy was one of the wonders of the world.

Then he undid the mysterious package which the little Huntington girls had been eyeing all the evening. That, too, was a present for Lucy, a perfect love of a gray bonnet trimmed with blue. Kittie, many years later recalled how Samuel set it on Lucy's head, himself, and spun her around the room in a scandalously un-Methodist fashion.

"I don't know if I like—" began Helen in a momentary silence.

"Whether," said her watchful father.

"I don't know *whether* I like," Helen corrected herself, "whether I like the piano or the bonnet best," as concerned about it as if the two belonged to her.

"I don't either, dear," said Lucy.

It was a late bedtime for an early rising family, and mother Huntington bustled them all away at last.

The traveler lit his wife upstairs with a tallow dip. Her arms full of bandbox and voluminous skirt, halfway aloft, she turned to say the phrase that was always to make a bridge for them from heart to heart across any difference of their brains:

"I love you, Sammy." Then she asked a question. "You will not leave me again, will you?"

The war was calling her husband. He knew now that the struggle between the North and the South was no three months' struggle.

He kissed Lucy, bewitching in the new bonnet. But Kittie, listening, heard no promise that he would not leave his wife again.

PART V

FORTH TO WAR

"There's but the twinkling of a star
Between a man of peace and war."

—BUTLER

CHAPTER I

BURYING AND MARRYING IN OSHKOSH

In the Fall of 1861, Samuel bent to the task of finishing his education out of books and people.

Collecting his Lucy, he traveled up into Wisconsin's lumber region to take charge of his first parish at Oshkosh, a picturesque spot, receiving station for the great trees torn from the forests farther north and thrown into the waterways.

Lumberjacks in caps of brilliant red or blue with shirts to match, like great, ungainly birds of brilliant plumage, rode the whirling logs with a song. Periodically, they gathered in Oshkosh, after pay day, and shot up the town.

To Lucy these wild men were a horror; to Samuel part of the flavor of the time, as was the old Indian Chief, Oshkosh, who, blanketed and feathered, stalked in occasionally to see how his namesake town was faring.

Dignified as a pine tree, tragic chieftain of a doomed people, he was fortunate to be gathered to the Great Father of the Forests, before his name, a sneeze in letters, made his town the irresistible butt of stage jokes and gave it national fame as the home of the wear-proof overall, an excellent article, but not to be mentioned in the epic class of Indian chiefs.

The little "sawdust town" of Oshkosh, chopped out of the surrounding forest, Samuel made his Theological Seminary.

Upstairs in his study, he set his vigorous mind at Professor Bowen's books—Theology, Philosophy, Mental Science, Poetry, Shakespeare and other great pieces of literature. He stored his memory full of quotations, the most beautiful thoughts he could find most beautifully expressed.

He wrote and rewrote sermons and wrote them again, searching for the right word.

"Hard writing makes easy reading," he would say to his wife sitting beside him, poring over his books, as she could find the time. "Hard writing makes easy reading, my dear."

When she was busy with household tasks downstairs, every hour or two she would hear his happy voice come booming down the stairs, always with the same request:

"Something gay on the piano, please, Lucy love, one of your sprightly pieces."

For laboratory practice, Samuel went out among his parishioners. He preached. He buried. He married—one couple for a fee unique in his experience, "a sack of potatoes when they was growed." The bridegroom liked the bride so well, however, that, before the month was out, he appeared at the parson's front door to pay his debt with a sack of old potatoes.

No Theological Seminary could have grounded the young minister better than did that Oshkosh year. But it gave him no degree after his name.

"How is it," a New Englander once asked famous circuit-riding Peter Cartwright, "how is it that your denomination has no doctor of divinity?" Quick as his finger on a trigger came Peter's answer. "Our divinity has never been sick and doesn't need doctoring."

Not then or ever did Samuel's religion know ill health.

While her husband was getting his training out of Brushwood College, as the Methodists liked to call their country parishes, Lucy was having hers in the exacting rôle of a minister's wife.

She remembered herself in those Oshkosh days as so shy that her knees would shake and her cheeks flame, merely because she had to open the door to a stranger.

Goodness was her vocation, the position of minister's wife its most prized expression. But only the courage of her fighting ancestors, the iron of her own resolve and the lift of her husband's love carried her through that year of development and adjustment which transformed her timidity into poise and charm at twenty.

Yet she delighted in that Oshkosh chapter, doing parish duties with Samuel close by loving her, guiding her mind, reading her letters and praising their composition and her beautiful handwriting. She prayed it might go on forever, even while she saw the leash that held her husband to his place of peace wear thinner day by day.

At the end of their first year in Oshkosh, after the summer of 1862, it broke. Samuel Fallows applied for the chaplaincy of the Thirty-second Wisconsin Infantry, a volunteer regiment, stationed at Camp Bragg, just outside of town. Before its men, on a blue and gold Sunday afternoon of September, the young minister preached his probation sermon.

Sergeant Leander Ferguson of Company B, sixty-one years afterward, recalled just how "Mr. Fallows stood upon an improvised platform, with a box for a pulpit. On one side sat Colonel James H. Howe, regimental commander, with his official staff, and in front of him were a thousand of us boys, all strange to him. Tall and erect, he stood in his young manhood and preached the word to us. At first he seemed a little embarrassed, but as he proceeded with his subject all trace of fear passed away and his face was illuminated, as I have often seen it since when he seemed inspired."

He won the boys then and there. They all wanted him for chaplain. Leander Ferguson liked his preaching because he was a Methodist, like himself; the others, whatever their denomination, because he spoke to their hearts.

He wrote to Lucy, at Cedar Bluffs:

OSHKOSH, October 1st, '62

MY DEAREST LUCY:

My election as Chaplain has been noticed in the Oshkosh paper. The people were thus prepared for it. Sister Davies had a cry over it. Others were very sorry. The soldiers were all glad. I have been in Camp nearly all day, took dinner and supper.

I find I am needed immediately and as I want to make a *good* Chaplain I must enter upon my duties immediately. I shall not be able to come home before going back to Oshkosh, as I must settle up affairs as soon as possible and then accompany my little pet home before the regiment starts. It will go probably in two or three weeks. Meet me at the Minnesota Junction on Saturday afternoon of this week, as I shall leave on Saturday morning. Be sure and do so, dearest. Sister Davies will be expecting us. I am in a great hurry as I start this A.M. for conference.

Good-by, love, for the present. Meet me on Sat. I feel *deeply* for my little love, but I see Providence in my going. God bless you, is the prayer of

SAMUEL.

CHAPTER II

BATTLES OF THE LORD

Chaplain Fallows, a flame of sacred zeal, marched away that Fall with the Thirty-second, to fight the battles of the Lord.

"This is a holy war, this war to free the slave and save the nation," he had said to the Lucy Huntington in Lucy Fallows, who hated war as her grandmother had hated it. The June before, with the ferment of patriotism working in his blood, the young Methodist had preached a sermon to an uplifted congregation.

"We, before our country's altar," he ended, "calling upon a mightier than Jove to witness our vow, swear unfaltering allegiance to the land of our adoption and our birth. Until the last vestige of this rebellion is wiped out, we must not give up the struggle. If need be, ministers and members must enter the militant ranks. Our pulpit may have to be the seat of war; our auditors the rebellious South; the singing of our choir the battle cry of freedom; our prayers the skyward rocket and the whizzing shell; our sermons the sharp and piercing bullet; and our benediction the bending of the forest of glistening steel and the resistless charge of the bayonet."

In such a transport of feeling for his adopted country, did Samuel take his place as chaplain of his regiment.

For all his self-mastering boyhood and his self-earned education, his vice presidency and his first parish, he was still

185

young in years—twenty-six—young in experience and with little knowledge of evil.

From the sheltered goodness of England, he had come into the hardy goodness of pioneering, thence into the academic goodness of the University, and so into the progressive goodness of the Methodist Church.

He thought he knew evil. Surely—surely. Had he not brought to heel the strong passions of his own stalwart body? Had he not observed the evil of the Forty Thieves, crooked political gang of Madison, carousing in their house of pleasure? Had he not read of evil in books? Had not living people confessed their sins to him—his parishioners, repenting of selfishness or the omission of their souls' duties?

The Thirty-second Wisconsin became part of General Sherman's command at Memphis, Tennessee, and moved southward with his army, through northern Mississippi, in General Grant's march toward Jackson.

With the first plunge into the life of the regiment, Samuel's test began.

"We were a rough and tumble lot," wrote one of the Thirty-second boys to his former chaplain, fifty years afterward. "But when it came to fighting, *how* we fought!"

The regiment was like most regiments, with the restraints of peace off—probably a little more so. It was recruited from the northern and eastern part of Wisconsin. With the boys of gentler living, were mixed miners and lumbermen, who for crude animal courage, crude badness and crude goodness, too, could not be excelled.

"I was prepared for a great deal of wickedness," wrote Samuel to Lucy, "but never, never for the sin I see."

It was one of the zero moments of the war. Antietam, the bloodiest day in American history, was only a few weeks back. Lincoln had made the Emancipation Proclamation, but it still seemed a very doubtful blessing. As for this being a holy war to free the slaves and save the nation, some way the glorious idea had wavered out of the spotlight.

"We are fighting we know not for what," said Samuel in his first letter.

"*All* want to go home and have the war brought to a close."

"Some miserable scapegraces of generals are perfectly willing to have the war continue while they are making handsome fortunes by speculating in cotton."

Negroes were flocking into the Union lines by hundreds, with little clothing, nothing to eat, some unable to work. "The Government cannot employ them all. . . . What they will do I cannot tell," he groaned.

He knew, already, that war was not a Pilgrim's Progress. Even the "seat of war as a pulpit," which he had preached about so eloquently in Oshkosh, was a blasphemous place. The regimental language would have astounded a Billingsgate fishwife. His own Colonel, with whom he had a pleasant friendship, could turn the air blue for miles around him.

The Chaplain held up his Methodist yardstick against the mountainous wickedness of that regiment. What could one young parson hope to do against it? But try he must.

He started with his Colonel, whose language he made the text for a personal sermon.

The Colonel, who was an expert at the game of war, explained. "You see, Chaplain," he said, "no regiment that isn't sworn at and prayed for is worth a—a—Confederate cent. We'll make a bargain. I'll do all the swearing for this one and you do all the praying."

The Chaplain repeated the remark in after years with a chuckle. But in 1862 the devil grinned.

The regiment was on the march most of the time at first. The Methodist parson did as many of his Chaplain's duties as he could. Services were impossible for men tramping all day Sunday.

"You are not preaching, you are not even holding **prayer**

meetings," wrote Lucy, recent Methodist. "I really can't see, dear, what you are accomplishing at all." Lucy was writing under the peaceful trees, trying to imagine war.

Her husband was sleeping in wet cornfields those days, with his coat for a pillow, and waking with a burning throat to drink water smelling like "sulphureted hydrogen." But he managed to show a cheerful face to his soldier boys. "If one of them dropped out," wrote a comrade of his, "the Chaplain found him a place in the ambulance. If that was full, he set the soldier on his own horse and walked himself."

As a method of turning a down-and-out sinner from sin to grace, an hour's ride on the Chaplain's horse was better than a hundred prayer meetings. But Lucy did not know that, and Samuel, as yet, only half suspected it.

In December, because the mails were so uncertain, he went North to carry the money of the soldiers to their wives and families. He saw Lucy and made patriotic speeches.

Laden with letters and Christmas packages for his boys, he went back to Tennessee. But Holly Springs, the Union base of supplies, had fallen in the meantime. Everything was demoralized. The regiment was not where it had been, and no one knew where it was. Wandering around, like Rip Van Winkle, he saw strange sights. "Soldiers rode on the tops of the cars, and darkies, darkies by the hundreds—some of them decked out in the plundered clothes of their mistresses. Poor strutting creatures, as happy with a scarlet dress and a black veil as a house and lot."

"What will become of them I do not know," wrote the Chaplain, on January eleventh, 1863. "They are all discouraged about the war here. I can scarcely hear a single hopeful remark from officers or men. They are sick of the mismanagement, sick of the incompetency and treachery manifest."

He found his regiment at last, divided and discouraged, and cheered them with gifts and letters and jokes.

All the time the soul, far within Samuel's house of deeds, was fighting its own battle with doubt and depression and despair.

Waiting "seven weeks for a letter from Lucy" did not ease the struggle. The mail carrier, too, was "one of the most moderate men" he ever saw. "He has to turn his whole body when he looks around." Before long, the Chaplain added to his other duties that of postmaster.

In the course of his work he exchanged horses so many times that his wife wrote him she dared not tell her father, for fear he might think her husband was a horse trader instead of a chaplain.

In camp again, with a regiment doing provost duty and hating the inaction, the young minister found his hands full of his legitimate work. Major General Hamilton wanted the Thirty-second and the Eighth regiments where he could lay his hand upon them at any moment. So wait they must.

Men were dying every day. At one time only four hundred and fifty out of the regiment of a thousand were reported on their feet. The Chaplain prayed with the sick and read burial services over the dead. He visited the hospitals. He preached. He held prayer meetings. He used the Episcopal service on Sundays because Colonel Howe desired it. Mrs. Harvey, whose husband, the Wisconsin Governor, was drowned while ministering to wounded soldiers, who had personally badgered the President into putting a war hospital at Madison, furnished the prayer books. But Samuel wished Lucy to be sure that the eighteen prayer books, even coming from so admirable a source, would not make an Episcopalian of him.

"I love liberty of conscience and opinion too much," he assured her, "ever to cut loose from the Catholic Methodist Church."

The Race Problem settled itself upon him one day in the form of Walker. Walker was a colored boy who had slipped in through the lines. He adopted Samuel as his own. The Chaplain put him into a white uniform, and he became the mascot and pride of the regiment and the Chaplain's charge to teach in any odd moment.

The idler the camp, the stronger waxed moodiness and wickedness. The hotter waxed the fight within Samuel, and the more he strove outwardly to sustain the morale of his boys. When praying seemed to be indicated, he prayed. At other times he staged gymnastic contests and ran races, himself. When the boys were tired and sick enough of everything to desert the next hour, he turned cook and got them to preparing a plum pudding, "of raisins carefully stoned, the currants washed in five waters, candied citron pared in wafer-like slices—suet finely shred, eggs, nutmeg, flour and sugar and water." News of the pudding went through the regiment.

The pudding bag was a pillowcase. The mixture was put in to boil for hours. Withdrawn at the proper moment, it ran all over the dish, a fizzle of a pudding. But the fun and the joking of it all had restored the morale of the soldiers.

The Chaplain was sick in body. He was discouraged with his work. He seemed to be making no headway. "You can scarcely understand what difficulties there are," he wrote Lucy.

In just such a humdrum of trivialities must souls sometimes fight their biggest battles. No beat of drums. No blare of trumpets. No cheering crowds. They must wrestle as did Jacob with the angel, in the dark. The young Methodist tied to a certain shibboleths might have emerged from his first plunge into the horror of war a cloistered parson, shunning evil because he feared it.

Instead, in the rough-and-tumble school of the Thirty-second, he learned the great truth which he was to spend the rest of his life unfolding—that creeds and formulas are not religion, but the definitions of religion; that virtue and sin

BISHOP FALLOWS' CHURCH

St. Paul's Church, corner of Winchester Avenue and Adams Street, Chicago, built by Bishop Fallows in 1886, where he preached for thirty-six years.

[*See Page 202*]

are relative terms, changing as men change; that good may live in the heart of evil and that all men under their differences are brothers.

While the Chaplain was accomplishing this new step in his spiritual evolution, his Lucy at Cedar Bluffs had gone through the miracle of motherhood. The news reached her husband as the days of his chaplaincy were drawing to a close. In a war which only shot and shell could win, a noncombatant's task was bound to be only a makeshift to a man of his active temperament.

"It would have been his temper," said General Charles G. Dawes, long afterwards at a memorial service, "when the fight grew hot to catch up a musket and fight with his men; to ram in the very leaves of his Bible as gun wadding if he had no other, to drive home the truth to the enemy."

The Chaplain was to have his musket, but it was not one thrown down by a dying comrade. Early Summer brought an acute attack of illness. That and the desire for more active service caused him to resign. He wrote a last letter to Lucy.

MEMPHIS, TENN., June 28, 1863,
Sunday Evening.

Another Sabbath, love, has almost come to a close. I had a very large congregation this afternoon and preached with a great deal of freedom from: "I am not ashamed of the gospel of Christ." This evening the attendance at our Prayer Meeting was large. We had a good time. I shall regret to leave the boys. They all feel sad at my prospective leaving. I have become much attached to them. But I am not sorry that I sent in my resignation.

. . . .

My little boy, Walker, is sitting at the table with me looking at the pictures in his Spelling Book. The more I see of him, the more I like him. I think he is a treasure. He makes funny mistakes in spelling yet,—not understanding fully the sounds of the letters. He was just now spelling the word h o g, and pronounced it pig. The picture of the animal was before him, and recollecting the name he had been accustomed to call it—pig came out, instead of hog. It almost convulsed me.

. . . .

Monday morning.

It is almost breakfast time and Silas will soon be here. How are my darlings this morning? God bless them. We captured some ladies the other day who were going outside of our lines. Upon searching them we found hidden away among their underclothing 8 large Revolvers. They were sent to the Irving Block—our Military Prison. Two of our men were captured by the Guerrillas—while picking berries just outside of the picket line. We have not heard from them since. I was out there a few weeks ago on the same errand but as you see was fortunate. It is a good hint to keep out of danger.

. . . .

The morning is pleasant—sun shining, but we shall probably have showers before night. I am looking forward with deep joy to our blissful reunion.

. . . .

I asked Walker this morning while dressing, if his Mammy ever taught him to pray. He said "No" but his Daddy was a Christian man, and taught him.

Good-by. God bless you both.

Walker was to go north with his Chaplain, to be brought up and given an education by his father. But on the eve of the departure, the eager little mascot ran out between two lines of the regiment at practice, was caught by the cross fire and fell, mortally wounded.

The regiment buried the little black boy with the honors of war. He had an earthly immortality, at least, in his Chaplain's memory. Years later, when he was making Walker's story an example to the school children of Chicago, he told them he could go with his eyes closed to the very tree under which his little friend was buried.

Chaplain Fallows had found strange things in the chaos of war, stark, unpleasant things. But they had only given him a new and wider definition of the brotherhood of man. They had only strengthened his enthusiasm for the battle of mankind. He went back to Lucy a Methodist in name, but a Christian citizen of the whole wide world in understanding.

CHAPTER III

THE CHAPLAIN LEARNS TO LEAD

In the Summer of 1863, Samuel left the Thirty-second a chaplain and a sick chaplain. Since it was necessary to finance his wife and baby until he could make his next war move, he accepted a parish at Appleton. On this pleasant oasis, fed with proper food, and reveling in his new parenthood, he gained strength rapidly. Acting as agent of Lawrence University, for a while, he made the evangel of college education a turning point in the lives of other young people, as the Reverend Jabez Brooks, speaking at the Porter schoolhouse, had made it in his.

In November, on the day before Lucy's twenty-third birthday, the wings of Anne Ashworth Fallows' valiant soul lifted skyward, leaving to her son, Samuel, ideals on which his conscience was built and a memory that ran through all the years of his life, like the subtle distillation of an exquisite spirit. For the grandchildren who never knew her, she became a sweet face in a raised black oval frame, in their father's study.

Soon afterward, Lawrence offered the ex-Chaplain a professorship which he accepted, but never filled. Before the time appointed to occupy the chair, he calculated that he had saved enough money to keep his family of two from starvation for a while and was ready for the warpath again.

Toward Spring, Lincoln called for two hundred thousand volunteers from the Northwestern States, to serve one hundred days. This was the hand of opportunity for a minister wanting to be a soldier.

Though the state had already been combed and recombed for soldiers, until it seemed as if every willing man must have been impressed into service long before, he had a plan for getting more. This he laid before the Governor. To him, also, it seemed so good that on the spot he offered Chaplain Fallows a colonel's commission, if he could produce his companies. Samuel's idea was to get them from the student body of the state.

Again, the glorious idea behind the war became his cloud by day and his pillar of fire by night. He visited every college and normal school in the state. Though he walked as other men walk, gray-haired veterans who were students at that time remember him as if he had been a spiritual Paul Revere, on a flying steed. John Taylor, of Black Earth, studying then at the University of Wisconsin, was one of a group of students idly sitting on the grass in front of the recitation building, on a warm Spring day, when the ex-Chaplain, came upon them.

"Even to this day," John Taylor wrote, "almost sixty years after, I feel the thrill of his burning words and his cry from the heart to his Alma Mater for help to save the nation. So profoundly were we moved, that we threw up our hats and enlisted in a body."

John Spooner, United States Senator-to-be, executive even then, raised a company and borrowed three hundred dollars with which to feed and board it. A thrifty provision of the government put the burden of these expenses on the man who raised a company until it was mustered into the regiment. If it was never mustered in, so much the worse for his purse. Under the spell of Samuel's patriotism, John Spooner took the risk. With such a spirit abroad in the University, no wonder the class of '64 graduated in the field!

Up and down the state went Chaplain Fallows, leaving

enthusiasm in his wake. In those days the magnetic force with which he was surcharged leaped at his hearers like a living force. Once, filled with a passion of eloquence, he saw his gesturing fingers tipped with little blue sparks. Afterwards, he took himself in hand. "Samuel, Samuel," he said, "this will never do. You have to last a lifetime. Conserve, my boy, conserve." Some way, after that, he learned the art of portraying great emotion without draining himself. In that strenuous war campaign he was as fresh at the end of a day of speeches as at its beginning.

The patriotism of an Englishman born was very appealing. Lads, enthralled by his words, signed their names to go to the front. Their parents came to him. He was Chaplain Fallows, still, a Methodist minister and a teacher. They could see how he loved the enlisting lads, just by the way he put his hand on their shoulders. All the older men had gone. These, the flower of youth, the seed of the future, were very precious.

"Lincoln needs our boys," the parents said to him, "schoolboys, our last born. We will intrust them to you, if you will be their Colonel. But keep them safe and keep them good."

And Chaplain Fallows, who knew the filth and wickedness of war and believed a good colonel could keep his regiment clean in the Inferno of it, said, as if he were giving a sacred oath,

"With God's help, I will."

With God's help, he might have. With a Governor's he did not.

Samuel, at the end of the recruiting campaign, with his companies promised, took the train for Madison. But money, eloquent in any war, had spoken its own language in the state capitol, while he was marching over the state, preaching patriotism.

A banker, with ambition and a few companies of militia,

had waited upon the Governor, not patiently, as one waits upon the Lord, but with an accent of authority.

"I have no idea," he said, "that that man Fallows will get his companies. Here are mine all ready. You'd better make *me* Colonel of the Fortieth."

Since it is not well to antagonize the plutocracy at any time, and especially in a war, the sinews of which it must furnish—the Governor did.

Chaplain Fallows went into the presence of his chief and made his report. The Governor hemmed and the Governor hawed. Finally he blurted out the truth. He had made a banker Colonel of the Fortieth.

"Banker! Colonel!" gasped Samuel, remembering how he had promised the parents of the recruited boys to keep them safe.

"I'm very sorry it has occurred," said the Governor. "You will be Lieutenant Colonel."

Since the suggestion of a Governor in military matters is a command, he was.

A storm of protest arose from all over Wisconsin. The Governor was besieged with petitions to make Mr. Fallows Colonel. Impressive with signatures, the petitions found their way, finally, for safekeeping, into the State Historical Society, where they are now. But they had no effect on the Governor's decision.

Samuel accepted the second place without bitterness. "Ours will be a splendid regiment," he wrote his wife. Since the technique of leadership demands that a man be able to obey, as well as to command, Lieutenant Colonel Fallows could be grateful that the lesson was forced upon him so early in the game.

The regiment left the state June the fourteenth, had a good meal at the Soldier's Rest in Chicago and arrived at Memphis on Sunday the nineteenth, "with the thermometer a hundred and two in the shade and the sun as hot as Marseilles in the first chapter of 'Little Dorrit.' " Dressed in heavy uniforms suitable for Alaska in Midwinter, the unseasoned youngsters marched a mile and a half in the broiling sun to their camp on Pigeon Roost Road.

The camp was a bitterly unhealthy place, hot and malarial. Samuel Fallows' heart ached for his schoolboys. What a Lieutenant Colonel could do to redeem his promises to the mothers who had trusted them to him, he did.

He gave them robust, man-to-man talks on Sundays, with a text for all the week. Wherever he could, he acted as buffer between the boys and the Colonel, who knew better how to manage dead dollars than live boys.

One morning Charley Devoll, of Company G, came in from twenty-four hours on picket, most of it in rain. He was wet to the skin, very hungry and dead for sleep. To clear out the water which had seeped into the barrel of his gun, he drew the ball, raised the hammer, pointed the muzzle to the ground and pulled the trigger.

The Officer of the Day immediately appeared and haled him away to the Colonel, because he had fired his gun in camp, against orders. Poor Charles protested that there had been no such orders when he went on picket. But the Colonel, nevertheless, ordered the Officer to bring the wet, hungry boy, sleepless for twenty-four hours, a shovel and set him to digging a hole back of his tent.

The Lieutenant Colonel happened to pass that way pretty soon. "What's the boy done who is digging that hole over there?" Charles heard him ask the Colonel in a low tone.

"Fired off his gun and it roared like a cannon," replied the Colonel.

"He's just in from picket, and wet through," ventured the Lieutenant Colonel. "It looks like more rain. Don't you think it might be better to send him to his tent?"

To the joyful amazement of Charles, the Colonel agreed and the Lieutenant Colonel approached him.

"I turned and saluted him as well as a green kid could do it," Charles recalled, with the details branded into his memory after sixty years.

"He said: 'Hello, son, how old are you?'

" 'A little past sixteen,' I answered him."

The boy explained again about the orders that were not when he went out, and were when he came back.

"Go to your tent," ordered the Lieutenant Colonel. "A good sleep will be better for you than digging this hole."

Charles did not stand on the order of his going. "You may be sure," he concluded his account, "that Lieutenant Colonel Fallows' stock in my company went up to 100 per cent plus."

In the little world of the regiment, surrounded by an enemy waiting eagerly to break through, Samuel Fallows' invariable thoughtfulness for his boys bulked large as a source of comfort. When the unhealthiness of the camp was mowing them down in August, his face, next to the devoted doctor's, was the one the suffering youngsters wanted most to see, his words the ones that soonest put cheer and courage into them.

On week days, he entered into the fun with which they kept their balance. There was fun, because the soldiers were boys whose spirits like yeast worked up through any situation, clever fun, usually, because they were Wisconsin's picked youths.

An advance agent of "Who's Who" could have gone into almost any group and picked future names for his book blindfold. Lucy's brother, William, a little shy and always modest about himself, would go into the book later, as a President of Boston University. Two future State Superintendents of Public Instruction were there. Judges and professors-to-be, prominent business men were almost too numerous for notice. James L. High, a slender, reticent boy, over six feet tall, with a square brow and a caustic tongue, was to make

Chicago and the country sit up and take notice with his High on "Injunctions."

The Lieutenant Colonel had a special liking for bushy headed Jack Spooner, whose round face was always creasing into ripples of laughter over a joke, and for his chum, John Taylor.

The rice, bacon, bread, beans and wormy hard-tack, their staple articles of diet, they often traded for an old black mammy's hoecake. This was a profitable diversion and not dangerous. Sometimes they borrowed vegetables from a rebel garden. This, too, was safe.

But, by the Colonel's ruling, milk from a rebel cow was taboo.

One culprit, already, according to report, had been confined in a wretched little pen for twenty-four hours, with no blanket or furniture, with the damp ground for bed and part of the time with a dead man for company. Rumor, doubtless, exaggerated that sentence, but, even so, rebel milk was about as safe in that camp as a keg of gunpowder over a lighted match.

Once, very early in the morning, the Lieutenant Colonel was returning to his quarters from a sick call. All but invisible in the thick mist, he heard John Taylor, on guard, challenge a shadowy figure emerging out of the fog.

"Who goes there?"

"Shut up," called John Spooner's voice, prudently muted. "Come on over and get some milk."

Not able to get his Colonel's fine distinction between rebel vegetables and rebel milk, Samuel, lover of real boys, closed his eyes and faded noiselessly into the mist.

If he ever discussed the ethics of the question with Senator Spooner in post-war days, it was in a closed committee meeting, with no reporters present.

The Fortieth seemed scheduled to pass its term of service

merely guarding trains of supplies to the front, acting as a watchdog to the enemy, and fighting malaria with fun and quinine. But destiny will nose a man out wherever he is. Destiny pounced on the old Samuel, asleep in his tent, one morning late in August, 1863, jerked him out of his cot to the long roll sounding for attack and into a new self-hood.

General Forrest, Confederate, picturesque cross between Robin Hood and Israel Putnam, clever enough to spike even Grant's plans once or twice, had broken through the guard and was attacking Memphis.

Four Union generals were gathered there. He hoped to bag one, anyway. In this he failed. They all escaped, though one, a dignified Wisconsin general, had to make his get-away, in his night gear, through the back door of the hotel, as Forrest's men came in the front.

But this meteoric raid had results enough for the Lieutenant Colonel of the Fortieth.

It gave his life a turn which sent it a different way.

The long roll sounded. Samuel Fallows, doorkeeper in the house of authority, second fiddle in the regiment, pegging away at his lesson of obedience, jumped into his uniform and over to his Colonel.

The Colonel was in a fever over the fact that the boys had only sixty-four rounds of ammunition.

"I'll go to Memphis for more," said he.

"You, Lieutenant Colonel Fallows, take charge of the Regiment."

So the Lieutenant Colonel led his regiment, which he had recruited himself and loved like a composite son.

He marched on the double-quick nearly three miles to the Hernando Road, where the enemy had entered the city. There the order was to support a battery which was engaged with the enemy.

Then those soldiers, those schoolboys, pride of their

mothers, hope of the future, lay down for an hour between the rebel line and the battery with the artillery duel of death playing over their heads. It would have tried the courage of veterans. The nerves of one of the lads snapped. He leaped up.

"For God's sake, let us shoot," he shouted.

"Lie down," the Lieutenant Colonel shouted back. "Or we'll shoot *you*."

Released at last from support of the battery, a flying figure of vengeance, he led his men another two miles down the road, after the departing enemy, who turned every few minutes to say good-by with bullets.

When he finally gave the order to halt, the regiment had to look far back to find its nearest follower.

The *Annals*, a paper published by the boys under cover, more merciless in its judgments than a court-martial, had its own description of the Lieutenant Colonel's part in the affair.

The regiment as a whole had come to esteem him highly before any fighting qualities were called into requisition; but when the regiment was formed to give old Forrest's Raiders a chase, the boys were all jolly glad when the Ray scampered for ammunition and left Col. Fallows in command.

And the rapidity and yet perfect good order with which he led them clear ahead of all other regiments, up into the music of shot, shell and miniés, and the utter coolness and fearlessness evinced by him during the whole action, won the admiration of every man in the regiment—those who had attended that kind of concerts before as well as those to whom the cotillion was new.—And when on their return to camp, he complimented the battalion for their heroic conduct, the cheers the boys gave him for his part of the glory they had achieved were but an expression of the enthusiastic regard in which he will ever be held by the men of the Fortieth.

Samuel went into that engagement, Methodist minister,

school-teacher, Chaplain and Lieutenant Colonel. He came out a Commander of men.

Back in camp, he made a speech of thanks to his boys for their courage. They threw up their caps and shouted for him. Charley Devoll remembered marching round with a shouting multitude singsonging the words to himself: "Up in front of us all the time. Red blood, every drop of him. Not a bit of yellow in it."

The Colonel, back from Memphis, glowered at his Lieutenant Colonel.

"Don't you know better," he rapped out, "than to praise men for doing merely their duty?"

"I am afraid," was the sharp retort of his second in command, "if one waited to praise men only when they had done *more* than their duty, one might never speak at all."

CHAPTER IV

HE COMES SINGING OUT OF HELL

The rest of Samuel Fallows' war record, the rest of his life, indeed, rolled out from Forrest's Raid like ribbon from a reel.

Back at home with the Fortieth, he soon raised another regiment with little trouble. He was commissioned Colonel, really Colonel this time, the latter part of January, 1865. He weathered the preliminary ordeal of turning down tactfully applicants for office in the regiment—farmers, ministers, drug-store clerks, horse traders and the rest, who because they had been unsuccessful in their own professions, felt perfectly sure that they could fill successfully any office in the Forty-ninth, from sutler to Lieutenant Colonel.

He appointed the officers he, himself, wanted. Edward Coleman, veteran, was Lieutenant Colonel. A ball at Gettysburg went clear through his brain.

"Colonel Coleman," said the surgeon then, "by all the laws of surgery, you are a dead man."

But he proved himself one of the livest soldiers in the army.

Major Noyes was kind, as well as firm. The other officers were men to bank on, including Adjutant James L. High, of the Fortieth, and First Lieutenant William E. Huntington, who had received his baptism of fire in Forrest's Raid by his brother-in-law's side. It was one of those pleasant by-products of the war that his salary as lieutenant afterwards paid for his college course at Wisconsin University.

Samuel Fallows was commissioned Colonel of the Forty-ninth on January 28, 1865. The regiment was recruited, organized, equipped and on its way to war in a little more than a month. The Colonel took his regiment out of Madison to the usual accompaniment of cheers and band music, hoping that its destination would be the eastern front. He held in his hand sealed orders. Opening them at the proper time, he had one of the sharpest disappointments of his life. The regiment was booked for Missouri—focus for guerrillas, bushwhackers, hard work and no glory. It was a salutary lesson for a man qualifying as commander. The Colonel took his medicine standing and made a sermon, presently, on sealed orders, for the comfort of other sufferers.

At Chicago, the soldiers were bountifully fed by the ladies of the Soldiers' Aid Society. Fifty years afterwards, the *Chicago Tribune* reprinted the item, but not the fact that the meal ended comfort for the Forty-ninth, and began misery.

Against every protest, the railroad officials, at the train the next morning, packed the regiment into freight and cattle cars. It was the dead of Winter and a blizzard was raging on the Illinois prairie.

The Colonel, himself, described what followed in an article for the *American Magazine,* many years afterward:

My men were freezing. Fingers caught it; ears did, and toes. Had I got myself into the state of inefficiency which worriers arrive at, the soldiers would have suffered severely by scores and hundreds. But I kept calm, and pretty soon, when our train pulled up alongside a string of cabooses, I ordered my men to raid the cabooses, take out some of the stoves, put them into our freight cars, chop holes for stove-pipes, and with fuel from the cabooses, fire up.

They went at it gloriously, I with them. Frantic railroad hands came running, and, in language not fit for a bishop to repeat, demanded to see the Colonel. As I had a common army overcoat on, they were unable to pick me out from the rest, so we finished our job and pulled through alive.

The matter was reported to Washington. A dapper little French major traveled out to Missouri with a tremendous claim for damages from the railroad, something like twenty thousand dollars. Samuel withered him with a blaze of righteous indignation. He got his surgeon to brandish a list of the frozen fingers, frozen toes and the lives lost from the exposure. The Major faded away, and that was the last of the damage claim.

Forty years later, Bishop Fallows told the story to his young assistant, Mr. Lepper.

"That railroad," he concluded with a chuckle, "has sent me a pass for the last twenty years. Perhaps they never knew I was the one who destroyed their property. But I prefer to think it was their sense of justice working belatedly."

Two qualities marked Colonel Fallows' new-found talent for commandership—any leader's natural authority which makes men obey, and that in him which made them love to obey. The cattle-car incident shows the first. The impressions of the Colonel of the Forty-ninth, gathered by his old friend Hosea Rood, from members of the regiment surviving after almost sixty years, are full of the record of the second.

Charley Lang, another little Charley, sixteen, like Charley Devoll, after the freezing jolting journey in the cattle cars, arrived at Rolla with the regiment, worn out, only to be put on picket duty at once. He spent four hours at it in an icy storm. When he was relieved at last, he and three other cold and hungry boys posted off to the town a mile and a half away to buy a hot breakfast.

Roll was called while they were playing hookey, and on their return they were haled before the Colonel. Slack discipline was no part of his creed. He gave the boys the severest kind of a rating. "Didn't they know that they were soldiers now, and had to obey orders?" he asked. "Didn't they realize

COLUMBIAN EXPOSITION—THE GRAND COURT AT NIGHT—ELECTRICAL ILLUMINATION OF MACMONNIES FOUNTAIN AND THE ADMINISTRATION BUILDING.—DRAWN BY CHARLES GRAHAM.

AT THE COLUMBIAN EXPOSITION

Bishop Fallows was the Chairman of the General Committee on Education of the World
Congress Auxiliary of the World's Fair in Chicago, 1893.

[*See Page 315*]

that guerrillas were lying in wait all around? That they might have had a bullet through the head, instead of breakfast?"

He told them what it meant to be a citizen of Uncle Sam's great Republic, in words they never forgot, and what it involved to be his soldiers. "Can I trust you now?" he asked. "Do you promise this will never happen again?"

They promised and went away his friends for life, the four of them. "For all he was so polite and nice," said Charley Lang, reminiscently, sitting in Madison, in 1922, with the second wife, to whom Samuel had married him, "we knew he meant what he said. We knew we'd better promise. But we *liked* promising," he smiled. A few days after the picket party, the boy was fixing his dog tent. It was a hard job, and he was using all the expletives he could muster. Along came his Colonel on his horse, quite unseen. Down, bang, came the flat of his sword on Charley's thumb.

"Never let me hear you use such language again," he snapped.

Charley's thumb "hurt like anything," but, because his adored Colonel had given the whack, he sucked it rather happily and watched the wheel of the "stylish gray horse."

This regiment, at least, its leader could make a reform school for its youngest lads. Tucked away among his papers was one, written in an unformed boyish hand, promising that the writer would abstain from tobacco in all its forms during the time of his service. He gathered his boys on Sundays for short talks, which left a long influence on their lives.

"Rated an excellent disciplinarian," Captain Dinsmore of Oshkosh remembered, "yet he was kind and courteous to all, as approachable by a private soldier as by an officer."

Captain Dinsmore was present at the jubilation over the surrender of Lee at Appomattox, especially significant to the Forty-ninth because of its Colonel's speech. To this celebration, arranged by the officers of the Thirteenth Missouri

Cavalry, the Forty-ninth was asked. Let Captain Dinsmore describe it:

"As a matter of courtesy they invited Colonel Fallows to the platform. When their officers had finished, and the audience was about to go, the boys of the Forty-ninth called for Fallows. The Master of Ceremonies asked him if he would say something, but he shook his head. Then our call for our Colonel became a roar, so the presiding officer asked that he step to the front and acknowledge the call even though he had no prepared speech. Well, Colonel Fallows stepped forward and spoke about ten minutes.

"I wish I could describe it, but no words of mine can do that speech justice. It was a concentration of fiery, patriotic American eloquence—such an outburst as I had never heard before, or have since then. It turned those Missouri cavalrymen and our boys into a cheering, howling happy mob of surprised, enthusiastic men. It was such a demonstration as I had never seen, and can never forget."

Years afterwards, Captain Dinsmore met Samuel when he was "Bishop Fallows." " 'I hardly know,' I greeted him, 'by what title to address you.' I told him that to me he was Colonel, but that since we had thus known him he had been made brigadier general and bishop, and I did not feel certain just what to call him. He replied that it did not make much difference to him; that, one day, a man in Appleton had hailed him from across the street with, 'Hello, Sam!' and that sounded pretty good to him."

Colonel Fallows was first commander at Rolla and later commander of the post of St. Louis and of the first subdistrict of Missouri.

He realized in the Forty-ninth his hope of a well-trained regiment. It "was retained in service in preference to Missouri regiments," according to Captain Hauser, "on account of its superior discipline and the popularity of Colonel Fallows as post and district commander."

Early in November the regiment started home. It could

have worn, as a feather in its cap, the letter from Brigadier General T. C. Smith, commanding the District of Missouri, to the Adjutant General of Wisconsin, which praised in highest terms the manly, moral and military virtues of its men.

The homeward journey had a touch of comedy.

Once more the Colonel and a railroad company locked horns.

At St. Louis, the officials tried to pack the regiment, like cattle, into box cars for Wisconsin.

"Don't get in," the Colonel ordered his men.

They swarmed over the platform and tracks like locusts, seeking what they might devour. The railroad officials were helpless. "What can we do? What can we do?" they groaned to Samuel.

"Get coaches for my men," he said.

"Can't be had," replied the railroad officials.

"Here we stay," replied the Colonel, "until they *can* be had. Make yourselves at home, boys."

They did, to the utter dismay of the railroad men. "Take them away. Take them away," they begged.

"Coaches," replied the Colonel.

Enough were finally conjured, out of the land of "Can't be had," to hold most of the regiment. But the number was still two or three short.

"Coaches for the men who are left," demanded the Colonel, remembering the frozen ears and toes and fingers of the former trip.

"At Alton—At Alton," pleaded the officials. "We will surely supply them there."

The Colonel, who always liked to act when he could as if mercy were the better part of justice, capitulated. His faith in human nature and the railroad company were justified by finding all the coaches he needed at Alton.

The War was the West Point from which Samuel graduated to the battlefields of peace. Out of that experience, which crushed so many men, he gained a tremendous release of energy. He emerged a happy warrior, with a song upon his lips. And he sang, partly because he could not help it, and partly because he knew himself equipped for his future work. He had learned to lead and to be abased. In the symphony of life, he could conduct the orchestra or play, with equal grace, the part of the humblest fiddler.

PART VI

THE BATTLES OF PEACE

CHAPTER I

A CURTAIN RAISER

The war completed Samuel Fallows' training for liberal leadership. It found him an obscure young Methodist minister with ambitions, in a lumber town. It left him brevetted brigadier general, trained in the handling of men, equipped for the battles of peace.

The Methodist Church, giving him a rare opportunity, appointed him to Summerfield, the strongest Methodist Church in the state and the most progressive in Milwaukee. A warrior setting out to fight provincialism could scarcely have found pleasanter conditions for his initiation, if he had chosen them himself.

After a long separation, he and his wife were united again to do the work they both enjoyed, in a delightful town, in a delightful church. They knew how hospitable it was from the moment they went up the parsonage steps and found the door unlocked.

"Burglars," gasped Mrs. Fallows. They were—the Summerfield kind. They had filled the pantries, loaded up the woodshed, built fires, lighted the house and left a sumptuous supper on the table.

A reporter of the *Evening Wisconsin* thriftily made news of this attempt at "reversed burglary." Milwaukee was small enough and friendly enough to enjoy the amusing item with its supper the next evening. But it also had size enough and age enough for a measure of culture, and it was full of the tang of growth.

A progressive church had a chance to grow in a city like Milwaukee. Summerfield was full of life. Its membership had representatives of all "the city's favorite activities," as the *Evening Wisconsin* liked to put it: George S. Austin and Alanson Follansbee, pioneer merchants; George W. Lakin and C. K. Martin, prominent lawyers; R. P. Elmore and George H. Foster, commercial leaders; Amherst W. Kellogg, secretary of the Northwestern Life Insurance Company; J. J. Tallmadge, former mayor. Walter H. Carter, already an eminent lawyer, father-in-law to be of Charles Evan Hughes, was superintendent of the Sunday school and leader of the choir during the whole time Samuel was pastor of Summerfield. Supported by such an able enthusiastic corps of workers and many others just as full of Western snap, the church flourished. Pews filled up and the debt dwindled.

But work was set to a merry tune. The pastor had a faculty of seeing fun in everything and making others see it. His delighted parishioners never knew just what he would do next. One afternoon, he whisked off Louise Kellogg and his own little Mamie to a photographer, and the next night he flashed the gingham-clad youngsters on the screen, when the program threatened to grow dull.

Dullness had little chance with him around. Those whose memories go back so far say that he was the life of the simple social occasions with which the Milwaukee of that day was well content. But, at least once, he yielded the palm to Topsy, the Elmore parrot. The Elmores, pillars of the church and of Milwaukee, were hospitable and gracious. Topsy was not. At an unforgettable Elmore supper party, Dr. Steele, President of Lawrence University, began the meal with grace. He thanked the Lord for the delicious food and kept thanking Him and thanking Him, while the food cooled by the minute. Finally, from the conservatory came a sharp decisive voice:

"Oh, pshaw now, old man, dry up! Dry up!"

Poor Dr. Steele came out of his trance of gratitude with a

jerk. The pastor of Summerfield, politely restraining his mirth until he was walking homeward with his wife, confided to her that it might improve long-winded prayer meetings to have Topsy installed as timekeeper in the House of the Lord.

Three years at Summerfield slipped by—beads told on a rosary of delight. That time was then the limit allowed by the Methodists to a pastor in one charge. General Fallows was next assigned to Spring Street, Milwaukee's mother church of Methodism. In the year and a half of his pastorate there he cleared off a heavy debt and built a new church. During those Milwaukee days the Methodist pastor was ever an advocate of freedom. He saw life as a unity, at a time when the popular religious conception of it was provincial and broken. Business, pleasure and worldly concerns had little connection with the church, except as matters of prayer.

In those days, Samuel Fallows had the seed thoughts which did not come to their final blossoming for fifty years. Even then, he might have transposed Terence to read: "Nothing that is common to man should be foreign to a Christian."

Acting on this belief, he persuaded the editor of the *Milwaukee Sentinel* to put illustrations in his paper; the first time, so far as is known, that any paper in the country made the experiment. National politics, just then under the Johnson régime, were an unwholesome brew. But the pastor-general told the young men who flocked about him that it was their civic duty to get into politics and clean them up. Ministers had their obligations, he declared, as well as laymen. His was no idle preaching, as he was very soon to prove. He also practiced temperance and defended it. In the journalistic language of the time, "he thrust a keen lance into the stereotyped phrase that temperance is a worn-out theme." Taking for a text, one Sunday, Paul's command to be all things to all men, he demonstrated practically what he meant by it before the week was out.

Susan B. Anthony and Elizabeth Cady Stanton came to Milwaukee to hold a meeting for Woman's Suffrage. They wished it opened with prayer and approached Samuel Fallows, as the pastor in Milwaukee most likely to grant their request. Having foolishly done ten men's work, the week before, he was flat in bed with one of the devastating sick headaches which were the toll he sometimes paid, in those days, for an orgy of effort.

The two suffragists went to five other ministers with the same request. Woman's Suffrage was anything but a popular cause just then. Each minister found an excellent reason for absence from the meeting. The news reached Summerfield's pastor while he was fighting forty devils of dizziness and the depression from his liver, which is worse than any depression of the soul. He pulled himself up by the bedpost and dressed and shaved. His wife, seeing how shaky he was, protested.

"My dear," said her husband, with the firmness of an early Christian martyr, "those women want to be prayed for. I'll open their meeting with prayer, if I have to be carried to it on a stretcher."

Interested in issues and causes himself, he was able to make each of his churches also a factor in the progressive life of the city. He preached a vigorous gospel, in which he sounded the new note of social brotherhood. It was a controversial issue, but he tipped his darts with love and his barbs with humor and carried his congregations with him.

A Pen Portrait by the Reverend Dr. English, printed in the *Sentinel,* describes the Samuel Fallows of that day as "lithe, graceful and finely organized, with a clear-cut, classic set of features, heavy, overhanging forehead, swelling out in the region of the reasoning faculties, thin and firm-set lips and bold, piercing eyes rather wide apart.

"Brother Fallows," Dr. English went on to say, "is one of the best illustrations of a self-made man in Wisconsin. Less than twelve years ago he was a penniless boy, working his way through college. To-day he stands in the first rank of pulpit orators in the United States. It is high praise to a young man not yet thirty-three years of age, but it is nevertheless the meed which those best qualified to judge freely accord him."

The friendly writer also pointed out the fact that, for three years, General Fallows had been preaching at Summerfield on the highest salary ever paid "a poor Methodist minister in Wisconsin," and had refused a number of calls from other cities at still larger salaries. Even so, the salary, perhaps $2,500, did not spell opulence, except to an optimist. But neither then nor at any other time was Samuel Fallows able to measure values in terms of the dollar sign. Service was the currency he liked best to use. Even that, he was more interested in giving than receiving—one of the reasons, perhaps, why so many boys flocked to his church in those Milwaukee days. Among them were two who were to figure in all of his later life. One of them, "Barney" Eckhart, worked in a•milling company at the end of a little siding, up which the other, a rising young brakeman then, ran his train. On week days the two had friendly squabbles. On Sundays they went to hear General Fallows preach. They liked the idea of his being a general and they liked what he said. He spoke a language they could understand.

The enterprising brakeman was Frederick D. Underwood, who later became President of the Erie. One day, looking back over a friendship of half a century or more, he told about the Samuel Fallows he knew in Milwaukee. He said:

"Young men went to him as naturally as a duck goes to water. His church was full of them. No one in Milwaukee ever drew them as he did. Denominations made no difference. My father, though he was a close-communion Baptist, never felt that General Fallows was proselyting. He was the point of contact between church interests and religious interests. He didn't look at the world through sectarian eyes.

"We were a provincial lot in those days. But he pulled us out. He gave us something to live by.

"He had so many human sides—like a diamond. He could always deliver what he had, too. I never saw him fail to come up to any situation. I suppose many men might have known as much as he did. Well, a miner can sit on his nugget of gold in the Klondike and starve. If he can't get it out and sell it for food, what's the good of it?

"General Fallows could always get it out.

"He endeared people to him. I don't know how he did it. He was the friend of man and dog alike. He was a human magnet. But he always imparted something of himself. Yes, he was like a sweet perfume."

Without the tremendous pressure of war, which unstoppered the commander within him, Samuel Fallows might have become merely something ministerial or professional, which looked like his pre-war destination. Instead, in 1866, he charged at the problems of peace and, for five years, carried the young men and the old men, Summerfield, Spring Street and Milwaukee with him.

After this pleasant curtain raiser, he was given a chance to try out himself and his theories in his first big battle against ignorance.

CHAPTER II

A SUPERINTENDENT MAKES HIS OBJECTIVE

The State Superintendent of Public Instruction, A. J. Craig, died in 1871, in the midst of his term.

Governor Fairchild, intrepid soldier, one armed out of the war, with ideals for Wisconsin, cast about him for a successor to the office. He wanted a man who would fight for big issues and who had influence enough to carry them through. His eyes rested on Samuel Fallows, and he asked him to be State Superintendent.

That meant going into politics. The pastor of Spring Street Church had seen the practical workings of the state machinery during the war. He knew that politics in Wisconsin, even under Fairchild, was not a rose-scented bath.

But he wanted something for the children of the state. "Thank you, Governor," he said, "I will accept," and dived in, headforemost.

He, himself, was a product of the cloistered system of education for the privileged few, a system started by the monks of the Middle Ages, which had seemed good enough to the world until the time of his own graduation. Learning, for learning's sake, was its god; the classics and academic philosophy, its priests.

Then the spirit of the French Revolution struck education. Whiff! Bang! Boom! Culture with a capital C went smashing through the window, and that utility on which the

219

education of to-day is built, came swashbuckling through the door.

By 1866, the University of Wisconsin, following the national lead, had changed from an educational Monarchy to a Republic. Science sat upon the throne. The classics were reduced to the ranks. For the first time in the world's history, the cow elbowed Cicero, the hen strutted next to Demosthenes, and the pig was arrayed next to Æschylus in the same curriculum.

Samuel Fallows, appointed Regent just at that time, defended the new order in a speech two hours long.

He proclaimed the rights of the farmer—the educated farmer who would be fitted by the university "to step from the farm to the Senate or the President's chair, to wield equally the hoe or the scythe or ax and the destinies of the State or the Republic."

He also championed the women students who had slipped in during the war and were looked on by the young gentlemen as a post-war pest. Though these ex-soldiers had braved death down South to give the negro freedom and education, in Madison they wanted to deny the "Normalites" the same things. When they could not, they passed the poor girls by on the other side and made faces at them behind their backs.

Regent Fallows, in 1866, told the young gentlemen, politely, that they could like the young ladies or lump them.

"By the organic law of the University," he said, "women belong in the University. If the State is under obligations to educate men, it is also under obligations to educate women."

So in 1871, the new Superintendent undertook his job, with a knowledge of the state and its needs. As to his own fitness for it, he was an individualist by nature, a conformist by immediate inheritance. He was instinctively authoritative, with an inborn tolerance that gave him a slant on the other person's way of looking at things. "His mind," as one of his associates expressed it, "worked like lightning. He could take an idea, bat it all over the ring, try it with uppercuts and undercuts, test its wind, knock it out or extend the right hand of fellowship, so quickly that when he said to an audience of one or a thousand: 'This plan is good and that is bad,' it seemed the judgment of intuition."

Looking over his field of battle he found the school system of Wisconsin as jumbled as the family clock when a small boy has ripped out its works and tumbled them into a hat. The higher education of the state was administered on a plan as happy-go-lucky as a country fair.

Left-overs of individualistic pioneer conditions, academies and colleges and mushroom universities ran their educational booths to suit their own sweet wills. They were largely denominational, since people in general shared the belief of the Honorable Amos Lawrence, of Boston, that a secular institution was freehold for the feet of the devil.

Anyone, like Mr. Lawrence, who had a fund and the backing of a denomination, could, at that time, set a college going in the wilderness. So, too, could a man with a vision like Judge Gale's persuade a legislature into making a township and giving him the county seat in which to start his university. Some of these institutions, such as Lawrence and Beloit, were excellent. Some were an abomination to the name of education. Good or bad, each was a law unto itself. Each made its own set of standards.

As for the district and secondary schools, everyone was a unit having no relation to the other units.

The State University sat high on its hill, detached from the rest of Wisconsin's schools. Legislators had looted it of its land. It was the ward of the state, a charity child, a thing without class. Students attended it because it was cheap or near home, not often from choice.

The new Superintendent drawing up his plan of campaign saw that one thing would make the helter-skelter aggregation of Wisconsin's schools into a smooth-running, efficient system—to make this despised University its head. He had advocated that plan in 1866 as Regent Fallows.

"I would like," he had said then in his two-hour speech to Ath. and Hesperian, "to make the connection between the University and the children of the State as binding as the sun to its planets."

As State Superintendent, in 1871, he fixed on this as his objective.

The technique of this, his first campaign, he adopted also for later engagements—to use what was left of the old broom, to get all the coöperation possible and to persuade rather than to compel.

Superintendent Craig had already established two normal schools. These, the new Superintendent strengthened. His predecessor had also inaugurated a few Teachers' Institutes in remote corners of Wisconsin. They were a substitute for our present Summer schools, except that the mountain went to Mohammed. The school moved itself, lock, stock and barrel, up to some remote county, gathered its teachers together in one place and administered to them, on the spot, lectures by distinguished educators. These Institutes were the strongest feeler toward standardization in Wisconsin's whole jumbled educational system. Superintendent Fallows proposed to push them to the limit.

For his campaign to put a college education in reach of every child in the state, he must have the backing of the legislature. But no action could be secured from that body without the coöperation of the voters, which meant getting a state of individualists to act as a unit. His first need then was to create public opinion

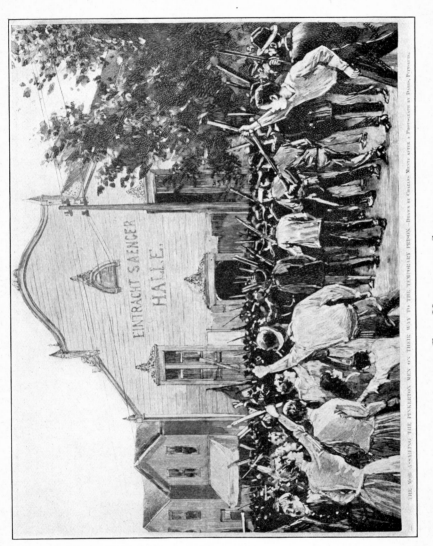

THE MOB ASSAILING THE PINKERTON MEN ON THEIR WAY TO THE TEMPORARY PRISON.—Drawn by Charles Mente after a Photograph by Dabbs, Pittsburgh.

THE HOMESTEAD STRIKE

Steel workers' strike near Pittsburgh, Pennsylvania, where Bishop Fallows preached on arbitration the day after the above scene.

[See Page 318]

Through Institutes, he reached the teachers. He not only had to convert them to his way of thinking, but with his associates, he had to make a great body of them, trained badly or not at all, into a smooth-running force to manage the new machinery. In his first six months of office he traveled six thousand five hundred miles, visited twenty-two counties and addressed Teachers' Institutes in twenty-one of them. Before the end of his term, he had stood on almost every one of Wisconsin's fifty-five hundred square miles of territory, had met personally almost every teacher and all of the county superintendents and had conducted examinations and visited schools in every county.

In the speeches at Teachers' Institutes, which were part of his propaganda for better standards and better teaching, the Superintendent never forgot to mix praise with criticism.

He told Walworth County, for example, that it had some of the best schoolhouses in the state and also some of the worst. What Walworth had to do was to get all its schoolhouses into the best class and make itself an example to the state.

The Walworth teacher he had in mind, was to be a compendium of all virtues and all knowledge. That paragon was to be wise, thoughtful, discriminating, a reader of the newspaper—above all things, a progressive teacher. "In the language of the Litany," said the youthful Superintendent, "good Lord deliver us from a *young* old fogy."

A couple of pages of his scrapbooks at that time give an idea of what he thought a progressive teacher ought to know.

The account of a Chinese banquet where Emerson spoke and Oliver Wendell Holmes read a poem follows a recipe for coating stoves, guaranteed to last a year or two.

A funny story of Pat, in the army, who didn't know

whether he stood five feet ten or ten feet five precedes a pathetic account of the melodeon's inventor.

An abstruse article on the "Unity of the Universe" is next
to a protest against high-heel boots. A sermon by Henry
Ward Beecher rubs elbows with the plan of an unrecognized
genius to revolutionize industry by the use of mouse power.

The Superintendent's mind closed on all this information
like a trap. It was there to use whenever and wherever he
pleased. Years later, he could discuss the article on the theory
of the universe with his friend, the philosopher-physician, Dr.
R. N. Foster, or laugh over mouse power as a substitute for
machinery with Debs or some other labor leader. It was quite
as easy to quote from Emerson's speech fifty years afterwards
as to get his wife to use the new coating for the stove in 1871
—much easier, in fact, since Lucy Fallows had her own convictions about blacking for stoves.

What Superintendent Fallows said to Walworth County
and the other counties spurred on pedagogical minds. But
his sympathy spoke louder than his words.

A little teacher, seventeen or so, in one of the crudest of
Wisconsin's half-finished counties, started her work with
dreams of being queen in a log-cabin schoolhouse, ruling her
docile subjects graciously to the music of a, b, c, and seven
times one is seven.

The horrid reality had no resemblance to her dream at all.
She boarded around. Mornings in an icy schoolroom she
built her own fire of corncobs and sticks of wood so green
that they fought fire as a cat does water. Stupid Franz,
mischievous Pat, dull Susie, obstinate Thelma—were these
the docile subjects of her queendom, these pig-tailed girls and
shock-headed boys, cased in flannel to their necks, blue-nosed
when the pot-bellied stove refused to draw, scratching at their
chilblains when it did? Little dummies who gagged at the
first of the three R's! And she was supposed to teach that

hopeless lot more subjects in a day than Uncle Sam had stars in the flag!

A schoolma'am typical of hundreds, she went to an Institute, crushed and hopeless. Somewhere on the program, Samuel Fallows spoke. He told those teachers that they held the future of Wisconsin in their hands. As they molded their pupils, their pupils would mold the state. He made each teacher feel as important as the President.

Afterward, the discouraged priestess of knowledge shook his hand. His sympathy, quite voiceless, said, "Oh, yes, my dear, I was one of the flock and I taught them. I know how you have to drill holes in their heads to get a fact through, and about the green sticks and everything. But keep right at it. You'll win in the end." All the schoolma'am's hopes were out of their cage again in a moment and flying about her head with songs. Back she went to the log schoolhouse, to do the impossible.

Forty-five years afterward, that teacher, at the time an important person in the educational world, walked up to Bishop Fallows, in a Chicago restaurant, and appropriated him. "I am what I am," she explained, "because he was my State Superintendent."

As part of the publicity campaign, the Superintendent accepted invitations to speak on all kinds of subjects.

He was a teacher with the teachers, a soldier with the soldiers. He made addresses, before huge audiences, on two of the earliest Decoration Days at Milwaukee and Waukesha.

Farmer with the farmer, he gave the principal address at a Waukesha County Fair, which "contributed as materially to the large attendance," a reporter said, "as the liberal prizes for the trotting matches and the best horses." He also talked before the State Horticultural and Agricultural Societies.

He was a Methodist with the Methodists. Tactfully, at an Oconomowoc camp meeting, he told the dear old believers in the "Brushwood College" that the great success of the Methodist Church had been due, under God, to her educated men, that Wesley, himself, was a graduate of Oxford.

As a pastime, he raised debts, little and big and middling sized; debts on parsonages; debts on churches; the debt of the Young Ladies' Steeple Society, a thousand-dollar debt for the little town of Reedsburg, where gifts meant no new clothes that year for the contributors; a nine-thousand dollar debt for a church in Boston where the pledges meant merely a check out of a fat check book.

But whatever rôle the moment demanded, the Superintendent was the watchful general with his eye on the University.

He might start a speech with the moon or the equator. It might be about turnips or the Kingdom of Heaven, but never did it end without some adroit reference which made the children of Wisconsin and their needs a living issue.

Doing this propaganda work, in his three and a half years he traveled fifty thousand miles in the state of Wisconsin, enough to carry him in a straight line twice around the world.

To journey a mile in comfort during those early seventies, a man needed armor. The roadbed gave the passenger worse punishment than a pugilist. It threw nim from side to side like a ball. Black and blue shoulders distinguished the traveler, as tattoos the sailor. By day he ate cinders and went through stretches of burning country with a wet handkerchief over his mouth.

By night the traveler swallowed the fumes from smoky oil lamps and bumped a little harder, because he was trying to get some sleep. No Pullman cars mitigated the rigors of night. In Summer he melted and in Winter he froze.

Pounded by the jolting train; watery eyed from smoke; short-circuited of sleep by an upright night; padded with newspapers inside his vest, before and behind, to keep out the cold; wrapped in his blanket shawl—the Superintendent was quite likely to tumble off the train to speak in a town and find that it had burned up the day before and that the inhabitants were starting to build a new one. He made a speech at a Cornell commencement which "rollicked in anecdote, soared in imagery," according to the newspaper, "and scintillated with beautiful utterances." Straying over into Iowa he gave his well-known lecture on "Idols" at Charles City. No account of it appeared in the next day's paper. "We were so interested," apologized the poor reporter sent to cover the lecture, "that we did not think of taking a synopsis."

A trip to Boston was an occasion for gathering educational ammunition. The G. A. R. was holding its meeting at the Hub. A letter to his wife describes the trip.

BOSTON, MASS., May 22, '71.

MY DEAR LUCY,

I am in Willie's room. He is absent a few moments in the chapel attending prayers, for *theological* students sometimes do such things.

. . . . . .

I reached B. at 9 P.M., hunted up 36 Bromfield St., rang the Seminary bell, was admitted by a gentleman, ascended two or three flights of stairs, came to a wicker gate, rang the bell— was admitted by a plump little damsel who showed me to Willie's room. I knocked, heard the well-known voice, walked in and squeezed him. The next morning we sallied out early, went to the Commons, rode each in a velocipede boat on the pond, which would have taken by storm Eddie and Mamie, looked at the Monuments and returned home after calling on Gov. Fairchild.

. . . . .

This morning we went to hear the oration before the Army of the Potomac in the Globe Theatre by Governor Fairchild. There was a most brilliant assemblage. Gen's. Sheridan, Kilpatrick, Meade, Burnside, etc., etc., were there. The Gov. did nobly. We felt proud of our noble state.

. . . . .

This morning I went before the oration to Harvard with

Brother C. Was introduced to President Eliot. Visited the buildings, etc. On our return from the theatre we found a scrap with the following on it—"F. D. Huntington, sorry to miss you." You can imagine how disappointed we were not to see him.

I go in a few minutes to Charley Fairchild's to tea. Gov. F. and wife are there. At 7½ P.M. I go to the Banquet of the Army of the Potomac with Gov. F. The Gov. is very kind. He takes the utmost pains to introduce me to the distinguished men of the time and makes it pleasant for me.

Your dear letter came yesterday. How glad I was to hear from you. The darling boy Eddie, my little shoemaker! How I laughed as I read your description of the scene. Mamie's sweet face looks down on me as I write. A thousand kisses for you all.

Of the Harvard visit he wrote again with more detail:

"I chatted for a moment with President Eliot. He is a young man, affable, scholarly, earnest. He believes in treating young men as *men*—giving them great latitude in the choice of studies, but asking for thoroughness in those selected. He was elected President in the face of great opposition, but is now 'master of the situation.' All concede his ability and fitness for the position."

Less than ten years before, Samuel Fallows had been turned away from Harvard. On this visit Governor Claflin furnished an aide to show him the different schools of the city.

Officially, the Superintendent visited also on this trip the schools of New York, whose Columbia, a decade earlier, would have none of him, and he called on President Woolsey, of Yale. Having seen a complete cross section of Eastern education in the earliest seventies, he was ready to apply what was good in it to his own state and omit what was bad. But he was more than ever committed to his own plan for Wisconsin.

The State Schoolmaster at first left his family in Milwaukee and shuttled over to them as often as he could. But he soon found valid reasons, besides his own desire, for moving them to Madison.

"We can save a hundred dollars on the house rent," he wrote to his wife, "and I can be at home three-fourths of the time and help with the care of the children."

Three-fourths of the time for domestic purposes! He underestimated his task. But, with that hope, he moved the family to Madison and established them in a pleasant house, which soon became a center of cheer and good will.

With a husband so peripatetic, Lucy Fallows had to administer the daily discipline of course. But it was uncanny how the father of the family would walk out of nowhere into crucial situations.

Sometimes he was a Day of Judgment. Once Eddie, believing his father to be on the shores of Lake Superior, tried smoking his first cigar, under a Madison culvert.

He looked up and, lo! there he was, standing over him.

But sometimes he was an angel of deliverance. In a rash moment, Mamie (who became Helen in her later years) invited some of her friends to a party, forgot to mention it and forgot it herself. On the proper day six small, befrilled, beribboned guests arrived on the scene. Her mother was house cleaning in a kitchen apron, with a towel round her head. Brought up on emergencies, she had them off and the makings of a party whisked together in no time. It was a great success.

But Mamie knew that punishment for so great an offense would be both swift and awful. She held on to the last guest, who stood between her and disaster like grim death. Just as this one hope tore herself loose, down the street came her father—not expected for days—swinging his big valise and laughing, to restore her, by some magic of his own, without disaster, to the Society of the Elect.

Even though the Superintendent went skirmishing all over

the state and out of it, it was no part of his tactics to neglect
his base.   As Regent, he was helping, all through his term
of office, to make the University as worthy of its position as
the schools that were to bow down to it.

The Normalities were still about as popular in the institution as spiders on a New England ceiling.   The girls had a
separate graduation, and they were granted some sort of a
certificate in lieu of a degree.   The Superintendent used his
influence to get an Easterner to move West as President of
the University.   He supposed, of course, the new man was in
favor of coeducation.   Commencement approached.   He and
the other advocates of the women were in high feather.
After the long battle, the Normalites were to have their
rights, at last.

Then two or three days before Commencement the President refused point-blank to graduate the girls.   "Never,"
said he, "will I be guilty of the absurdity of calling young
women bachelors."

No argument moved him.   The day before Commencement
the Superintendent and one of the professors had an inspiration.   They looked up "bachelor" in the dictionary and read,
to their inexpressible relief, "Bachelor, an unmarried woman.
Ben Jonson, Obs."   That settled it.   No college president
could go back on Webster.   The girls got their degrees.

Samuel Fallows served out Dr. Craig's unexpired term as
Superintendent and was twice elected.   The people wanted
to elect him a third time.

"He would come into the house," said his friend, Professor
Gilman, who was a boy then, "sit down to dinner with us all
in the kitchen and talk cheerily about usual things.   But
when he had gone, we found he had always left us something
to remember.   All over the state he was doing that.   His feet
were everlastingly on the ground, but he always flew his kite
in the fourth dimension.   No wonder Wisconsin wanted him
for another term."

The Superintendent would like to have kept on being State Schoolmaster, perhaps, but the special thing he had in mind was accomplished.

A letter to his brother-in-law, Mr. Brooks, tells the story.

"I wish you would notice in *The Courant* the important educational progress we are making in Wisconsin.

"I have had the honor of introducing and carrying to a successful conclusion measures by which the State University has been brought into practical and vital relations with the public schools. For twenty-five years it has been isolated having no more connection with them than any other institution . . . so all that I have done is something of importance in this direction. The plan is as follows: The graduates of the graded and High Schools of the State who have completed a course of study prescribed by the faculty of the University and have passed an examination satisfactory to the faculty *at the school* from which they graduate are entitled to enter the college class for which they are prepared, or the sub-freshman class without further examination and without *any charge for tuition.*

"Thus we shall be enabled to grade all the schools of the State upon a proper basis and secure the unity we have so much needed. The measure is looked upon as one of the most important ever adopted in the State by educators and the press."

A college education, tuition free, for every Wisconsin boy or girl who wanted it—that was the result of Samuel's work as Superintendent, that and order out of educational disorder.

In the formative period of Wisconsin's history, he had the privilege of helping to shape a school system which, essentially the same to-day, is rated as one of the best in the country.

Governor Fairchild, about this time, offered his Superintendent the position of military secretary, left vacant by Vilas.

Four small colleges begged him to shoulder their burdens as president. Change was in the air.

CHAPTER III

THE SEEDS OF CHANGE

The war inclined men to appreciate authority, order and ritualism. Obedient to the technique of leadership it had taught, General Fallows had helped to straighten out the educational system of Wisconsin. Now it was the turn of religion and his own soul.

The Methodism of those early Seventies was full of zeal and accomplishment. Its virtues were positive and wonderful: the warmth of heart which made of most unlikely units spiritual brothers and sisters; the strength of arm which reared up colleges for the young out of sacrifice and the trees of the wilderness; the humility which kept its members earning their way to heaven each day of their lives. The Methodists had a simple form of worship, the fervor of which had been the salvation of pioneers living repressed lives. Occupied with the stern task of subduing nature, they had little time or desire for an æsthetic expression of religious emotion.

What was excellent for pioneers did not suit so well the needs of a more sophisticated society. This, many Methodists realized. But many mistook the letter for the spirit. They rejoiced in their limitations, instead of their possibilities. They condemned any attempt at beauty as worldly, even to an excess ribbon on the bonnet of the minister's wife, and much innocent fun as harmful, even croquet for the minister. These less advanced Methodists gloried in an uneducated ministry which learned what it knew from Brushwood College —an excellent substitute for the seminary in pioneer times,

232

but not so good for 1870. They forgot that Wesley, himself, held a college degree. They took too literally their founder's original program "to manage their lives by rule and method," and resisted normal change and growth.

Samuel Fallows, dearly loving the church into which he had been born, was one of those who saw its limitations and its possibilities. His Oconomowoc camp-meeting speech advocating theological training for Methodist ministers marked him a progressive. Fresh from his victory in the educational field, with the schoolmaster tingle in his fingers, he must have longed to help the Methodist Church toward beauty and liberalism.

The House of Bishops of the Protestant Episcopal Church in 1852, sent Bishop Whitehouse, against his desire, to Chicago. The result, by a devious path, was the Reformed Episcopal Church, twenty years later, the most significant church split of the century.

Bishop Whitehouse was a superfine kind of human being. He was scholarly, logical, skillful as a poet, musician and painter, eloquent enough to preach the opening sermon at the Pan-Anglican Synod in the chapel of Lambeth Palace, wise enough to receive honorary degrees from Oxford and Cambridge.

They sent this estimable man, who would have graced the most ritualistic position they had, this rigid High Churchman with his ecclesiastical eye on the letter of the law, steeled in traditions, aristocratic—they sent him to Chicago—Chicago fresh as new paint and as impatient of conventions as a bucking broncho.

Bishop Whitehouse did not wish to become Bishop of Illinois in 1852. He tendered his resignation in 1855. The House of Bishops, however, against his earnest protest refused, at that session, to accept his resignation. Again they made him Bishop of Illinois. Again they sent the unwilling

Bishop, with his classical mind and his Lambeth Palace cut of theology, back to Chicago, where an occasional Indian proclaimed its mush-room origin, and even the wind so far forgot its dignity as to blow a ship up on land one morning and poke its nose into the breakfast room of a lake-shore mansion.

Chicago was an incredible hotbed of rude, democratic activity just then. No one cared what his neighbor knew, as in Boston; for his pedigree, as in Philadelphia; or the size of his bank roll, as in New York. "What can you do?" was the question. Importance was measured by the size of a man's biceps, his aristocracy by what he accomplished.

Imagine Bishop Whitehouse in this mad rush of seething force! Sooner or later, the irritation of his misfitting would catch him. The inevitable was bound to happen. It did. Bishop Whitehouse and Mr. Charles Edward Cheney came to grips.

Samuel Fallows, pastor in Milwaukee then, was deep in Methodist concerns. But that encounter between the Bishop and Mr. Cheney was one of the forces which lifted him out of his own church.*

Mr. Cheney was the popular young minister of Christ Church on the South Side. A classmate of Phillips Brooks and broad also in his theological views, he had taken over Christ Church in 1860 at the time when Samuel was having his first brush at a career as Handy Man at Galesville.

Mr. Cheney, with patience and zeal, built up his church out of Chicago's splendid pioneer stuff—men like John Ben-

---

* This encounter was one of a long series in which the liberal forces within the Protestant Episcopal Church were arrayed against the conservatives. The bitter fight involved so many intricate vital issues that it cannot be reported fully here. But a summary of it has been prepared by the Reverend Dr. William A. Freemantle, Editor of the *Episcopal Recorder*. This account will be found in Appendix A.

ham, Thomas Crouch, Samuel McRoy, D. W. Keith, Melville W. Fuller, the Maxwell brothers, E. G. Keith and George F. Brown. During the years when Samuel Fallows was learning generalship out of raw war, Mr. Cheney was lifting his struggling church successfully from crisis to crisis.

The young Protestant Episcopal minister was as completely the antithesis of his Bishop as the limits of the church would allow. He was as Low Church as Bishop Whitehouse was High; as evangelistic as his superior was sacerdotal. He was magnetic and lovable, with the rounded dome-like forehead of a man who will fight for his opinions. The gray-blue eyes, black under excitement, behind his eyeglasses saw the world as his friend. He was sympathetic and impetuous. He had a quick, nervous mind. His mouth was wide and generous. Under provocation, it set like a trap. So, also, did his convictions.

He saw human behavior largely in the terms of his personal reactions, which made him an ardent defender of a given cause rather than a statesman or a diplomat. But for almost ten years, he was successful in avoiding an issue with Bishop Whitehouse. Then restrictions became so disagreeable and the High Church tendencies so marked in the affairs of the Synod that some of the clergymen wrote a protest to the Bishop decrying the Romanizing trend of his management. Mr. Cheney and several other ministers signed this protest. Thus was the explosive planted which helped to blow the Reformed Episcopal Church from off the parent church. The gentle gossip of a prominent Baptist clergyman of Chicago set the match. This friendly man of God had an excellent luncheon, one day, with Bishop Whitehouse at the Episcopal residence. In the pleasant hour of expansiveness following it, he said in substance:

"I met Mr. Cheney in a bookstore the other day. Fine man. We had a good talk about infant baptism. I was somewhat surprised at his views. You know when he baptizes a child he never uses the part of the service in the Prayer Book which asserts that spiritual regeneration is infallibly tied to baptism."

In May, 1869, Bishop Whitehouse called on Mr. Cheney.

The Bishop said, in effect: "Can it possibly be true that one of my clergymen is omitting words from the Baptismal Service?"

Mr. Cheney, knowing how much company he had, for nearly all of the Low Church ministers did the same, said: "It is."

Mr. Cheney said firmly, but respectfully: "I'll keep on baptizing babies as I have done."

"Very well," said the Bishop, "you will be tried and deposed from the ministry."

"But, Bishop," asked the culprit, "how can you tell beforehand that I will be deposed?"

"Because," he replied, "I shall not allow any man to be on the court who has signed his name to a certain document." He referred to the Protest which had served as the first declaration of hostilities.

Mr. Cheney was tried. As the Bishop predicted, so it was. The arraigned could take his pick of five judges out of ten. But all ten were High Churchmen. Which one he picked, therefore, made very little difference. An injunction was granted, which stayed the trial for a number of months. It then proceeded with four triers instead of five, as one of the original members of the court had been made a bishop and had moved away in the meantime. Mr. Melville W. Fuller, afterward Chief Justice of the United States Supreme Court, defended Mr. Cheney. He protested against having his client tried by a diminished court. Bishop Whitehouse overruled him. It proved a fatal decision for the Bishop.

Mr. Cheney was pronounced by this court guilty and suspended from the ministry until such time as he "should express contrition for the past and conformity for the future." Contrition for obeying his conscience! As if a man could cut over his convictions and his principles to suit each new bishop! No vital rule of the Church, even, was at stake, merely the interpretation of a rubric—one of the directions in the Prayer Book for the convenience of ministers.

Because Mr. Cheney's interpretation did not square with his Bishop's, a young man with a zealous congregation and a tremendous capacity for service was suspended from the ministry, four years after the war, in a country torn by reconstruction, in the state of Lincoln, in a booming town with enough raw energy, properly harnessed, to run a spiritual world.

Mr. Cheney paid no attention to the judgment of the court. He simply went on preaching and doing his parish work, more loved by his people than ever before, but shunned entirely by his Bishop. A second trial charged him with "contumacy"—the church word for obstinacy—in disobeying the command of the first court, and the sentence of deposition was passed upon him.

Then it became a moot question which owned Christ Church—its parish or the Diocese of the Protestant Episcopal Church. Each claimed the property. This disagreement took the whole matter into the civil courts and finally to the Supreme Court of the state. That august body gave Christ Church to the parish.

Moreover, the Supreme Court ruled that the first court of all, which began as five men and ended as four and which suspended Mr. Cheney until he should say he was sorry and promise to repent was "a body of amiable gentlemen, no doubt," but not a court according to the canons of the Protestant Episcopal Church, itself. The court further ruled that, therefore, Mr. Cheney, Dr. Cheney, now, was not amenable to the decision and penalty of the second court, the decision of which was wholly conditioned on that of the first.

Translated, it meant that Dr. Cheney was still, and had been all the time, by the laws of the land and the laws of the Church, a Protestant Episcopal minister, with a church and a congregation of his own.

Dr. Cheney was deposed for his interpretation of a rubric. Absurd, we say, with a world waiting to be saved. But can we afford to be so superior? Have we not recently had our good bishops deposed for their opinions? Have we not had our spectacular trials over unessentials—stones of doctrine about the religion of Jesus thrown to a world crying for the bread of life?

Why blame Bishop Whitehouse, unable to get out of the orbit where nature set him?

His dust, by now, is, perhaps, the rooting ground of lovely flowers. His Cathedral, in one of the spots left sad and forlorn by the changes making a slum of the section of the West Side where it stands—his Cathedral of stone and plaster— was burned a while ago. But the Cathedral Shelter, run in its name, succors the poor and forlorn of the city. A few of its inmates, the poorest of the poor, found an unruined spot in the artistocratic Bishop's Cathedral, and they wrought out of it a chapel, with hands of love. They made its benches with their own hands. They gave it stained-glass glory, with bits of paper pasted on the common glass. The Christ of the carpenter bench walks there. Time has done its healing.

CHAPTER IV

A METHODIST GOES HALFWAY

The tug which lifted Samuel Fallows out of the Methodist Church was no simple pull of one event or motive. Denominationally, he was always a potential cosmopolitan. Methodist because he was born into the church and was converted in it, he could regard it, even in those early denominational seventies, as one of his Commander's battle fields, from which he might easily be called to serve in another. As long as he was fighting always under the same banner, the kind of battle field seemed to him of secondary importance.

With responsibilities heaped upon him, feeling in himself the tremendous force let loose by war, he could scarcely escape the knowledge that he would make any sector in which he commanded hum with action. As he was drawn strongly toward authority, form and ritual, there is no knowing to what camp his feet might have led him had it not been for his wife's strict Methodism and Dr. Cheney's spectacular persecution.

Much about the Church of England was sweet in his memory—days in the parish school in Pendleton, the moments with his mother in the stately Warrington church, looking at the tombs of the nobility. Her Methodist soul had sometimes expressed to him a yearning for the Church of England which had baptized and confirmed and married her, to which a vague desire of his own gave echo.

In Hadley, on his first trip East in 1860, the hungry-minded Methodist had talked much with Lucy's uncle, Frederic Hunt-

239

ington, who was just then feeling the first ecstasy of turning from Unitarian into Protestant Episcopalian. That same Uncle Frederic was now a Bishop, high in the councils of a great Church.

In the war, at the request of his Colonel, for the first time Chaplain Fallows had read in public, out of one of the eighteen Prayer Books furnished by the Governor's widow, that wonderful service of the Episcopal Church with the authority of all the years of history behind it. The rhythm of the stately prayers was in his ears even while he wrote to his wife that she need have no fear that he would ever submit himself to the authority of the Episcopal Church "because he loved the freedom of the Methodist far too well." Without the counterbalance of the Cheney trial, his Methodist mate and an innate something of his own, Samuel Fallows might have found more than merely tempting that Protestant Episcopal camp, the only Protestant Church in the United States using the Book of Common Prayer.

But he did have to reckon with that dear wife of his who, so recently for love, had made her terrific fight against her Unitarian convictions and her family. In the new Church after all, she found herself a prisoner of joy because of her husband's presence. But there she wished to stay. One soul battle was all she wanted. Any hint of a move from the Methodist Church put a stricken look into the eyes.

Now, the religion of a banker's wife may be his or her own —or of a doctor's wife or a lawyer's, a baker's, a beggar's or a candlestick maker's. It makes no difference with his business. But a minister's wife is his spiritual partner. Unless the two see almost eye to eye, the ship of success goes on the rocks. Samuel was only free to change the aspect of his religion as he could get Lucy to change hers. He might have remained in the Methodist Church and fought out his fight there. The attraction of the home Church was very great, almost as great as the pull toward religious beauty and form. Having faith in his powers of persuasion, he might possibly have tried to graft his wife on the Episcopalian tree, if Bishop Whitehouse and the devil had kept their hands from Dr. Cheney.

At this time, the Methodist minister was State Superintendent, facing a decision about his future. Should he stand for another term? In answering that question, his wife was probably the decisive factor. She, as well as he, had helped to secure a free college course for the children of Wisconsin. But hers was the grubby part—keeping the home fires burning, cooking meals herself when the hired girl refused to be hired, and disciplining three active children with her soft-soled slipper.

He must not make permanent such a life, for one of her mind and talents. Summerfield had taught him both her desires and her capabilities. She had a special vocation for being a minister's wife. Whatever he did in the future must provide her that.

Should he stay in the Methodist Church, then?

Turning the question over and over, on a trip to a remote Teachers' Institute, in the jolting train murky with kerosene fumes, he had a vision that seemed to open heaven. He saw a new Church with the old, beautiful Liturgy, a Church opening its pulpit to other ministers, bidding all Christians to its communion rail. He beheld it Episcopal and evangelical, stately but loving, combining the virtues of Episcopalians and Methodists, omitting the faults of each. He even saw its name! The Reformed Episcopal Church.

After that, events came thick and fast.

Bishop Cummins, Assistant Bishop of Kentucky, Low Church and greatly in sympathy with Dr. Cheney, was goaded to the breaking point by the High Church faction. At a conference of the Evangelical Alliance in New York, Bishop Cummins took part in a union communion service held in the church of Dr. John Hall. He, a Bishop in the Apostolic Succession, had dared to administer communion in a non-Episcopal Church to any pleb of a Christian who wished to take the sacred bread and wine. The whole Episcopal Church was in commotion. Scathing letters appeared in the public press. This last straw of intolerance broke the Bishop's patience. He wrote a letter to the Presiding Bishop of the Church where he had served twenty-eight years, announcing his withdrawal from that body.

On December 2, 1873, with Dr. Cheney and other clergymen and laymen, Bishop Cummins organized a new Church, the counterpart of Samuel's vision even to its name—the Reformed Episcopal Church. It seemed like an answer to prayer. The Superintendent sent a telegram of congratulation to Bishop Cummins.

At this first meeting of the Church in New York, Dr. Cheney was elected Bishop. In December, Bishop Cummins went out to Chicago to consecrate him, and on that consecration rests the claim of the Reformed Episcopal Church to the Historic Succession.

Bishop Smith, Presiding Bishop of the Protestant Episcopal Church, after various other expedients had failed, telegraphed Bishop Cummins, at Chicago, that he must not consecrate Dr. Cheney. This action showed that he thought the Bishop of the new Church qualified to do it. By the ruling of the Protestant Episcopal Church, the Presiding Bishop was not vested with the right to forbid Bishop Cummins to perform his office. "Once a bishop, always a bishop."

Dr. Cheney, by the judgment of the court, was still a clergyman of the Protestant Episcopal Church. Bishop Cummins had not been deposed from the Episcopate of the Protestant Episcopal Church. Technically, he was in good standing and in full orders. Why the historic Episcopate was not transmitted to another communion on that occasion, it is difficult to see. The Reformed Episcopalians, however, regarded it as a beautiful and historical rite, but not endowed with mystic power.

Whatever one side or the other believed, the stubborn fact remained that the Reformed Episcopal Church made the first break in the Episcopal ranks since the Reformation.

About that time, Lucy's uncle, Bishop Huntington, a powerful man of the Protestant Episcopal Church, came out to Wisconsin. One day, in Madison, he ordained his older brother, William Huntington, into the Episcopal Church. At the end of the day, Bishop Huntington had a serious talk with his nephew-in-law, Samuel. It was very apparent to so good a judge of men as the Bishop that this young man had a bright future before him. The responsibilities already heaped upon him presaged that. The rumor had got about that Samuel Fallows was inclining toward the new church.

Bishop Huntington wanted him in his own and asked him to join. No man with the Superintendent's experience could fail to know that this powerful backing would mean swift advancement to a place in the sun within the Episcopal Church. But he gave no answer, then. He declined to run again as State Superintendent and accepted the Presidency of Illinois Wesleyan University, a Methodist Institution at Bloomington. Denominationally he was still unsettled.

In the days that followed, battling with the question of his future, he flung out into the open, as he did so often, to think it over. He sought the Madison woods, which had seen him through his boyhood decision and talked with his close friends—a very few, since he was given to keeping his own counsel. Dr. Louise Kellogg remembers that her father and Samuel Fallows drove for a whole afternoon in the country, discussing the question of whether he should leave the Methodist Church or not. Louise, sitting on a stool between them was such a little pitcher that they did not suppose she was taking in a word. Mr. Kellogg did not wish his friend to leave. But Samuel Fallows wrote to Bishop Huntington that he could not join the Protestant Episcopal Church and pledged himself to the new Church.

At last, in the Reformed Episcopal Church, he had the form and ritual his war-self craved and the freedom the Anglo-Saxon individualist in him demanded. But he had more, much more than he had dared to hope was possible in an imperfect world—a Church, to begin with, as loving as Christ and as broad as the world, a Church that would take the young giant of the growing West and mold it with beautiful hands. The Church was also to have a great university very soon. Ripe in experience, he was to head the educational work. How he and Bishop Cheney had dreamed of such an institution as they visited together in Chicago! All their letters were full of it. The University of the West!

His wife could not fail to be at home in this new Church. It was beautiful with form, but cleared of all the "Romishness" which she feared. She, seeing how raptly happy he was, forebore to speak her doubts.

The Methodist minister entering the new Church saw with his imagination and felt with his heart. But he thought with his head. Through the eyes of his brain, the future of the Reformed Episcopal Church looked very bright. It would attract Methodists who had outgrown simplicity. It would draw Episcopalians who were tired of restrictions.

Phillips Brooks had intimated that he would cast in his lot with the new denomination. That would probably mean that the whole Low wing of the Church would swing in with him. Samuel Fallows, himself, told this to his own son, Edward, years afterwards. In the seventies, he scarcely dared to think what it would mean to work with Phillips Brooks. They were spiritual brothers in aim and intention. With one in the East and one in the West, what might they not accomplish!

The pressure brought to bear upon the Eastern minister by the leaders of the Protestant Episcopal Church was apparently successful. For reasons still unknown, Phillips Brooks, big-hearted lover of freedom, changed his mind and did not enter the Reformed Episcopal Church.

Samuel Fallows felt that the new Church was destined for great numbers and a special mission. He was profoundly convinced that it offered the greatest opportunity of the age.

PART VII

BISHOP IN A CHURCH

CHAPTER I

COLLEGE PRESIDENT

Samuel Fallows' life fell into two halves—before Chicago and Chicago.

The presidency of Illinois Wesleyan was a hyphen between these divisions of his career—a short but significant hyphen.

The Wesleyan University, at Bloomington, Illinois, was a scrap of canvas compared with the state of Wisconsin. But, using the same methods, the new President accomplished in miniature there what he had done on a big scale as Superintendent of Public Instruction. He strengthened the organization of the institution and set new forces going, which are operating in education to-day.

The student body, composed largely of ambitious farmer boys and girls, was the kind of unspoiled human material with which the new President loved to work. His creative schoolmaster eye saw his pupils as the stuff out of which to-morrow's society would be made. "We will do our best for the University while we are there," he wrote Lucy.

Pledged to the Reformed Episcopal Church, though his decision was as yet unannounced, knowing that his time at the University would be short, he worked as if Wesleyan were his for life. He started a Music Department and founded a Law School, the first in the state to be connected with a university. His unusual contribution to the cause of education was the outcome of a wish to give struggling Methodist ministers an incentive to study in their spare time at home. To this end,

249

he induced the University to grant degrees to such of them as passed satisfactory examinations.

This granting of degrees *in absentia* raised a small tempest. Some of the Methodist brethren, even, held up their hands at the innovation. Dr. Allyn, evidently some one of consequence in the educational world, indulged in a spasm of protest. Primarily for Methodists, the course was open to any who could prove themselves eligible. Such democracy of opportunity seemed the end of the educational world, almost, to Dr. Allyn. He and the President had hot and heavy discussions in the press.

"This has never been done before in the United States," argued the Doctor, voice of the conservatives.

"True," said the President. "But could you have a better example than London University? The custom of that institution is to grant degrees *in absentia*. All that is necessary is to safeguard the high standard of the course and the examinations."

The new departure proved very popular. Not only ministers but others all over the country, enrolled for these courses. The experiment, embodying the sympathy of a far-sighted man for the hungry-minded, so far as is known, marks the beginning, in the United States, of university extension work, which no important college of to-day is without. The President, though he did not know it then, had thought out very much the same sensible system which French and German universities had developed.

But academic information was only part of what the President was providing for his students. The reports from those days are full of his human relations with his boys and girls. By precept and example, he was trying to teach them to be all-around men and women. He wanted no cloistered recluses among his graduates.

"You must vote," he told the young men. "You must talk and act and control by all lawful influence the votes of others.

If you shrink from duty as politicians in the best sense of that most abused term, you are unworthy of your diplomas and a place among Americans."

Edward Maxwell was one of President Fallows' boys for a term only—all he could manage in a self-supporting career. Afterward, he went to Chicago, became one of its important men and a member of Bishop Cheney's church. As a member of the President's Rhetoric class at Wesleyan he "fell in love" with him for life. "He charmed the students," Mr. Maxwell testifies. "They all adored him." It was partly because their interests were his. He roused the students to enthusiasm over debates. He fostered an intercollegiate contest of oratory, which brought much glory to Illinois Wesleyan. He encouraged sports. In the ample "President's House," set in a whole block of yard, he and his wife entertained the students in little groups and larger groups. At Commencement, they hung the yard with Chinese lanterns, borrowed two locomotive headlights and "spread a table outside with all the delicacies of the season, which made all within a man," as the reporter expressed it, "heave with pleasant sensations of delight."

After the second Commencement, the pleasant Bloomington episode came to an end. The University was well organized. It had more money than ever before and more students. In the full tide of success, the President accepted the rectorship of St. Paul's Reformed Episcopal Church in Chicago, at a salary of one thousand five hundred dollars less than his salary at Wesleyan, announced his intention of entering the Reformed Episcopal Church, handed in his resignation to a stunned faculty and made his regretful farewell to the students.

"My resignation," he said, in his last chapel address, "is not because of any dissatisfaction with the students or faculty or trustees of the institution; not for the sake of gain or glory; but because Providence has brought about what has been the hope of my life—an opportunity to preach to the masses of a great city the Gospel of Christ, and to train laymen and laywomen for the same great work."

With that hope, Samuel went to Chicago, which had been calling him all his life. It was the call of an expanding city to an expanding personality.

CHAPTER II

DR. FALLOWS GETS A TOE HOLD

In this Chicago, where one was playwright, actor, manager, carpenter, scene shifter, ticket collector and audience all at once, Dr. Fallows began to experiment with his own special world first. He needed to master its technique, its rules of thumb, if there were any, so that he might break them intelligently if occasion arose.

He preached his first sermon at St. Paul's on Sunday, the Fourth of July, 1875, twenty-seven years to a day from the time he had landed on the Milwaukee dock, in his funny, hot, clumsy English clothes. The sermon was on the "Rights of Skeptics." He had never read the Liturgy publicly before, except as Chaplain in the Civil War, at the request of his Colonel, out of a Protestant Episcopal Prayer Book. He had never before had a Reformed Episcopal gown upon his unaccustomed shoulders.

His wife, in her demure bonnet, sat in one of the front pews, with the children in a row beside her. Although, during the whole fifteen years of her married life, she had never known her husband to fail in rising to any given occasion, her throat was sympathetically dry, her hand in the black silk mitt sympathetically clenched, in the face of this unique ordeal—preaching to a strange congregation, in a strange church, in a new denomination just minted by the hand of time.

But Samuel Fallows was feeling, once more, the primal thrill of his guiding hand pushing the plow blade through unbroken earth. Everybody's Church, in that first sermon, was making its first furrow beneath his steady grasp. Where might not that furrow lead—East, West, across the seas, over the world! The dream of its greatness was in his voice. After a few minutes, the congregation swayed a little this way and that way with his gestures, like wheat in a light wind. Then his wife relaxed against the hard back of the pew, assured that she could safely leave the rights of skeptics to Samuel and a kind Providence for the rest of the sermon.

It was a day, too, when skeptics were a cross between an unbarred convict and an object with invisible horns and a tail. They and women were in the same category as to rights. A timid man would not have cared to preach about them. The *Tribune,* the next morning, printed the new minister's sermon on skeptics in full. By this act, it admitted him to the hierarchy of Chicago's popular and liberal preachers— a pleasant ægis behind which he worked for almost forty-seven Chicago years.

The spiritual world of Chicago was full of bubbling, provocative, creative energy.

The earthquake moment in history which had heaved up a new slaveless America was also pouring a new spirit of religion into old bottles. Nowhere in the country, probably, was the effort more intensely centered at the moment than in Chicago. Three heresy trials in three different denominations in about as many years marked the cracking of the bottles.

Samuel Fallows, looking deeper than the surface, found it possible to rejoice in the religious commotion about him. Upheavals followed Pentecost and Luther and the Wesleys. After each of them, religion had stretched itself, revalued itself, added a cubit or two to its stature and flung out a few outposts, before it sank into a lethargy of routine again.

(From Leslie's Weekly, 1895)

TWO OF BISHOP FALLOWS' ACTIVITIES IN SOCIAL SERVICE

(Above) The exterior of the People's Institute, founded by Bishop Fallows in 1894 as a community center. It was one of the first in the United States. [See Page 321]

(Below) The Home Saloon, founded by Bishop Fallows in 1895 as an experiment in temperance. [See Page 328]

Organized religion is a big body, and forward marching is heavy work, requiring a mighty and reiterated impetus. The late President of Wesleyan knew that. He realized that it was time for another application of impetus. And he could see it given by the Reformed Episcopal Church.

From the period of turmoil which had tossed Professor David Swing and Dr. Thomas out of their denominations into independent down-town churches and Bishop Cheney into a new church, he had faith to believe that something new and American was emerging.

Personal salvation had had its long day, from the Middle Ages on. Under that belief, a Christian's main business simmered down to getting himself on a safety raft, lest he drown in a brimstone ocean.

The slow inexorable pendulum of progress was swinging away from that spirit—Tick!—Tock!— At the tick of personal salvation for that long, long historical moment, it was describing its inevitable arc, now, toward the tock of brotherhood. All the forces of reaction were trying to pull the world back to tick.

Bishop Whitehouse had tried Dr. Cheney because he refused to say that baptismal water on a baby's head regenerated its spiritual nature.

"Keep him at tick. Keep all the people at tick. That tock is the place of perdition." So said Bishop Whitehouse and set about building a Cathedral.

Dr. Patton demanded the trial of the poet-preacher, David Swing, who shed sweetness and light in that crude young city, as if a Christ fire were lighted within him, because he had dared to preach in a Unitarian Church and to couch his Christian thought in language that did not accord with Dr. Patton's vocabulary. Dr. Swing, tried by his Presbyterian Church, was left with a verdict so ambiguous that he stepped out of the home church which he loved, to preach in Central Music Hall, bidding people to hurry on to tock, while Dr.

Patton was trying to pull them back to that outworn tick of time.

Dr. Thomas, convicted by the Baptists of being progressive, started his independent congregation down town. Full of the clash of conflict was that spiritual world of Chicago, where heretics of the day were being made into the saints of to-morrow. A fine field for a man who loved greatly and could fight as greatly!

And Dr. Fallows preached his first sermon in Chicago on the Rights of Skeptics!

CHAPTER III

BEES, RAMS, LUCY FALLOWS AND THE APOSTOLIC SUCCESSION

The new minister's first week in Chicago was a pacemaker.

There was the house to settle at odd moments. He began to edit the *Appeal,* the Church paper, and had consultations with Bishop Cheney about the University of the West.

He went to Bishop Cheney by horse car, a neighborly thing in those days. The passengers became acquainted, as on a long sea voyage. One man drove and collected the fares. When the car got off the track, as it frequently did, all the male passengers filed out and helped it on again. In cold weather, it was half-filled with hay, to keep people's toes from freezing. An impeccable West Side young lady jumped up midway of one trip, shrieking and dancing about as if she had delirium tremens, because a friendly little garter snake mistook her ankle for a slender sapling.

Getting down town by car was such a leisurely process that Dr. Fallows, walking swiftly for exercise, found he could sometimes outpace the vehicle to State Street. When bad weather or weariness made him a passenger, he used the car as an extension to his study. Having learned to make his brain do one thing while his tongue was doing another, he frequently took a text at his home street, chatted with the other passengers on the way and jumped off at the end of the trip with a sermon all prepared.

He bettered his own record for quick work in his first seven Chicago days. Between Sundays, he and his congregation

257

bought the American Reformed Church on Washington Street, and moved out of their old cramped quarters into that spacious structure on a dignified street.

Preaching on skeptics one Sunday, on the next, with Bishop Cheney's help, Dr. Fallows dedicated the new church. It was to be, he said, "a church for the people where rich and poor could meet on an equal footing, not a focus for an exclusive set nor a church club. Over its portals would be written 'Welcome to all.' "

Those three words, WELCOME TO ALL, expressed his idea of the new church as a receiving station.

Thirteen more words carried his conception of it as an outreaching, conquering force. "Go ye into all the world and preach the gospel to every creature."

After pledging himself to the Church, before entering it even, he had been compelled to relinquish his cherished dream that it was to be a Church of overwhelming numbers.

The law of spiritual gravitation, which keeps people to a familiar footing, even a distasteful one, held the cultured Methodists whom the new Church hoped to attract, in their own denomination. The decision of Phillips Brooks and the valiant efforts of the Protestant Episcopal Church to hold their own kept all except the boldest Low Churchmen from leaving the home fold.

But the initial lack of numbers was merely a stimulant to a courageous man's hope for his Church. It meant a greater heave of the shoulder at the wheel—that was all. He had no doubt, then, that this Church, beautiful but free, could conquer the great West for righteousness. With the University of the West for minds, and its churches for liberal souls, he still had his empire-building dreams of making the Reformed Episcopal denomination a great factor in national life.

In the meantime he had Chicago. He was heady with the joy of it. Loving people as the sailor loves his sea, crowds were an elixir. They never drained him. They made the simplest trip down town an excitement. He liked to brush against people in the street, in secondhand bookshops where he was finding material for the *Appeal,* at church, anywhere. In Chicago, teeming with life and excitement, where a man of leisure would have felt as lonely as Robinson Crusoe, the quality of crowds was more exhilarating than anywhere else.

It was good to have that enjoyment in his first weeks of big-city life. For there were offsets. Not even he, tireless as he was, could keep up his swift pace without the penalty of weary moments. But things, on the whole, were moving as well as he could possibly expect.

Then, like a thunderclap in August sunshine, came the news, one morning, that his spiritual partner, his stay and his helpmeet, was not really a convinced Reformed Episcopalian at all.

A letter brought the word from his wife, visiting at the farm with the children. She wrote her missive on the same little wooden table, in the upstairs sitting room by the window overlooking the apple orchard, where she had poured out her troubled Unitarian soul to her Methodist lover nearly eighteen years before.

Again she wrote out of the clash and fray of souls in conflict. Again the kitchen rocked with the discussions between her mother and herself.

Mrs. Huntington's contention was the same as of old. All her dear family was going toward Rome and destruction. Eighteen years before, she had been fighting the step from Unitarianism to Methodism. Now it was from Methodism almost into the Pit.

It seemed to Lucy Fallows, herself, as if all the men folk of her family had been caught in an earthquake and heaved out of their former spiritual positions. There was her father, intellectual, ironical Unitarian at first, affronting Samuel's warm boyish acceptance of all things Methodist by calling a camp meeting no better than an Indian powwow; afterward, almost ninety-nine-hundredths Methodist himself! Then, that last strange step, only a little while before. Ordained by his brother, Bishop Huntington, her uncle Frederic, as a clergyman in the Protestant Episcopal church. Not only that, but he had gone to Dakota as a minister-missionary.

Here was Samuel, a Methodist for forty years, with not a worldly reason missing to keep him in his home Church the rest of his life, part of a new denomination with all its struggles before it.

William, her brother, after a course in theology at Boston University and a couple of years of Methodist preaching, was on the verge of joining the Reformed Episcopal church; likewise Fred, the brother just graduating at Wisconsin.

Lucy Fallows wondered if men were a different race from women, that they could take a wrecking process so easily and slip into a different denomination as if it were a new coat.

They were merely red-blooded Christians, of course, responding to the stimulus of progress which had heaved up a slaveless America, toppled an old system of education from its perch, broken new churches off old ones and generally made things ready for the new brotherhood of man which was to keep her husband busy the rest of his life.

If Lucy Fallows could have grasped the significance of all this, she could have saved herself much agony of spirit. That was impossible, of course. We could have no civilization at all, if it were not for pathfinding race-fathers—in both sexes —and tradition-keeping race-mothers—also in both sexes— who set their beliefs like candles in the windows of their souls, that any wanderer lost in the dark may find his way back to safety.

So she, of the latter type, attended by her New England conscience, sitting at the Cedar Bluffs window, looked at the green apples in the orchard, ripening themselves with no thought of the morrow, and tumbled out all her doubts and fears in a letter to her husband.

When the postman gave that letter to the master of the house in dusty Chicago, he smiled to think how happy his family must be at the clean farm, with the air full of good-smelling clover. But when he had read the pages packed with doubts and fears, he did not smile at all. He sat down and wrote his wife a letter which expressed his philosophy of service for the remaining forty-seven years of his life, as well as for 1875.

CHICAGO, ILL., Aug. 16th. '75 Friday.

DEAR LUCY,

I enclose Mrs. Willing's letter. It is a good one. The best thing to do is to try and help others, to forget *self,* and go out to bring others in. That was Paul's plan. He trampled all his prejudice under his feet, became a Jew to the Jews —a Greek to the Greeks—a Roman to the Romans, all *things to all men,* that he might win some to Christ.

Now in coming into the Reformed Episcopal Church there is no sacrifice of *principle.* The mere custom of gowns, surplice, service, or a thousand other things are *nothing, literally* nothing.

I'll wear twenty gowns if need be, if in that way I can lead men to a higher life. Our prayer meetings *I* enjoy as much as I ever enjoyed any meetings in the Methodist Church, camp meeting, class meeting or anything else.

I am in the church, one of its acknowledged leaders. The foremost men, some of them in the M. E. Church, are wanting to come in too. It's *no time to look* back. Progress was never made that way. I have no regrets. I have an absorbing ambition to build up a church of Christ loving men and women. They may view life differently, have different ideals of amusements from mine. With that I cannot interfere except in the way of persuasion. It does not trouble me a bit. God is blessing our work. To weaken, faint, to hesitate, to halt, to fluctuate will be disloyalty.

I am in. There is no alternative. By God's help the church must win a grand success. I am thorough and radical in my convictions. I cannot go by uncertain feelings. It is impossible to have things our own way. It was a greater prejudice for me to overcome, when I first saw American Christians reading newspapers on Sunday to believe in their Christianity than it was later on to reconcile dancing with a high Christian profession.

And yet a glass of English ale *we* could take without wincing. But it would be hard to make some American Christians believe in beer drinking. Many good English ministers take a glass of wine. I don't believe in the practice.

Prof. Jaques has a holy horror of secret societies or did have. Some good Christians are carrying on a crusade against them in a most virulent unchristian spirit. Brother Miller was fiercely attacked by these zealots and his piety denounced.

My standard I cannot make the standard of all. If persons profess to love Christ and by their *daily walk* show they do it, that is all we can ask. And as for being troubled over it I have something infinitely more important to look after.

But I want full sympathy in my work. I am conscious I am carrying a tremendous load,—my sermons; my pastoral work; University plans. Debts press upon me. But I can carry it all and not grow weary by God's help. But you must be a *help meet*. It would be adding to the strain if I have to carry you too.

We had a glorious sociable last night, the largest we have had. Several new families I took down yesterday.

Will write more particulars soon.

Love and kisses to all.

Very affectionately,

SAMUEL FALLOWS

But, sensitive to his helpmeet's human weather, he felt from her reply that he had not settled her doubts, after all. His wife's coöperation was more essential to his peace of mind than anything else, so between Sundays he slipped up to Cedar Bluffs to see what he could do about it.

The day of the settlement began appropriately with butts. Little Ellery, the youngest brother, had a pet ram which ran amuck in the morning, and, taking the little boy in the rear, knocked him down. Evidently feeling that the Day of Judgment had backed up against him, and that it was no use to resist, Ellery stood up and went down again twice before he thought otherwise, and badly damaged made the house by scuttling crab-fashion from tree to tree.

That seemed calamity enough for one day, but it remained for his Uncle Samuel to cap the climax. That he did in the afternoon, returning from some farm errand with the light wagon, when the restive horses crashed into one of the bee-hives near the house.

It was while his wife, in the pleasant farm kitchen, was easing with mud plasters the woe caused by the angry bees, that her husband probed for her own trouble.

"It's the Apostolic Succession," said Lucy Fallows, torn by all those discussions with her mother. "Has the Reformed Episcopal Church that Popish thing?"

This was no girl of eighteen he had to convince, but a woman grown, with strong opinions. She had pulled away from her beliefs once for love. So much the harder was the second yielding.

"Yes, my dear," her husband said. "I think the Apostolic Succession is ours. But its significance to us is as a very beautiful historic rite. It is not mystic."

In the next half hour, he was able to persuade her that the devil and all his works had been driven out of the new Church. He made her see that there was no Popery in its service or in its gowns and that the Christ of the carpenter bench was as truly in its midst as in the Methodist Church.

When Mrs. Huntington, a little later, entered the kitchen to make biscuits for tea, she found her daughter sitting by her son-in-law, the convinced Reformed Episcopalian she would always thereafter remain.

One of her delights, from that time on, was to keep black satin gowns in beautiful order and, presently, when the Bishop's robe was part of the equipment, to make a picture of herself for her children's memory.

CHAPTER IV

THE BIBLE, BERNHARDT AND A SHOE CLERK

With his wife walking whole-heartedly beside him, the new minister of St. Paul's organized the church work. The two together also made the parsonage a center of idealism in the midst of a practical city.

To Annie Walker, Mamie's age, one of the church girls who went in and out of the house on Fulton Street like a daughter, the household seemed like "something out of a story book." They never measured values at 530 Fulton Street in terms of the dollar sign or the stock market, but by standards of goodness and badness. Yet the house was a merry place. Let Annie Walker draw her own picture of that time:

"The Bishop could make people do anything in the world he pleased. He was full of charm. Everyone went down before it. Mrs. Fallows had just as much but hers was different. She was very beautiful in those days and exquisite as always. She was cordial and gracious and yet in her presence you felt as if you must take a step up as to a queen.

"Afterwards she absorbed herself so completely in the Bishop's needs and in his work that she seemed almost part of his background. But it was a voluntary subordination. With her mind and talents she might have shone as an individual anywhere. But she elected to become the Bishop's third arm as it were.

"Once I remember her cultured and learned father was visiting at the house. After supper when we were sitting around in the back parlor, he said something in French. We

264

all looked at each other, uncomprehending, the Bishop, too.

" 'You said,' spoke up Mrs. Fallows serenely, 'it is a pleasant evening and we have had a good meal.'

"She had a rare gift of expression. Her feeling for wards was as accurate as the Bishop's. I used to love to sit in a corner and listen to the music of her voice.

"She was always ready to help the children with their lessons. Her husband said she spelled better than the dictionary. Eddie was sure she knew more arithmetic than his teacher. She kept house beautifully. In those days it meant doing much of it yourself. She was a power in the church. I never understood how she accomplished so much.

"As to the relation between her and the Bishop it has stood to me all my life as the most beautiful married life I ever knew. If they ever differed, I, who was in the house half the time, never knew it. Theirs seemed to me as nearly perfect a love as human beings ever have.

"It did not mean in the least, either, that Mrs. Fallows did not stand up for her opinions. Just before they left Bloomington, burglars broke into the house and stole the watch which one of the Bishop's parishes had presented to him. During the first year in Chicago, a pawnbroker wrote the Bishop, who was not a Bishop yet, by the way, and said: 'I can get your watch if you will send me fifty dollars.'

"I happened to be present during the family council. The Bishop wanted the watch very much. He was quite inclined to accept the pawnbroker's offer. Mrs. Fallows shook her head at him.

" 'Why, Sammy,' she said, 'don't you realize that it would be compounding a felony?' Then with one of her delicious practical after-thoughts she added. 'Besides where would we ever get the fifty dollars?'

"Another time, the Bishop gave a tramp his winter overcoat.

" 'What will you do?' said Mrs. Fallows, 'for a coat yourself next winter? Even the Bible, you knows, says "charity begins at home." ' "

The new minister of St. Paul's was finding the world a friendly place just then. The Methodist Church and the

Methodist press were still mourning his loss. But he was dismissed from the Church of his birth to another field of service in the kindliest possible way. Blessings followed him, not curses. The new Church, of course, was open-armed in its welcome. Chicago took him to its heart like blood kin. Chicago, scrambling about like a venturesome Newfoundland puppy finding its legs, remained a constant delight. It was so young and so grown up all at once.

Demon Rum was having a very bad time, just then, all over the state. Samuel was making it all the trouble possible. In Bloomington, he had helped start the woman's crusade for state-wide temperance. The women were as versatile in expedients then, as they are now. They had their own version of tag day when young ladies went out with "their pretty devices and winning ways" not to get dollars for sick babies or poor people, but to induce clerks and other young gentlemen to sign the pledge. The most popular girls collected signatures, like favors at a German.

The members of the Senate at Springfield even took a recess to allow the ladies to get their signatures. The House, not to be outclassed, did the same.

Out of all this agitation came a most drastic law. Under it, a licensee had to give bond for three thousand dollars, with two good sureties. He was obliged to pay damages not only for injuries received by an intoxicated person, but to members of the intoxicated person's family who might have been injured "in person or in support." Not only that, but the owner of the property from which intoxicating liquor was sold was conjointly responsible with the man who sold it.

The hands of white ribboners rang the church bells when that law was passed.

If it had ever been enforced, actually enforced all over the United States, Volstead would have gone to his grave, unknown, unhonored and unsung.

In all this effort at temperance, Dr. Fallows took an active

part. He was a fast friend of Frances Willard. His voice
was raised for the National Women's Christian Temperance
Union, founded in 1874. He enrolled himself as a member in
the oldest Lodge of the Good Templars in Chicago. By his
presence, he supported the meetings of John B. Gough, reformed drunkard himself, and one of the dramatic sensations
of the religious world, in those days.

In spite of the generous mind toward a glass of English ale,
expressed in his "twenty-gown" letter to his wife, he had quite
another mind toward Demon Rum. Chicago, at that time, was
wide open, with the worst tenderloin in the country. No one
could take a walk through down-town streets after nightfall
without the risk of being knocked over by toughs or drunkards.

"Down with Demon Rum," cried Samuel Fallows, seeing
no better remedy. He was all chaplain and guardian of
souls on the liquor question. In due season, he found a way
of fighting it by substitution rather than denial. That was
when he was twenty years older in experience and wisdom.

On another question which was agitating Chicago, however, he was rather remarkably Paul's Jew with the Jews, his
Greek with the Greeks, and a cosmopolitan citizen with the
citizens. In the Fall of 1875, the School Board took up the
question of retaining Bible reading and the use of the Lord's
Prayer in the school programs. By a unanimous vote, they
dropped both. Then the storm broke. The Chicago Presby-
tery deprecated the action of the School Board. Methodist
ministers petitioned that it be rescinded. A great public mass
meeting passed resolutions condemning it.

Only three ministers in the city raised their voices in favor
of the Board's decision, and Samuel Fallows was one of
them. As State Superintendent, the new minister of St.
Paul's had met the same situation, in a Wisconsin log schoolhouse. Some parents, in Wisconsin, had objected to their
children hearing the Bible reading at the opening of school.

"Very well," said the Superintendent, "keep them away until it is over."

Though personally he desired greatly to retain Bible reading in the schools, he took the broader view.

His decision, now, was in line with that.

"The School Board is right," he said, "in dropping the Lord's Prayer and the reading of the Bible from the school programs. This is an America for all nations and all religions. State and Church must be separate. In schools supported by taxes imposed on all, it is unfair to have religious observances not approved by all."

This opinion coming from a man who was an authority on education and, already, one of the religious leaders of the city, undoubtedly strengthened the hands of the School Board, and the Bible was kept out of the schools.

Social life in 1876 was divided largely along Church lines. Socials and watermelon parties provided very well for the effervescing spirits of the young. But Lillian Russell, merely Lillian Leonard then, made them stale upon the palate of a minister's young son for many a long day.

The Leonards lived across the street from the Fallows and were quite the last word in metropolitan gayety. Hacks stood in front of the door when they had a party—sometimes as many as three or four at once.

Lillian, getting friendly with Eddie, invited him to one of the entertainments,—a sheet and pillow-case party. Next to Barnum's Circus, it seemed to the small boy the choicest amusement possible.

But in the family conclave held to decide about the invitation, Eddie's mother shook her head.

"It's very worldly," was her verdict.

"But a sheet and pillowcase party, my dear," ventured Eddie's father, seeing his disappointment. "It sounds very innocent."

"It wouldn't do at all," decided Lucy.

He rarely reversed her judgments about the children. But what he could do, he did. Eddie had been saving and earning money in all sorts of little ways to buy a toy theater for five dollars. When the mother of the family had gone out to superintend supper, he drew a silver dollar from his trousers' pocket and handed it to Eddie.

"For the theater, my boy," he explained.

But the greatest thrill of his small son's life, his father, himself, provided unwittingly, a little later, when he took him to a benefit performance for something or other held at Central Music Hall.

In the middle of the program, an enchanting little person in pink came out on the platform and spoke French words in a wonderful voice. She was Sarah Bernhardt. Eddie almost wore his palms out clapping. The horse car on the way home was filled, for him, with visions in pink.

Now all actresses were children of the devil, in his mother's estimation, the "divine Sarah" a little more so than the others. Nevertheless, so possessed was Edward by her charm that he organized a club of five boys, the next day, for the sole purpose of drawing up resolutions to congratulate Bernhardt on her success in America!

These resolutions he engrossed himself. Then he took them down to Bernhardt's hotel and knocked at her door. It was opened by her manager, who accepted the resolutions with a French bow. One glimpse of his deity, at the far end of the room, was all the little boy caught. But it was enough to live on for days.

When a very moral Chicago left Sarah stranded at a reception in her honor, circling about her at a distance, but not daring enough to approach, she might have remembered, with wistfulness, the genuine admiration of five small boys. Later still, when she came into her own and the city knelt before her, and she called Chicago "the pulse of America," she might have chuckled over the perfectly American temerity of an unknown club of youngsters congratulating a world-famous actress on her success.

But she never could guess the terrific courage it took for Lucy Fallows' son, denied even a sheet and pillowcase party, to knock at the door of Sarah Bernhardt.

Not often in the Fallows household did such ribald things occur. Channels for surplus excitement were provided along more legitimate lines. What camp meetings had done for the pioneers, revival meetings did for Chicago in 1875. Samuel Fallows was very much at home in them, on the platform with the revivalist, in the little room afterwards, talking his "sanctified common sense" to those just about ready to do a spiritual right about face.

As camp meetings provided a safety valve for our forbears, repressed and restrained by the hardships of conquering primitive life, revivals made an escape for their descendants, walled in by materialism. Circuit Rider and revivalist, alike, waked them out of spiritual catalepsy into action.

The great revivalist, Dwight L. Moody, had one of his most signal triumphs in Chicago in 1875. He and Mr. Sankey held their first meeting in the city at eight o'clock on a Sunday morning. They opened exactly on the hour, but in that "Godless" city of the West, an audience of seven thousand sang the opening hymn.

Moody was fresh from his amazingly successful campaign in England, Philadelphia and New York. The Chicago seven thousand went to hear him, partly out of genuine concern for their souls, partly because he was a Chicago product. Not many years before, he had started life as a shoe clerk in one of the city's well-known shoe stores.

In those early days he rented five pews in his own well-to-do church and filled them with spiritual mongrels every Sunday. Applying at a mission for a class to teach, and told to

THE BISHOP AND HIS BEER

For the purpose of proving that beer could be clean and pure and contain a small amount of alcohol, Bishop Fallows invented and brewed the popular beverage known as Bishop's Beer.

[*See Page 332*]

go out and get his own, he appeared the next Sunday with
half a dozen ragamuffins, out at the elbows, but clean because
he had washed them and dressed them himself. Those were
the days of color, when he naïvely made the announcement
that, having just become engaged, he could not be depended
upon to see the girls home from meeting any more. They
were the days of that choice incident when Moody put his
hand on the arm of a stranger going into a basement saloon
and said:

"My friend, you are going straight to Hell."

"Just my luck," answered the man.

"A great human!" Drummond called **Moody.** "Very great
in goodness," said Samuel.

Part way, Samuel went with Moody very gladly. The
springs of action, he knew, lay in the emotions. Religion,
he said many times in many ways, was out of the heart, not
out of the head. If you have a man with his feelings alive,
you have something to direct. Nothing can be done with a
corpse. Because Moody was past master in waking up dead
sinners, Samuel prized him. He loved him for his tireless
executive fearless self, his consecration and because mighty
enthusiasms for humanity speak the same language across
any differences of belief.

CHAPTER V

THE BISHOP STARTS HIS BUSINESS GOING

In the Spring of 1876, Bishop Cummins, founder of the Reformed Episcopal Church, died suddenly. At the next General Council, held that summer in Ottawa, Canada, Dr. Fallows was elected bishop.

On the evening of Sunday, July the seventeenth, with the Reverend Edward Cridge, he was consecrated "to the office and work of a Bishop." He was presented by the Reverend Joseph D. Wilson and the Reverend James A. Latané. Presiding Bishop Charles Edward Cheney, D.D., was assisted by Bishop William R. Nicholson, D.D., Bishop Albert Carman, D.D., Bishop of the Methodist Episcopal Church in Canada, the Reverend Messrs. Joseph Young, of the Methodist Episcopal Church in Canada; Hunter, of the Wesleyan Methodist Church; Faris of the Presbyterian Church and seven Presbyters of the Reformed Episcopal Church.

That the candidate had anything to do with the details of his own consecration is improbable. But the occasion was so illustrative of his policy of inclusion that it seemed as if he must have had. This was the first time in Canada that any members of other churches had taken part in the consecration of a bishop.

Dr. Fallows became a missionary bishop, with a roving commission to build up the Church at large. Nothing could better have suited his inclination and his capacity. But the new honor was to provide hardships for a wife who liked to work by his side.

272

He whisked Lucy off the next Fall to the Centennial celebration at Philadelphia and back again. He put affairs in order at St. Paul's, and by Spring was ready for the Crusade which was to mark the zenith of the new Church's growth.

CHAPTER VI

A WHIRLWIND CRUSADE

For the next three years, the new Bishop had the uplifted joy of a leader in a great Crusade. Now, more than ever before, he was the happy Christian soldier, leading the war against all kinds of provincialism. The world was his battle ground, the Reformed Episcopal Church his weapon.

He carried the message of his Church north, south, east, west and to England and Bermuda. The tempo of his life was set to the rumble of trains and the chug, chugging of boats.

The Winter after he was made bishop, he visited all the Canadian churches and started new friendships which were to last all his life. That Spring of '77, he left St. Paul's to other hands and began his missionary duties with a trip to South Carolina, to visit the colored school and the sixteen negro congregations of the Church. This work had a special appeal for a Northern general, as it was conducted by the Rev. P. F. Stevens, a Southern gentleman of Charleston's bluest blood. He had been a brigadier general of the Confederates and was credited with having fired the first shot of the war at Fort Sumter.

Mr. Stevens was devoting his best energies to the unpopular task of uplifting the negro. For all they had fought on opposite sides, the minister and his bishop saw eye to eye on post-war negro questions. A letter to Lucy describes a typical visit to the colored churches.

CHARLESTON, S. C.
April 27th, 1877.
Friday, 8 A.M.

MY DEAR LUCY:—

I have just returned from the country, having visited several of the colored congregations with Mr. Stevens.

My trip has been a very interesting one, so much so that I cannot give you a full account of it in writing. We went to a point of the R. R. 45 miles from Charleston, then took a buggy drawn by a poor, shambling horse, owned by one of the colored brethren, and rode ten miles among the pines. At 12 o'clock we had services, a large congregation of enthusiastic hearers. I confirmed 27 at the close.

In the evening the two colored deacons talked and preached and I gave afterwards a short account of the progress of the church. This was the Church of the Redeemer at Pineville.

We stopped with an old Planter, S. W. Palmer, Esq., living alone with his colored help. The bed was so high I had to get on a chair to climb into it. What would Allie think of such a bed as that?

The next morning we took a ride behind a mule over cross roads, on which scores of pine trees had fallen, prostrated by the gales wh. sweep very often over this country. They were the pitch pine, or turpentine pine. I will tell you all about it when I come home. These are the trees from wh. our resin comes. We reached Immanuel Church at 11 A.M. where I preached and had the colored friends shouting happy, and confirmed two persons. We then went to Nazareth Church where I confirmed nine persons and administered the Sacrament.

We began at 5 P.M. and closed at 8. We then rode four miles to St. Stephens, the depot on the North Eastern R. R., got some supper and went to bed. This morning I had to rise at 3.30 and take the train for Charleston. I have just had breakfast and must now start for Atlanta, Georgia.

The Northern General and the Southern General loved the white souls of the poverty-stricken black congregations, who could have taught wealthy ones a thing or two about meeting their obligations. These black folk, with a sense of humor, a conscience and very little else, put money on the collection plate, if they could, and eggs, if they could not. When the collection seemed inadequate to the colored minister, he told his flock so. "We will wait here, my brethren, till we gets what we needs," he told them, "if we sits here all day." Then they turned their pockets inside out and robbed their lunch baskets of more eggs, until their spiritual judge was satisfied.

Only once, in all this visitation, did a congregation fail to produce its quota of eggs. A colored brother supplied an explanation which convulsed his white friends. A clerical conference had recently been held in the neighborhood.

"Nothing is left to lay," said the darky. "The chickens has all done entered the ministry."

From Charleston, Bishop Fallows went to Fort Sumter. There he wrote his wife, who was never long out of his mind wherever she might be, how privileged he felt to be the representative of a wonderful new Church. All its dignitaries, he said, had fallen in love with her. He had promised she would be at the Council to be held at Philadelphia in May.

"So you must be sure to come," he wrote. "Get a new dress, if you need it, black silk, or otherwise. Have some nice ruching about your dear neck, and a nice necktie. Get a new bonnet, too, if you need it."

At that Council, in 1878, the missionary Bishop was made Presiding Bishop of the Church.

Then began the whirl of his travels, which were to cover fifty thousand miles in two years. Deck chair and car seat were his study.

He revisited his native land, for the first and, as it happened, the last time in his life, and covered ground like a native American in the two or three weeks he was in Britain. Preaching at the Brunswick Wesleyan Church, where he had tried to be a Christian at seven, he showed the Sunday school children the thick red book of Wesley's hymns which his teacher, Mr. Ashton, had given him. He had an interview with Gladstone. He also rode on the Southport donkeys for auld lang syne. A kindly welcome was extended to him by the Archbishop of Canterbury on a Sunday morning, and in the evening he assisted Mr. Charles H. Spurgeon, of the Metropolitan Temple—taboo to the conservatives—in the administration of the Lord's Supper. A day or two later he slipped up to Edinburgh for a religious meeting and met Henry Drummond. Having accomplished, as well, the work for his Church which was the purpose of the trip, he took the steamer home again.

Back in the United States, in the early Fall, he began again his spiritual wanderings.

North, south, east, west, in an almost incredible spirit of Christian brotherhood, other Churches went out of their way to help the new denomination. Baptists, Presbyterians, Methodists and Lutherans offered their churches for its services. The Presbyterian Church in Montreal gave not only the use of its building, but fifty dollars to help on the work of the Church.

On a March Sunday, in Jacksonville, the Lutheran Church loaned its building for the morning service, the Baptist for the evening service; and in the afternoon, the Reformed Episcopal Bishop preached to the colored people in the Presbyterian Church. It seemed as if Church unity were just around the corner.

Samuel Fallows went to bed in sleeping cars in those days —the joggly ones of the late seventies—and waked at the place of his next appointment feeling almost as if this beloved Church of his were about to bring in the Kingdom of Heaven.

A vigorous young apostle of joy, he preached for the Reverend J. E. Rankin—who was soon to write "God be With You Till We Meet Again"—at the Congregational Church at Washington, D. C., and made the opening prayer at the morning session of the House of Representatives on February 4, 1878.

In May, he reported to the General Council that he had traveled twenty-seven thousand miles during the year and had never missed nor been late for a meeting. The Council rose and sang "Gloria in Excelsis" and elected him Presiding Bishop for the second time.

Having moved the family to Brooklyn, the traveling minister went at his work with new vigor. One day, he made a special address to the colored waiters of the Prospect House, at Nyack, New York. Almost the next day, he preached a sermon to a huge gathering of the camp meeting at Ocean Grove.

All that year, Bishop Fallows went on traveling up and down the eastern world, dipping back to Chicago, up to Canada and down South, as he had before. Churches sprang up behind him. It seemed the Golden Age of the Reformed Episcopal movement.

Then a great calamity happened. To carry on this extension Crusade, funds were necessary. Thomas H. Powers, of Philadelphia, a very generous contributor to the Church, died suddenly, without making any provision for his ecclesiastical enterprises. Ten churches in Philadelphia, in the process of construction, were heavily involved.

The Council which met in May felt itself unable to swing the Crusade movement longer, with finances as they were.

What Samuel Fallows wished for with all his heart was to make the Reformed Episcopal Church a strong, aggressive factor in the life of the time.

It could be. He had traveled over the field of the Church from side to side and from end to end and knew its appeal to cultured people and common people alike. No other denomination so combined beauty of form, liberality, inclusiveness and a sound Evangelical basis. He could see his church, thus equipped, reaching out and conquering the new West to the Pacific.

For such work, it was imperative that at least one bishop should be free to build up the work already started and push its limits farther. Finances or no finances, Samuel was ready for the venture. But his brethren, burdened with the load of the present, could not see as he saw.

St. Paul's in Chicago, owing to unfortunate leadership, was in a very bad way. The Council, feeling that so important a parish should not be neglected, asked Bishop Fallows to resume the rectorship of it and do what he could as Bishop in his left-over time.

CHAPTER VII

Chicago's material achievement was unmatched in history. This is not a rhetorical statement, but founded on statistics. A year's pigs, set nose to curly tail, could have girdled the world. Yesterday's town of logs and clapboards was sending lumber to the ends of the earth—enough in one year to freight a continuous line of vessels two hundred miles long or to load a train stretching fourteen hundred miles. Operations in real estate staggered the imagination of even the most frenzied boomers. Just on the edge of the eighties, Chicago sold more real estate in the year than New York, Philadelphia and Boston put together, with St. Louis thrown in for good measure.

In those achieving years, it made a river run backward, uphill and over another hill. As the African cleric said: "It knew the unknowable, did the undoable and unscrewed the inscrutable."

But for all its size, the Western metropolis was a village city still in 1879, where almost everybody went to church, the gentlemen in broadcloth and silk hats, the ladies in those costumes which Lucy always described to her dressmaker as "something suitable for calling and church." Vice was obvious enough but the newspapers still printed sermons in full and gave more space to reports of religious interests than to crime and scandals.

The city's hospitality had the village mixture of incongruity. The banquet to Grant, on his way round the world,

280

where Samuel sat at the speakers' table near his old Commander, was an effort worthy of New York. But soon afterward, the city sent a stiff English earl to the theater with his hotel keeper. At the theater, the audience rose and sang for the titled British subject, "God save the Queen." As the poor man's training had given him no clew to the correct form of response for this upside-down city, he could only sit, dumb as an oyster, in his box and look unhappy.

Since Chicago's population was so largely recruited from villages, its activities naturally reflected village culture. Boys, by the hundred, came in from other parts of the state with their clothes in a bundle and their capital under their hats, bringing their small-town psychology with them.

They hunted up a church and joined it, as a matter of course. It was the center of their soul life, also of their social life, and the place for courting, unless a girl back home was the favored one.

Presto! Change! Almost before it seemed possible, these lads were magnates and industrial lords. Emerging into millionaires, they increased their contributions on the plate each Sunday. Their voices grew more important in church councils. Knowing very little about art, music or literature, when they felt an urge to give, they did something for the church. Chicago's endowed churches of to-day, almost all of them, date back to that period.

But successful men of business, while they must develop vision and farsightedness along their own particular line, may still remain provincial small-town boys in matters of religion. This was to make the crux of some of Bishop Fallows' later battles. But it did not appear in the last year of the seventies, when he returned to Chicago to resume the leadership of St. Paul's

Lucy Fallows, weary after the Brooklyn year, was dropped off, with the girls, at the Dansville Health Resort to catch her breath. Her husband, in the meantime, selected a pleasant house on Adams Street, not far from the church, opposite the Melville Stones and in the midst of other pleasant neighbors. After five months, his partner returned rosy and fit. She had a disconcerting idea, at first, of serving two meals a day, following the sanatorium dictum, but it soon evaporated, and the Fallows home life took on its usual aspect.

The West Side was still a charming place to call home. It held its own, even though the competition of the other sides of the city was sharp. Ashland Avenue was the West Side Gold Coast for millionaires. But Washington Street was also popular. There, on the corner of Ann Street stood St. Paul's. The Church which its pastor and his wife built out of the Chicago of the early eighties was a lusty vital happy thing. It grew rapidly. Former parishioners returned to their allegiance, and new members came from many quarters —charming people, cultured people, "like Summerfield," said Lucy Fallows, and could pay no higher compliment.

The pastor gathered to himself a group of vestrymen from the strongest and most promising men of the West Side. Among them were Mr. Everett St. John, coming President of the Rock Island Road; Mr. John Bradshaw, building up a profitable business on South Water Street; Mr. John Walker, pioneer type, man of iron, fast climbing up the financial hill as a commission merchant; Mr. J. L. Fulton, piling up dollars out of making superior pavements for a growing city; Mr. Gray; handsome Mr. James Ball; Mr. A. S. Smith; Mr. A. M. Wright, one of the Presidents of the Board of Trade; Mr. Bernard A. Eckhart, of Summerfield days, in the milling business, who would one day need a quarter of a page in "Who's Who," to list his directorships in various enterprises.

"The Merry Vestrymen," they called themselves, in those high and happy days of high and happy actions. Then there were all the enthusiastic lay members with names from a to izzard—a host of workers. They were all young and invincible together—the vestry, the parish, the West Side, Lucy Fallows, Samuel, forty-four in years, twenty at heart.

Other churches, doubtless, were as warm and friendly as St. Paul's. A few, perhaps, enjoyed themselves as much, though the congregation did not believe it. They were one big family, with their Bishop the father of them all, responsible for their welfare. That they remained for the forty-four years of his pastorate. When the list of his activities was so long that an expert stenographer spent an hour and a half copying it, his attention to his church family was as close and loving as in those early days when his outside interests could be numbered on the fingers of two hands.

Quite literally, he was all things to his people in those burgeoning years of the early eighties. He shared the ambitions of his men, was at home with the grandmothers and played with the babies. His adaptability made him fit into any situation. Mrs. J. L. Fulton loves to tell the story of a dinner to which she invited her pastor and his wife. She wanted to make it a proper and formal function, but in the middle of the meal the waitress came in shrieking that the cook was having a fit. Mr. Fulton rushed out for a doctor. The ladies went to the cook. The guest of honor hearing the wail of the baby, turned nursemaid. Later, during that same hectic evening, he went to the desk for a piece of paper. As he opened it, out fell piles of poker chips. "Playthings for the children," gasped Mrs. Fulton. They had been salvaged by Mr. Fulton after one of Chicago's raids on a gambling den. But Mrs. Fulton felt sure that only a man as understanding as her Bishop would have believed her.

Skimming the cream of his strength for St. Paul's, during his first two years back in Chicago he made twelve hundred parochial visits, raised $15,000 on the $27,000 debt and arranged for the payment of the rest within the year.

Those facts he reported to the General Council, which met

in May, 1881.   In addition to his duties as rector, he had
also performed all of those falling to his share as Bishop of
the West and Northwest and, in addition, had made a month's
visit to Colorado.   He still saw the possibility of the Church,
as a great missionary force, to follow the plow and conquer
the West.   He tried to make his brethren see it.   He protested
with all the eloquence he had against the policy of tying
bishops to parishes, with so much extension work to do.   But
heavy responsibilities made the Council cautious, and he could
not carry his point.

"To preach the Gospel to the masses" had been one of the
strongest motives, to draw Bishop Fallows into the Reformed Episcopal Church.   When the outlet his denomination provided for his missionary spirit seemed insufficient,
he helped to organize the Christian Army, an organization
something like the Salvation Army, whose object was to gather
in the human flotsam and jetsam that drifted by its modest
headquarters on West Madison Street and to carry the Gospel into the ill-favored quarters of the city where the toiling
thousands were paying the toll of the city's greatness.

His sympathy was for all humanity, not for any section
of it.   The West Side, with its prosperity, its Gold Coast,
its men who would one day be the future overlords of the
city, was one of Chicago's incubators, excellent for its own
purpose.   In his bishop's robes, the pastor of St. Paul's
phrased his hopes and ideals for one section of society in
language appropriate to that section.

Then he shed his bishop's robes and, in the slums, from
boxes and cart tails, talked to the men and women who were
then the oppressed and the lowest of the low.   He sensed
the miracle of Western civilization—under dog to-day, leader
of the pack to-morrow.   He sensed also the unity of society—
that it was only strong as all of it was strong.   So he gave
those Christian Army street congregations brother-to-brother

kind of talk, hoping it might become a part of the working philosophy out of which they would frame the city of to-morrow.

People's exteriors were only interesting to him as identification marks. He enjoyed meeting a president or a tramp, because his sympathy was a divining rod that found their souls. He saw an Italian shoeblack against his inheritance of the beauty and splendor of his native land. He saluted the dignity of the ancient Hebrews when he greeted a Jewish peddler. Even a criminal he saw as a potential good man. With his sympathy about him like armor, he was safe in the most dangerous parts of the city. In Hell's Knuckle, one of the toughest districts in America, where the Chicago police went in fear of their lives, Samuel could walk the streets at midnight and preach to its people with no fear.

In the eighties, as always, though he was a bishop in a church and giving his best efforts to building up a denomination, his efforts to help humanity knew neither race nor creed. He was working with Bishop Cheney for the good of the city, but also with those other idealists, Dr. Swing, Dr. Thomas, Rabbi Hirsch, Bishop Ireland, "Father Tom," who could manage Hell's Knuckle as if it were a kindergarten, and anyone else, religionist or layman, who was trying to make the world a better place to live in.

Of the latter class, were the members of the Veterans' Union League, founded to improve the government of Chicago, which was happy-go-lucky enough in the free and easy eighties. Made up of veterans of the Civil War, who just then were in the political saddle all over the country, this organization had its own importance. It managed General Logan's campaign for president and did good work in reforming some of Chicago's worst abuses. But adapting itself to the customs of the times, the League never insulted its members by asking them to drink the health of anything in mere water. It maintained, for their convenience, a very respectable little bar.

A League President, Col. James J. Healy, remembers well how one day he and Bishop Fallows visited headquarters together. Colonel Sexton, later to be postmaster, and several other members were there.

"Come on," said Colonel Healy, "all have a drink with me."

Some one made frantic gestures behind his guest's back.

"Are you so dense," asked the Colonel scornfully, "that you suppose for a moment the Bishop doesn't know you drink?"

"What will you have, Bishop?" he asked.

"Cider," was the prompt reply.

Perhaps because he was wise enough not to try to speak the word out of season, he was given plenty of chances to speak the word in season. For years he served the Veterans' League as Chaplain, and at the banquets of that body probably began the practice which he described years later to his assistant, Mr. Lepper. Soldiers' dinners, all through that time, with no restraining Eighteenth Amendment, were anything but dry.

Mr. Lepper, who knew the Bishop's temperance principles, asked him how he managed at the banquets.

"Oh," said his chief, "I always turn my glass upside down and stay till the end."

"But don't the soldiers sometimes get under the influence of liquor?" pursued Mr. Lepper.

"Yes, yes, frequently. Then they ask me for a sermon."

"What do you do?" asked his assistant.

"Why, preach to them, of course," was the reply. "That's when they need it. One must always stick by the comrades, Lepper."

This spirit and an eloquent tongue made a militant Bishop popular among the veterans. Even in the eighties he was

—Chicago Tribune Photos

[See Page 353]

EVERY DOOR A SALOON

A small section of a mile-long street of saloons in the Red Light District of Chicago in 1906 before Samuel Fallows helped clean up the city.

well along on the first lap of the Marathon which, by 1915, had won him the reputation of having made "more patriotic speeches and dedicated more soldier's monuments than any other private citizen of the United States."

Scarcely a week went by that his wife did not inspect her husband's coat for spots and his bag for clean collars and handkerchiefs, and brush his soft military hat corded with gold about the crown, and call out messages to his inattentive coat tails as he went flying off out of the city to speak on Decoration Day or the Fourth of July, or at a reunion of one of his Wisconsin regiments, or of the three of them together, or at the State G. A. R. or the National G. A. R. or the dedication of the Kenosha Monument or something else.

In Chicago, military engagements were part of the regular schedule—at his Post, the Grant, one of the oldest in Chicago, at the Loyal Legion, at the Chicago Sons of Veterans, the Veterans' Union League and the rest.

But of all the soldier meetings, that of the Grand Army of the Republic, each year, was the most significant. With the Civil War veteran so important a factor in national affairs, these meetings, though not so advertised, were naturally hotbeds of politics. They made and unmade as many candidates in those days as did the party conventions. Plums seemed to fall into the mouths of Civil War soldiers. Presidents, postmasters, Federal officers by the score were all veterans. Possibly the ex-soldiers did monopolize political honors a trifle. Still, they would probably have held the offices they did if there had been no war. Only the stronger men went to war. Their plums were the reward of the ambitious.

The Grand Army reunions of the seventies and eighties were pageants of conquering youth. Heroes came with their heads up, bringing their brides beside them, for the honeymoon—hundreds of couples. The procession was a thing for a small boy to dream of, all his life—up in front were the generals, on horseback with their clanking swords. Back of them were all the soldiers on foot.   Away behind, somewhere, was one soldier who should have been in a museum. He really was more wonderful than the generals, because there were so many of them and just one of him.   He had an eight-foot beard which he trailed in the dust in front as a lady dragged her dress behind.   He could have used it as a smoke screen at Antietam or an ambuscade at Gettysburg.   That beard would have made him a fortune as a prophet.   Not only small boys, but even Samuel Fallows never forgot it.

Busy though he was, the pastor of St. Paul's rarely missed a Grand Army reunion, but, for some reason, his special branch of the Grand Army, the Army of the Tennessee, did not discover him until he spoke at their banquet during the reunion of 1881, at Cincinnati.   The banquet was a brilliant affair.   Ex-President Hayes was a guest.   If any generals were absent, on that occasion, it was because they were dead or not in Cincinnati.   Sherman, Sheridan, Pope, Cox, Hunt, Hickenlooper, Force, Belknap, Warner, Gresham, Dawes— all were there.   Judge Taft was present.   Colonels, majors, captains were as thick as blackberries in August.

Bishop Fallows "invoked" the blessing.   "The dinner," according to a reporter, "then transpired at the leisure of the participants."

It kept transpiring until eleven o'clock, when General Sherman announced the "dinner proper as transpired," and the toasts began.

Eighth on the program, Bishop Fallows responded to the toast: "The Loyal Pulpit."

"Something reverential, mild and dull," the comrades confessed afterwards, was what they expected from a minister.

What they received was a twenty-minute "whirlwind of eloquence," that lifted the audience out of itself like a charge of dynamite.

Little Rufus Dawes looked on from the corner where he had been deposited by his father, General Dawes.

"I never saw anything like it in my life,' remembered Rufus Dawes forty-five years afterwards. "The audience stood up and shouted. They shook their napkins at him. They crowded around him so you could not see him for five minutes at a time. They shrieked themselves hoarse. Never before, nor since have I heard anything like that speech."

General Sherman said that never in his life had he witnessed such enthusiasm. The papers, the next day, were unrestrained in their commendation. The episode was a pleasant one. Its effect, so far as the Army was concerned, seems to have been that comrade Fallows was seldom allowed to keep silent through the whole of any subsequent reunion. But the importance, for his future work, of having a sympathetic audience of men from all over the country was much more than honorary to a man interested in fighting for great causes. His influence as a future righter of wrongs was increased by every soldier whom he made his friend that night. Once and for all, that night, he established his reputation among the veterans as a minister who was a human being first.

CHAPTER VIII

IN TRAINING FOR TROUBLE

A man who has any wish to change things from what they are into what they ought to be must acquire the muscle to make disappointments into opportunities. The next decade was to give the Mid-West Bishop much practice in that art. Hitherto, though heavily beset sometimes in the process, he had been able to make his dreams come true in the end. Now he was to find his progress barred by walls of prejudice and shortsightedness.

Take the dream of the University of the West. That was a gorgeous thing—a dream beautiful enough with its sister dream of preaching to all the world, to draw Samuel Fallows from the beloved Church of his birth into the Reformed Episcopal.

From 1875 on, for a few years, it was never possible to make the University of the West more than a dream on paper. Then Mr. Martin, of Red Hook, New York, offered one hundred and sixty acres of land near Chicago on which to build the institution. Its name was changed to the Martin School of Theology, but it was the same old wonderful dream. In 1883, the General Council of the Reformed Episcopal Church voted to accept Mr. Martin's offer, and the vision seemed about to become a reality. A very jubilant Bishop Fallows returned to Chicago after that Council.

But the General Council of 1885, alas! reversed the decision of the Council of 1883. Certain conditions about Mr. Martin's offer made it appear to a cautious majority a very risky venture. To a man who was a general as well as a bishop, these conditions seemed merely a challenge of faith in the success of the Church and in the quality of its workers, a sharpener to put the edge on opportunity.

He said to the Council:

"In my judgment, no church in the country, at a corresponding period of its history, ever had such a munificent offer on terms so advantageous and feasible. Brethren, after looking at this matter from every point of view, I am thoroughly convinced that *the* golden opportunity for our church to care for its future ministry and prepare them for the great work to which God has called us is at this moment before us."

A committee of five had the matter in charge. Three opposed accepting Mr. Martin's offer. Samuel Fallows and Mr. Beers signed a minority report favoring it.

"In the strength of God, in the loyal love of our united church, east and west, north and south, go up and possess the land," the Bishop begged his brethren.

But Chicago was a long way off and wild and woolly, anyway, in the eyes of Philadelphia. No one dreamed, then, that it would become the second largest city in the Union and the fourth in the world. The possibilities of the West were not sensed in the East, and the dreamer of dreams and seer of visions had to endure the disappointment of seeing his beloved Church close the door on what seemed to him its greatest opportunity.

Though Mr. Martin's offer had been disapproved by the Council, the Synod of Chicago could still have rescued the project. Mr. Beers, of Bishop Cheney's church, and Samuel Fallows did their best for it. Somewhere around that time, Bishop Cheney was preaching to thirty millionaires every Sunday. But they could not see as did the signers of the minority report.   To them, as to the Council, the risks of the offer seemed too great.

Which side was right and which was wrong, is, at this distance, a matter for conjecture.   But it would seem as if Samuel Fallows, a minister of the Gospel and not a business man, while he was flying his kite in the fourth dimension, again had his feet solidly on the ground.   Years later, he stopped his assistant, Mr. Lepper, down town, opposite one of Chicago's greatest hotels.   The building stood on a small piece of the land offered to the Reformed Episcopal Church by Mr. Martin.   Even so much of it would have made the church rich beyond the dreams of avarice.

Bishop Fallows, by that time, had come to be a symbol of cheerfulness in the mind of the city.   But the pain of that old disappointment was still in his memory.

"My boy!   My boy!" he broke out.   "Mary Tudor said: 'When I die, you will find Calais written on my heart.'   When *I* die, you will find written on mine: 'The University of the West.'"

The dream of ten years went down to defeat in 1885.   But the dreamer did not go down with it.   He buried his hope for the University of the West decently with the honors of war.   Blocked in one direction, he found forty other places to use his figthing arm.   Such a technique for meeting disappointments made them his slaves and swiftly and surely pushed him on to the wider ministry which was his destiny.

Unable to make the General Church see what he felt was its larger opportunity, he redoubled his efforts with St. Paul's.   The neighborhood around the church was changing. Recognizing the Western trend of the population, he induced his congregation to sell the Washington Street property and build a new church a mile farther West, in what seemed, then, the far suburbs.   Scarcely was the church built before its interior was burned out.   Nothing daunted, almost before the flames had died down, its pastor began to solicit funds for rebuilding. So much was the church identified, even then, with the interests of the community, that a Jew headed the subscription list. The members old and new took hold with a will. Only a list of the entire church membership could comprehend the helpers who in a few weeks made St. Paul's habitable again.

No pursuit of the dollar could be made to seem really exciting to anyone with the virus of service in his blood. But a practical man in a practical world must make the ends of his budget meet, some way. Books helped somewhat. He had published two, which he did as fancywork in spare moments—"Bright and Happy Homes" and "The Home Beyond." In 1884 he brought out "Synonyms and Antonyms," which, revised and enlarged, is still serving cross-word puzzlers, to-day.

He even tried a building venture, from the burden of which the Elevated Road, passing through the back of the property eventually delivered him. He then moved the family to a house on Monroe Street, three stories high, with a fine basement playground for little Charles Samuel, the latest addition to the family. The spacious parlors were the battle-ground where the head of the house fought battles for all kinds of souls; the informal court from which he dealt out justice and mercy until the shortage of domestic help during the World War compelled a move to smaller quarters.

Lectures on the Chautauqua circuit were a profitable diversion. Vacations for others he considered essential. A change of work made his. A letter written in the Summer of 1884 to Lucy, summering in Worthington, Massachusetts, on his caligraph, an early species of typewriter, in his special kind of shorthand, indicates his idea of what a vacation should be for her.

328 W. Adams St.,
Chicago, Aug. 1, 1884.

My dear Lucy,

I am about 2 start for Chaut. I hav just b een
lookng at e Moquette. It z a bigger bundl that u think. I am
not quite clear that t z best 2 try & snd t. It crtainly wll
not b v e rit siz, & t wld b mor bothr thn t z worth, 2 rip
t up & rearrang it. It wld keep u simply trying 2 get thngs 2
rights insted v resting & enjoying mattrs. I am afraid t will
b e old story, e wa thngs ar looking. of your being n a whirl
v business for sombody els. I thnk u had best settl down e res
& b content wth what u hav, & let evrythng take care v itslf.
If u stll clng 2 e idea, aftr this lettr, writ 2 Will, immediately. & he will hav thngs n train, for it 2 go off next week.
I still thnk i t z a tsk, that u hardly need undrtake, this
tim. I wll gather e other thngs togthr & send or bring them n
some wa. Mr & Mrs Fairbanks go 2 Chatauq. wth me this aftrnoon
Mr Muncey cam a few minuts ago, 2 tell me that Hiram died yes
trda. He had been ill only 2 days. He & som othr boys bought
som bananaas, plums, pears, &c, & ate them freely. He died v
inflammation v e bowels. Th funeral will take place Sunday.
    Tha will hav either Mr. Burke, or Mr. Morrison. Hav e chil-
        dren b very carful v their diet.
I must go now. Good by. Remember I objct most decidedly 2 ur
being e mothr v a numerous family wth its cares. That will
    keep me awa most surely. If u can get along wthout e assump
tion v them, all rit, but if not t z all wrong. Please let
me kno positively & solmnly, bfor I return 2 Madison.
I want u 2 hav a REST, & I shall b provokd byond mesur, IF IT
    IS OTHERWISE. I am emphatic on this point, so much so that
it will essentially alter my plans. Now let me kno e honest
truth n e mattr my darling girl. U dont ofn dceiv me , n thes
thngs, but I want e plain truth.
            Lov & kisses 2 u all.
                Your Affectionate Husband,
                    (Signed) Sam Fallows

Mrs Lucy B. Fallows,
    Worthington,
                Mass.

P.S. Tell Fred I will lectur for him on Talent for Growth,
(Provided thngs ar as I wsh thm 2 b regarding ur relations
2 e whol mattr.)

A Time-Saving Letter

His next letter, written three days later from Chautauqua, shows how his own vacation combined business with pleasure.

MY DARLING LUCY,—

We reached here 4 P.M. Saturday after a pleasant ride.

I am in the midst of the enjoyment of this unique place of intellectual, moral and religious resort. The woods are full of fair women and brave men, the former clothed in diaphanous outside material looking wondrous sweet and some of them wondrous wise.

I conducted the opening Liturgical service yesterday morning. It is a very nice service framed by Dr. Vincent, who thinks our church almost an ideal church.

Yesterday I enjoyed a good rest and listened to two discourses and Dr. Vincent's talk at the Vesper Service. I find very few I know but am beginning to see some familiar faces.

The Amphitheater is a fine one. It will hold, they say, four or five thousand and yet one can be heard in it with perfect ease.

I shall leave Wednesday morning, reaching Chicago 8 Thursday morning and shall start at 11.30 for Madison.

I receive fifty dollars and railway pass, but pay my own way here. I am living at a nice place for $1.25 a day. The hotel charges $3. I shall clear about $40 from the trip. I am glad I came here. It is a treat in many ways.

I am counting the days until I shall be with you. Love to you all. Squeeze my pet boy for me. A special warm embrace for my darling wife.

During the next few years, Bishop Fallows more and more was reaching out into the life of the city. The need of the masses were pulling at his heartstrings. Far ahead of the founding of Hull House, at a Baptist Social Union meeting, he made a plea for a settlement for them. He wanted the ecclesiastical emancipation of women. He was also pleading for consideration for that most boresome of objects, the

Book Solicitor. He talked on the dangers of food adulteration, on child labor and on the problems of great cities.

The problem of Chicago was very much on his mind. The town was full and growing fuller by the minute. It was wide open and getting more so every night. Down town had its army of boys coming to the city with two or three dollars. Stranded without a cent after a day or two, they had no place to sleep, so at night they huddled, as many as could, in the entrance to the *Inter Ocean* office, which had two openings. When the police drove the sleepers out at one end, they merely walked around the block and came in at the other. The saloon free lunch fed them. Painted ladies stood ready to give them cheer. The cappers in front of the gambling dens were as cordial as brothers.

Let Mr. Titus, one of the small-town boys, working at Field's, just then, with Harry Selfridge, not yet dreaming of London stores, tell his effect on the youth of Chicago, at the beginning of the nineties.

"You have no idea how we flocked about him. At this distance you can hardly realize his influence over us. One night he was to speak at the Y. M. C. A. A friend and I wanted to stay down town and hear him. That meant buying dinner. We had just fifteen cents between us. For ten you could get a soft drink at any saloon and a good meal. By a little scheme of our own we made one nickel do double duty, had a hearty meal and then went over to hear the Bishop.

"He was a very important man in the city, one of the big ones. But we boys felt we could go to him with anything and he would understand. We could tell him things we wouldn't to our own father. He was like an uncle. He saw things as we saw them. He never tried to make us go his way. Fathers do. The Bishop helped us to do what we wanted in our own way, to work out our own salvation, you know."

Somewhere around that time, three good fighters for civic hygiene came to Chicago—the sons of his friend, General Dawes, reaching back to his University of Wisconsin days.

"Our father's stories had made Bishop Fallows one of our heroes," said Rufus Dawes. "We boys were much excited to think that we were to be in the same town with him."

Not very long after that, Charles Dawes asked some of the important men of the city to meet a young Captain Pershing, just back from the Philippines, who seemed to be made of promising material. The young Captain made his first speech that night. "It was a modest speech," Rufus Dawes remembered, "as a hero's speech ought to be."

"It wasn't a speech at all," said General Pershing, Commander in Chief of the armies, sitting in the War Office at Washington, many years later. "I couldn't make a speech, then. I can't now. I wanted to sit down after five minutes, but Ferd Peck pulled my coat tails and said 'go on,' so I went on. The Bishop was as kind about that speech as if it had been a real one. I began to love him from that night, on."

For a creative mind, no occupation was so alluring as building its ideals into the builders of Chicago—the boys and the men down town, the workers whose faces turned up to him as he talked from wagons and soap boxes, the endless commencement audiences, the soldiers, the Second Regiment boys whose Chaplain he was—a myriad of people. Saint or sinner, millionaire or pauper, Jew or Gentile, Democrat or Republican, they were all alike in Samuel Fallows' eyes, souls in the making.

That attitude endeared him to individuals at the time when his various civic accomplishments were making him important in the city's life. More and more, Chicago was turning to him on important occasions. The Republican Convention met that year in Chicago, in June, and nominated Benjamin

Harrison for President. Samuel was Chaplain of the Convention. In his prayer, he earnestly invoked the divine blessing upon the President of the United States—a Democrat.

The leading Democratic paper of the city, in a facetious little editorial, the next day, said that never again would Bishop Fallows be asked to officiate at a National Republican Convention, since he had prayed for a Democratic President. "Things have come to a pretty pass," retorted the leading Republican paper the next day, "when a President of the United States is past praying for."

In the last year of the eighties, Chicago trebled its size and its problems by the simple device of taking in its suburbs. About that time it acquired the largest telescope in the world, "to be able to see," as Charles Dudley Warner put it, "to the end of its suburbs."

CHAPTER IX

HE MEETS HIS VESTRY

"O human race, born to fly upward, wherefore at a little wind dost thou so fall!"—DANTE.

The pastor of St. Paul's, after a full and happy day, turned homeward late one afternoon, with a head full of visions—visions of a Chicago yet to be, visions that needed the pen of the writer of Revelations to make them as splendid as they seemed to him. The Vestry was to meet that night. Though the West Side was slipping in popularity, and the church had had some hard sledding, things seemed to be set for better times, now. After dinner, swinging down to Winchester Avenue, he stopped to admire, for the thousandth time, the beauty of the church into which he and Lucy had built their hearts and their hopes.

A cheerful fire of cannel coal was burning in the little room of the church where the Vestry met. Its members gathered rather promptly. They were prospering in their different ways. That pleased their pastor. He entered into their success as if they were his sons and brothers. To send men with ideals out along the material highways and byways of Chicago he regarded as an excellent piece of work.

The meeting seemed the usual kind through the routine of opening. Not until everyone had laughed and joked a little did it stand forth as the testing ground of a man's integrity. With just what words the drama was set it is not possible to know, since the deliberations of vestries are not for pub-

lication. But the significance was plain enough. Samuel's
Merry Vestrymen, wrestling with their problems in terms
of the balance sheet, were possessed by the material point of
view. They wanted to see St. Paul's run like a factory. They
saw the church merely as a unit, not as a weapon for the
larger fight against provincialism. They wanted their pastor
to give up his "outside" interests and concentrate on the
church.

"If you would, Bishop Fallows," said one of them, "you
could make ten thousand dollars a year."

He needed no vestryman to tell him he could be a ten-
thousand-dollar man if he wished. Offers from other
churches, which he had refused to stay with St. Paul's and
had never even mentioned to his congregation, told him so
much.

They talked far into the night. Samuel Fallows sitting
in his armchair across from the fire, must have felt as if
he were in a dream. Then, if ever in his life, he must have
prayed his Master's prayer after him; "Father, let this cup
pass from me." These were not strangers, but his own
church family, in the church they had built together, putting
this bitter draught to his lips. Seeing them, out of his
tolerant love for them, he must have said also: "Father, for-
give them for they know not what they do."

Finally, the issue leaped out clearly into words. If the
Bishop would promise to give up his outside interests and
concentrate his energies on St. Paul's, the vestrymen would
stand by. Otherwise they would resign—not all, but enough
to cripple sorely a church already afflicted by the changing
conditions of the West Side.

Here was the crisis at last, the crisis every man must
face who tries to bring down fire from heaven for his fellows. Like all the lesser crises of his life, this, which would
leave him bound or free, for all time, met him in the routine
of his day's work, in a West Side vestry room of Chicago.

The issue was clear. The pastor of St. Paul's labored under no delusion. On one hand was ease, comfort for his family, the support of strong men, ten thousand dollars a year. On the other, sacrifice, perhaps not even a living wage, but freedom—freedom to try to make actual an idealist's vision of the world waking from the "long, bad dream, that makes her mutter and moan," waking to the glorious reality when,

> Suddenly all men arise to the sound of fetters breaking,
> And everyone smiles at his neighbor and tells him
> his soul is his own.

Standing among his vestrymen, opposite the cheerful, crackling fire, in an instant that seemed as long as eternity, the warrior fought his battle. Smug comfort for himself? Prosperity? But the price! An army of youth, E. H. Titus and a host of companions, his Second Regiment boys and the rest, marching into the future to make the America of to-morrow lacking something beautiful that he could have given them. The multitude of the workers with one champion less. Oppressed ones—Gentiles, Jews, negroes, all the exploited ones—fumbling mutely from misery to misery, when his tongue might have set them free.

He flashed out his answer.

In just what words, the minutes do not say, but they meant:

"Away with your dollars and your kingdoms of the earth. I am here to do the will of Him that sent me. *He* did not say preach the gospel to St. Paul's, but to all the world. There *are* no outside things."

Battles take their toll. A vestryman who did not resign watched his pastor start on his homeward way. For once, the Bishop's step was slow. At the street crossing, he lifted his foot to the curbstone like an old man.

Lucy Fallows, wakeful and apprehensive, heard her husband stumble up the steps of the house as if he were carrying a heavy weight. She stole downstairs in her bath robe, trimmed with blue because he liked blue, and found him in the kitchen, heating over the oil stove the bedtime milk always left ready for him, talking to Dick, the gray cat, waiting expectantly for his saucerful. Never, she said, had she seen her husband look so tired and gray. His brave smile hurt her.

Always, when he could, he spared her the hard things. But he told her the story of the Vestry meeting. This it was her due to know. She must share the hardships of the way he had chosen.

There was silence in the kitchen for a moment. Then he spoke to her as if he had gone back thirty years to the days of their courtship. "Would my Lucy have had me answer differently?" he asked.

She took his tired gray face between her hands.

"My dear, my dear," she replied. "What else *could* you have said?"

That encounter with his Vestry seemed a rout for the forces of liberalism and freedom. But it was only seeming. His idealism worked its leavening influence in the lives of even his dissenting vestrymen. In the last year of his life, when only one of all the Merry Vestry was left alive, Mrs. J. L. Fulton, the wife of one of them, spoke of the disagreement and its consequences. "Every one of that vestry," she said, "every one, without exception, came to acknowledge that the Bishop was right."

PART VIII

THE PULPIT IN THE MARKET PLACE

"Like the bird that pausing in her flight
Awhile, on boughs too slight,
Feels them give way beneath her and yet sings,
Knowing that she hath wings."

—Victor Hugo

CHAPTER I

JOY IN THE MORNING

Lucy Fallows, after a night of troubled dreams and many wakings, rose early. Heavy eyes looked back at her from the mirror while she was doing her hair. She sighed as she tiptoed down the hall at last to her husband's door.

For thirty years, she had looked after his creature comforts. She had darned his socks and sponged spots from his clothes and told him when his hair needed cutting. She had seen that his breakfast oatmeal was cooked at least twenty-four hours, and she allowed no fresh bread on the table, except her currant buns, which even he could not resist. Outside the pulpit, this man was her husband, also the boy she had loved who must sometimes be admonished, and the father of her children, a subject for coaxing.

Inside the pulpit, he was another person—her Ambassador to God. He had been that for thirty-two years. For almost fifteen, she had knife plaited the ruffles of his bishop's robe. It seemed as if she must know him in all capacities, through and through and in and out. But he was always surprising her. He did, now.

She went down the hall with the devoted feeling of a Sister of Charity about to offer aid to a stricken one. She was prepared to say: "Sammy, my darling, lie still and I will bring you some nice oatmeal and toast and bacon and postum cereal with lots of cream."

She had the words on the tip of her tongue. Then, as she neared his door, she heard the wall exerciser being pulled for all it would stand. Her husband began on a hymn at the top of his lungs.

"Come, thou fount of every blessing," he shouted.

She opened the door. He held out his arms and she went into them. "But, Sammy," she said, "last night—"

"Was last night, my dear," he interrupted. He waved his hand toward the back yard, rather stark in the sere and yellow leaf of Autumn, but full of morning light:

> " 'And now, the shadows fall apart,
>   And now the west winds play,
> And all the windows of my heart
>   Are open to the day.'

"Our work is ahead of us, Lucy."

Then they went down arm in arm to breakfast.

CHAPTER II

THE CHEERFUL GIVER

Chicago, about to enter the thoughtful nineties, was a ripe field for a man with a vision of a larger ministry. After a gorgeous period of wild-oat sowing, the city had stopped short and begun to think how the other half lives. Never doing anything by halves, she awakened thoroughly. The poor in her midst were skewered on a large pin and examined. The Charity Organization, founded about that time, laid down rules of conduct. Good citizens must not indulge in helter-skelter relief. They must not give money to beggars at the door. The practice merely made more beggars. The problem of the tramp class was scientifically met by a wood yard to the upkeep of which the charitably inclined contributed. The contributors were given books of tickets. When a tramp appeared at the door with a hard-luck tale, he was handed a ticket. For so many chops he could get a meal; for so many more, a lodging.

The Bishop, handicapped by the habit of tempering justice with mercy, but believing in the wood yard and its principles, tried to obey its rules. He and his family presented dozens and dozens of tickets to needy callers. So few of the recipients ever turned up at the wood yard that the guileless dove might have turned suspicious. But the head of the Fallows family was long since suspicion-proof.

One afternoon, opening the door himself to a tramp with a most pitiful story of hardship and illness, he instinctively put his hand into his pocket. Finding no change, he seated the man in the hall, and going to his desk in the back parlor,

307

wrote a note asking the wood-yard manager to give the poor fellow his meal and a lodging for nominal work. Even while he was writing the note, the feeble brother slipped the Bishop's daughter's opera glasses from the hall table to his pocket.

Did it disturb her father's belief that it is more blessed to give than to receive? Not in the least. To the robbed one bewailing the lost glasses, he said cheerfully:

"My dear, I would rather give help to ninety-nine unworthy persons than to miss one who really needed it."

This daughter, subject to many spasms of unrighteousness in those formative days, reflected that it might be a very excellent sentiment. Still they were not *his* opera glasses.

But, a few days later in that open season for rascals, she beheld her father quite as optimistic when it was his own shoe that pinched. On a Sunday afternoon, a mythical son of a clerical brother in the East wheedled out of him ten dollars, which seemed like a hundred in those days of heavy demands on the family budget. The man was scarcely out of the door when certain flaws in his credentials revealed him a cheat.

"But I would rather give help," his benefactor began, "to ninety-nine unworthy—" Then that unregenerate daughter of his slipped out of the room because she knew that her Winter coat would have to be ten dollars cheaper as a result of the misplaced charity.

In those first conscientious days of impersonal giving through a society, her father guiltily slipped a coin one day into a street-corner beggar's cup. Knowing how he was advocating the Charity Organization, his daughter meanly pointed out his inconsistency.

"But you see," was his excuse, "you see, my dear, it was an old soldier."

Lacking the old soldier, he always had some other good reason for charity. The biblical seventy times seven was merely a beginning in his arithmetic of forgiving. He accumulated in the course of his life enough experiences to fill a volume of "Tales of My Neighbor and How He Undid Me." Almost without exception, his Reformatory boys gave back what they borrowed. But of the other hundreds to whom he had lent money, two only, he said, ever returned what they borrowed—a woman and a Jew.

He made the statement, during the very last year of his life, as cheerfully as if he were announcing an unexpected stock dividend.

The new emphasis of that day on social service was being expressed in many ways. One day, Bishop Fallows came home to lunch with the news, that a young woman, Miss Jane Addams, with her friend, Miss Starr, was planning to start a social settlement called Hull House, on Halsted Street.

He himself began about that time the first of his original series of experiments for social betterment, by founding the American Society of Patriotic Knowledge and a magazine, its official organ, called the *Home, School and Nation,* to teach children patriotism. Seventy-five per cent of the city's children, he discovered, largely foreign born, escaped from school before they were twelve years old, with not much more knowledge of United States history than if they were living in Russia or Hindustan.

The magazine was a good one, to judge by its reception. The first number brought to its editor a deluge of letters from men all over the country, prominent in National Affairs, in literature and education, among them Cardinal Gibbons, of Baltimore, the Reverend Dr. R. S. Storrs, of New York, and Dr. Oliver Wendell Holmes.

Besides editing the magazine and running the society, Samuel Fallows was Presiding Bishop of the Church that year, with the supervision of the entire Church. He was Bishop of Canada and the West, which meant several months away from St. Paul's, also his charge. He was preaching every Sunday when he was in Chicago, and was keeping up his parish work.

As an incidental, he took on the making of Webster's Encyclopedic Dictionary, which involved examining almost as many words as there are sands of the sea. In the midst of his task, his three children, on a Massachusetts hilltop, and his wife's brilliant brother, Fred Huntington, were stricken with typhoid fever. Through nerve-racking weeks, he thought of them week days and prayed for them in church on Sundays. Free at last, he sped East like an arrow, arriving just in time to see his beloved brother-in-law make a triumphant exit from the life he had graced so well.

His children were spared to him. But the anxiety over them told on him. Then his bank failed and his Sunday school superintendent absconded. Under the accumulation of tasks and worries, for the first time since the days of his chaplaincy, his physical machinery faltered and his physicians ordered him to a rest cure sanatorium, conducted on Weir Mitchell principles, by the Forsyth sisters, Miss Jessie and Miss Christina.

The theory of the rest cure was that food padded tired nerves and that the patient must eat everything on his tray, if he died for it. The poor Bishop, always a dainty eater, found the rule a hard one. On a certain memorable day, he had a large amount of mashed potato on his tray. As soon as the nurse had gone, he opened the window and dropped nine-tenths of the potato into the garden. Miss Christina, happening to be sitting just below, heard it come plomping down. Straightway she procured twice as much potato carried it up to her clerical patient, presented it without a word and chatted with him cheerily while he ate it.

"More potato, Bishop?" she asked.

Then they both laughed irrepressibly.

The patient saluted. "It's a poor General, Miss Christina," he said, "that doesn't know his superior officer when he sees her."

The cure was complete.

CHAPTER III

THE CONQUEST OF THE BOY

Governor Fifer, in 1890, responding to the new social emphasis on brotherhood, looked at the Illinois institution for keeping naughty boys out of mischief and found conditions very bad. He turned to his old Grand Army friend, Bishop Fallows, and said:

"Bishop, please be President of the Board of Trustees and see if you can't do something about it."

Full of desire to preach the Gospel to every creature, he was on tiptoe for just such a difficult mission.

"Of course, Governor," he said, "of course," thereby committing not only himself but Lucy Fallows and the children and Bridget and Dick, the cat, who liked his meals on time, to twenty-one years of opportunity for growing in grace.

The new President's dominant belief, radical for that time, was that bad boys were not small depraved lumps of iniquity but boys like his son or your son who had slipped a cog and could be brought back to normal living by kind, rational, firm treatment.

To teach the boys to control themselves was his aim for the whole twenty-one years during which the Reformatory grew from a feeble little institution to the second largest in the United States. That aim led to his advocating occupation, education and the teaching of trades to the Reformatory boys; the cottage system approximating the family group; the Junior Republic, with its self-government idea, unique at that time in reformatories. Above all and over all, the head of the Reformatory Board believed in the indeterminate sentence and the parole system, which let a boy out under supervision until the institution was sure of him.

Under this indeterminate-sentence law, a boy was found a job with an employer who would be responsible for him. He was also obliged to report himself to a probation officer at stated intervals until he was discharged from the care of the state.

In 1900, with Senator Deneen in the Governor's chair, and the storm center of a political attack, the parole law was violently assailed. At that time, a comprehensive investigation of most of the reformatories in the country was directed by the President of the Board.

He then answered the question, "Do Reformatories Reform?" with a mass of facts.

"Yes," he said, "even on a basis of dollars and cents." Reformatories and juvenile institutions, more than a hundred in number, justified an outlay of over twenty-five million dollars on buildings and grounds, and an annual expenditure of more than six million, he declared. Why? Because by careful calculations, he computed that the graduates of two only of the ten adult reformatories in the United States, Pontiac and Elmira, were then earning six billion dollars per year, an amount equal to the annual expenditure of all the reformatories and industrial schools in the United States.

Addressing the National Prison Association, at Omaha, the next year, the Bishop made the statement that of the eight thousand boys who had gone out from the Pontiac Reformatory during his term of service, seventy per cent became law-abiding citizens.

For the whole twenty-one years of the Reformatory dispensation, the house on Monroe Street, in all seasons and at all hours, was a runway for the Pontiac boys and their mothers and their fathers and their sisters and their cousins and their aunts.

As for meals, the uninterrupted ones of the whole twenty-one years could have been counted by a child who knew first-grade arithmetic. Even Dick, the Maltese cat up in the study who sat by his master at mealtime, understood that the bell rung for dinner simply announced to the head of the house, probably busy with a caller, that food was ready. Only when his master sharpened the carving knife was the wise cat down the stairs like a gray streak and up on his chair ready for action. But often before he had even a tidbit the doorbell sounded.

Bridget, returning from answering the ring, always met her Bishop's questioning look with the same standard, useless answer.

"I towld thim to wait and they said they would. Now, Bishop," (with that pleading Irish lilt to her tone,) "just finish this chop. *Lave* them wait. It's only wan of thim Pontiac people!"

Up would go his protesting hand. Down would go his napkin. Out of the door would go himself. Into the warming oven would go his chop.

Downstairs in the back parlor, day after day, in hours and out of hours, he held a Pontiac confessional for his boys and their kin. Some of his best and tenderest bits of eloquence went into his unrecorded attempts to make these rebellious relatives glad to have the prisoners stay in the Reformatory until it was wise to let them out.

Upstairs, in his study, he dictated letters about the boys, files and files of them. For he investigated every case. What he meant to the "cases," perhaps no man understood better than the probation officer who worked with him many years, Mr. Clem Reed—kind, big-hearted "Daddy Reed," friend of the boys and trained by the President of the Board, himself. Going over those days, he said:

You can hardly put into words what the Bishop meant to those boys. No one else was like him. He would go down to Pontiac for Board meetings two or three times a month. He never failed to go out and speak to the boys on the playground. They would drop their bats and gather round him, and follow him about. They wanted to get near enough to him to touch him, even his coat.

They'd say to each other: "Say, if the Bishop's your friend, you gotta chance."

The relatives would write him asking him to parole their boy. He would refer the case to me. I'd look it up. Then he'd go to Pontiac, usually a day ahead of the Board meeting and he'd see each boy that was up for parole with all the facts in his mind and have a talk with him.

"Get a boy's confidence, Daddy Reed," he'd say to me, "and you can do wonders with his reformation." Nine times out of ten, he'd parole the investigated cases, not because he was soft but because he knew those boys were ready to go out.

Mr. Ralph Bradford, brother-in-law of Major McClaughry, a great Pontiac superintendent, was full of stories which gave a picture of the President of the Board in action at the Reformatory.

One day while the Bishop was down, the pigs got out into the cornfield. An Italian boy and a Polish boy from Chicago were sent to corral them. The corn, shoulder high, made an excellent screen. The little scamps, instead of turning all the pigs home, drove two to the other end of the field and sold them to a farmer. With part of the proceeds they bought the tobacco for which they were crazy.

The boys were not found out until months afterward. The President persuaded the Board then not to punish the boys but to find the farmer who was the real offender and deal with him.

One of the culprits afterward became a Court interpreter in six languages. Two other brothers sent to the Reformatory also made good. The Bishop suggested to the father that, as Pontiac made such an excellent family finishing school, he had better send the other brothers on his own account!

The happy faculty of putting himself in the place of the boys made his justice human, not academic. Mr. Purdunn, I remember, one of his good friends on the Board was walking with him across the grounds after a meeting.

"Purdunn," he said, with that disarming smile of his, "don't you think sometimes it's a shame to punish boys for using tobacco when you go along spitting all over the sidewalk, always chewing something as big as a hickory nut?"

"Bishop," said he, "I'll never cast another vote to punish a boy for using tobacco."

Whatever else the busy President of the Board might be doing in those overfull years, his boys were never off his mind. Inside the Reformatory or out, they were his responsibility. He and Daddy Reed had many a splendid tussle over a Reformatory boy, with a salvaged life as their reward.

Thousands of boys to-day living straight and happy lives are the reward of their faith and self-sacrifice.

These Pontiac graduates would spring up to greet the President of the Board wherever he wandered. At a National Encampment of the G. A. R., he went into a room where a score of correspondents were at work for their papers. One of them came forward and shook his hand.

"I see you don't know me, Bishop," he said.

"No," was the answer.

"I'm one of your boys," explained the newspaper man.

Getting into trouble during the World's Fair, he had spent eighteen months at Pontiac. He was, at that later time, the correspondent of a leading New York paper.

On a corner of a San Francisco street another boy came up with another story of making good; in Chicago street cars; on Broadway, New York; out in the Philippines; everywhere, they stopped Bishop Fallows to tell him their stories, sure that he would rejoice with them.

"Don't ever," he said to Mr. Reed, when they first began to work together, "hesitate to call on me if a boy needs a temporary loan. An ounce of prevention is worth a ton of cure."

Daddy Reed lent one ex-Reformatory boy out of work five dollars. Of a good family, discouraged and feeling disgraced, the boy decided to commit suicide and bought a revolver from a pawnbroker for three dollars and a half. A plain clothes officer, seeing him buy the weapon, promptly arrested him. The prisoner asked his jailers to send for Bishop Fallows. He reached the boy as fast as the street car could carry him, and heard his story. The next day he went with the prisoner and Daddy Reed before the judge, explained the situation and secured the boy's release. The three of them first returned the revolver to the pawnbroker, with a piece of Samuel Fallows' mind, which was more militant than clerical.

"The Bishop found the boy a position in a big printing firm," said Daddy Reed, continuing the story, "and lent him money to get started. To-day that boy is the head of one of the largest printing plants in one of our largest cities. Two years ago he took me out to his home in his own Pierce Arrow.

" 'Except for Bishop Fallows and you,' he said, 'I'd be a tramp printer now in a strange country from which people do not come back!' "

He was just one of the retrieved thousands.

"The Bishop loved to marry the boys," said Daddy Reed, "but they had to start right. I remember one boy had been in Pontiac for stealing. He and his sweetheart came to me to get the Bishop to marry them. 'Has he told the girl?' he asked, 'about his trouble? It's much better for him to tell her himself.' " The boy had, so Daddy Reed took them out to the Bishop. "The groom had quite a little roll," said Daddy Reed. "He flashed it at the Bishop and handed him a ten. The Bishop handed it to the girl. He always did. He saved the boys.   Then he married them.   Then he christened their babies.

"My, but I did love that man," the probation officer broke out.   "There was something so wonderful about him.   I was a Bloomington boy, you know.   Twenty years after he had gone, they would always fill the church for him.   His memory was sweet, there.

"When he went off the Board, I didn't know how I could go on with my work.   He never failed you, you know, when you leaned on him.   The judges and the business men all did what he wanted.   Everybody did.

"Sometimes I wish I could put into figures what his saving the boy meant to the country.   Nobody knows, either, better than I do, how much he helped to better the police machinery for dealing with the boys.   There were no children's courts then or children's judges.   A paroled boy was caught and he hadn't a show in the world.   He was just a cat's paw in the hands of the parole officer and back he went to wherever he came from.

"They couldn't put that over with the Bishop.   He was too important a man to ignore.   He paved the way for the Children's Court, which he helped to found, and a lot of the other reforms that give bad boys a halfway decent chance to-day."

CHAPTER IV

HE TAKES UP THE CUDGELS FOR LABOR

The Homestead strike at the Carnegie steel works, near Pittsburgh, was one of the first dramatic clashes between capital and union labor fighting for recognition.

Samuel Fallows, attending a Christian Endeavor Convention in New York, read about this struggle in the papers.

He stopped at Homestead on his way back to Chicago, to see what the trouble was about, stepped off the train, interested as any humane person would be in the workingman, and stepped on again, a few hours later, with another cause under his official arm.

The strikers, when he arrived, were holding a great secret meeting at the Opera House to consider relief measures. The visiting Bishop sent in his card. Chairman Hugh O'Donnell welcomed him and asked him to speak, and ushered him to the platform, the boards of which were mottled with dark stains where the wounded prisoners had bled a few days before. Here he faced an audience novel in his experience—three thousand discontented workers jamming the building from wall to wall.

What happened, the *Chicago Herald* correspondent described for his paper.

"Bishop Fallows . . is beyond all manner of doubt, the most popular man in Homestead Borough. It is safe to say that at ten o'clock to-day not more than half a dozen citizens of the Borough even knew of the existence of the big, deep-voiced man from Chicago, but before high noon every

318

BISHOP SAMUEL FALLOWS,
CHAPLAIN IN CHIEF GRAND ARMY OF THE REPUBLIC,
. . . AND . . .
MAJOR GENERAL FRED D. GRANT, U. S. A.,
VICKSBURG, MISS., NOV. 7th, 1907.

BISHOP FALLOWS AND THE SON OF GENERAL GRANT

[See Page 357]

mother's son of the twenty-eight hundred locked-out mill men were lauding the bishop's varied merits and doing their level best to turn the clerical gentleman's head by the most extravagant flattery ever meted out to mortal man.

"The story of how the Bishop acquired this phenomenal popularity in less than half an hour is easily told. He made a speech to the men, a twenty-minute speech, which set the big audience frantic with delight. In those twenty minutes he talked law and arbitration and the rights of labor. . . . He talked wonderfully well according to those who heard him. Sad to relate the oratorical and logical beauties of this much talked of speech cannot be made public for reporters were rigidly excluded from the meeting. Even the Bishop himself was present only while delivering his remarkable speech. . . .

"Chance brought the Western divine to Homestead and the invitation of Hugh O'Donnell brought him into the meeting. His eloquence and his agreeable arguments did the rest."

He went on to Chicago that night, to be ready to preach on Sunday. The account of his Homestead visit Lucy Fallows read in the morning paper, and she went rather blindly about her duties for a few minutes. Daniel had been thrust into the Lion's Den, but her Samuel had thrust himself voluntarily into a meeting of men who had fought one of the bloodiest battles in labor history a few days before. What might they not have done to him as he stood on the "dark stains where the wounded prisoners bled!"

When she heard his key in the door, she flew to the hall as if she had been twenty-one, instead of fifty-one, and received him like a returned warrior. "There, couldn't be *two* Homestead strikes in a lifetime, could there, Sammy?"

Not understanding the personal bearing of her question at all, his face grew grave.

"I'm afraid, Lucy," he said, "there will be many strikes before labor and capital learn that they are brothers and two halves of the same social machine."

Future events proved him right. Chicago, itself, struck and struck until he cried out: "Chicago, with all thy strikes, I love thee, still!"

Conservatives and aristocrats blamed him aplenty for taking up the cudgels for labor at Homestead. But their recriminations troubled him not at all then or later. In the stockyards strike, in the early 1900's, he was the only minister in the city, Miss Mary McDowell said, to help her in her fight for the strikers. He not only preached for them, but went among them incognito, studied conditions and fought the harder, afterward, to get them a living wage. He preached arbitration in 1890, and he preached it until his voice was stilled in 1922. He preached it for the laborer and for the capitalists. Being fair-minded to both, he came, in time, to be regarded as a kind of official balance wheel in many a bad situation.

CHAPTER V

THE PEOPLE'S INSTITUTE

Once a teacher, always a teacher. The next venture of a pioneer of the Social Gospel proved the adage.

Preaching to Chicago from pulpits and cart tails, addressing it at banquets, meeting it in masses and classes and gone wrong at Pontiac, he saw education as the city's great need. During the early nineties, he was playing all his rôles except that of schoolmaster. He was Presiding Bishop, plain Bishop, Pastor, President of the Reformatory Board, Chaplain of the Second Regiment, champion of Labor, and of any civic cause that needed bolstering. In odd moments, as author, he was working away at a book called "Past Noon."

How this man of many interests could lend even a finger to help along the city's education did not appear. But one day, when all his other selves were taking a rare moment of rest, the uneasy schoolmaster in him slipped out with such a beautiful idea that his adventure as State Schoolmaster of Wisconsin and as President of Illinois Wesleyan paled to insignificance.

The People's Institute was the result—a great community center, one of the pioneer community centers in the whole United States. Enchanted with the glorious game of setting things free from limitations, its founder added this to his other labor as if the enormous task were play.

The People's Institute endeavored to reach not only young people, but the whole family and those who had no family. Good entertainments at small prices, athletics and

321

patriotic celebrations were part of the program. On Sunday afternoons, undenominational religious meetings with fine speakers were to be held, and the Second Regiment Band was to play. The Institute offered, also, courses of study, making one of the first demonstrations in the country of the University Extension idea.

As its author dreamed the People's Institute, so it materialized and became a vital factor for years in the life of the West Side and of the city. Its quarters at first were the Wigwam, a building with a seating capacity of three thousand, on Van Buren Street, in the heart of the West Side. The idea caught the fancy of the people at once. They flocked to the Institute meetings.

Professor Richard Green Moulton, of the University of Chicago, led off the Sunday afternoons in the Fall of '92 with a recital of the book of Job which remains memorable today in the minds of those who heard it.

Those who did hear it were as many as could get into the building.

"More persons might have been put in the Republican Wigwam on Van Buren Street and Irving Avenue," the *Herald* commented the next morning. "But such a procedure would have necessitated piling them up in layers like dried figs. Certainly no such assemblage ever before gathered in this city for such a purpose. The big auditorium was solidly packed with chairs, even the aisles being obstructed after the other seats had been taken. Every chair contained a listener, and what was more to the point, an interested listener."

Some years later, Dr. Moulton showed his friend, the Bishop, the long shelf in his study, filled with the Modern Readers' Bible, interpreting all the books of the Bible as he had interpreted Job. "You are responsible for all those volumes, Bishop," he said. "I followed your suggestion of People's Institute days."

CHAPTER VI

THE WORLD'S FAIR

The World's Fair, set like a bit of fairyland in Chicago, the great divide between the old city and the new, seemed to Samuel Fallows, seeker of unity in diversity, a Master Key of brotherhood.

It was pure delight to see a flat marshy waste on the Lake Shore blossom overnight into a city of white, intersected by the blue lagoons along which gondolas made their singing way. It rejoiced his heart to hear beauty-hardened Europeans catch their breath over that square mile of loveliness, the White City, to listen to their "Oh's and "Ah's," as the buildings after dark were outlined in living fire and played upon by searchlights.

Still, what made the Exposition seem almost stupendous to a Mid-West minister who thought in continents was its exhibition of brotherhood. He had always been wanting to tie the four corners of the earth together, and here he found them tied. The endless exhibits, tracing the material progress of mankind, with their international implications were a positive joy. The six acres of the gold-domed government building were no more terrifying to his feet accustomed to tramping, than his own back yard. He rode in the Ferris Wheel. He went through the Midway with the relish of a boy. But from all the strange folk living in it—the Egyptians in the Streets of Cairo, the Alaskans, the Cowboys in the Wild West Show and the funny little Samoan people— he gathered information for future use.

323

But the material exhibits and the Midway were his diversions, not his concern. His special responsibility was with the World's Congress Auxiliary of the Exposition.

The Auxiliary was planned to do for mind what the other departments did for matter—to show the progress of the mind of mankind; to establish fraternal relations among the leaders of mankind; to review the progress already achieved; to state the living problems now awaiting solution and suggest the means of further progress. It aimed—

> To make the whole world one in Sympathy;
> To make the whole world one in Mental Aim:
> To make the whole world one in Moral Power
> *Learning and virtue passports to all lands.*

It seemed a wholesale order. But this was Chicago in 1893, in the day of wholesale orders.

The Auxiliary was to be a "Summer University of the world," a "Convention of Conventions," a "Congress of World's Thinkers." Some of the subjects discussed were: Education, Temperance, Moral and Social Reform, Labor, Literature, Law Reform, Commerce and Finance, Agriculture, Arbitration and Peace, Music, Art and Women's Welfare. The list must have made Samuel Fallows feel as if he had gone back to the old "Ath." days in Wisconsin, when the year's program was limited only by all the discovered knowledge there was.

His work was as chairman of the general committee on Education. He was also chairman of a special committee on Public Instruction.

The first week of the Educational Congresses of which he was general chairman was divided into thirteen sections, dealing with all branches of knowledge. The discussions were divided between the old and the new in education, that work which had been already thoroughly demonstrated, and inno-

vations, such as Kindergarten and Psychology. During the
two weeks, the General Chairman talked on every subject
under the sun, and behind each talk he put the strength of
his knowledge and the fire of his personality. The two weeks
had meant much effort for him and Mrs. Wilmarth, who was
in charge of the Woman's part, and all the rest of the committee, but the results were more than worth while. "Never
in the world was held such a congress on Higher Education,"
said three Olympians of Education who happened, just after
it, to be standing together—United States Commissioner
Harris; Seth Low, President of Columbia College; and
James B. Angell, President of Michigan University.

No phase of the Fair was unbrotherly. But some were
more brotherly than others. On the Fourth of July, for instance, bands from Arabia, Serbia, Vienna, Cincinnati and
Iowa played "Yankee Doodle" at the Exposition with one
hundred thousand American flags floating in the wind above
their heads and the air "thick with oratory and smoke." That
was merely the first syllable in brotherhood, compared to the
Parliament of Religions organized by Dr. John Henry Barrows, held for seventeen days in the month of September and
devoted to religious congresses.

Samuel Fallows, like other liberal ministers, had been
working with his might for the Parliament. Its first meeting
gave him and the others who attended it the feeling of a nine-
teenth-century day of Pentecost. All the religions of Christendom were gathered into one room in Chicago, crowded to
its last inch of space. All the races, almost all the nations,
clothed in almost all the colors of the rainbow, spoke from
one platform. They spoke the language of the soul, of the
verities that united them, not the unessentials which divided
them. Those who attended said they could feel the sense of
brotherhood almost as a palpable thing. It moved them so
that they laughed and wept and waved their handkerchiefs
and broke into tumult after tumult of applause. The black

brother rubbed elbows with his white brother; the Jew with the Gentile; the Brahmin with the Free Methodists.

No wonder it seemed millennial to a minister whose ideal was a puplit in the market place, to preach the Gospel to every nation in the world!

CHAPTER VII

BISHOP'S BEER

After the Fair, Chicago went through a period of gloom and depression which made every day seem a terrible blue Monday. Panic gripped the city. Armies of men were out of work. Hundreds of them, well-to-do only a few months before, would wait hours on the chance of earning fifty cents "suping" in a theater. A thousand men a night slept on the floor of the City Hall. Except for bread lines and soup kitchens, established by all sorts of charitable agencies, men, women and children would have died off like flies.

To add to the general discomfort, William T. Stead, an English journalist and reformer, visited the city, investigated it and in a sulphurous book called "If Christ Came to Chicago," told the result with such eloquence that poor Chicago could not sleep nights for thinking of its iniquity.

Bishop Fallows bore his part in the civic effort to relieve the temporary distress and to clean up the city and its government. He was one of the early members of the Municipal Voters' League and the other bodies formed to cope with the problem. He worked with a will for the general weal.

But by the late Winter of '95, he was ready to try out another original idea in his series for making the Gospel socially practical.

The People's Institute, now in a fine building of its own, was providing a social outlet for many West Siders. But he desired something simpler, a portable People's Institute, as it

327

were, which could be set down on any street corner and become a poor man's club, competing with the saloon.

His plan was to open a sample temperance saloon, called the Home Salon, so furnished as to make the poor man feel at home, and serving a kickless beer which would cheer, but not inebriate. If this sample saloon was a success, he wanted to see it duplicated not only all over Chicago, but all over the country.

The plan was shrewd and sagacious. It was based on the remarkably successful English Coffee House movement, sponsored by the Earl of Shaftesbury and the Duke of Westminster, with its hundreds of coffee houses of all grades, buying their flour by the cargo from the United States.

A chain system of Home Salons all over the country would make possible the economy of large buying, a business procedure since demonstrated as sound by restaurant keepers, drugstore men and the creators of the five and ten cent stores. This large temperance project, however, brought the fighter against saloons, squarely up against the liquor interests, with their unlimited capital and influence. They adroitly killed the movement in the end, short-sightedly and stupidly, perhaps, as far as their own interests were concerned. If they had coöperated with the Home Salon idea in 1895, instead of opposing it, the poor man, as well as the rich man, might have had his club to-day, and the United States have become temperate, even without the Eighteenth Amendment.

Not blinking the fact that human nature *is* human nature, Samuel Fallows, in the mid-nineties, was possessed by the conviction that men, being social animals, would have a place to congregate, a decent place if they could get it, but, anyway, a place. He saw the saloon as the only agency giving the poor man what he wanted.

"What," he asked, "has the Church or the Temperance Movement to offer in a material way to compete with the saloon? Nothing. . . . People want light and warmth and a place where they can feel they have a right to be. I believe such a work as this, if it proves successful, will be worth fifty years of purely intellectual temperance work."

"The Saloon," it seemed to him, was the "poor man's or the average man's clubroom, cosmopolitan, instinct with the spirit of democracy. The very prompting which brings business men together in their Somerset Club or their Union League club leads the laboring man into the clubs furnished by the saloon." It was also, he said, the chief labor bureau in nearly every large city, the place where the jobless man went for temporary relief and for another job, rather than to a charity organization. He believed that the American saloon was one of the most powerful factors in American social life. There, for a small sum, the workingman could have large privileges. Homeless, he could find a home; friendless, a friend or a pretended friend. He could meet there his fellows on terms of equality, play games, read newspapers, write letters. The saloon, he concluded, was meeting a great need of civilization in a wrong way.

In a speech to the Somerset Club he gave his views:

"My theory is a very simple one. It is to adopt the best features of the saloon with the best features of the restaurant, and so to blend them that we shall have the excellencies of both.

"You must remember we are drinking animals. Gentlemen, your ancestors and mine were men who used to drink every other people on earth blind. We inherit this thirst. Any attempt to ignore it is a fatal attempt, and the result of the attempt is found in the fact that there are to-night nearly seven thousand saloons in the city of Chicago, and nothing of any kind to antagonize them. Bishop Potter, of New York, week before last, at a meeting of business men, while he did not say anything about the Home Salon by name, yet urged the formation of a company to furnish to the people what in a small way we have been endeavoring to furnish; in the first place something to drink that should be wholesome and not alcoholic, and second, food at the lowest possible price.

"I have before me now a little map; it extends from Halsted Street to Michigan Avenue, and from Lake Street to Harrison Street. There are 541 saloons north of Harrison Street on the South Side, and 359 on the West Side, between Halsted and the river, or 900 in all in this district. Nine hundred saloons and one Home Salon! Gentlemen, it won't do. . . .

"There ought to be a thousand Home Salons in the city of Chicago. I like the word 'Salon,' as it distinguishes the place from the saloon. We may not be able in four weeks, or even in a year, to reform the whole of Chicago, but we may be able to do for Chicago what old Peter Cartwright said had been done for him. When asked by Bishop Hamline who was a little put out at the levity of the old hero of Kentucky and Tennessee and Illinois, 'Brother Cartwright, are you sanctified?' Cartwright said: 'Yes, Bishop, but in spots.' We may not be able to sanctify the whole of Chicago but we will sanctify it in spots.

"Let me say now as a humble representative of the church, it is useless for the church to wrestle with the liquor problem unless we put something in place of the saloon. I do not know but that it would be wicked in some cases to eliminate the things which the saloon has unless we put something better in their place."

The Home Salon was opened in February of '95 in the basement of 155 West Washington Street, formerly occupied by Jerry Sullivan's saloon. Said one paper:

"The new institution started off with an immense boom. Though away under ground, though approached from the sidewalk by narrow, steep steps, and though advertised outside only by a modest sign reading 'Home Salon,' the rush began at an early hour. . . .

"It was a part of Bishop Fallows' plan to make the salon a saloon in everything except its evils, and the effort was a complete success. There were the stuffy basement, the little round bare tables, the lunch counters, the sawdust two inches deep on the floor, the bar, and the barkeepers. The bar especially was a stunning feature. The former occupant of the premises would have noticed no change. The wall was covered with mirrors, in front of which were rows upon rows of tumblers, mixers, and bottles of what looked like Old Tom gin and Old Crow whisky. There stood the same tall bar with the foot-rest in front of it and with the white-aproned 'beer-slingers' behind it flopping the drinks down.

"But, by way of saving grace, pasted on the mirror were life-sized likenesses of Neal Dow and Frances E. Willard.

"On the opposite side of the room within an inclosure a couple of cooks were kept busy ladling out to customers the 'free lunch,' consisting of bread and butter, a piece of meat, and peas or potatoes. When a customer had been served and had paid 10 cents, he took his lunch to the barkeeper and then received a drink of beer: so that it was really a 'free beer' instead of a 'free lunch.'

"The customers were an average Chicago crowd. The Rev. J. P. Brushingham and a few other ministers dropped in to wet their whistles; a few nice-looking elderly women sat in the back part of the place with their beer, and the rest of the throng who climbed over each other's heads, as if the Bishop were serving eternal salvation instead of beerette, were hungry men of all ages.

"The personnel of the management is intresting. First of all came the Rt. Rev. Samuel Fallows, D.D., Bishop of the Reformed Episcopal Church, proprietor; then there was L. T. O'Brien, late President of the Retail Clerks' Union, manager; then F. L. Newman, the famous bartender in other years of Delmonico's in New York, who presided over the bar. Newman was ably assisted by George Bradley, formerly colored porter at Hannah and Hogg's and Chapin and Gore's; George Wilson, late saloon hustler for George Fisher; and G. Castles, a former bartender but late of the Painters' Union. The chef was George Brown, the former popular cook of the steamer *Virginia* of the Goodrich Line, who was assisted by one plain cook and two carvers."

Only temperance drinks were served, of course. The chief of these was a new drink, with a very small per cent of alcohol, developed from pure hops by a chemist retained by the founder of the Salon. It was dubbed almost at once, "Bishop's Beer."

The attendance on that opening day varied from two thousand to eight thousand, according to the reporter. It reached at least the two thousand mark. The start of the venture was memorable to the man responsible for it in more ways than one. As a gentleman from the *Tribune* put it:

"The congregation was composite. Church people were there to see that stock in the new church venture was not a drug on the market. And it wasn't. The beer all ran out at high noon, despite brewery contracts for perennial refreshment. The sporting gentry was there to give the bishop a friendly tip about encouraging a homelike atmosphere in the place. Laborers came and some women, too, because a good lunch was got at cut rates. Saloon-keepers peeped in to see what graft the bishop had on his advertising. A delegation of the Bartenders' Association inquired if Bishop Fallows expected to recognize any but union labor. Knights of the green cloth eyed unoccupied nooks in the saloon with gloating and it is whispered will make the proprietor a proposal to start games under the sidewalk.

"In anticipating the great rush at the opening of his churchly enterprise Bishop Fallows and his helpers reached the Home Salon very early yesterday morning. By 8 o'clock scrubbers and scullions were running hither and thither in a bustle of preparation. Cooks started to cook for the multitude. Bakers' and brewers' and grocers' wagons drove up and delivered their goods. Six swift-footed messenger boys stood in line and were alternately dashed out on expeditions for commissaries.

"When help ran short Bishop Fallows hung his hat and coat over the bar and started in with a scrub brush himself. After accomplishing that feat he polished the bar with a cloth until he could see the reflection of his white shirt sleeves. Then a wail from the kitchen caused him to rush to the help of the chef brigade, where for ten minutes he was kept busy stirring a caldron of bean soup that threatened to scorch.

" 'Ain't the bishop a handy man, though?' said the chief bartender to the head female waiter.

" 'My, but he's perfectly lovely—a regular home man that knows more about domestic duties than a suburbanite,' replied the girl.

"And from the soup caldron the master of ceremonies was called to direct a green hand about the artistic way of knocking bungs out of a beer keg.

" 'He's on to everything,' muttered the bartender; 'wonder if "Doc" Parkhurst hasn't told him about some of the ways he's seen in Manhattan. Now, what parson would 'uv pulled a bung out by pounding on the barrel? Shades of Murphy —but he does it just perfect.'

"It was encomiums for the bishop everywhere. He was immensely popular. They liked his free, easy way, his advice, and his garments. This fact was driven home to the bishop when he returned to don his discarded apparel. It was gone. Coat, overcoat, hat and gloves had been appropriated by some sneak thief who doubtless had received a lunch with a glass of beer for nothing. By chance, the bishop's valuables had all been retained on his person, so that the loss was confined to clothing.

"In the press of early noon business, therefore, the hatless, coatless man was compelled to borrow garments from one of his force and sally forth to a clothing emporium.

" 'Bless them that despitefully use you,' was the ejaculation of the church leader when he learned of his loss. 'If that man continues to trade here we will give him so much for his money's worth we will make him ashamed of himself. I hope he did it by mistake, not malice.'

" 'They'll take surplice and surplus both if you give them a chance, doctor,' volunteered the head bartender.

"At 12:15 the crowd had reached its maximum. They couldn't reach any more. They filled the saloon, the rear room where lunches were served, they blocked the entrance and pavement. A phalanx, organized and expectant, stood four abreast ready for admittance. The news that the beer had been exhausted did not cause many to turn back. There were still concoctions of unknown consistency, there were all the softer drinks, and lunches and pastries galore."

The liquor interests did not take this innovation lying down. They began, apparently, trying to knife it at once. The very day that the Salon opened, a case of Weiss beer was slipped in with a soda water order and served over the counter before the mistake was discovered. Weiss beer contained eight per cent of alcohol and was taxable. Curiously enough, revenue agents were on hand just at the crucial moment, ready to take for analysis samples of the drink presumably being served in the Salon. The word of a Bishop was sufficient to convince the government that the Weiss beer was a mistake. The analysis of Bishop's beer showed only the per cent of alcohol claimed. The Home Salon took out a license, to be on the safe side, and banned the soda water firm which had sent the Weiss beer—which closed that incident. But there were others.

To keep it legally alcoholic, Bishop's beer had to be put in kegs very soon after it was made. The next move of the liquor interests was to tinker with the coopers who furnished the kegs. These men cheerfully promised kegs and then failed to deliver them, which was much more embarrassing than if they had not promised them at all. But the management scoured the state for kegs, tided themselves over temporarily and eventually secured a bottling plant, so that this attack also was successfully met.

"It is foolish," said Samuel Fallows, pragmatist, "for saloon keepers to make war upon us. If the sale of our beer is more profitable than the sale of theirs, all they have to do is to keep our beer for sale. We shall be glad to supply them. We have orders for it from one ocean to the other."

The press rollicked with the comedy of the experiment, from coast to coast. That also, undoubtedly, was liquor interest propaganda. But it was proof positive of the position which the Mid-West Bishop occupied in the newspaper world that it was comedy, not irony, and that in most cases the serious import of the experiment got, at least, a paragraph.

IN THE PHILIPPINES

From left to right:—Bishop Fallows (in black) ; Hon. Dean C. Worcester, Secretary of the Interior, Philippine Islands; General Bell, commanding Philippines Department; Raymond Robins, social worker, in black coat and white trousers; Bishop C. H. Brent, Episcopal Bishop of the Philippines and Edward H. Fallows, son of Bishop Fallows and President of the American Company (in gray suit on right).   [See Page 391]

The next attack on the ground that Bishop's beer was harmful, was quashed by a sworn statement from the manufacturer that the beverage was made of pure malt and hops and contained absolutely no harmful ingredients.

Even in the face of opposition, the Salon idea proved itself successful. At the end of five weeks, the manager and secretary signed a certified statement that the net profits of the business had amounted to more than a hundred dollars a week.

For a couple of years, the Home Salon thrived and flourished and was copied in other parts of the country. It was difficult to perfect the beer so that it could be kept for any length of time or shipped without developing alcohol beyond the temperance limit. But with capital, it would have been entirely possible. Capital, the Bishop did not possess, and the brewers were clever enough to see that he did not get it.

To make the Salon a continuing success, an executive was necessary, strong enough to down the liquor interests. That, again, was impossible to secure, for the brewers had two hundred million dollars with which to buy brains, to the Home Salon's pence.

Some students of the temperance question, looking back to-day, feel that if Samuel Fallows, with his boundless energy and his influence through the country, could have dropped everything else and have thrown himself into the fight to make his rational temperance experiment widely successful, the history of temperance in the United States might have been materially altered. But such a campaign would have required an immense fund, and none was forthcoming.

Therefore, having demonstrated that his idea was practical and that, under any normal circumstances, it could continue successful, the Bishop-brewer reluctantly conceded the right of other pressing responsibilities, and turned the key on his vision and on an experiment for the benefit of a section of his fellow men still neglected to-day.

CHAPTER VIII

THE JOURNALIST

If the desire to get things out of traps and cages had not so possessed Samuel Fallows from the beginning of his career, he might conceivably, have become the head of a metropolitan daily.

The value of a gallery he appreciated from the moment he cocked his six-year-old eye at his schoolmates across the dye ditch. He was also able to gather information from everything and everybody. After attending a long exhausting session of a Church Council, for example, he spent the noon hour of rest turning the mind of a little Greek newsboy inside out. "It was entirely characteristic of him," said Dr. Freemantle, who tells the incident. "The next time the Bishop made a speech on Greece, he had that boy's information at his tongue's end."

The editor's power of producing copy, standing or sitting, sleeping or waking, was likewise his. Never sure of an uninterrupted hour, half a dozen times on his quietest morning, he would be called down from his study to see a caller. But his different thought trains never went off the track. He could eat his dinner, answer the telephone, keep up a conversation and, at the same time, be writing a speech on the back of church entertainment cards, with his inch-long pencil. One day, he showed a visitor a little book called "Don'ts." "I received a hundred dollars for that," he said, "and I wrote every word of it on street cars." The mechanism of his mind was such that, after two years, he could take up a conversa-

336

tion just where he had dropped it. Dr. Freemantle testifies that he heard him do it more than once.

But the busy Bishop could not have produced fifteen or twenty books, including dictionaries and a Biblical encyclopedia, in addition to sermons and articles by the score, without a talent for swift organization. He gathered about him a trustworthy staff, one of whom was Myrtle Reed's mother. And they were ever ready at the drop of the hat. A hurry call from a publisher was always a delight. Could he have ready, in three weeks, a life of some distinguished person just dead? Time was his slave. Certainly he could! By afternoon, he would have a wagonload of material on the third floor, the work apportioned and his staff busy. With promptness one of his virtues, he never failed to have the book ready on time.

Usually, literary work was confined to the upper story. But during Summer vacations, with the family away, it crept downward. His wife, returning unexpectedly one Fall, found her sacred lower floor possessed of the literary devil. The kitchen tables were in the front parlor, the ironing board in the back. Every inch of space was covered with books and papers, systematically arranged. Flatirons were in use as paper weights; kitchen pans as paste pots. Half a dozen people were at work. The dining room was littered with files and manuscripts. It was proverbial among the Bishop's friends that nothing ever caught him up a tree. Nor did this serious situation.

"It's all right, Lucy, my love," he said soothingly. "It's all right. You go right upstairs. We are making a Supplemental Dictionary to prove that slang is English on probation, you know. We'll have it finished in a minute now. I'll call you as soon as we are through."

Possessing so much editorial instinct, Bishop Fallows could not resist using it now and then, as in editing the *Home School and Nation*. For a number of years, also, he was

associated with Dr. Shailer Mathews on the *World Today.*
His most extensive task of editing was in connection with
the University Association, which, with Dr. Bonney's co-
operation, he founded soon after the closing of the Home
Salon. Its object was "fraternal association in small,
local centers for the purposes of intellectual and moral
culture."

This meant that a group of people in Portland or Podunk,
Tampa, Shanghai or an island in the South Seas, could get
together with a leader, receive courses sent out by the Association, be examined in them and, if the course was satisfactory, receive certificates to that effect.

The plan was to draw heavily, for the Association courses,
on the mass of papers and speeches left over from the World's
Fair, which the Government could not be induced to publish.
But the material, after all, did not lend itself to consecutive
courses; and Samuel Fallows found that, as Editor-in-Chief,
he had a heavy task on his hands. The first year's course
covered universal history, the second, universal literature and
religion, the third, political economy, political science and
sociology.

The Association enrolled sixty thousand people in two
thousand centers. As part of his strenuous recreation, the
founder of the Association visited centers here, there and
everywhere. He had the true editor's gift of shedding care.
A well-known business executive of to-day remembers his
delight when the Bishop, who had given an Association lecture in his home town the night before, lifted up his dignified
coat tails and rode downhill with him on his bobsled. Never
was an industrious man more pushed than during the life
of the Association. But its Secretary and Treasurer,
Mr. W. E. Ernst, said that day after day the Bishop
came into the office as cheery and apparently carefree
as if he had nothing more than a game of golf on his
mind.

Samuel Fallows, it happened, was a bishop and not an editor. But his editorial instinct helped materially to make him the kind of bishop he was.

As a publicist, he was very well aware that if you could get enough people inoculated with an idea at the same time, you could overturn the world in sixty seconds. In his program for spreading the social gospel, therefore, he stressed any method of broadcasting which would reach a great number of people at once. The schoolmaster in him—perhaps the little boy as well—welcomed processions, as one of the surest and most interesting ways of convincing the crowd through its ear and its eye, as well as its mind.

Chicago, delighting in the spectacular, was able, always, on the slightest pretext, to produce a procession—a procession of patriotism or protest, of welcome or farewell, a procession of joy or a funeral march. All of them Samuel Fallows encouraged, and in most of them he marched—with the soldiers, with the ministers for some civic cause, with the laymen, anywhere that his presence would help to drive home the idea behind the procession. The march never seemed to tire him.

Charles Cheney Hyde, Bishop Cheney's nephew, has a recollection of being utterly fagged out, merely watching one of these processions halfway through, and of seeing Bishop Fallows march by him as fresh as if he were twenty. "Daddy Reed" said that marching beside him was work for an athlete. When the probation officer did it, he had to run like a little boy, to keep up with his chief. Bishop McDowell remembers that once, when his own parishioners wanted to make him ride, he saw his eighty-year-old friend come down the street like a young Viking. "When Bishop Fallows rides," he said, "I will, too."

Preaching the gospel to every creature did not mean to him, either, a pulpit in a corner, but a movable rostrum that could be set up wherever the creatures were. A Boston paper named him as one of the six or seven notable examples in the country of ministers who carried their pulpits into public affairs.

One of his first experiments in religious publicity was to make his church a forum. Mr. Thomas Wilson, his organist for years, was convinced that "no church in the West had so many prominent men speak in its pulpit as St. Paul's. Dukes, Earls and Princes were included in the collection." An African King visited the church once, sang a Gospel hymn in the African language and told the congregation the story of an English curate who visited his tribe and begged its members to repent. "Eat, drink and be merry," was the preacher's text, "for to-morrow ye die." Obediently, the Africans ate, drank and were merry. The next day they sat around waiting to die and, when nothing happened, almost lost their faith in this new religion.

But the pastor of St. Paul's believed that the newspaper provided the best method of spreading the gospel of religion, as well as of fact. Preludes on current topics before his Sunday morning sermons carried his ideas all over the country. For months, he wrote sermonettes for one paper. Another time it was prayers. One of his daughters, hurrying to her father's room with a message one morning, was stopped by her mother standing at the door with a reverently bowed head.

"Hush, my dear," she whispered, "your father is giving a prayer over the telephone."

"The Bishop was a minister who understood the value of publicity," said "Dick" Finnegan, friend and editor of the *Journal*, who, as a small boy, had delivered papers at the Monroe Street front door. "I went out to the house one night after dinner to go with him to the Baptist Church where he was to speak. As we walked along he turned to me and said:

" 'The press and the Church must meet each other face to face in the dark street of life and then go arm in arm like two soldiers of the night, guarding the highways and byways for the security of others.

" 'Even though the Church is full to-night we will still speak to a handful of people compared to the hundreds of thousands of readers who will get the message from your newspaper story. Some clergymen do not appreciate the value of close coöperation with the press. I have found the papers not only willing, but anxious, to link arms with me.'

"The Bishop was a good diplomat. You couldn't put him in a corner. I was impressed by that when I went to his La Salle Street office before the Negro Semi-Centennial celebration and found him besieged by rows of colored people, all wanting money. He talked and joked with them awhile and then sent them away happy though unsatisfied.

"His point of view was big. He knew human nature, and his cloth never got in his way.

"No one ever called him a crank, because he was never so overzealous for a cause that he lost his balance. On questions of right or wrong, no one could get him to compromise an inch. But on other things he compromised intelligently.

"With his great enthusiasm, people might have thought he had staked everything on one project. . . . But I who worked with him so often knew he never did. Did he think any one thing would bring the Millennium? Not at all. He was contented if a plan would pull the world even an inch along.

"His general information was always surprising me. I re-member, once there was a fight on against the Mormons. People were trying to get funds at a church meeting to extend Christian work in Mormon territory. The speakers were supposed to be experts on the subject. It was merely a by-product with the Bishop, but he told more about Mormonism in five minutes than the rest had in an hour.

"I used to meet him long after he was eighty, going to late dinners when it seemed to me he ought to be resting.

"I said, one night, 'You shouldn't let people impose on you, Bishop.' 'No, no,' he said, 'it isn't that. Young people keep me young.'

"Something did. He had seventeen years of usefulness after most men are on the shelf. The Bishop was unique, in my experience."

His versatility of information was the undoing of a reporter, Mr. A. Pegler, on the Hearst newspapers, who, for several years, had many assignments involving the West Side minister.

"He was most picturesque, you know," Mr. Pegler recalled. "That back parlor of his, a little dusky, was like a stage. He usually began speaking before he appeared, and when he swept in he was very like what you might imagine George Arliss would be, if he made up as a bishop. He was as friendly and informal as a man could be. Yet, you felt instinctively there was a place beyond which you must not go.

"I never found a subject he couldn't tell me something about, from vegetation on the Andes to the best food for chickens. But one night I thought I had caught him. Moving pictures were just in their infancy. I took the Bishop to a meeting where moving picture men were speaking who were supposed to know the game from *a* to *z*. I asked him to speak, and I thought to myself, 'Well, this is where I have put one over on you.' He spoke. I declare, he knew more about the subject than the movie men themselves.

I was so surprised I backed off the platform into the potted palms and fell all over them."

This same versatility was a source of delight to another reporter who was campaigning for Taft, at the time when he was running for President. The newspaper man turned up a speech made by this "mere minister," endorsing the candidate, which he said would have done justice to a campaign manager and, thereafter, used it for ammunition.

Dr. Norton, the religious editor of the *Tribune* and a friend for years, said that the Bishop was his most satisfactory subject for interviews, because he could call him up any hour of the day or night, ask him for an opinion on any subject and get it without a moment's delay. This power of instantaneous response, said Mr. Curley, managing editor of the *American,* made it part of the regular procedure in any newspaper office, if anything important came up, to telephone Bishop Fallows to get his opinion.

Mr. E. S. Beck, managing editor of the *Tribune,* who knew Samuel from the days when Chicago was wide open and shameless, through her days of repentance and fruition, down to the end of his life, declared he could ask him about anything, from primordial protoplasm to the best way of preparing pork.

"He was a man first and a clergyman afterward. I could name some bishops in this town who would send a deputation down to demand what we meant by asking them some of the things that we applied to the Bishop about as naturally as possible.

"His dignity was native, not anything he put on with his coat or his robe. He was genuinely interested in anything that concerned his fellows. He never cheapened himself. But he had an open mind to everything.

"Nothing in the city, all those years, was complete unless he had a hand in it.

"He could fight abuses and wrongs like a heavyweight champion. We called him 'the fighting Bishop,' you know— a spiritual Roosevelt. Yet he was not always battling. His attitude was not dictatorial. Out to fight gambling and vice, tooth and nail, he was able to disarm the opposition, even of the men with gambling houses. They loved him."

"Why?" Mr. Beck was asked.

"Because," he said thoughtfully, "he was able to get people to reform themselves."

This tolerance endeared him to Fremont Older, editor of the San Francisco *Call,* who took the Mid-West minister, during one of his California visits, to a great labor gathering to hear Bill Haywood, the radical labor leader.

"Bill Haywood," wrote Mr. Older, "was anathema to all

our respectable people and I was rather timid about taking your father to the meeting. I sat next to him and shuddered every time Bill Haywood said something I feared might shock him. At the finish of the talk we passed out of the hall silently, not a word spoken till we got well out on the street."

"Well, Bishop, what did you think of it?" was Mr. Older's apprehensive question.

"I liked it immensely," said Samuel. "It sounded to me like true Christianity."

"I cannot conceive of the life of this man being written," Mr. Older wrote further, "without it being almost a history of the finer side of American life during the period of his activities.

"I recall a vivid story he told of his crusade in the state of Wisconsin, I think it was in 1856, battling against all the old prejudices that existed there then, that still exist in our state to-day, favoring the abolishment of capital punishment. He won that fight, and went on with his Christian work. When I say 'Christian work' I do not mean church work. I mean trying to carry out the full spirit of the Sermon on the Mount. More than almost any other churchman I have ever known, Bishop Fallows lived and practiced the Christian doctrine, making church forms quite secondary and inconsequential."

The newspapers, according to one of Samuel Fallows' editor friends, gave to him, during his lifetime, more space in actual inches than to any other citizen except presidents. He thought it was partly because the fighter against provincialism saw the newspaper as his most effectual weapon, partly because his big-heartedness made him automatically a friend of every newspaper man he met.

"He was a boon to every cub reporter," to quote Dick Finnegan, who had been one himself. He never failed to help them out. He was a trifle kinder to the poor cubs, trying to find their journalistic feet, than to anyone else. One of those whose troubles he had solved, as he went down the steps, paid his spontaneous homage to that little touch from the fourth dimension in a bishop's humanism, which was its distinctive quality. "That man," said the boy to his companion, "never puts up his hand to feel if his halo is on straight. But you know it's there, all right."

No matter what time the cubs might appear, he was always ready to help them out. A callow youngster turned up at the Monroe Street house one night about eleven-thirty requesting notes for his out-of-town paper on a speech to be delivered the next day. The speech was not written, and the subject of the request was very weary after a late engagement. But he sat down then and there, in his dressing gown, and wrote out his speech in full for the grateful youngster. In 1922, that reporter, then the editor of his paper, recalled the incident as his tribute to the memory of a man departed.

The cubs never seemed to tax his patience too far. He even forgave the one, detailed to report his sermon, who produced a sermon for the next day's paper which he had not preached, on a text he had never used.

"Aren't you going to do something about it, Bishop?" asked one of his indignant parishioners.

His pastor smiled his inscrutable smile.

"It was a good text, wasn't it?" he asked.

The parishioner had to admit that it was.

"And a good sermon?"

Again the parishioner had to concede its quality.

"It was a good thing for the young man to have to think out a sermon like that, wasn't it, and to keep his mind on his soul for a while?"

Once more, the parishioner had to admit his pastor's excellent logic.

"I think we'll let it go at that," concluded Samuel Fallows with a wave, dismissory, of his long-fingered hand.

CHAPTER IX

HE DEMONSTRATES BROTHERHOOD

Chicago's Fall Festival unexpectedly gave Samuel Fallows the privilege of saving his beloved city's face and doing a dramatic bit of arbitrating.

The city, in '99, was in one of its worst labor tangles since the time of Debs. Various building trades had struck. Employers retaliated by locking out labor, and there was trouble enough. Chicago, so far as development was concerned, was as stagnant as a pool in the middle of a marsh.

The new post office, then in the process of construction, seemed to offer a solution of the problem. Its construction would provide employment for hundreds of men. Some public-spirited citizens decided that the laying of its corner stone should be an occasion to outdo all Chicago's other occasions, barring none. McKinley was to be invited to lay the corner stone. Sir Wilfrid Laurier, of Canada and Diaz, President of Mexico, were to be asked as guests.

Plans were laid, at a Horseshoe Banquet at the Grand Pacific, which, should have carried the enterprise through any amount of bad luck. Influential guests represented every branch of the city's activity—President Harper, Commissioner "Ferd" Peck, Penn Nixon, Fred B. Upham, Barney Eckhart, Daniel M. Lord and about ninety-five others. "Bathhouse John" was there and, near him, Samuel Fallows, who, as a long-visioned citizen, had had to fight the Bathhouse's personal politics all his life. But the Horseshoe Banquet was a merger of differences. The Irish fourth of the Mid-West

Bishop smiled into the agate eyes of Bathhouse John, and they knew each other for lovers of their fellow men, however their methods of handling their fellow men might differ.

"True religion is cheer," said the Bishop in his speech. "Men were not intended to go about with their heads bowed down like bulrushes, making abject apology for having been sent into the world. I want this Fall Festival to demonstrate that there is a universal church among men and that a common humanity stalks among us all."

Bathhouse John clapped. He thought then what he said later: "He's a regular fellow, this man, a lovable fellow, not like a parson at all. He's full of nature, a man of the people, like McKinley."

The Bathhouse, otherwise known as Alderman Coughlin, made his maiden speech that night, in six feet of full evening dress. He said he had come "to listen and learn and get religion," and he promised that the special traction ordinances would "slide through the council easy."

Bishop Fallows clapped him. Then they both listened to the plans which were to make Chicago's Fall Festival as notable— no, more notable—than the World's Fair. Four million incandescent lights and three thousand arc lights were a detail. There were to be arches and arches of lights, and fireworks almost by the ton. Lorado Taft and fellow artists were to provide statuary enough to fill a museum. A bicycle parade was to contain hundreds and hundreds of bicycles. A dragon, invited from San Francisco, was so huge that it would require three hundred Celestials to carry its tail. There were to be great receptions and meetings, of course, with McKinley as the special attraction.

After such a send-off, it seemed as if any Fall Festival would be mannerly enough to glide to success without a hitch.

Samuel Fallows accepted the chairmanship of the committee on religious services. Having arranged a couple of meetings on a big scale, with enormous choruses of school children, he went up very comfortable in mind, to perform his Episcopal duties in Canada. He returned to Chicago, only ten days before the date set for the Festival, to find the project about as peaceful as a den of wild beasts.

Labor was rebelling as never before in the history of the city. The crux of the difficulty seemed to lie in the fact that the post office, a Federal building, was in charge of a Republican government, while the Fall Festival Committee was Democratic. But the real issue was a duel between capital and organized labor.

The government had given the contract for building the post office to an Eastern man named Pierce, with permission to use any kind of labor he chose. He chose to use cheap nonunion labor and to do all the work in his New England quarries.

Labor discovered this and was furious. The work would have employed Chicago men for years to come, and would also have put something like two million dollars in circulation among them.

"Let McKinley come, if you want to," said the labor leaders. "But if he takes a trowel in his hand and, as a mason, lays the corner stone of a building being constructed by nonunion labor, we will advertise to the world that he is in favor of unorganized labor."

Then the fat was in the fire. With politics mixed in, the question became a national one. Election day was coming on apace. McKinley could not afford to be put in any such position.

Committees and one influential man after another had tried to smooth out the trouble. Dr. Graham Taylor, outstanding friend of the workingman, had done his best with labor, in vain.

Everything was ready for the celebration, even to a beautiful silver trowel for McKinley. William G. Edens and

Volney Foster were at the White House, inviting him politely to be present. McKinley, moistening his restless lips and shifting his restless eyes, said:

"Is this a fight or a fête you are asking me to attend, Mr. Edens? I will not go a single step unless a united Chicago invites me."

It looked as if the city must stand disgraced before the nation. Then the official peacemakers turned in desperation to a minister.

"Bishop Fallows," they said, "see if you can't do something about it. We will abide by what you think is fair."

"I'll try," was his answer. That was his chance to test out conspicuously the principle of arbitration, the form of brotherly love which he considered the ideal solution for labor troubles.

With Patrick O'Donnell and Father Murray, who was close to labor, he set up an arbitration board. He summoned labor and he summoned capital. Each side aired in a safe place all the grievances it had been smothering. Reporters were excluded, and what was said had the secrecy of the confessional.

The result was a triumph for the principle of arbitration. In a few days, the two sides had reached a conclusion which both could accept. The deadlock was broken. McKinley came.

"The Bishop," said Mr. Patrick O'Donnell, "with McKinley, was the principal figure at the Festival. He solved the immediate problem. But those meetings between capital and labor had a much more far-reaching effect. They made the two sides understand each other so that, very soon afterward, the grievances of the Building Trades were settled and everybody went to work."

Mr. O'Donnell, at that point, threw back his head and laughed out of his Irish eyes.

"The Bishop rubbed in the lesson," he went on. "He made

capital pay for a get-together banquet. I never went to another like it in my life. Everything was there from dress suits to jumpers—and everybody. When they were all fed and comfortable, the Bishop gave them the neatest speech on arbitration I ever heard in my life."

It was such occurrences that won the fighting Bishop the friendly title of "the Great Pacificator."

"At stormy church councils," said Dr. W. R. Collins, his successor at St. Paul's, "we used to say of the Bishop:

" 'He always had an oil can in each hand.' "

CHAPTER X

THE COAL STRIKE

Bishop Fallows, in the Fall of 1902, was offered the happy chance to serve, at one and the same time, as a defender of labor and as a journalist. Those were the days of the terrible coal strike in Pennsylvania.

Coal went up to twenty-five dollars a ton in Chicago, which was about the same that sixty dollars a ton would be to-day. The Pennsylvania coal miner who refused to mine it, suddenly became the city's next-door neighbor. If he struck much longer, the city would have to burn greenbacks for fuel. Greenbacks were impossible fuel for the poor who were already suffering terribly. Something had to be done about this labor problem of the anthracite coal region deposited on Chicago's very doorstep.

At a great mass meeting, over which Samuel Fallows presided, a Miners' Relief Committee of One Hundred was appointed to secure action. This committee, which represented all the classes and the masses of the city, from mayor to hodcarrier, from minister to brewer, delegated the presiding officer to investigate conditions in the coal fields and make a report. Anxious always to bring about a better understanding between capital and labor, he gladly welcomed the chance to study on its home ground the most serious strike up to that time.

"Meet me in Pennsylvania," he telegraphed his younger daughter. He then procured a camera, which he fondly hoped would take pictures, put a few more inch-long pencils

into his vest pocket, changed five dollars into pennies, packed
a bag and donned a soft military hat now the only kind he
wore. A short time before, in the midst of a house-cleaning
bout, his wife had brought him his last high silk hat in a
dusty box.

"Take it away, my dear," he said. "Take it away. It's
no use to me. Give it to one of my colored brethren. He'll
think he is Solomon in all his glory."

The clerical coat and vest, which completed the uniform,
tricked many a good Catholic into paying him reverence and
kissing his ring. The General-Bishop combination of attire
was a good one for the coal fields, teeming with foreigners
who would admire his democratic hat and respect his cloth.

The ordinary reporter broke into the strike region, feeling as if he took his life in his hands. What news he obtained, he got on the sly. But all barriers were down before
the deputy of the Miners' Relief Committee of Chicago.
Labor and capital both said: "Come and see."

For a week the representative of the Relief Committee
looked. What his blue eyes missed, under his thatch of
iron-gray hair, was not much. Visiting President John
Mitchell at his headquarters in a cheap hotel, he found him
a pallid monk in the ghastly unshaded light, talking the gospel
of arbitration for his laborers. Under his direction were
thousands of hot-blooded foreigners who thought no more
of sticking a knife in an enemy than into a pig. Bishop
Fallows could not restrain his admiration.

"Never," he said, "was a disciplined army managed with so
little disorder as this mass of ignorant strikers."

He spoke with Mitchell at a huge meeting of the miners,
most bloodthirsty, according to report, and found them as
peaceful as a St. Paul's picnic. At a schoolhouse full of
miners and their families, he helped to dedicate an American
flag. In the villages, he visited in the homes of the miners

and heard their first-hand accounts of their grievances. Groups of children, who never could resist him, gathered about him. He talked Americanism, gave them pennies, fed them peppermints and tried to take their pictures with the camera which, alas, played him false. He caught their mothers going to get the food supply allowed by the union. He learned what he wanted to know, first-hand and through interpreters. Visiting the homes of the operators, he listened to their side. He especially liked John Markle, who was human and near enough the seat of the trouble to know something of the miners' point of view.

All through that week of investigation, the Chicago Committee's deputy toured the coal region in a rickety hack, making thirty miles a day. He began the morning with ardor. At the end of the day, on the last tenth of the thirtieth mile, he would spy something, a group of men, perhaps, away over beyond a culm pile, and stop the driver, leap out and make his way to them with the springy step of a boy.

At first, the District President, a local strong man, told off to accompany the investigator, tried to keep up his pace. One day, after the forty-fifth stop, he leaned back against the cushions exhausted and rolled a despairing eye at his charge's daughter.

"Doesn't your father *ever* get tired?" he groaned.

Weariness had no place in Samuel Fallows' body just then. There was something to do. When the District President was sleeping the sleep of the down-and-outers, the deputy of the Miners' Relief Committee washed off the soot that made of him, like his negro friends, "God's image cut in ebony." Then he wrote his daily stint for the papers and filed it with the telegraph company. Finishing the sixteen-hour day which would have kept him out of any union, he climbed very gingerly into the bumpy small-town hotel beds, with ancient bedding and terrible entomological possibilities.

The next morning he was as ready for the fray as ever.

Continuing his trip, the investigator went to Philadelphia to call on Mr. Baer, President of the Reading Railway and one of the largest coal operators whose attitude was one of the most irritating things to the Chicago public, paying twenty-five dollars a ton for coal. When he went into Mr. Baer's office, in Philadelphia, he could have had no hope of converting him. But, after a tour of the coal regions, it was so easy to see how simply the situation could be met, if the two sides could consider themselves neighbors for five minutes, that the optimistic Mid-West Bishop had to see for himself if there was any hope of inducing Mr. Baer to consider arbitration.

There wasn't.

The final call of the tour, which ended in New York, was on Frederick D. Underwood, President of the Erie and also an operator. It was like honey after quinine. Mr. Underwood had come from the bottom up. He knew how the workman felt. He had a feeling for his wrongs and his rights and an understanding of his mistakes. The investigator, having known him from the time he was a brakeman on the road, could discuss the national crisis with him as friend to friend. In Mr. Underwood, he found a believer in his theory of arbitration.

"If the operators had let Fred Underwood handle the strike," he said to his daughter after that interview, "it would have been settled long ago."

In the end, it took Roosevelt and his big stick to turn the trick. But his solution was along the lines the two discussed that day in Mr. Underwood's office.

PART IX

THE VELVET YEARS

CHAPTER I

SEVENTY YEARS YOUNG

So traveling over many paths, a busy pilgrim reached man's allotted threescore years and ten and passed into the first of his velvet years.

The gayest day was gay for him, but so was the dullest. He had never lost his gift of putting wings on sandals. He could get a lift from the stupidest task of a stupid routine. He could make a dictionary or a Haroun al-Raschid excursion with equal zest. So he did not go limping with a cane over the Psalmist's threescore mark, which all men secretly dread, but flying like a happy boy.

How does he keep so young and joyous? People were beginning to ask that question even in 1900. Sometimes they caught a hint of the reason. "My dear," he said once to his younger daughter, who was worrying about something. "Don't cross the bridge till you come to it, and be sure to burn it behind you."

A man who likes to sit under the Juniper tree of circumstances could have found plenty to worry about, if he had been pastor of a West Side church at the beginning of the century. That section of the city had fallen quite away from the glory of its ancient days. It was getting grayer and dingier every year. "Rooms to let" signs filled the windows of the houses which had once been prosperous family mansions. Still the minister of St. Paul's, with a congregation smaller but devoted, saw as many people to help as ever and refused to be troubled.

357

"Most of my millionaires have moved to Heaven or to Evanston," he explained cheerfully to a new assistant. "It is hard to keep track of the rest. But in the army we utilized whatever we had. If we had no pillow, we used our saddles. If we had no saddle, we used a log or anything. So it is with our work here. We have to adapt ourselves to conditions. Your first task will be to make out a new directory."

People and positions tried again and again to tempt him away from his habitat. Frank Hall, accustomed to sunny clean Madison, visiting at the house one day, said: "Bishop, this West Side is terrible. *Why* don't you move?"

He never forgot the reproach in his old friend's earnest blue eyes.

"Frank, Frank," was his answer. "Would you have me desert my duty? This is one of the outposts. I must help to hold it."

He could be humorous about his beloved West Side on occasion. Mrs. Frederick Grant sat down with him at one Grand Army Reunion. "Now," she said, "let us talk about Chicago, wonderful Chicago—its beautiful South Side, its beautiful North Side, its dreadful West Side."

"That's because it has been subjected to my influence so long."

For a man always looking at to-day and to-morrow, no condition seemed hopeless. His reporter friend, Mr. Pegler, told him one day of "Red Barrett," a "lifer," at Joliet, sent up for killing a policeman. "The prisoner believed he shouldn't be there," said Mr. Pegler, "and was very low in his mind. The Bishop at once began a correspondence with him to cheer him up, which he kept up several years. I saw one of the letters. It was great, you know. The Bishop found something for him to be thankful for, even shut up for life."

Red Barrett is out now, so his case was a beautiful demonstration of the expediency of cheer!

With the same spirit of making the best of things, Samuel

THE GOLDEN WEDDING

Bishop Fallows and Mrs. Fallows fifty years after they were
married. From a photograph taken in 1910. [*See Page 379*]

Fallows was working away, as always, for the good of
Chicago. The older chieftains had passed on. But now
he was fighting shoulder to shoulder with their successors—
Dr. Frank W. Gunsaulaus, Dr. Graham Taylor, Dr. John
Timothy Stone, Clifford Barnes, Dr. William E. Barton, Dr.
Herbert L. Willett, Dr. Preston Bradley, Dr. Howard A.
Johnston, President of the Church Federation; Bishop Charles
P. Anderson, Rabbi Joseph Stoltz; his Catholic friends; Judge
Landis, Judge Tuthill, the rest of Chicago's good judges, Ella
Flagg Young; Mrs. Harry Hart, Harriet Vittum, Mary
McDowell, the George Dixons, Charles Wacker, Arthur
Burrage Farwell, Dr. Ernest Bell and all the other civic
soldiers.

Said his friend Governor Barrett O'Hara: "He always
tried to turn smaller things to the bigger cause he was working for. If by some chance the devil had been elected Mayor
of Chicago, the Bishop would have called upon him at once,
and said: 'Your Honor, the Devil, I know you are not half
as black as you're painted. I believe you are going to make
your administration the best this city has ever had and I mean
to help you all I can.'"

"Bishop Willard Brewing, of Toronto, one of his ministers,
tells this story of the Gipsy Smith campaign:

"The Gipsy decided to carry out a parade through the
Red Light district. The day before the parade the Chicago
papers announced: 'Bishop Fallows disapproves of the Gipsy
Smith parade.'

"But it was carried out, and in the morning the same
papers announced: 'Bishop Fallows approves of the Gipsy
Smith parade.'

"That evening Bishop Cheney and Bishop Fallows met, and
Bishop Cheney was greatly disturbed over the apparent viola-
tion of consistency. He said to Bishop Fallows: 'What is this
I see? In the evening you approve, and in the morning you
disapprove?'

"Bishop Fallows, laying his long and eloquent hand on his friend's shoulder, said: 'My dear Cheney, "to be or not to be, that is the question."' And then: 'When I disapproved, I had not seen it, but when I had seen it, I approved.'"

"Only once," says Bishop Brewing, "I recall him showing some irritation. It was over a minister prematurely old who was retiring from active burden bearing too early, and talking of age and death. The Bishop, with an unusual flame in his eye and an unwonted edge on his voice, said: 'Why is he talking of dying? Why doesn't he spruce up?'"

This habit of making the best of things over a long series of years was one of the secrets of his unshakable poise. He practiced it in little things and big. Bishop Brewing was with him when they missed an important train. He, himself, was much perturbed. But his Bishop made merry over it. "The soul is too great and important an instrument for us to allow it to be upset by a missed train," was his conclusion.

Chief of Police Collins remembers how, years ago, he and the Bishop scrambled off the same train for a twenty-minute dinner at a station. The waitress was very slow. "The Bishop complained mildly," the Chief explained. "The waitress said: 'I could eat all *I* want in five minutes.' The Bishop didn't get mad. He just said, 'You must have a double row of teeth, then.' He was so cute about it he set her and all the rest of us laughing, and she hustled the food on, like anything."

The first trip of the Christian Endeavor Society to California for a great convention provided another chance to make the best of things. The excursionists were a huge body to move, and the railroad company was new to the business. For the sake of those with scruples, it had been arranged that there should be no Sunday traveling. But the railroad company found they could not get the train to the coast in time for the convention without it.

"The officials referred the matter to the Bishop," said

Mr. William Johnston, who was on the train. "I think we should get there on time," he decided. "Then, to take the curse off, on Sunday, which was also the Fourth of July, he preached a patriotic sermon from a little platform we rigged up for him between the car seats."

If not seriously, then humorously, he extracted the best from a situation never more neatly than in a trivial conversation with Mrs. Wilbur E. Fribley. Let her tell about it.

"One day, while lunching with the Bishop, I was admiring the wonderful way he always said exactly the right word at the right time and the even flow of perfect language he commanded. I said I so longed to be a fluent speaker. In his kindly way he patted my hand and said:

" 'Why, child, don't let that trouble you. Perhaps people respect you more just as you are.'

" 'But,' I gasped, 'how could they?' In his calm way he said: 'Well, when you go home just read the directions that come with your fountain pen.'

"I could not wait to arrive home but stopped at the nearest drug store and asked to see pens. Imagine my surprise when I read:

> " 'If the ink in this pen flows too
> freely, it is a sign it is almost empty.' "

While nothing was too small for his making-the-best-of-things philosophy, nothing was too great. Even the Iroquois Fire, greatest disaster of Chicago's history, only temporarily shook his optimism. By some strange chance, he was in front of the Iroquois Theater when the flames first burst forth. The firemen allowed him, first of all civilians, to enter the hideous death hole behind them. All the afternoon and evening he helped to carry out the wounded and render last consolation to the dying. Late that night, he returned home haggard and looking ten years older, for the terrible experience. Not even in the Civil War, he said, had he seen such frightful scenes.

Nevertheless, on the following Sunday, while the entire city was still stricken and dumb, he was able to preach a sermon so full of hope that he lifted the entire congregation out of its gloom. It was not a sickish-sweet piece of easy philosophy. It had the flavor of courage and high conviction, with a rousing quality which stirred his hearers to an effort to prevent any repetition of such a calamity.

"Divine discontent" was the state of mind which he preached and for which he strove, himself. It was contentment with all the slothfulness left out and all the dynamics of growth left in.

CHAPTER II

THE CLEARING HOUSE OF SORROW

Having learned to make the best of things himself, Bishop Fallows, in the last few days of 1907, began, on a large scale, to teach other people how to do it, too.

One night, early in January, waylaid, as usual, after dinner by Dick, the Maltese Czar, he drew a paper wad teasingly through the parlors and the hall, round and round, and, while puss recovered his honorable and very ancient wind, played a crashing bit of Wagner on the player piano with virtuoso gesture. This done, he dropped into an easy-chair, poked the back parlor fire thoughtfully and made a place for his cat on his knees.

Turning to his wife, sitting near at the big roll-top desk, adding up belated Bazaar receipts to report at the next meeting of the Ladies' Association, "Lucy, my love," he said, "I have decided to preach a series of sermons Sunday evenings on the power of the mind over the body and call it Christian Psychology, and I will turn the midweek prayer meeting into a health service."

"Sounds interesting, my dear," she replied, absent-mindedly.

Just so casually did a man with his hands full take on the Health and Happiness movement which set Chicago ablaze, spread over the country like wildfire and added thousands of souls to his unofficial parish in the United States, Canada, even Mexico, England, Australia and Japan.

His interest in mental therapeutics, however, was anything

363

but new. It was at least as old as the engagement letter to
Lucy Huntington, in 1858, which recorded that Professor
Read, illustrating the power of the emotions, had covered his
pupil with confusion by asking whether he had ever been in
love. From that time on, one of his minor specialties had
been the study of all sides of mental science. He, himself,
with the vigor of twenty at seventy-three, was a living illus-
tration of the power of the mind over the body. As a member of the Society of Psychical Research, he had investigated
any number of cases of psychic phenomena. Whole drawers
in his study were given over to memoranda on them.
Thought transference was a favorite subject.

The club to which Samuel and Rabbi Hirsch, Professor
Swing, Dr. Thomas and many other liberal leaders belonged
had spent some of their time investigating mediums and
discovering frauds.

Some time before, he had published a book called "Science
of Health," expounding his own views and showing how they
differed from Christian Science. The psychological corner
of his library had all the latest books on the subject. For a
number of years, also, he had been giving lectures on Mental
Science at Bennett Medical College.

He began the movement with a sermon on the last Sunday
evening of the old year.

His sermon that night on Christian Psychology did not in
the least minimize what the mind harnessed to suggestion and
religion could do to the body. By Monday night, Chicago
was ringing with a new sensation. Bishop Fallows had come
out as a Faith Healer or something. By Tuesday, his telephone was tinkling every minute. Questions poured in as fast
as the wire could carry them. Some appeals for help were so
desperate that he agreed to see three or four people at the
church on Wednesday.

After lunch, therefore on that day, he and his daughter
Alice swung down Adams Street to the church, around to the

chapel entrance, expecting to meet the three or four, and opened the chapel door to find the room packed to capacity and a newspaper camera pointed at them over a sea of faces.

With no more warning than that, a busy man was plunged into his attempt to help solve one of the most acute problems brought about by the mad rush of modern civilization—the problem of those who cannot go ahead under their own steam.

Funny, pathetic, tragic, they all fixed their eyes on him. One woman was in a wheel chair. A Jew with a red nose and a roving eye explained his loss of memory to his neighbor. He always forgot the name of a certain street "quicker and quicker every day—" the sad result of domestic troubles, he thought.

"They say the Bishop demands doctor's certificates," he ended mournfully. "I haven't got one, but I can prove by any conductor on the line that the only way I can get off at that street is to wait till I see the female wooden Indian in front of the cigar store on the corner."

Out at the elbows, in costly furs, suffering greatly or mildly, they kept coming and coming. By three o'clock, the hour appointed for the clinic, the chapel was overflowing, and lines of people crowded the hall.

At that point the Bishop, according to a newspaper report, spoke to them:

"I cannot hope to treat you all. The best I can do is to define the purposes of the movement to you and to tell you what it is not, as well as what it is. The name commonly accepted for it is Christian Psychology. You might also call it Religious Therapeutics, or Applied Christianity. Probably the first name is, etymologically speaking, the most precise.

"There is, however, no relation between Christian Psychology and the various other 'ologies' and 'isms' that have connected themselves with the Christian religion.

"I have no sympathy with any doctrine of healing which seeks to eliminate the physicians. On the contrary,

I say to the physicians: 'We can't get along without you.'

"The question is entirely apart from them, or, rather, the new movement is something added to the field of medicine. For ages the functions of the physician and the priest were blended in one. The priests of the early church were the doctors of the community. They attended not only to the spiritual needs of their parishioners, but to the bodily needs as well. In spite of the lack of science and the prevailing ignorance of the times, they accomplished wonders.

"Then the progress of science brought about a differentiation in the functions of the priest and the physician. The man trained in anatomy and therapeutics took entire charge of the body and the man trained in theology took entire charge of the soul.

"For a while that was satisfactory to the people, but progress has gone on until the world has come to appreciate the fact that the work of the doctor overlaps that of the clergyman and the work of the clergyman overlaps that of the doctor. They are thoroughly interdependent.

"What we desire to do is to bring about this proper union, the doctor to aid the clergyman in correcting bodily evils and the clergyman to aid the doctor in putting the mind and spirit right.

"So far as this work is concerned, you needn't be an Episcopalian, or a Presbyterian, or even a Christian, but I do believe that the man or woman who has the right perspective toward things divine, who can see over and above the universe the great central power which is in everything and which is everything, will be the man or woman who will receive the largest benefit.

"I do not profess to be able to correct any disorders which are purely diseases of the body, although I do think that by putting the mind into the right mood, the work of the physician and surgeon may be materially aided.

"That is not our main object, however. There are thousands and thousands of people who are suffering to-day from melancholia and hysteria, and that most common of human ailments with the uncommon Greek name, neurasthenia.

"One of our eminent nerve specialists said to me the ohter day:

"'Bishop Fallows, the world has no idea of the number

ı—Chicago American

VETERANS OF TWO WARS

Bishop Fallows and an American Doughboy celebrating
Armistice Day, 1919.   [*See Page 396*]

of nervous victims who are dragging themselves about their daily work, miserable and disheartened. The physicians can't begin to take care of them all.'

"Thus, you can see the field of the Christian psychologist. We are simply beginning where the doctors have been compelled to leave off. It is not a new discovery I am trying to put into effect here. It is simply that I am trying to do my part to get the pastors and the doctors together again, and to get back to first principles.

"There is not a thing in Christian Psychology which requires that you should change your views concerning the Deity, or concerning faith, or hope, or love. You are not required to think one whit the less of your own individual church, whatever it may be. In fact, I would consider it very wrong to promulgate any movement of this kind which would make it necessary for a man to fall away from the faith of his fathers.

"We merely want to be helpful to those who need help. Auto-suggestion needs reinforcement from some other mind or soul. Whether that suggestion be the suggestion of mind or soul is a metaphysical distinction which is not pertinent now.

"You need the suggestion; that is the main point. I think I can give it to you, and you can be of assistance to one another. My original intention was to give up one afternoon a week to personal conferences, but I see that one afternoon will not be enough. I shall make it two afternoons and cut out some other work. You can come to me with your troubles and we will go over your case in detail and I will apply the suggestion which I think applicable to you. If suggestion fails, we will try persuasion."

He invited everybody back for the evening service and begged all to leave, except the six with whom he had appointments. The meeting broke up, but nobody went. Instead, they flocked around the healer Bishop, caught at his hand and touched his coat, as if mere contact helped them.

His patience was unending. One buxom lady preëmpted him for five minutes, because she was the good friend of his good friend, Mrs. ——.

"One of the well ones, I see," said the Bishop. A dismal sigh was his answer. He told her to come and be helped, also a pathetic little old lady who clung to him as her last straw.

"We are helped already, Bishop," they both declared and went away happy. That was also what the six clinic patients said. One of them, ill for years, declared she was entirely well.

While the Bishop treated his patients in his study, his daughter took down, by the dozen, the names of the people who wanted future appointments.

The service in the evening, the inaugural of the Happy Club, which took in the whole audience, was almost a repetition of the afternoon. A social hour followed the formal meeting, and coffee and cake were served.

So ended the first day of that amazing year, natural and scientifically explainable. Yet a mystic quality pervaded it, which impressed even the newspaper reporters, than whom there are no sincerer skeptics. Said the one from the *Examiner:*

Perhaps the Temple in Jerusalem, on one of the days when Christ was performing miracles, may have presented a similar scene, but no recognized church in Chicago has ever contained an audience like the one that gathered in St. Paul's Reformed Episcopal Church yesterday afternoon to attend Bishop Samuel Fallows' first psychological clinic.

As Christian Psychology started, so it continued. Eight days after the initial sermon, the papers called the "newly launched system of Christian Psychology the most generally discussed topic in religious and scientific circles in the United States." Interviews with various progressive clergymen, with Rabbi Hirsch, Dr. Harold Moyer and other nerve specialists, proclaimed these men heartily in favor of the new movement. Several Christian Science leaders, on the other hand, had spicy and derogatory opinions. On that eighth day, a bushel basket of out-of-town letters was received in the first two mails and the leader of the movement confessed that he had a pile almost two feet high, besides, which he had only partly read.

Indeed, Christian Psychology completely possessed the house of Fallows. It kept the telephone constantly atinkle. Even night was no silencer. People called in the wee small hours to plead for just five minutes' talk with the Bishop. Callers came in a stream. The postman made trip after trip. The master of the house kept three stenographers busy answering letters.

His daughters, both fortunately fitted with special psychological training, took a leave of absence from their own work to stand by the ship. His younger son, Charles, was also borrowed from his business in New York and impressed into the service.

Within two weeks, the machinery of the new movement, organized by his older daughter, was running as smoothly as clockwork. The Bishop preached on Christian Psychology subjects Sunday evenings. On Wednesday evenings, when the Happy Club held its meetings, he talked on the same subject, more informally, or had outside speakers. Dr. W. A. Evans, health commissioner, was one whose sensible, merry talk captivated the audience. Light refreshments were part of the Wednesday evening lure. On Tuesday afternoons, another general meeting was held, with special features, in addition to the brief talk about some phase of mental hygiene. A gymnastic teacher gave lessons in relaxation, gratis, and people with special talents often contributed some bits of entertainment.

The actual clinic work was confined to two afternoons each week, and Bishop Fallows was booked up with appointments four weeks ahead. In organizing this part of the work, he had the generous counsel and coöperation of many physicians and, especially, of the leading nerve specialists of the city, such as Dr. Hugh Patrick, Dr. Sanger Brown, his old friend Dr. Harold Moyer, and others. But Dr. Sidney Kuh, who ranked second to none of them, agreed not only to give advice but to diagnose free of charge, before the Bishop saw them at all, the patients applying for treatment. The precision and accuracy and thoroughness of Dr. Kuh's work gave the Christian Psychology movement a thoroughly scientific, as well as a spiritual, basis.

All sorts and kinds and conditions streamed through the church clinic. One man came who had suffered business reverses, felt desperately ill and had decided to commit suicide. The Bishop took him alone with him into his study, talked with him, prayed with him and sent him out remade for good.

Another discouraged brother thought he had heart disease. Big and strongly built, he was helped into the study by his wife and daughter. His face was haggard and his shoulders drooped. A physician, some time before, had told him he had a serious case of heart trouble, and he had been living down to that verdict ever since, though other physicians had tried to assure the poor man that he had no trouble. Dr. Kuh's diagnosis showed that his only trouble was in his mind. But the patient, nevertheless, was getting weaker and weaker. He had made his will and prepared to die. His latest doctor sent him to the Bishop.

"He told me he had done all he could," said the patient. "He told me you could speak to me with authority. I am here as a last hope. What can you do?"

"Through God's grace, I can cure you absolutely," said the leader of the Health and Happiness movement. "But stand up straight, my friend. Don't you know man was made two-legged instead of four-legged to keep his spine perpendicular and look at the sun? Now look up." The man lifted his bowed shoulders for the first time since he had entered.

"Take fifteen or twenty good deep breaths," pursued his

healer. "The air is the symbol of God's Spirit. Spirit means breath. God has breathed into us his Holy Spirit. There is no more fitting symbol of His Spirit than the free, pure air around us.

"Fill your lungs full of it consciously every day, for it carries health and life. Your mind and body are wonderfully interrelated; they act and react upon each other. No idea has ever entered your consciousness except through your senses. Every sensation which is caught by your sense is registered automatically upon your mental and also upon your physical being."

Then he went on to make clear to him how suggestions of disease may creep into the mind, and once there, how insidious their action is.

"And now," he said, "I have spoken to you. I have told you all that a man can tell you. I am going to stand aside now and let God speak."

And he opened the Word and read to him: " 'For the Lord God is a sun and shield; the Lord will give grace and glory; no good thing will He withhold from them that walk uprightly. . . . If thou wilt diligently hearken unto the voice of the Lord thy God, and wilt do that which is right in His sight, I will put none of these diseases upon thee, for I am the Lord that healeth thee. . . . Bless the Lord, O my soul, and forget not all His benefits. Who forgiveth all thine iniquities; who healeth all thy diseases; who redeemeth thy life from destruction.' "

The man went away cured.

A nerve specialist sent one case to the head of the church clinic, instead of to the asylum, on the slender chance that he might break the vicious circle which was making the man insane and convince him that he had not committed the unpardonable sin and was not doomed for eternity. A warrior battled for the life of a man's soul and his mind behind the door of his study that day and won. The patient came out looking transfigured. His letters, received from time to time for years afterwards, were pæans of joy and thanksgiving in broken English.

An old man, suffering from a form of melancholia, declared he had no power of mind or body to do anything and must go to the hospital. After a single treatment, he testified the next evening that he had gone to work, instead of to the hospital, and felt like a two-year-old. A most estimable gray-haired wife and mother came to confess that the desire to commit suicide had dominated her and darkened her life for months. She was soon delivered from her obsession.

The director of the healing work exercised a wise discrimination in his suggestions, prescribing sometimes nothing more than fresh air and sunshine, good food, exercise and self-forgetfulness. One zealous woman, over emotional about her religious life, was told to stay away from church for six months.

Reëducation, which could only be accomplished slowly, was also part of the work. The nervous patient, medically speaking, is on the road to recovery as soon as he has the conviction that he is going to be cured, but he is only well on the day when he believes himself to be cured. The long analyzing talks required to bring this happy result about with the more obstinate cases, the Bishop and his assistants understood and practiced.

But sometimes the cures were almost breathlessly and unbelievably dramatic. A poor old codger came to the clinic, late one afternoon, dragging himself along with a crutch. One arm and one leg were apparently paralyzed, and he seemed an utterly hopeless cripple. He had no appointment, but, as a patient failed to appear, the Bishop's daughter who was keeping the door, slipped him in that he might have at least the comfort of a talk with her father.

The man came out, still dragging his leg, but looking happy

and murmuring to himself: "The Lord is the strength of my salvation. Whom shall I fear?"

At the next Happy Club meeting, the Bishop's younger daughter, sitting with her back to the chapel door, heard it bang. Some one with a swift firm step came up behind her, reached for her hand and squeezed it in a grip of iron and shouted, "I'm cured! I'm cured! Look at me. Praise the Lord!" It was the poor old hopeless cripple, crutchless, swinging his arms and leaping about.

The cure was reducible to a scientific formula. All the cures were. Everybody was trying to keep things down to a perfectly normal plane. But for all that, such an experience made one feel as if prophets and apostles were abroad and miracles possible at any moment.

As for the leader of the movement, never was his peculiar magnetism more apparent. The force which showed as little blue flames at his finger tips when he was a boy preacher; which cured his wife's headaches and the sick doctor, his tent-mate during the war exerted its influence on his patients so that many felt the strange force of it even in his handshake.

During those months when Christian Psychology was at its height, he lectured on the subject to ministers' meetings of all denominations, to doctors and to laymen, in town and out of town, several times a week. Returning from one of these strenuous trips at noon, after a fifteen-minute nap, he would go down to his clinic, electrify patient after patient all the afternoon, return for dinner fresh as a schoolboy and deliver another lecture in the evening.

The minister and the doctor were to coöperate in meeting this great need of nervous sufferers. The problem was their united responsibility. Man had a body, as well as a mind. Only one disease in four might be real, as an eminent doctor had said. But that fourth one needed medicine and

perhaps a surgeon's knife.   Since the Bishop knew his
God to be in all and through all, in man and in the least
electron, he saw no logic in conceding divine power to purely
mental healing and denying it to medicine and the surgeon's
knife.

It was a consistent attitude, theoretically perfect as far as
its exponent was concerned.   But his own abounding health
made any personal experience of the knife unnecessary and
the use of medicine very infrequent.   If his physician, Dr.
White, had not been a military man, he could never have
managed his patient at all.

About medicine and all other things, Samuel Fallows, now
grave, now gay, was his dearest and most human self during
that astonishing Health and Happiness experience.

Nothing at all that was common to man was foreign to him.

At one Happy Club meeting he showed physiologically and
psychologically why man should be ashamed not to live to be
one hundred and twenty.   Metchnikoff had just brought out
his book advocating sour milk as an antidote for the harden-
ing of the arteries, which is the meanest foe known of perpetual youth.

These, as reported, were a Christian Psychologist's rules
for living one hundred and twenty years.

Drink sour milk or pure buttermilk two or three times a
day.

Avoid too strenuous living.

Go to bed early.   Get up with the rising sun.   Take plenty
of exercise of a kind not associated with your employment.

Obey rigidly the laws of hygiene.

Keep a clear conscience.

Love God and be square with your fellow man.

Drink some more sour milk.

The papers, all over the country, snatched eagerly at this

fresh item of news and, of course, featured heavily the sour milk and buttermilk aspect.

No one of the Bishop's readers was more impressed with his recipe for a youthful age than the two little boys pasting in the back parlor the clippings which came from coast to coast.

They discussed the matter with bated breath. Being in the house so much, they knew that he took his own medicine, in this case, and was always slipping into the kitchen for a drink of buttermilk or the milk which Minnie was perpetually souring.

"Betcha he could pitch a ball," said one small paster.

"Must be most a hundred," said the second.

"Most!" from the first.

"Sour milk did it," the second.

"Must of drank it all his life," number one.

"Let's *us* ask Minnie for some." They both started for the kitchen, while the subject of their discussion, hidden in the front parlor, laughed loud and long.

Yes, very human and natural was the head of the Christian Psychology movement, during those uplifted days. To relieve Dick, the cat, having a devastating time with fleas, he applied a highly recommended remedy which nearly killed poor puss. Between two tremendously busy days he spent most of the night in the furnace room sitting beside his pet, a little gray mass of misery. He only left the sufferer when the pain was eased and recovery sure.

The prejudices which made him lovable and human were as strong as ever. Ticking clocks were his pet abomination. On one official visit to a distant city, where he was entertained in a very beautiful home, he was kept awake by a clock in his bedroom, with a voice like Old Ben. Rolling up the noisy little monster in a comforter, he stowed it away on the top shelf of the closet, shut the door on it and forgot all about it.

After he reached home, he had a telegram from his host:

"Valuable heirloom clock missing.   Did you borrow it?"

In a primitive world of tents and food-bearing ravens, the pleasant experience of healing the sick without money and without price might have gone on forever.   No one connected with the work failed to feel the uplift, and no one was willing to commercialize it by taking fees from patients.   But with collections which hardly met the cost of the light refreshments, almost the only sure source of income, the question of financing the movement was a serious one.

The Bishop's younger son had long since gone back to his business.   His daughters could no longer neglect theirs.   His wife could not be taxed much farther.   Mrs. Inez Deach, Miss Touzalin and all the other splendid workers in the church could carry on the extra work only for a limited time.

Some adjustment was imperative.   One could no more desert the throngs coming to the church for help than push hands off a life raft.   The head of the movement published a book called "Health and Happiness," which was the first attempt at a solution.   Its chapters were not lectures, but talks —clear, vigorous and easily comprehended, accurate scientifically, but suitable for an average reader seeking help.   As in his personal dealings with his patients, the author put religion first.   He wrote of the "Science and Practice of Prayer," calling autosuggestion a kind of prayer.   He discussed faith as "A Dynamic Force," "The Presence and Power of God," "The Power of Love," and gave a little sermon on "Love's Therapeutic Value."   "Doubt," "Fear," "Cheerfulness" and the other emotions he discussed in the same informal way, ending with "Watch Words of Right Living."

"Health and Happiness" aimed to open up to the reader an understanding of the big essentials of sane, wholesome living. "The Book is not an apology," said one Boston reviewer, "it is a guide. And it is brief—beneficently brief." It offered for patients a safe course in self-treatment.

To garner more fully the enthusiasm for efficient living generated by this movement, Bishop Fallows had two plans. The first was to establish a school of some kind to train psychological religious healers. The need of them was real enough. He had proved how great a number of incapables could be made capable by simple suggestive treatment.

He had also discovered that neither a clerical robe nor a medical diploma by any means fitted every minister or every doctor to cope with nervous cases—partly mental, partly physical, partly spiritual, requiring for successful results the infinitely delicate touch of a human watchmaker. This fact limited the scope of the Christian Psychology work as a universal branch of church work. But there were hundreds of sufferers needing just such help as it gave. Three diseases out of every four, eminent doctors agreed, were not bodily and could be relieved by suggestion. Yet just these cases were shunned by both doctor and minister. Neither theological seminaries nor medical colleges offered adequate courses, at that time, to prepare any except neurologists to deal with them. But the neurologists were very few, the cases very many.

The Bishop widely extended the Christian Psychology movement through an association called the "League of Right Living." "A child of the Emmanuel Movement," one editor described the League, "but destined," he thought, "to outgrow its parent many times." Its object was to lessen the misery and increase the efficiency of the world. Its new contribution to the religious life of the time was this—to advance health and happiness by a scientific combination of psychology with piety.

The teachers who wrote for this course were the world's masters in the field. They were Dubois, of Berne; Janet, of Paris; Jastrow, of the University of Wisconsin; Angell, of

the University of Chicago; Royce, Putnam, Cabot and Southard, of Harvard; Peterson, Miller and Woodworth, of Columbia; Hinkle, of Cornell; Professor Batten, of the General
Theological Seminary; Professor Geer, of the Hartford
Theological Seminary; Professor Ayer, of the Philadelphia
Divinity School; and Professor Tolson, of the Pacific Theological Seminary. Men like Drs. Lloyd Tuckey and Milne
Bramwell, of London, and other specialists from the world's
most famous names were thrown in for good measure.

Bishop Fallows continued to carry his evangel of Health
and Happiness wherever he went. The movement, in general, did several permanent and important things. It aroused
doctors and ministers and the general public to the fact that
nerve victims were a social responsibility. As a result, many
theological seminaries provided psychological courses, and
medical colleges sent their graduates out better prepared to
cope with nervous patients. This widespread attention to ab-
normal nervous conditions also, indirectly, had a marked influence on the latter-day treatment of criminals and the whole
subject of reform. For the victims of nerves, themselves, the
Bishop's work and his book suggested a method of mental
hygiene and self-treatment as effective to-day as it was in
1908.

CHAPTER III

A GOLDEN WEDDING AND A VACATION

The next few years held two novelties for the Bishop. The first one was his Golden Wedding, in 1910, celebrated at his elder son's house, in Dobbs Ferry, with many old friends and new to make it merry. Even the yellow forsythia in the yard came out days ahead of time. Lucy Fallows, as on her wedding day, wore a gray bonnet trimmed with blue. Everybody that year was humming the Golden Wedding song, "Put on Your Old Gray Bonnet." The wedding guests sang it to the couple.

Before Dr. Huntington, their sons, daughters, "daughters-in-love," and the one granddaughter, Annette, the two promised once more to love and to cherish one another. Long since, Samuel Fallows, wise in human nature, had begun to omit from the marriage service the bride's promise to obey her husband. Years before, when Mr. Clark, now editor of the San Francisco *Chronicle,* came to him to be married to Miss Jenkins, daughter of his old Civil War friend, he said:

"Mr. Clark, I'm not going to put that 'obey' in the service. I've been married a great many years and I know it's no use."

From then on, he omitted the obsolete word, and when re-married himself, after fifty years, he saw to it that his Lucy did not promise to obey him, during the rest of their years together.

In 1913, the busy Bishop made a trip to the Philippines

with his son, Edward, his son's family and a party. This excursion to the East enlarged the geographical area of his experience by about twenty-one hundred miles; his social area by two civilizations—and the Philippines; his personal area by contacts enough to make his brain a portfolio of all the races.

CHAPTER IV

SANTA CLAUS AND SANDWICHES

By the things that people asked of him, you could see that the Bishop had now become a kind of Santa Claus for grownups.

One old lady from out of town asked him please to hunt her a room in his neighborhood, and to meet her at the train, because cities frightened her. A young lady wanted a piano. A dame of fashion desired a new hat. A worthy young farmer wished a position found for him, with short hours and little work. Wives were anxious to get helped away from their husbands and vice versa. His beloved Pontiac "graduates" were full of requests. The mother of a daughter bade him find a school for her daughter, who was a little difficult. The request of the mother of a son made him laugh until the tears came. This son caught cold easily, and he hated to wear an overcoat. Would the Bishop please make it his business to see that Dicky wore his overcoat whenever the thermometer dropped below fifty? Some people think there is no drama in a minister's life! Any member of the household on Monroe Street knew better.

Bishop Fallows came home about midnight, one zero night, and routed his housekeeper out of bed.

"Minnie," he said, "there's a gang of men at Western Avenue working on the Madison Street car tracks. If you'll make sandwiches and some coffee, I'll carry them out to the poor fellows. Keep them out of the saloons, you know."

Minnie complied, of course.

381

One night, a ministerial looking gentleman, wearing the look of a saint, Minnie said, called with a friend. The master of the house closed the front door behind them and came down the long hall with little explosions of laughter.

"Know who that was?" he asked Minnie, setting the table for breakfast.

"No, Bishop."

"Pat Crowe. Kidnaped the Cudahy child, you know. Picturesque rascal. He hid for months right here in Chicago. The police never found him. Wants to build a lodging house, now. Asked me for a recommendation."

"But could you give it, Bishop?" asked Minnie.

His answer held a whole philosophy of mercy. "Well," he hesitated, "well, I *could* say that he seemed to be a changed man, and I believed he meant well. Never kick a man when he is trying to reform, Minnie, never. It's a hard enough job at best."

One day a Black-Hand letter came through the mail, stating that unless the Bishop carried a large sum of money on a certain night to the Park and put it at the foot of the Lincoln statue, his life would not be safe. As Minnie remembered it, the threat was one of those blanket affairs which included the family and the house. Anyway, it was violent enough to make her feel that she might face a pistol whenever she opened the front door or receive dynamite in any back-door package.

Mrs. Fallows, fortunately, was in the East, which lessened her husband's anxiety at least ninety-five per cent, and increased Minnie's feeling of responsibility almost as much.

The evening after the letter was delivered the Bishop conducted a wedding on the far South Side, a very fashionable one, where the hats of the gentlemen guests were numerous enough to be checked, but not too carefully guarded—at least in the officiating clergyman's opinion. For when the last

THE UNVEILING OF THE GRANT MEMORIAL

Bishop Fallows presiding at the dedicatory exercises at Washington, D.C., April, 1922. From left to right: Confederate General Julian S. Carr; third from right, Vice President Calvin Coolidge; Colonel C. O. Sherrill; Bishop Fallows; Princess Cantacuzene; Secretary Weeks; General Pershing; Secretary Hughes in the background.

[See Page 420]

guest had departed, and he went to claim his hat, he found left, a headpiece like his own in shape, but broken, smudged and utterly disreputable. "The joke of a scamp!" he declared. He tied a handkerchief under his chin to keep his hair clean, set the hat on top of it, and departed as nearly wrathful as he could be.

Minnie and her husband were watching for him at the front window, tense with anxiety over the Black-Hand letter. Minnie spied the handkerchief almost before he was out of the cab, and had the front door open and the Bishop pulled into the safe hall in a twinkling.

"You're hurt, Bishop, you're hurt," she cried almost in hysterics.

He laughed. *"I'm* all right. But some scalawag stole my hat. Look at this," showing the wreck of a hat.

It was Minnie's turn to laugh.

"It's your own, Bishop. Your furnace hat. You took it by mistake. I tried to tell you when you started out, but you went too fast."

The Black-Hand episode had an equally happy ending. On the night appointed, a detective, smuggled surreptitiously into the Monroe Street house, emerged in one of the bishop's overcoats and the soft military hat—not the furnace one—which was part of his accepted uniform. The detective carried a dummy package to the Park and laid it at the foot of the Lincoln statue. No one took it, and nothing blew up. Mrs. Fallows never heard of the episode nor did anyone else for years afterwards, lest some way it might reach her ears.

The individuals in difficulties, like Pat Crowe and the wives and husbands and sons and daughters and mothers out of kilter with the world, Samuel Fallows settled in his odd moments, even to the mother whose baby had swallowed a button and wanted a remedy and the little boy whose dog was sick and who asked the Bishop to pray him well. He looked after them, as Santa Claus, with the happiness of a nation on his shoulders, might stop at the foot of a chimney to mend a broken toy.

The Semi-Centennial of Negro Freedom, for which as chairman the Bishop had worked three years was held at the Coliseum in 1915. It showed the progress of the colored race from the beginning to the present, with exhibits and pageants and entertainments on a heroic scale.

He was also the Grand Army Department Commander of Illinois in 1914 and 1915 and in that capacity traveled all over the state and visited posts and commanderies and soldiers' reunions of every kind—more, even, than usual. His vitality met every demand upon it. One night he walked off a stair landing in the dark, fell in a heap at the bottom of the long flight of steps and insisted on speaking the next day at a county fair ten or fifteen miles away!

He found time the year he was eighty, to give lectures on the Chautauqua circuit. He met, besides, all the usual church demands—the duties devolving upon him as Presiding Bishop and pastor, his obligations as member, executive or officer of the Y.M.C.A., the Y.W.C.A., the Central Howard Association, which looked after discharged prisoners, the Church Federation and the numberless other societies to which he gave allegiance.

A list of his engagements shows how completely he was entering into the different phases of Chicago's activity. He made addresses to the Life Underwriters, for example. He believed in Life Insurance and, as their Chaplain, told them so, year after year. When he died, with his other policies, he was carrying one for a thousand dollars which he took out for his bride when he went to the Civil War.

He talked to the schools. He made speeches to little circles of the Grand Army women and to big circles. Around that time, he was working to get a Sunday holiday for the members of the theatrical profession. He seemed to have more weddings and funerals than ever before. His sympathy knew no discrimination. He was as tender speaking at the funeral of a hodcarrier, in a Chicago tenement, as in conducting the funeral of Colonel Fred Grant, at West Point, in the presence of the nation's most noted men.

"A race man," his friend, Graham Taylor called him, "interpreting the common mind, giving as his Master did, a new currency of meaning to ordinary things."

CHAPTER V

LUCY FALLOWS GOES

At one of the pinnacles of his joy in life, Samuel Fallows sprang out of bed on December 13, 1915, with a song on his lips. It was the twenty-nine thousand and two hundredth time he had so sprung and so sung, deducting only the year of babyhood when he could neither leap nor sing.

Whatever the wear of the day might be, the night was always kind to him. Morning met him renewed, as ready for adventure as a schoolboy Columbus. But even at that, not every morning found him eighty years young and feeling like a two-year-old.

He splashed and sponged and rubbed to the hymn, "Come Thou Fount of Every Blessing" and pulled at his wall exerciser like a happy athlete. He shaved, as usual, made a speech to the flourish of his razor, and, tying the cord of his dressing gown, went springily down the long hall for his wife's birthday greeting.

Lucy Fallows was more exquisite than ever, just then, with the lamp of the spirit burning brighter and brighter behind the flesh. But she was frail. Her husband would not let her go down town alone, and he took her, himself, each month to the meeting of the Society of the Dames of the Loyal Legion, of which she was a charter member, and of which he was the Patron Saint. His care of her was so tender that the Dames, old friends all, wiped their eyes when the two were out of sight. The services at St. Paul's, Lucy Fallows never missed, but the walk down and back tired her now. House-

386

keeping was difficult. So her daughter Helen came home to take charge, with her husband, the Rev. E. S. Williams, of California, known lovingly up and down the whole Pacific coast as Everlasting Sunshine Williams. The dark months that followed were constantly lightened by his spirit of cheer.

Letters, telegrams, flowers and calls marked the eightieth birthday of the head of the house. Mr. McMahon, his baker and his friend, sent over the usual birthday cake. Lucy Fallows was smiling and loving and merry at the last birthday dinner she and her husband would have together.

Ten days afterward, in the midst of Christmas preparations, she was taken ill. She did not rally under the doctor's treatment. One morning Samuel Fallows made his supreme effort to draw back the wife who had walked beside him for fifty-five years. He went into his own room first and closed the door. He must have prayed, for his face shone so when he walked into the sick room and stood by the patient's bed.

"Lucy, my love," he said, "arise!"

Lucy, who was part of Samuel, as his soul was part of him, without whom he could never have been what he was—Lucy listened.

"Try, Lucy, try. Come, we will try together, as we have, dear, all our lives."

The alien note of agony in his voice was like a sharp knife turned in the hearts of his daughters and Mrs. Seaborne, the nurse.

He took her hands. "Try. Try."

All the strength that the unremitting years of service had left to Lucy Fallows sprang to obey the voice she had never refused. It was not enough. Halfway she rose and sank back.

"Thy will be done. Thy will be done," her husband murmured.

They knew, then, that they must ease the patient as gently as they could through the Valley of the Shadow, until it opened into light at the other end. Samuel Fallows, as a good soldier must, kept at his work and met his engagements, but with half his heart back there in the room where his wife lay.

In July of that year of 1916, Wilson sent the National Guard down to Mexico. The boys of the Second Regiment wanted Chaplain Fallows to go. But his wife was so deep in the Valley of the Shadow, then, he scarcely dared to slip away even to say good-by to the soldier boys who were like his sons.

On the last Sunday of the month, just at the hour when, for forty years of Sunday mornings, she had made her way to St. Paul's, Lucy Fallows' sweet spirit left her body for time and eternity.

"No black. No black," said her husband. He always raised his voice against crape and mourning, believing as he did that death is a step to life.

So Mrs. Seaborne dressed Lucy Fallows in her golden-wedding gown of white. Helen put a rose in her fingers. Only hands that loved her touched her who had been so loving. The case that held her like a precious treasure was of gray.

Until the day when they took her to the church of whose soul she was a part, as she was part of her husband's, she lay restfully in her own room. The last night, in the shaded light, with the electric fan rippling her soft hair, and the hint of a wild-rose flush in her cheek, she seemed just ready to wake. Samuel Fallows closed the door on all the rest and watched with her the whole night through.

CHAPTER VI

THE OLD ORDER CHANGETH

The soldier, still at battle, did not falter in his stride after Lucy Fallows was gone. But Sunshine Williams, who had never failed in the hour of need, had a collapse. His wife took him to Evanston for rest and quiet, and her sister took her place as housekeeper in the Monroe Street house.

Outwardly, her father was the same as always. He sang before breakfast and pulled his wall exerciser and came running downstairs in the morning with a joke on his lips. All day long, he went out inspiring people, returned for dinner just a little weary, slept for fifteen minutes, waked a rosy youth and started off buoyantly for his evening engagements.

Perhaps, his daughter thought, if a man keeps busy, busy, busy, he does not miss so much, after all, the wife he had loved for fifty years and more. He almost tricked her into believing his invariable cheerfulness was something he could not help.

One day she learned better. Sitting at the foot of the stairs, she was too weary to mount, playing with the little ring her mother had pulled so often to summon her father from his study, she heard him pacing the hall above, back and forth, back and forth. Suddenly he broke the silence with a cry:

"Lucy! Lucy! My love! My love!"

It was the cry of a man in mortal pain. His daughter stole out of the house softly, that her father might be alone in it, as he thought he was, carrying with her the knowledge that

389

he was a man as other men, full of grief, but practicing the principles of optimism he preached.

Difficult things came in a series, that year of 1916. Bishop Cheney, after a happy breakfast in comparatively good health, was suddenly gathered to his fathers. His old friend went white at the news. A man's fortitude is not invincible. It trembles, for a moment, when the associate of forty-five years goes out like a puffed candle. The loss weighted Samuel Fallows' heart and doubled his work. But work, to a warrior, is merely an opportunity, even at fourscore. Doing the big things and the little things that fell to his lot, he carried on.

Then 1917 moved swiftly on to its April sixth. Over the wires from Washington came the fateful news. War!

CHAPTER VII

MILITANT AND TRIUMPHANT

War once more possessed the land.

The veteran of the Civil War went to the recruiting station nearest his house as soon as it was opened.

"I want to enlist," he said.

"Age, Bishop?" asked the officer.

"Over twenty-one," came the answer, like a shot.

"Don't look it." The officer shook his head. "Can't accept you till you go home and ask your mother."

The would-be recruit entered into the joke, and drew out the little notebook he always carried in his pocket for easy reference. He turned to the statistics, so often quoted by him, on the ages of the soldiers in the Civil War, and to the page about the Battle of Gettysburg. So many thousands were under eighteen, under sixteen even, that it seemed as if the brunt of the battle must have been borne by lads.

"You see," said he, acting his part, "every boy counts one."

But the officer still shook his head.

For the first time in his life, this conqueror of age resented his years—eighty-two of them. They kept him away from France, out of the front-line trenches, where he would like to have struck blows for freedom beside his boys. Then he faced his age and the ills of the flesh. "Away with you. Begone!" he cried. "I'll do my full-time service at home for all of you. A hundred and twenty is the span of a man's life. What is eighty-two? Back, weakness; back, weariness. Back, foes, I say, back." He brandished the sword of the

391

spirit at them. That ancient weapon was as good as a modern machine gun. He never acted as if he were more than forty, the whole war through and no one ever seemed to remember that he was.

If a man for whom everybody has a use decides to accept every call for service, he can keep almost as busy as a regiment. Samuel Fallows did.

First, they asked for his help on Roosevelt Day. "Surely," was his answer. He and the Colonel had been friends ever since Edward, his son, Roosevelt's floor leader in the Assembly, during his Governorship, had introduced them in Albany. The two men had taken to each other like chemical affinities. Both of them believed the world was no fit place for anyone to live in until it was fit for everyone to live in, and both of them were ready to battle for it.

During Roosevelt's Presidency the fighting Bishop of the Mid-West had helped him wield his big stick with a will. He had thrown his influence against impure foods—modern Herods, he called the manufacturers of them. He had fought for the rights of children and better hours for women, and decent treatment for the laborer.

When the fight had been won at last, Roosevelt, talking with Raymond Robbins one day, banged down his Presidential fist on the desk.

"It's men like Bishop Fallows," he said, "who have made this legislation possible."

Bishop Fallows, remembering his many meetings with the Colonel, said again to the committeeman asking his help: "Surely."

He met the ex-President early in the morning at the station, marched in the parade, sat near him at luncheon and bandied words over the best way to break into this exclusive war. He helped the guests at the luncheon to pass resolutions asking Congress please to let the Colonel take over some men and fight the Germans. Through a Chicago gone wild with enthusiasm, he trailed Roosevelt, the tireless, all the afternoon.

At night, in the Stockyards Pavilion packed as full of humanity as a sardine can, the "General-Bishop" stood on the front row of the platform in his Civil War uniform and, for an hour before the Colonel arrived, like a cheer leader at football, helped the audience to sing war songs.

He opened the meeting with a three-minute prayer, thrilled to one of Roosevelt's greatest speeches and arrived home at midnight. After sixteen hours on duty, he turned to his daughter, sprightly as a small boy just waking up ready for breakfast, and said:

"Now, my dear, do you think we might have a little something to eat?"

Soon afterward Joffre and Viviani came to Chicago. Again the Committee on Arrangements said: "Bishop, can we depend on you?" Again he said, "You certainly can."

Only cripples and the inmates of the county jail stayed indoors when Joffre and Viviani came to town. Governor Lowden loosed all the military units to do them honor. Three hundred thousand school children were let out of school to see them. It was a high spot of the war when the Marshal of France and its Minister came to Chicago. The soul of the multitude was lifted into a superworld of emotion. The processions and receptions, the Auditorium meeting seemed held on another plane. At the Pavilion meeting, seventeen thousand gathered to greet the heroes of France. The multitude split the air with their cheering.

Samuel Fallows, on home duty, moved forward to give the invocation.

"At sight of the Civil War medals covering the Bishop's chest," a *Herald* reporter wrote, "the seventeen thousand let out another wild yell. It was a wonderful prayer—the choicest bit of inspired English during the whole two days. It was the keynote to which every listener was attuned. From the galleries came a resounding 'Amen!' Then the hall burst into cheers, applauding the invocation."

Very soon, the fighting Bishop was unofficially appointed Town Chaplain. The telephone hummed with requests: "Bishop, will you make a prayer for this? Will you pronounce the benediction for that? Will you speak for the other thing?" Always the conversation ended up: "Oh, Bishop, would you please wear your Civil War uniform?"

Before long, the occasions for acting as everybody's war spokesman became so frequent that they established themselves as part of the daily routine, like shaving or singing to the wall exerciser or morning postum or evening prayer.

The little book which held his engagements and the vest-pocket inch of pencil which recorded them were overworked. The precious engagement book, without which he would have been a rudderless ship, he carried always in his trousers' pocket.

"Why not in your coat pocket, Bishop?" his assistant asked, once, curiously. "You see," was the answer, "sometimes, Lepper, I change my coat. But I always keep my trousers on."

Any day that did not have its three or four speeches was a novelty. The home soldier spoke to everything and everybody. War was always his theme. He talked to white soldiers and colored soldiers, to native soldiers and foreign soldiers. He said good-by to the regiment of which he had been Chaplain so long, now the Hundred-and-Thirty-Second. He talked to mothers and fathers, to Church members and atheists, to Jews, Gentiles, Mohammedans, Czechoslovaks, Poles, Greeks, Turks—anybody and everybody.

He was on the committee for Save and Sow Sunday. Summoned by Hoover, he went to Washington to confer about

Food Conservation. He asked the divine blessing on every-thing from Taft and the Grain Dealers' Association and the Credit Men of the Nation, to the Expressman's Mutual Bene-fit Association and Alexander Hamilton, whose statue was unveiled in Grant Park. He rarely prayed more than five minutes. But he could not have packed more patriotism into an hour.

Edward, his elder son, rejected for active service because beyond the age limit, undertook at the request of the Lord Administration "to cover the country five feet deep with cocoanut oil" because of its fourteen per cent content of glycerine essential for munitions.

Charles, his younger son, living now in California, and quite above the draft age, said good-by to his wife and the babies and entered the first Officers' Training Camp possible. His father found it easier to fulfill his own commission in the Chicago trenches after all. He charged at the days with the zest of a general doing battle and he liked them full and difficult.

Slackers got no quarter from him. At a meeting, one night, where he was to make an invocation, he came up behind Mr. Thomas, of the Central Trust Company, who was on the committee of arrangements. Some one important to the pro-gram had failed him, and he turned the air blue telling what he thought about it. Looking back he saw Chaplain Fallows, and was covered with confusion.

"I beg your pardon, Bishop," he began.

"Say it again for me, Thomas," interrupted his friend. "Say it again for me," he chuckled. "The occasion demands it."

With the Kaiser gripping his teeth in the throat of the world, pacifists seemed to an ex-General about as effective as a regiment of muzzled bulldogs. Pacifists menaced the safety of the boys in the trenches. That he could not abide.

"The greatest pacifist," he said in an article for the Sunday *Herald* on "Is war ever justifiable?" "is the American soldier. He never creates war. Whenever he fights, he fights for peace. He is the man behind whom every pacifist would go on the double-quick for safety in time of danger. He is the embodied flag. He is the incarnate country. Multiply him. Honor him. This is not militarism. It is the truest patriotism.

So believing, he advocated universal military training and, summoned before a United States Senate committee, testified in its behalf.

As in the Civil War, the Chaplain in him never let him forget the welfare of the boys at the front. Whatever added to their comfort, he favored. With Evangeline Booth, one of his adopted daughters, he helped send over Salvation Army lads and lassies, to ease their lots, and the Y.M.C.A. boys, of course. A reformer, who ranked the unpardonable sin and cigarettes in the same class, heard that the Salvationists and the Y.M.C.A.'s were furnishing cigarettes to the soldiers.

"Bishop," she said, "*you* would never give cigarettes to the soldiers, would you?"

The proceeds from the sale of Samuel Fallows' "Story of the American Flag" were being applied, at that moment, to buy tobacco for the boys in France. He did not use it himself. He saved his tobacco money to buy books. He took the expensive cigars they pressed upon him at banquets and sent them, when he remembered about it, to his brother, Daniel, who usually complained that he had kept them so long they were spoiled. He never considered the use of tobacco a praiseworthy habit. But he looked at the lady reformer with wrath in his eye.

"Madam," he said, "if any soldier in France asked me for a cigarette, I'd give him one as big as a hose pipe if I could find it. You would, too, if you had the least iota of an idea what real war is like."

Perhaps some one might have invented a demand Samuel

Fallows would have refused. But it did not happen during the war.

One night at 2 A.M., a man's voice woke him to ask if he would marry, at 3 A.M., a soldier leaving immediately for the front.

"Certainly, certainly," promptly answered the Bishop, who had not done more than eighteen hours of work the day before.

He arose, and so did Buster, the pedigreed cat, successor to Dick; they waited down in the back parlor, and shivered and shivered and waited. No soldier and his bride appeared, so at five o'clock the two went back to bed again.

"Poor chap," was all the sleepy minister said. "Probably she wouldn't have him."

Some way, he found strength for every demand. No one applied for help or counsel and went away empty.

Between times, he even made a war garden in a corner of the back yard. "I cannot ask other people to do what I am too lazy to do myself," he said, as he turned the shovels of earth.

Just once, at the end of a week fairly barraged with speaking engagements and house calls, the beast of mortality which he was holding so well at bay caught him.

On Friday noon, he made an address to his University of Wisconsin boys at their regular weekly luncheon. His enthusiasm so gripped them that it pulled them out of their chairs a cheering mob. But, going home in the car, he was stricken. The conductor got him into a cab. The driver of it helped him up his own steps.

Mrs. Seaborne, friend and nurse, happened to be at the house. Her quick remedies and the grace of God pulled him back from the jaws of death.

"Dear me," he exclaimed, as soon as he was able to speak at all. "I really should remember that I must not eat when I am going to speak." What he had eaten at the luncheon

Tuesday, May 15th, I made a brief address before the men of the various Reformed Episcopal churches, held in Christ Church, Chicago.

Saturday, May 19th, I made a patriotic address before the Daughters of Veterans of Chicago.

Wednesday, May 23rd, I made the invocation at a great Red Cross meeting in the Auditorium, Chicago.

Thursday, May 24th, I made a patriotic address before the Mystic Athletic Club of Chicago, at the greeting of the volunteers of that organization in the service of their country.

Sunday, May 27th, I delivered the address on the dedication of the building of the Young Men's Christian Association at Fort Sheridan, where four thousand young men were training as officers of the new National Army.

Tuesday, May 29th, I delivered a Memorial Day address before the Association of Commerce of Chicago, which has enrolled more than four thousand members.

Wednesday, May 30th, I gave the Memorial Day address at Naperville, Ill., the heart of the great German Settlement of Du Page County of Illinois.

Saturday, June 2nd, I acted on the Reception Committee to greet the Italian Commission on their visit to Chicago.

June 6th-8th, I attended, as Past Department Commander for Illinois of the Grand Army of the Republic, its Annual Encampment at Bloomington, Ill., and made a patriotic address.

Friday, June 8th, I made a patriotic commencement address at the graduation of the pupils of the Morton High School at Cicero, Ill., composed largely of young people of foreign-born parents.

Sunday, June 10th, I preached the annual sermon before the Lawrence College at Appleton, Wis. In my early days I was a student at this institution, and afterwards its Professor-elect of Natural Sciences.

Monday, June 11th, I gave the invocation at the commencement exercises of the Kent College of Law, Chicago, where nearly two hundred young lawyers were graduated.

Thursday, June 14th, I made a patriotic address before the Men's Club of Trinity Reformed Episcopal Church, Chicago.

Friday, June 15th, I made an address at the Flag Day celebration in Washington Park, Chicago.

Tuesday, June 19th, I attended the commencement exercises of the University of Wisconsin, my Alma Mater, at Madison, and addressed its Alumni Association on the War.

Wednesday, June 20th, I addressed the State Encampment of the Grand Army of the Republic at Kenosha, Wisconsin.

Sunday, June 24th, I preached in St. Mark's Reformed Episcopal Church, Chicago.

Friday, June 29th, I met the survivors of the Thirty-second Wisconsin Regiment, Volunteer Infantry, in Oshkosh, Wis., and marked with an appropriate corner stone Camp Bragg, where we were mustered into the United States service fifty-five years before.

Wednesday, July 4th, I gave the Fourth of July oration at Ashland, Wis., on the shores of Lake Superior.

BISHOP FALLOW'S ENGAGEMENTS AT EIGHTY-TWO YEARS YOUNG

—*Chicago Evening Post*

ONE OF HIS LAST SERMONS

Bishop Fallows preaching to the noonday crowd from a ladder in
a Chicago Street.   [*See Page 415*]

was barely enough to satisfy a good-sized canary, but not for worlds would he have referred that collapse to fatigue.

On the following Sunday morning, a class was to be confirmed at Bishop Cheney's church. With all his war duties, the Presiding Bishop of the Church was still performing his regular church functions and because of the shortage of men, he was still carrying on his old friend's work, as well as his own.

Ten o'clock Sunday morning found him weak, but unshaken in his determination to preach and confirm the class. When the service was over and his work finished, the visiting Bishop had a faint spell in the vestry.

His daughter brought him home and put him to bed, with Mrs. Seaborne to watch him and Dr. White to lay down the law.

"Don't you know, Bishop," he said as severely as a jolly-faced man could, "that you never lose time sharpening saws? You are to stay here at least a week and sharpen saws."

But did he?

He was scheduled to give an invocation at some great war meeting the end of the week. Two days before, a reporter called up to inquire whether the Bishop would be able to attend the meeting.

"No, indeed," replied his daughter over the dining-room telephone. "He's in bed."

"Certainly I'll be there," boomed her father's voice through the bedroom telephone, always at his elbow.

He was. His doctor, with a stimulant in his pocket, and his daughter, with smelling salts in her hand, sat behind him.

But as the Prophets of old called down fire from heaven, so did their patient seem to call down strength. Tottery and feeble an hour before, with nothing but an eighty-two-year-old body and God to sustain him, he lifted up that audience to the Throne of Grace as strongly as if he had been a young Methodist minister of twenty.

CHAPTER VIII

A SHIFT OF BASE

When the laundress, the housekeeper and the faithful tender of the Fallows' furnace all served notice within twenty-four hours that they were giving up their present occupations for war work, the rest of the household, in that time of labor scarcity, were left with no alternative except to move into an apartment for the Winter.

They found one on Adams Street, just off Ashland Boulevard, which, all told, would have fitted nicely into the two parlors of the Monroe Street house. With the apartment furnished and the stripped house barely habitable, its master lingered there on any pretext. Better wait for the move until he was a little freer! There was so much four-minute speaking to do! New nations, too, were getting themselves born almost at the rate of one a day—twenty-one or so of them. No celebration of a nation's birth by its Chicago subjects seemed to be quite complete unless he took part in it. The smallest excuse sufficed for delay.

His daughter contracted flu and forced the move or they might never have gone, but the farewell to the old house was a solemn occasion.

Foch, obliged to cut himself loose from all his food supply and march with an army into the wilderness, would have known how Samuel Fallows felt the day he moved from his base of over a quarter of a century. He bounded up to his third-floor study.

Three or four thousand books, nearly a ton of sermons

400

and addresses, manuscripts of books, old newspapers, letters by the thousand crowded the upper story to the last inch. Even the halls were filled with shelves of books from top to bottom. He had no catalogue of his books. But he could go up and put his hand on the book he wanted in the dark.

"A general scholar," Graham Taylor called him once. He would have thought so if he could have seen that library. Everything on every subject in the world seemed to be in that library.

His daughter heard him come downstairs and go into her mother's room. Through the window, she saw the remains of his war garden, the withered potato plants, discouraged by the soil and the smoke. Then he was beside her in the back parlor, his stage, his confessional, his battle ground, his human laboratory where he made lives over.

She ached to see the unaccustomed droop of his shoulders, as he looked over the two bare rooms.

"I feel," he quoted,

> " 'Like one
> Who treads alone
> Some banquet hall deserted,
> Whose lights are fled,
> Whose garlands dead,
> And all but he departed.' "

At the apartment, he surveyed his new quarters. Spatially, they were not quite so ample as the log cabin which was his first home in America. He looked at the bedrooms, the kitchenette, the dining room. Then he stood in the middle of the living room floor.

"I don't know," he reflected, "that you would have room to swing a cat around here." He glanced affectionately at Buster, who was smelling over every object with his little pink nose. "But then," he added cheerfully, "I don't know that you'd *want* to swing a cat around."

So, expressing his beautiful philosophy of adaptability, he settled himself at his desk in his sunny bedroom. Buster curled up beside him, and life went on into another velvet year.

CHAPTER IX

TAFT AND THE EMPTY HOUSE

When the paper boys, almost the day after the move to the apartment, shouted the great news of the Armistice under Samuel Fallows' windows, he sprang out of his bed, sang the Doxology to Buster, curled up at the foot of it, put out his big flag and went forth into the madness and gladness of that day.

At noon, with other men who had been carrying heavy war burdens in Chicago, he met Taft at luncheon. In the supreme exultation of the moment, he patted his old friend gently on the shoulder:

"Our next President!" he said.

Taft shook his head. "No, no," he replied, "there are three bills that never come back—Bill Hohenzollern, Bill Bryan and Bill Taft."

After lunch, through crowded streets, Taft and he started in an auto for the Coliseum where they were both to speak.

Chief Justice Taft, occupying a spindle-legged sofa with the safe bravado of a man who has learned to eat and grow thin, described the incident, long afterward, in his Washington house.

"We would move a foot and stop," he said, "then another foot and stop. We sat with our watches in our hands and fidgeted. We liked to be prompt, both of us. We pictured that great audience waiting. Ten thousand, at least, would be there, they told us.

"Finally, we reached the Coliseum and hustled ourselves
403

into the back door and onto the stage, ready for the roar of the multitude.

"There were three people in that vast building, I think. Otherwise it was empty as a church belfry. The Bishop and I were accustomed to speaking to audiences—audiences, you know," said Taft, with the chuckle which would make a morgue seem cheerful. "I looked at him and he looked at me and then we both laughed and laughed and laughed."

When Samuel Fallows reached home for dinner that night, he laughed again, over the incident. It was easy to laugh on Armistice Day.

Then the telephone, always beside him as he ate, tinkled softly. Over its wire came a message from California, that Helen's Sunshine Williams had been gathered that day to his Fathers. Because his life had been so rounded and blessed and cheerful, it seemed to fit the victorious spirit of Armistice Day that this happy soul had been borne out on the wings of the great peace.

In the streets again, after dinner, Samuel Fallows worked his slow way through the throng, gone mad with joy, west a mile to the old home ground of thirty-five years. On Madison Street, at Oakley, a block or so from the Monroe Street house, the mob stopped him, lifted him to a soap box and demanded a speech. His shoemaker friend across the street, who loved him, saw it as a picture:

"The crowd lapped up against the Bishop like a sea. He stood above them and talked. His face was so joyful that it shone like a lamp, and the people looked up at him as they would at a saint."

So ended the World War in the thirteenth of his seventeen velvet years.

CHAPTER X

WE THAT ARE STRONG

Samuel Fallows and Chicago accomplished their swing from war psychology to peace psychology together at a Coliseum meeting, held ten days after the mad jubilee of the Armistice celebration. This was the city's reverent pæan of victory, set to superbly ordered music and oratory which lifted the assembled ten thousand cheering to their feet.

That night, the Chaplain of the meeting reached the hall on time, through orderly streets, in company with Governor Lowden; Samuel Insull, Chairman of the meeting and of the State Council of Defense; Clarence Darrow and General Barry—escorted by a thousand bluejackets from the Great Lakes and the Eleventh Illinois Infantry.

"Bishop Samuel Fallows," the *Tribune* said, "struck the note of the evening in his invocation. He returned thanks for the victory past, and prayed for help with the problems to come."

"Let us," he said also, "give our enemies the food they plead for, that they may have strength to pay to the last farthing the indebtedness to the ravished countries they have desolated."

"The problems to come!" The man who had lived through three wars and almost three-quarters of a century of America in the making watched with fixed attention the "calling of the Nations"—a feature of the program. Forty-three nations responded, all in Chicago's melting pot, each represented by its ancient or its present flag, carried by a color guard in national uniform or costume. When all the flags were grouped in front of the speaker's stand, they were exchanged for the Stars and Stripes.

In the tiny hallway of the apartment, late that night, he hung up his hat and coat thoughtfully.

"Forty-three nations in Chicago," he mused. "Their problems. Our problems. The problems of reconstruction. The world problems."

"Oh," he exclaimed. "What a glorious time to be alive and at work!"

From then on, he shouldered his part of the work of peace, alongside of the men in Chicago who were doing heavy work.

He swung high on the trapeze of hope over the League of Nations. He fought for it and talked for it and landed with a dull thud against reality at its failure. He saw the hash that post-war selfishness was making of soldiers' lives, and lifted his voice against it. But in the welter that events made of everybody's dreams, his faith in the ultimate righting of a crazy world stood like a rock. He had seen the horror of reconstruction before.

Peace times were as full of duties as were war times, but set to pleasanter tunes. His zest in meeting them was unabated.

Like the big house on Monroe Street, the little apartment up one flight at 1618 Adams Street, became the focus of unnumbered trails of want. Little shoes, big shoes, shiny shoes, shabby shoes, pompous shoes, humble shoes, all the kinds of shoes society makes marched up the steps.

After two days of work which should have put a Bishop of eighty-four to bed for a week, "I do not feel the slightest fatigue," he wrote his son, Edward. On Mercier Day, he told him he had six engagements, two of them concerned with his Eminence. The evening banquet consummated a pleasant incident of the war.

When Mercier, standing against Germany, had been held

practically a prisoner in Germany, Samuel Fallows had been moved to write a blazing letter of protest for the Chicago *Herald*. The letter, also a warm appreciation of the great Prelate, was copied into most of the Catholic papers of the country. Reprinted and sold at the Allied Bazaar, it did its financial bit for the Cardinal Mercier fund. In time, a cordial letter of thanks, written at the Cardinal's dictation, slipped by the censors and reached the Presiding Bishop of the Reformed Episcopal Church.

At the banquet, on the night of Mercier Day, his Eminence personally thanked his Chicago defender and added that his letter was preserved in the Archives at Malines, testimony of the hopeful fact that enthusiasms for humanity know neither nations nor creed.

Before Bishop Fallows called his day's work complete, another incident, not officially recorded, was to prove that his sympathy knew neither high nor low. At home, that night after the long hours on duty, he slipped into a bath robe, piled up the pillows at the foot of his bed and prepared for the luxurious half-hour of a mystery tale which should wind down the tension of the day.

The telephone rang.

Somebody, a woman, wanted the Bishop to come over to the Cook County Hospital at once to see her dying husband.

"Do I know your husband?" he asked gently.

"No."

"Or you?"

"No."

"I've had rather a long day. Would any other minister do?"

"Please, no. Just you."

"Very well, I'll be over at once."

His daughter spoke. "One o'clock! Daddy, *beloved*, you *aren't* going."

Her father said, sometimes, but purely in fun, that it was

the age of obedient parents, also even more jokingly that he was the Bishop, but his daughter was the Archbishop.

The Bishop now began to put on his outside clothes and the Archbishop stood helpless.

"She wants me," said her father, simply.

His daughter looked at him, shining with the same radiance she had seen in the Cardinal's face, earlier. She thought of the Scotchwoman sending for Henry Drummond under similar conditions, another unknown woman she was, with an unknown husband. "But I'd like the feel of ye aboot him, while he's deeing," was the excuse to Drummond. The poor wife at the County Hospital meant the same thing, but she said it in American.

Going out the front door coated and hatted, Samuel Fallows turned back and spoke to his daughter, much concerned about him.

"We that are strong, you know," he said, "must bear the infirmities of the weak."

PART X

HE GOES SINGING O'ER THE HILL

CHAPTER I

The Winter Samuel Fallows was eighty-five his daughter suggested that he should take a vacation in the South.

"Vacation?" he looked at her blankly. "With all the things there are to do in Chicago? I'm perfectly well. What fun would a vacation be?"

"But at eighty-five!" she said.

"My dear," he said, *"can't* you understand that the older a man grows the more he has to do, and the greater his responsibilities are?"

With such a guiding notion, his days were as full of delightful projects as a juggler's hat is full of surprises. Face forward, he filled all his old rôles and played in any new one that came along.

One day a reporter asked him to turn the clock back. This champion of causes with his flashing blue eyes and black hair only tinged with gray, comrade to everyone who called, had had to fight every inch of the way up. Life had lashed at him. Disappointments had tried to hold him in traps. At eighty-five, how did he feel about it all?

The newspaper man had his group of questions:

If you suddenly became a boy—once more—
If through some miracle you were given your life to live again—
What would you do?
Would you follow the same life work? Or would you
411

really act upon the feeling so many have that "any other work would have been better"?

Some of those things you did that stand out like milestones, —big mistakes, and big achievements—would you do the same things again if you could do them over?

"Would you be a minister again?" the reporter asked.

"Yes, by all means, yes," he said, sixty-five years a preacher of the Gospel. "There are no financial rewards. The sacrifices for a man and his family are countless. But the rewards are as great. At every point I have done the best I could and I am satisfied. If I were to live my life again there is not one of the important milestones I would change."

Full of youth, he called to youth; and the younger generation answered. They never could fool him with anything they put on their faces out of boxes and bottles and tubes. Nor with anything they wore. Nor with anything they said out of their scientific young heads. He knew them for what they were, specimens of the same old human nature that began in the Garden of Eden. Human nature loves and hates and works and tires and is sad and glad in the given vocabulary of a given time. But what it always seeks is happiness.

Bishop Fallows had the secret of it. He had something that kept him young as a boy at eighty-five. So, like their grandparents and their parents before them, the younger generation took to their hearts this man who held life's choicest secret. He saw through them with such kindly eyes!

A one-way reformer who could look only backward irritated him very much, one day. She portrayed the young people of the present as black little monsters, until his patience was gone.

"Madam," said he at last, "call *us* the names. We made them and the world they live in."

A paper asked him for an interview on good roads.

"Certainly we need good roads," he said. "They promote courtship. A bad road discourages a young man. Good roads by all means."

His opinion was only half facetious. He liked to get young people together to do the business of life. He knew the interview would go all over the country. He hoped it would start some of the bashful ones thinking.

When Jessie Shepherd, President of the Chicago Wisconsin Alumnæ, asked him to talk to her girls, he gave them a talk about love, so charming that they felt they should find bridegrooms at once and apply to their Bishop to marry them.

One morning he came away from the telephone with his face broken into little crinkles of love and humor.

"A flapper!" said he to his daughter. "The paper wants me to define a flapper. Now what *is* a flapper? Buster, what *is* a flapper?" he asked of the gold-and-white Persian cat occupying three-quarters of his desk. He thought a moment or two.

"She's short-skirted, of course, with dancing feet and dancing eyes, bless her. She's about five feet of vital youth, I should say, done into the latest fashion of the hour."

How he did rejoice in the little flapper! Alice Bemis H'Doubler, one of his Wisconsin daughters who sat near him often on the Commencement platform, said that he smiled a little when the young men graduates passed by him, but he patted his hands softly for every girl graduate. Perhaps he was thinking of their flapper grandmothers and the early seventies when he and Webster's "Unabridged" won their fight for degrees with the President who refused to call a young lady a Bachelor of anything.

At his Wisconsin Commencement, in 1921, he told the flapper graduates that he liked their short skirts.

"Women are not growing less moral," he said. "They are just beginning to enjoy their privileges. The short skirt is no lowering of standard." He chuckled at that because the thing he was talking about was rising so fast. He had always hated the germ-gathering length of other days. "It is making the world a better place to live in," he declared.

The news went all over the United States. "Bishop Fallows Approves of Short Skirts."

"A few million Americans will not agree with him, that short skirts show the world is getting better," said one Duluth editor. "He is the antithesis of Voliva and Dowie trying to dominate the world by their rule of thumb. Insensate crying down of short skirts is but a form of intolerance. Bishop Fallows has made a courageous protest."

Now, with grandmother and granddaughter indistinguishable and the long skirt extinct, it seems impossible that the world took them so seriously in 1921.

With his happy faculty for taking only serious things seriously, he never found fault with the clothes of the younger generation, their cosmetics or their slang. What they took out of hip-pocket flasks was a different matter. As a man conserving the interests of the race, he did not approve of it at all. He told them why, when he had a chance. "The world of to-morrow is yours," he said. "The life of the race is in your keeping. You will bear it with your bodies. Can't you keep poison out of them? Can't you make them fine and strong for a task like that?"

He told the Illinois Dental College students what he, at his age, thought was worth while for them to do at their age. He talked to the Lewis Institute soldier students. He shared in the merriment of a merry party on Armistice night, so very merry that Colonel McCloskey, who had a serious speech to make after midnight on the meaning of Armistice Day, wondered how the noisy, thoughtless mob could ever be made to listen. Even he who knew the power of personality so well marveled at what happened. "On the stroke of the hour," he said, "the Bishop stood up on the platform and

BISHOP FALLOWS' FUNERAL

stretched out his hand over them, merely stretched out his hand. The shouting, dancing throng stood quiet, and in five minutes he prayed them into a sober company ready to remember the boys who had died to give them Armistice Day."

Very kind was the God of Fulfillment to His follower during those, the last, of his velvet years. They were a time of finishing patterns long since begun. Interest after interest was rounded to completeness. St. Paul's presented him with a birthday flag in the presence of the soldiers of the three wars in which he had worked for the flag. In the Summer of 1921, thirty years after this pioneer of the social gospel had carried his pulpit into the market place, he preached from a ladder at noonday in one of the most crowded streets of Chicago.

His liberality and plasticity seemed to make him a universal man who belonged to everybody in particular.

The Millennialists who believed in the Second Coming of Christ said, "He is one of us."

Spiritualists declared, "He is really a Spiritualist! but it would not be wise for him to say so." Once he preached a series of sermons on "Immortalism." An English paper reported that he had started a new cult which was spiritualism with the curse left out.

"Bishop Fallows at heart is a Christian Scientist," said some followers of that religion, and read his critical and Biblical Encyclopedia.

The Jew said: "He is ours."

His friend, Governor O'Hara, said: "I suppose he belonged to some denomination, but I never knew what it was."

Fundamentalists, not then so named, declared: "He is in our ranks, of course." Modernists claimed him as well.

Frank Hall, when he was asked which camp his friend would have joined, smiled wisely: "He would have waved his long-fingered hand and said: 'None of these things move me!' Religion was what he preached, not the chatter about religion."

A Chicago editor's estimate bore out that opinion. "He was the unofficial Chaplain for thousands of us," he wrote after his death, "the shepherd of our souls. He never preached religion to us. He lived it."

In the Fall of 1921, he spoke before the Dill Pickles, a club of young radicals in Chicago, famous for its soft collars, its hard thinking and free speaking. His subject was the Ku Klux Klan, just coming to the fore again. As he had fought it after the Civil War, he hammered at it now with all the force of his eloquence. He admitted that the intention of its members might be good. But their methods he could not abide.

"If American life has grown so morally desperate," he said, "that violators of the law must have secret warnings and night visits by shrouded men; if the courts have become so impotent that a secret society must try offenders, then God help this country. The Ku Klux Klan is the greatest disintegrating force in the country to-day. It is unworthy of America."

1922, the last of this pilgrim's adventurous years, found him, eyes front, full of plans and the expectancy of life. With his ever recurring interest in teaching the power of the mind over the body, he gave the twentieth-century version of it in lectures at the Training School for Home Nursing, conducted by Dr. John Dill Robertson, Health Commissioner.

Work for the Grant Memorial kept him busiest. Started seventeen years before by General Dodge, this tribute of the Army of the Tennessee to its Commander was to be dedicated in April. Succeeding to the Presidency of the Army after the death of General Dodge, a few years before, General Fallows, with the Commission, had had the task of bringing the project to completion. In connection with the final preparations, he went to Washington between Sundays, as he might commute to Evanston.

On those Washington visits, he left an impression behind him, of deathless youth and vigor. "All fire," said Col. C. O. Sherrill, executive officer of the Grant Memorial Commission, after watching him win Secretary Weeks, Senator Brandegee and the Grand Army of the Republic Committee to a plan of having Confederate representation at the dedication of the Grant Memorial set for April twenty-seventh, in Washington.

I should like to make this mean a new union of the North and South," said Bishop-General Fallows. Harding remembered him as the youngest and most joyous person who visited him in those days; Pershing as a "Warrior-Saint."

Reaching Washington in the early morning, the President of the Commission would fly about from engagement to engagement all day and take the night train for Chicago.

"Aren't you tired out, Bishop?" asked Colonel McElroy, editor of the *National Tribune,* late one afternoon.

"This isn't a very lively gait for a man eighty-six years young," was the laughing reply. *"Pax vobiscum."*

Off he tramped to see his friend, Commissioner Gardner, at the Pension Office. Joe, the gray-haired office boy who had chaperoned the Pension Office for thirty-four years, looked at his feet. The day was damp. "You ought to have your rubbers on, Bishop," he said. "The moisture will go into your body."

"Oh, it doesn't hurt a seasoned old fellow like me," said the old campaigner.

"Whenever he came in," said Joe, his old friend, "he brought the sunshine with him—a flood of it. When he shook hands, he shook hands with his whole heart. Yes, sir, he did."

One morning, for the thirty-seven thousandth seven hundred and fortieth time, or thereabouts, he pulled his exerciser and sang his morning tune.

The day was cold and windy, with a rain which became icy sleet by night. The Bishop had promised to speak at a negro meeting away off somewhere. No taxi was available. So he took his pet umbrella, which hooked over his arm, and went out into the wild blowy night.

"He ought not to have gone," said Louise, from Nottingham, faithful keeper of the household, shaking her head.

"No," agreed his daughter. Buster blinked his protest.

He came home very late—without his umbrella, and shivery.

By the next morning he was in the grip of flu and afire with fever. It was a bad case. Everybody, too, had requests to make of the patient, sick as he was.

"Try Biloxi, Mississippi," ordered his doctor.

The Southern sunshine helped. But the after-flu weakness persisted. Business about the Grant Memorial followed him, even down there. Could a man of eighty-six, his daughter wondered, gather himself, after such an illness, and preside so soon at that great affair. A man of twenty would find it almost impossible.

But the spirit of youth was still in his veins. On the way back to Chicago, he and his daughter planned a Summer trip to California. The venerable play boy had always delighted in motoring.

"We will buy a little Ford," he dreamed, with his daughter, "as soon as we get to California and ride and ride wherever we please!"

His doctor looked him over in Chicago. It was only a few days before April twenty-seventh.

"I wish the Bishop didn't have that Grant Memorial," said he. Knowing the mind of his patient: "You can't ask a General to desert his army," he added.

With everything packed and the taxi ordered, on the very

last morning, the patient had flu symptoms again, and temperature.

"Keep him in Chicago, if you can," was the doctor's advice, over the telephone. "If not, save him as much as possible."

"Shall I telegraph to Washington that you won't go?" his daughter ventured to ask him.

"Telegraph? Not go?" He looked at her in amazement. "Fail them? I? What can you be thinking of? Telegraph that we will arrive on the train arranged."

Then he got up and dressed and once more received the marvelous accession of strength which had never failed him in any great crisis of his life.

A beautiful place for finishing patterns was Washington in April, 1922, at its symphony moment of Spring. The days before the Memorial were a round of joy. The New Ebbitt lobby was full of friends, veteran boys from all over the country whom he had known as Chaplain and Lieutenant Colonel and Colonel, the widows of Generals, the Dames of the Loyal Legion. He had luncheon with his old friend, Mrs. Fred Grant, and her daughter, the Princess Cantacuzene. He went to Mrs. General Logan's reception. His church was with him in the person of Bishop Robert Rudolph, on whom his mantle as Presiding Bishop was so soon to fall. Dr. William Huntington, President Emeritus of Boston University, was in Washington to remind his brother-in-law of the old, old days at Cedar Bluffs. Edward, his son, was there with his wife Julia and his daughter Annette. Meetings, dinners, receptions were merely a roll call of friends. For him, an internationalist now, neighbor to every nation, comrade to all the world, friendships widened like concentric circles. At the center of his new patriotism was loyalty to America. At the center of his universal friendliness was loyalty to all his old associations.

Spare him! His daughter tried in vain. Buoyed up by determination, he came to April twenty-seventh, that proudest of all days for the Army of the Tennessee, when the Memorial for their beloved Commander was complete.

That afternoon, in a corner of the Botanical Gardens, the "General-Bishop" reviewed ten thousand soldiers of three wars, led by General Clem.

Later, presiding at the great Memorial gathering, over Coolidge's head and past Dr. Huntington's kind face, he beamed at General Julian Carr, Confederate, sitting on the front row of the platform to make his speech. Sheer will was driving his body that day. But there was no falter in his voice through the long exercises. For him this was more than the unveiling of a Memorial. It was the new union of the North and South. It was the fulfillment of one of his most persistent dreams.

A month later, he was summoned to Washington to serve as Chaplain at the dedication of the Lincoln Memorial. That unforgettable May day rounded out his life as a soldier and a patriot. He had next to finish the life of the Great Liberal who dwelt within him. June saw him do that, when he went to his last Commencement at the University of Wisconsin.

He made all his usual ports of call: on Mrs. Fairchild, widow of the Governor; Judge and Mrs. Burr Jones; Professor Parkinson, who was in college with him. He marched in the Alumni procession, looking like a prophet at play, said Professor Parkinson's daughter. There he spoke for the last time at the Commencement of 1922, to defend his Alma Mater attacked for its progressivism.

"The teaching of this University," said the man who had known it for sixty-eight years, "is and has been from the beginning such that the pursuit of science has meant the glory of God and the relief of man's estate."

Commencement over, still charged with the spirit of youth, he ended his duties as churchman with an ordination of a young friend at Mr. E. J. Sonne's church, also full of the spirit of growth.

Then, at last, he was ready for a real vacation. No work! Just rest and play! So to California he went.

It started off gloriously, that vacation, at Three Oaks, lovely dream spot of the Saratoga Valley, home of his younger son. There the eighty-six-year-old play boy had the treat of a lifetime. A letter from his "daughter-in-love," Eda, tells the story.

In the village one afternoon, "Grandpa Biffet" found a circus,—by courtesy, in a vacant lot off the highway, made up of a father, mother, several children, a tamish wild cat, two dogs and six cute little Shetland ponies. At the moment it was a circus in process, but a grand performance was set for the evening.

He insisted on taking the whole family. You can imagine what the poor little third-rate entertainment was like with the mangy wild cat and sleight of hand tricks even Pats could see through, a sad Punch and Judy show, and the spiritless children on the Shetland ponies which really were cute.

We sat on six-inch planks,—the family, a lot of blasé little boys who knew a real circus when they saw it, and a few others. After every feature, Daddy led and exhorted the applause as if it were a Methodist camp meeting.

At the end he went down and congratulated the performers personally, on their splendid performance. You know how he made them feel, as if no four ring circus in existence could hope to be in the same class with them.

On the way home, with his voice much more eager than any little boy's, he said:

"Great show. Great show. I broke a fifty years' fast from circuses on that splendid entertainment to-night."

After this indulgence, the vacationist grew serious. One morning he was caught selecting books to take with him on a trip to Carmel.

He held up a treatise on geology.

"A very interesting science," he said. "I've never had much time to look into it. I think I'll just take this book along."

His son threw up his hands:

"Dad, dad!" he said, "don't you even know a vacation when you're in it?"

In spite of the loving care of his daughter, Helen, Carmel the beautiful, held menace for her father. After two weeks there, his other daughter found him very happy, but very white. He panted going up the little slope to the library where the librarian, as in Chicago, saved for him all her best mystery tales. When he went out after supper with his little granddaughters, "Queen Bess" and "Princess Pat," to feed the small dog the trio loved, he came back spent.

So they took him up to San Francisco. "Quiet!" said the doctor.

"Can't we go to Chicago—to-day?" It was the patient's eager question every morning.

The doctor shook his professional head, but spoke out of the soul of his understanding:

"If you do not take him to Chicago, I am afraid you will regret it all your life."

The great railroad strike was on. At any moment, on any road between San Francisco and Chicago, any train in the middle of the desert, wherever it was, might have its wheels stopped dead.

But that haunting question!

"Can't we go to Chicago—to-day?" His children took the risk.

CHAPTER II

HIS WESTMINSTER

The brazen night closed down over Chicago and the traveler back in the little apartment. Morning came with a blaze of heat. After a day or two, a reporter made the news of his illness public property. Then the doorbell and the muffled 'phone were never still. All the people who loved him and needed him were calling or asking for more news than the papers gave. A veteran editor said, over the wire, with a voice that broke, "All the world wants to know how Bishop Fallows is. We need him."

The city turned the traffic away from the block on which his windows faced. Outside, at the entrance to the house, a man sat all day and far into the night watching. Years before, he had come out of the hospital weak and sick. "The first person I met," he explained to anyone who would listen, "was the Bishop. He said, 'What's the matter? What's the matter?' that cheery way he had. Well, I told him I was sick and broke.

"He said a lot of things to brace me up. Then he felt around in his pocket and fished out a silver dollar. I sort of thought he didn't have many of them, himself, just then.

"He looked at it kind of lovingly. 'Guess you need it more than I do,' says he. 'Go along now and get a shave and a hair cut and something to eat.' You could do it all for a dollar, then. 'Don't forget to hold your head up and look the world in the eye.' Then he was off down the street, on the sunny side of it, walking on the soft ground like he always did.   And say, that silver dollar turned my luck and it's stayed turned ever since.

"No, sir, you know the world can't spare that man.   He *has* to get well."

So his ministers felt and spoke to him of the Golden Jubilee of the Church, due in a few months.   "I believe he will be with us again," reported Dr. Ochsner to the Wisconsin boys, after a call on his old friend.

But those closest to the patient felt him slipping, slipping, day by day, back into the inner fastnesses where the spirit makes its last stand.

They tried to anchor him to the present with little things, the gifts overflowing the apartment—flowers, fruit.   Buster's happy days had rounded to a close while his master was away.   So they carried in, each morning, the janitor's gray kitten for his long kind fingers to caress.   Mrs. Deach tugged down in a basket, Renée, her soft shaggy Angora, next best to Buster.   Buster's master smiled at Renée sitting on Buster's blotter and waving her tail.

But the little things were not enough to hold a spirit setting sail.

Once he heard the muffled telephone.   "What is it?" he asked.

"Some one wanting your views on the Ku Klux Klan," explained his daughter.

"What did you say?" breathed her father.

"That you would answer when you were well."

His mind looked at her out of his eyes, clear, but an æon away from the Ku Klux Klan.   Not important things, either, could delay him, homeward bound.   But his heart beat warm for those he was leaving.   He sent his love to his children, East and West, to his St. Paul's family of forty-seven years, by his assistant the Rev. John Foster, to his comrades.

Each day found him a little weaker.

"Bishop," said his doctor.   "Never have I known you to

throw down your weapons. Aren't there things you still must do?"

His patient shook his head.

"The Bishop is using every ounce of his magnificent vitality just to keep alive," he said to those outside. They understood why. His son, Edward, was speeding to Chicago, and his father knew it. The next morning he arrived.

"There is just a chance for father," his sister told him. Longing for his parting benediction: "We must talk only of life and happy things," they decided.

So, sitting by his father's bed, his son recalled the time when he was taken to a big soldiers' meeting and laughed out loud and clear in the middle of his father's prayer. The patient's eyes, for an instant then, had their delightful impish flicker, and again, when he was told about the taxi driver of the morning, stopped at Ashland Boulevard by the guard who turned the traffic from Adams Street. "My father is ill," his passenger explained.

"Must be very notorious," said the driver. "Who is he?" Edward told him. "Oh, yes," he replied, "he *is* notorious."

Trying to lure him back to the ways of mortality, his son planned another rainbow trip to the Philippines. Would his father go? Speech was too difficult. But Samuel Fallows, Columbus of the spirit, said "yes," with a pressure of his sensitive hand, and his face lit up with a last gleam of his love of adventure.

His flame of life, under the stimulus of the visit, flickered up again, so that it seemed safe for his son to take a three-days' trip to New York.

They persuaded the patient to take a grape or two sent by one of his Wisconsin boys, Israel Shrimski. "Israel, Israel, my son Israel," he whispered as if he were speaking of the whole human race which he loved.

That very afternoon a change took place. The infinite reached into the finite for a soul. The still figure on the bed, in the little room in the little apartment on the West Side of Chicago, wore the look of Elijah when he felt himself called of God.

"So many people need you," begged his daughter in a last plea. "Won't you help us hold you?"

He shook his head.

Once, his daughter Helen asked him what he would do when he took the next step.

"I will explore the universe," he answered.

He could not speak, but his triumphant eyes told the same message now.

"My earthly work is over," he seemed to say. "My work is over."

And the next day at dawn it was.

Samuel Fallows, with a guard of soldiers at his head and feet, in his Bishop's robe, the military medals on his breast, lay in state in the church he had built. It was draped with flags and hung with purple. Black could have no place there. All the morning the stream of people, high and low, rich and poor, came and went.

In the afternoon, at the last service, the church was crowded to its last inch of space with the people who loved him. The congregation sang triumphant hymns. President Birge of Wisconsin, Bishop Rudolph, Bishop Brewing, and the assisting ministers sounded the note of hope. "It does not seem like death but like a coronation," said one to another.

Before the funeral procession, the city the happy warrior loved cleared the way to the cemetery. There the Church held its last services. There his colored brethren sang. There, at length, the veterans of the Civil War, after their ritual, sounded "Taps."

" 'Lights are out—the soldier sleeps.' Taps of the Finite—

Reveille of the Infinite; an Invitation to God's eternal camping ground."

The papers of the country carried accounts of Samuel Fallows' life. Men high in Church and State voiced their tributes. Societies and institutions, by the score, which he had founded and helped, expressed their sorrow. So full of love were the letters and the resolutions that they seemed to make a new vocabulary of sympathy.

But not all of them together were more eloquent than a little Jewish ragman out of the alley that ran by the apartment. He came through the back door to buy the piles of papers the master of the apartment no longer needed. He tied them into bundles and weighed them, stuffed them into gunny sacks and paid the few cents they were worth—just a peddler.

Then he stood there dangling his scales, and the far-away look of a Hebrew prophet came into his eyes.

"The Bishop was a friend of mine," he said. "I miss him. Everybody misses him. That morning he died, I was in a street car. Some one next to me said: 'Bishop Fallows is dead.' It went up and down the car. People began wiping their eyes. They were doing that all over the city. Made things seem kind of dull and empty to have him gone. I'd wonder what was the matter. Then I'd think. 'Oh, yes, I ain't going to get that nice cheery bow from the Bishop any more. I don't believe he ever bowed to the President any nicer than he did to me in the alley. Say you know it made you feel sort of set up, as if you was somebody, to have a friend like him.

"I read in the papers the telegrams Harding sent about him and Taft and Pershing and Evangeline Booth—I forget them all. And General Dawes managed the military part of the funeral. All the big folks were doing something. I thought: 'yes, they were all friends of his, but so was I.'

"Knocked off worked the day of the funeral. I couldn't get into the church and I stood outside jammed into one of the biggest crowds I ever was in. But I read about it all. Say, I guess any man that made a stir in the city that wasn't there, that day, was on a vacation—the Mayor, and judges and bankers and ministers and everybody. They'd put flags around the church. The Bishop loved the flag. When he kissed it sometimes, it made your heart turn over. Sitting up in the Chancel were Rabbis and Roman Catholics and all kinds of Christians. They seemed to forget they were anything but a friend of the Bishop's that day.

"And to think of it, *I* was his friend, too. Us Jews had a meeting the other night—hundreds of us. We spent three hours just talking about him, what a friend he was to the Jews. 'We'll never have another friend like the Bishop,' we said."

The ragman dabbed at his eyes and blinked through the storeroom door at the great accumulation of outworn possessions a busy man had dropped behind him as he rose higher. "Everything belonged to him, I guess," he said, "and he belonged to everybody. He was everybody's friend."

To go on living in the hearts and lives of men—that was the Westminster of Everybody's Bishop.

APPENDIX

SAMUEL FALLOWS' CHRONOLOGY

1835. December 13th, born in Pendleton, Lancashire, England, son of Thomas and Anne (Ashworth) Fallows.

1848. Emigrated with parents to Wisconsin. Settled on farm at Deansville, Wisconsin.

Early schooling at home, at Aztalan, and Sun Prairie, Wisconsin.

1853. United with Methodist Church.

Taught first school at Fountain Prairie, Columbia County, Wisconsin.

1854. Licensed to preach.

Entered Preparatory Department of the University of Wisconsin.

1855–6. Divided time between University of Wisconsin and Lawrence University.

1857–9. Student at University of Wisconsin.

Assistant tutor in University.

Medina town superintendent of schools.

Assistant pastor of Madison Methodist Episcopal Church.

1859. Graduated at University of Wisconsin, valedictorian.

1859–61. Vice-president and principal of Galesville University.

1860. April 9th, married Lucy Bethia Huntington of Marshall, Wisconsin, daughter of William Pitkin and Lucy (Edwards) Huntington.

1861. Pastor of Methodist Episcopal Church, Oshkosh, Wisconsin.

1862. Granted M.A. degree, University of Wisconsin.

September 25th, Chaplain of the Thirty-second Wisconsin Infantry.

1863.   June 29th, resigned as Chaplain.

Appointed pastor of Methodist Episcopal Church, Appleton, Wisconsin. Also professor-elect of Natural Sciences at Lawrence University.

1864.   May 20th, appointed Lieutenant Colonel of the Fortieth Wisconsin Infantry, which he had largely recruited.

1865.   January 28th, appointed Colonel of the Forty-ninth Wisconsin Infantry.

October 24th, brevetted Brigadier General of Volunteers, "for meritorious services."

1865–8.   Pastor of Summerfield Methodist Episcopal Church, Milwaukee.

1866–74.   Regent of University of Wisconsin.

1868–70.   Pastor of Spring Street (Grand Avenue) Methodist Episcopal Church, Milwaukee.

1870–74.   State Superintendent of Public Instruction of Wisconsin.

1873.   Honorary degree of D.D. granted by Lawrence University.

1874–5.   President of Illinois Wesleyan University, Bloomington, Illinois.

1875.   Entered Reformed Episcopal Church; accepted rectorship of St. Paul's Church, Chicago.

1875–7.   Rector of St. Paul's Church, Chicago.

1876.   July 17th, at Ottawa, Canada, elected bishop of the Reformed Episcopal Church.

1876–1922.   Member of U. S. Grant Post, Chicago, G.A.R. Served terms as Commander and Chaplain of Post.

1876–1922.   Member of the International Order of Good Templars.

1877.   Visited England, in the interest of the Reformed Episcopal Church.

1877–9.   Presiding Bishop of the Reformed Episcopal Church. Engaged in church crusade.

1878.   Removed to Brooklyn.

Visited Bermuda.

1879.   Resumed pastorate at St. Paul's Church, Chicago.

1879–1922. Rector of St. Paul's Church, Chicago.

1882. President of Cook County Temperance Union.

Promoted the Christian Army and its organ, *The Battle Cry.*

1883. Vice-president of Chicago Red Cross.

Aided in organization of Associated Charities.

1886. New St. Paul's Church built on corner of Winchester Avenue and Adams Street, burned, and rebuilt.

Elected member of Victoria Institute, London.

1887. Member of Evangelical Alliance.

Director of American Medical Missionary Society.

1888. President of Northern Illinois Chautauqua Union.

1889–94. Presiding Bishop of the Reformed Episcopal Church.

1890. Founded the American Society of Patriotic Knowledge and its official organ, the *Home, School and Nation.*

Vice-president of the National Temperance Society.

Board member of the American Institute of Sacred Literature.

1890–1916. Chaplain of the Second Regiment of the Illinois National Guard.

1890–1922. Trustee of the National Society of Christian Endeavor.

1891–1912. President of the Board of Managers of the Illinois State Reformatory at Pontiac.

1892–3. Chairman of the General Committee of Education of the World's Congress Auxiliary of the World Columbian Exposition.

Founded People's Institute, West Side, Chicago.

Member of Municipal Voters' League.

1894. LL.D. granted by University of Wisconsin.

1894–1908. Lecturer on Mental Science, Bennett College of Eclectic Medicine and Surgery, Chicago.

1895. Opened Home Salon in attempt to meet the liquor problem.

1896. Founded and became Chancellor of the University Association which enrolled 60,000 members in 2,000 centers.

With clergymen of other denominations ordained General Ballington Booth as minister-at-large in St. Paul's Church.

1897–1900. Presiding Bishop of the Reformed Episcopal Church.

1898. Member of National Prison Association.

Tenders services for Spanish-American War.

President of Brigade Association composed of members of the 29th, 40th 41st, 48th, 49th and 50th Wisconsin Volunteer Regiments.

1899. Arbitrator of labor troubles in Chicago preceding the Fall Festival; also Chairman of Religious Exercises.

1899–1922. Vice-president Christian League for Promotion of Social Purity.

1901. Member of Executive Committee of the Chicago Federation of Religious Workers.

1902. Investigator of coal strike regions in Pennsylvania for Chicago Miners' Relief Committee of One Hundred.

1902–22. Presiding Bishop of the Reformed Episcopal Church.

1903. Representative at National Prison Congress and National Conference of Charities and Corrections from year to year.

Aided in rescuing Iroquois Fire victims.

1904. Director Illinois Anti-Saloon League.

Chairman Religious Committee of International Olympian Games.

Investigated strike at stockyards.

1905–7. Chairman Standing Committee on Discharged Prisoners of National Prison Association.

1905–12. Director Beulah Home and Memorial Hospital.

1906. Thirtieth Anniversary of election as bishop celebrated by St. Paul's Church.

1907–8. Chaplain-in-chief of the National Grand Army of the Republic.

Commander Military Order of the Loyal Legion, Department of Illinois.

1907–22. Trustee of the Chicago Church Federation.

1908–9. Patriotic Instructor of the National Grand Army of the Republic.

1908.   Inaugurated in Chicago movement for religious healing known as Christian Psychology or Religious
Therapeutics.

Assisted in founding League of Right Living.

Director of Central Howard Association for aid of
discharged prisoners.

Chairman of the Advisory Committee of the Temperance Law and Order Parade.

1909.   Address on Mission of Healing at Alaska-Yukon Pacific Exposition.

Member Advisory Committee of the National Peace
Congress.

Director of the Citizens' League of Chicago for the
Suppression of the Sale of Liquors to Minors.

Manager of the Chicago Bible Society.

1910.   April 9th, golden wedding anniversary celebrated at
the home of his son at Dobbs Ferry-on-the-Hudson.

1910–14.   Director of the Frances Juvenile Home Association.

1911.   Member Advisory Board Civic Federation of Chicago.

1912.   September 28th, President Civic Welfare Parade.

1913.   January-May, visit to China, Japan and the Philippine
Islands during which he investigated the educa-
tional, penological, social, industrial, political and
religious conditions of the archipelago. Went with
the strong personal recommendations of Taft, then
President, and with the hearty approval of General
Wood, Chief of Staff.

1913–15.   President of the Illinois Commission for conduct of
Celebration of the Semi-centennial of Negro Freedom, culminating in a great exhibition held for a
month in the Coliseum, Chicago.

1914.   On Standing Committee for Simplified Spelling.

October, presided at celebration of Peace Sunday,
Chicago.

1914–15.   Commander of the Department of Illinois of the
Grand Army of the Republic.

1915.   Dedicated tablet marking birthplace of Grand Army
of the Republic at Decatur. (Same flag used for

tablet dedicated to Samuel Fallows in 1923 presented to Illinois Wesleyan University by the Illinois Chapter of the Women of the Grand Army of the Republic.)

On committee of National Defense for Security League.

1915–18. World War activities.

1916. Honorary Vice-president of the National Young Men's Republican League.

June 3rd, Marshal, Clergymen's Division of the Preparedness Parade.

July 30th, death of Lucy B. Fallows, wife of Samuel Fallows.

1916–22. President of the Army of the Tennessee.

Chairman of the Commission for the Grant Memorial at Washington.

N.B.—Following years were so crowded with interests and activities that typical ones only have been chosen.

1917. President of the Wisconsin Society of Chicago.

On the Advisory Council of the Anti-Capital Punishment League.

Member of Committee on International Justice and Good Will of Federal Council of Churches of America.

Testified before United States Senate Committee on value of universal military training.

1918. Member of the General Wartime Commission of the Chicago churches.

May 23rd, dinner given by alumni of University of Wisconsin to Samuel Fallows, their oldest graduate, to celebrate sixtieth anniversary of his graduation.

1919–22. President and lecturer, Chicago Training School for Home and Public Health Nursing.

1920–22. Trustee International College for Music and Expression.

1920.   Patron of Relief for Jewish War Sufferers.
1921.   July 19th, open-air preaching from stepladder in Chicago Loop.

September 19th, with ex-Senator J. Hamilton Lewis, made address at opening of the Greater Fort Dearborn Hospital and Training School for Chicago Colored People.

September 26th, dedicated tablet marking place where first Grand Army of the Republic Encampment was held in Indianapolis.

November 5th, dedicated site for Memorial Union at University of Wisconsin.

November 13th, Armistice Day Service at St. Paul's Church addressed by Commander McCauley of the American Expeditionary Forces and General Milton Foreman.

1922.   April 27th, presided at dedication of the Grant Memorial at Washington.

May 30th, chaplain of the day for the Grand Army of the Republic at the dedication of the Lincoln Memorial at Washington.

June, spoke on Value of Science at University of Wisconsin commencement.

Visited California.

September 5th, died at Chicago.

Buried with his wife, Lucy B. Fallows, in Forest Home Cemetery, Chicago.

SAMUEL FALLOWS' LITERARY WORK

Editor, *The Appeal,* 1875ff.
Author: "Bright and Happy Homes," 1877; "The Home Beyond,"
1879; "Synonyms and Antonyms," 1884; "Handbook
of Abbreviations and Contractions," 1884; "Handbook
of Briticisms, Americanisms, etc.," 1884; "Liberty and
Union"; "Supplemental Dictionary of the English Language, 1887.
Editor, *Home, School and Nation,* 1890ff.
Author: "Webster's Encyclopædic Dictionary," 1891; "Past Noon,"
1892; "The Bible Looking Glass," 1898; "Life of Samuel Adams," 1898; "Splendid Deeds," 1900; "Popular
and Critical Biblical Encyclopædia," 1901; "Story of
the American Flag," 1903; "Science of Health," 1904;
"Christian Philosophy," 1905; "Memory Culture,"
1905; "Health and Happiness," 1908.
Editor-in-chief of the Human Interest Library.

CHILDREN OF SAMUEL FALLOWS

EDWARD HUNTINGTON FALLOWS: married Julia Haughton Kit-
tredge; daughter, Annette Richards.
HELEN MAY FALLOWS: married Rev. Edwin Sidney Williams, who
died November 9, 1918.
ALICE KATHARINE FALLOWS.
CHARLES SAMUEL FALLOWS: married Eda VanLeska Bruna;
daughters, Elizabeth Bruna and Patricia Edwards.

THE REFORMED EPISCOPAL CHURCH

By Dr. William A. Freemantle

Editor of "The Episcopal Recorder"

On December 2nd, 1873, at ten o'clock in the morning, there met in the Y. M. C. A. Hall, corner of 23rd Street and 4th Avenue, New York City, a group of clergymen and laymen who founded at that time and place the only Episcopal, Liturgical Church of the Reformed Faith using the English language. This apparently sweeping statement is borne out by the fact that the Reformation in England was never completely consummated, either in the sense of dealing with all the matters in question or in the sense of finally settling and legally adopting even those matters that were dealt with. The early death of Edward VI called a halt and the "heats and divisions" issuing were not healed owing to the succession of monarchs with varying allegiances to the English and Roman Churches. While the Anglican Church is known as the Reformed Church of England, it is reformed only in the sense of being separated from the Papacy. The present heated discussion which is going on in England with regard to the Prayerbook Services substantiates this statement.

It was this partially reformed Church that was brought to this Country by the Colonists and which, after the American Revolution, became the Protestant Episcopal Church in this Country. The original proposed Liturgy of 1785 was Protestant and upon it as a basis Dr. White of Philadelphia and Dr. Provoost of New York were consecrated Bishops by the Archbishop of Canterbury. Before the Church could settle down into a thoroughly Protestant Church, Dr. Seabury of Connecticut, uncanonically elected Bishop by the Connecticut Tory priests, no laymen voting, and refused consecration on that ground among others by the Archbishop of Canterbury, was consecrated by the non-juring Bishops of Scotland with the distinct understanding that he would medievalize the Church in America. The union of the Seabury Episcopalians with the Protestant Episcopalians, brought about lest there should be two Episcopal Churches in the Country, led to the shelving of the proposed Prayerbook of 1785 and opened the way for sacerdotalism to creep back into the Church.   Forty-four years later the Tractarian Movement led by Pusey, Newman and others, began in Oxford and spread to this Country.   Its purpose was to restore the teachings and practices of pre-Reformation days.   The House of Bishops of the Protestant Episcopal Church was petitioned again and again to arrest this tendency.   These petitions were at first firmly rejected and then finally unheeded.

The Evangelical Party in the Church was fighting three things: sacerdotalism, ritualism and exclusiveness.   The first they considered Romish; the second childish and the third unbrotherly and un-American.   They could not be Romish.   They did not wish to be childish.   They were determined to remain brotherly and American.   The issue therefore was clearly drawn and the cleavage apparent.   The controversy was a bitter one.   The Revd. Stephen H. Tyng, Jr., was tried for daring to preach in a Methodist Episcopal Church in New Brunswick, New Jersey, and the Revd. J. P. Hubbard of Westerly, Rhode Island, for exchanging pulpits with a Baptist minister.   The Revd. Charles Edward Cheney of Chicago, who had doubtless won the enmity of Bishop Whitehouse his Diocesan because he had signed one of the Evangelical Petitions, was placed on trial because, for conscience's sake he had undertaken to change a sentence in the Baptismal Service which clearly taught Baptismal Regeneration, and being condemned was placed on trial a second time for "contumacy" for presuming to continue his Ministry at the unanimous requests of his parishioners.   The matter ultimately reached the higher Civil Courts which decreed that the Ecclesiastical Court was not properly constituted and its findings therefore null and void.   These trials show the condition in the Protestant Episcopal Church at the time.

In 1873, during the month of October, the Evangelical Alliance met in the City of New York.   On the twelfth of that month a memorable Communion Service was conducted in the Fifth Avenue Presbyterian Church of which Dr. John Hall was then Pastor. Bishop George David Cummins, Assistant Bishop of Kentucky, took part in this Service, assisting in the distribution of the wine, as did also the Revd. Dr. R. Payne Smith, Dean of Canterbury. This action created a furor which issued in a treatment little short of persecution, and it became apparent to those within the Church, as also to those without, that the Protestant Episcopal Church had become committed to a form of worship essentially sacerdotal and a policy essentially exclusive.

Bishop Cummins therefore, resigned from the Protestant Episcopal Church on November 10th, 1873, and wrote to Bishop Benjamin Bosworth Smith, of Kentucky, in part as follows: "As I cannot surrender the right and privilege to meet my fellow Christians of other Churches around the table of our dear Lord, I must take my place where I can do so without alienating those of my own household of faith. I, therefore, leave the Communion in which I have labored in the Sacred Ministry for over twenty-eight years, and transfer my work and office to another sphere of labor." It was frantically stated at the time "that Bishop Cummins had stolen the Episcopacy and run off with it." The transfer of work and office to which Bishop Cummins referred was completed on December 2nd, 1873, when the Reformed Episcopal Church was organized in conformity with the following Declaration of Principles, Bishop Cummins being elected Presiding Bishop and the Revd. Dr. Charles Edward Cheney being consecrated Bishop shortly afterwards.

DECLARATION OF PRINCIPLES
OF THE
REFORMED EPISCOPAL CHURCH
ADOPTED DECEMBER 2, 1873

I. The Reformed Episcopal Church, holding "the faith once delivered unto the saints," declares its belief in the Holy Scriptures of the Old and New Testaments as the Word of God, and the sole rule of faith and practice; in the creed "commonly called the Apostles' Creed;" in the Divine institution of the sacraments of Baptism and the Lord's Supper; and in the doctrines of grace substantially as they are set forth in the Thirty-nine Articles of Religion.

II. This Church recognizes and adheres to Episcopacy, not as of Divine right, but as a very ancient and desirable form of Church polity.

III.   This Church, retaining a Liturgy which shall not be imperative or repressive of freedom in prayer, accepts the Book of Common Prayer as it was revised, proposed and recommended for use by the General Convention of the Protestant Episcopal Church, A.D. 1785, reserving full liberty to alter, abridge, enlarge and amend the same, as may seem most conducive to the edification of the people, "provided that the substance of the faith be kept entire."

IV. This Church condemns and rejects the following erroneous and strange doctrines as contrary to God's Word:

First. That the Church of Christ exists only in one order or form of ecclesiastical polity.

Second. That Christian ministers are "priests" in another sense than that in which all believers are a "royal priesthood."

Third. That the Lord's Table is an altar on which the oblation of the Body and Blood of Christ is offered anew to the Father.

Fourth. That the presence of Christ in the Lord's Supper is a presence in the elements of bread and wine.

Fifth. That Regeneration is inseparably connected with Baptism.

It is thus seen that the Reformed Episcopal Church returned to the position held by the early English Reformers and completed the work which they had only partially accomplished.   Therefore it is stated that the Reformed Episcopal Church is the only Episcopal Liturgical Church holding the Reformed Faith using the English language. .

The Church therefore witnesses to the great and eternal doctrines of the Protestant Reformation: to the unity of all believers in Christ Jesus by whatsoever name they may be called and to the parity of all properly constituted Ministeries in the Universal Church.   Upon this witness the Church has consistently acted by receiving into its membership without Confirmation, unless it is desired, those who come from other Churches; and by receiving into its Ministry without re-Ordination such as have been regularly Ordained in other Churches. Such re-Ordination is uncanonical..

In polity the Church is thoroughly democratic, providing for direct Parochial representation in its Councils and all such representatives voting as one House.

In oversight the Church is Episcopal, retaining whatever may be of value in its historic succession from Canterbury and according to Bishops their usual functions with spiritual and ecclesiastical leadership.

In worship the Church is Liturgical, using a revised Book of Common Prayer based on the original Book of 1785, and at the same time it not only permits, but encourages, the practice of extemporaneous prayer on all occasions of Public and Private Worship.

The Church therefore holds a strategic position between the Episcopal and Liturgical Churches and the non-Episcopal and non-Liturgical Churches. It witnesses, as it was founded specifically to do, to the possibility of Protestant reunion; and by its doctrinal position, its Episcopal yet democratic government, its Liturgical yet free Worship, it suggests the ultimate basis of reunion for Protestantism. Dr. W. A. Curtis, Professor of Systematic Theology in the University of Aberdeen, in his "History of Creeds and Confessions of Faith" states concerning the Declaration of Principles: "The Principles are obviously such as would form a basis of any reunion of Episcopal and Presbyterian and other Evangelical Churches."

It was inevitable therefore, that Samuel Fallows, Protestant to the core, broad in his sympathies, brotherly with a human inclusiveness, a lover of dignity and freedom in worship, should be drawn to the point of fascination to this Church of which he ever spoke with glowing face as "the Church of my earlier and latest love."

To the above statement the writer feels honored in being permitted to add a personal word.

Samuel Fallows is beyond all praise. It is not for me to eulogize him, but to pay a tribute of appreciation, sincere if inadequate, to his memory.

As a scholar, his knowledge was deep and broad. No mere pedant, he had a wide knowledge of men and life. Gifted with a mind keen to the point of subtlety, he absorbed knowledge. Many institutions of learning honored themselves by honoring him.

As a preacher he was unusually gifted. A splendid presence, a magnetic personality, a keen eye, a voice capable of any inflection, and movements marked by unusual grace, he preached the full Gospel of the love of God, mediated to us in the face of Jesus Christ. His lips were cleansed and consecrated to a tuneful eloquence that now and again became a lightning flash against wrong, and yet again a clarion call to arms on behalf of the oppressed.

As a bishop he was wise in counsel and brotherly in helpfulness. Few presiding officers were his equal, and it is to be doubted if any were his superior. His decisions were instant, and unlike many instant decisions, right. Always courteous, he was always firm. His grasp of a situation was comprehensive, and at times there was an almost playful friendliness about his presiding over a Council's deliberations.

The secret of it all was in the faith in which he accomplished his warfare. As expressed by himself that faith was "that love to God and to man is the essence of all religion, . . . the regeneration and uplift of the world therefore depends upon the regeneration and uplift of the individual. The march of mankind is ever upward and onward because Divine intelligence and love are the very heart of the Universe."

INDEX

Abbott, Lyman, 27
Addams, Jane, 309
Albany, 27
Allied Bazaar, 407
Allyn, Dr., 250
Alton, Ill., 209
Alumni Association of University of Wisconsin, 398
America and England contrasted, 47ff
American Magazine, quoted, 205
American Society of Patriotic Knowledge, founded by Samuel Fallows, 309
American working girls in 1848 contrasted with English, 30
Amherst, Mass., 174
Anderson, Bishop Charles P., 359
Angell, James B., President of Michigan University, 325
Angell, James R., President of Yale, 377
Anglican Church, 439
Annals of the Fortieth, quoted, 202
Anthony, Susan B., 216
Antietam, 186, 288
Apostolic Succession, 263
Appeal, The, 259
Appleton, Wis., 89, 103, 108, 194, 398
Arabia, 325
Armitage, Sir Elkanah, 6
Army of the Potomac, 227
Army of the Tennessee, 416, 420; reunion at Cincinnati, 288
Ashland, Wis., 398
Ashton, William, of Pendleton, boyhood Sunday School teacher, 277

Association of Commerce, Chicago, 398
Athenæan Society ("Ath"), 102, 113, 115, 119, 130, 131, 222
Atlanta, Ga., 275
Austin, George S., 214
Australia, 363
Ayer, Prof. Joseph C., 378
Aztalan, Wis., 36, 84, 86ff, 89

Baer, George F., 354
Ball, James, 282
Baltimore, Md., 24
Baptist Social Union, 295
Baptists, 51, 277
Barnard, Chancellor Henry, 161
Barnes, Clifford, 359
Barnum's Museum, 27
Barrows, Dr. John Henry, 325
Barry, Gen. William F., 405
Barton, Dr. William E., 359
"Bathhouse John." *See* John J. Coughlin.
Batten, Dr. Loring W., 326
Beaver Dam, Wis., 89
Beck, E. S., quoted, 343
Beecher, Henry Ward, 224
Beers, Thomas, 291
Belknap, Gen. William W., 288
Bell, Dr. Ernest, 359
Beloit College, 221
Ben Lomond, 24, 26, 43, 72
Benham, John, 234
Bennett Medical College, 364
Bernhardt, Sarah, 269ff
Biloxi, Miss., 418
Bird, Colonel, 37
Bird's Ruins (Marshall), 35, 37, 68
Birge, President E. A., 426

"Bishop's Beer," 332ff
Black Earth, Wis., 128, 195
Black Hand letter, 382ff
Bloomington, Ill., 265, 266, 317, 398
Bonney, Dr. Charles C., 338
Booth, Evangeline, 396, 427
Boston, 103, 106, 170, 221, 234, 280
Botkin, Alexander, 125
Bowen, Prof. Francis, of Harvard, 176, 181; gives advice, 173ff
"Bowlegged Dicky." See Richard Maymon.
Bradford, Ralph, quoted, 314
Bradley, George, 331
Bradley, Dr. Preston, 359
Bradshaw, George, 6
Bradshaw, John, 282
Bragg, Camp, 398
Bramwell, Dr. J. Milne, 378
Brandegee, Senator Frank B., 417
Brayton, storekeeper, 86ff, 89
Brewing, Bishop Willard, 426; quoted, 359ff
"Bridget." See Mrs. John Morissey.
"Bright and Happy Homes," published, 293
Brooks, E. P. (brother-in-law), 231
Brooks, Mrs. E. P. ("Helen" Huntington, sister-in-law), 137, 142, 158; quoted, 164, 177
Brooks, Rev. Jabez, 89ff, 199
Brooks, Phillips, 234, 258; and the Reformed Episcopal Church, 244, 244ff
Brown, George, 331
Brown, George F., 235
Brown, Dr. Sanger, 370
Brunswick Street Chapel, 11
Brunswick Wesleyan Church, Pendleton, 276
Brushingham, Rev. J. P., 331
Bryan, William Jennings, 403
Buffalo, 27, 31

Burnside, General A. E., 227
Butler, Samuel, quoted, 179

CABOT, DR. RICHARD C., 378
Calais, 292
Calhoun, John C., 105
California, 360
Callao, Peru, 23, 71, 74
Cambridge University, 20, 101, 170, 233
Camp Bragg, 398
Camp meetings, Americanizing agents, 53; Americanizing effects of, 55ff; description of, 56; horse-trading at, 59
Canada, 278, 348, 363
Cantacuzene, Princess, 419
Canterbury, Archbishop of, 277, 439
Carman, Bishop Albert, 272
Carmel, Calif., 421ff
Carr, Prof. Ezra S., 126
Carr, Gen. Julian S., 420
Carter, Walter H., 214
Cartwright, Peter, 53, 182, 330
Castles, G., 331
Cathedral Shelter, 238
Central Howard Association, 384
Central Music Hall, 269
Chalmers, Dr. Thomas, 139
Channing, William Ellery, 118, 133, 139, 156
Charity Organization, founded, 307, 308
Charles City, Ia., Samuel Fallows lectures on Idols, 227
Charleston, S. C., 274, 275, 276
Chartist Movement, 23
Chautauqua, N. Y., 295
Chautauqua circuit, Samuel Fallows lectures on, 293
Cheney, Bishop Charles Edward, 234, 239, 240, 241, 244, 255, 257, 258, 285, 291, 339, 359, 360, 399, 440, 441; minister at Christ Church, 235ff; and Bishop Whitehouse on Infant Baptism,

236ff; first trial of, 236ff; second trial of, 237; elected bishop, 242; consecrated bishop, 242; consecrates Samuel Fallows bishop, 272; death of, 390

Chicago, 67, 89, 197, 205, 249, 251, 252, 261, 278, 291, 297, 299, 343, 351, 422, 440; in the '50's, 234ff; in 1875, 253ff; religious unrest in, 254ff; street car travel, 257; characteristics of, in '70's, 258ff, 266ff; Bible reading in schools, 267ff; revival meetings, 270; at end of '70's, 280ff; West Side, 282ff; West Side, characteristics of, 284; Hell's Knuckle, 285; problems of, in late '80's, 296; Republican Convention in, 297ff; trebles its size, 298; West Side, slipping in popularity, 299; wakes to needs of other half, 307; World's Fair, 315, 323ff; strikes in, 319ff; processions in, 339; experiences trouble in building postoffice, 346ff; Fall Festival, 346; West Side in 1900, 357ff; a melting pot, 405

Chicago Alumni Association, University of Wisconsin, 397, 413

Chicago American, 343

Chicago Church Federation, 384

Chicago Examiner, quoted, 368

Chicago Herald, 407; quoted, 318ff, 322, 393, 395ff

Chicago Inter-Ocean, 296

Chicago Sons of Veterans, 287

Chicago Tribune, 254, 342, 343; quoted, 205, 332, 405

Chicago Wisconsin Alumnae, 413

Children's Court, 317

Christ Church, Chicago, 398; ownership in question, 237

Christian Army, purpose of, 284

Christian Endeavor Convention in New York, 318

Christian Endeavor Society, 360

Christian Psychology, 364, 368,

369, 370, 373, 375, 377; explained, 365ff; treatment of cases, 370ff; reëducation of patients, 372

Christian Science, 364, 368

Christy's Minstrels, 27

Church clinic, 370

Church Federation, 139, 359

Church of England, 239

Cicero, Ill., 398

Cincinnati, 325; G.A.R. Reunion, 288

Circuit riders, 52ff, 85, 117, 270

Civil War, 185ff; Antietam, 186, 288; Emancipation Proclamation, 186; 32nd Wisconsin Regiment part of General Sheridan's command, 186; fall of Holly Springs, 188; 8th Wisconsin Infantry, 189; 32nd Wisconsin Regiment, 189; Hundred Day Call, 194ff; 40th Wisconsin Infantry, 197ff; Forrest's Raid, 201; 40th Wisconsin Infantry in Forrest's Raid, 201ff; 49th Wisconsin Infantry, 204ff; 13th Missouri Cavalry, 207; veterans of, 285; Gettysburg, 288

Claflin, Governor William, of Massachusetts, 228

Clark, A. H., editor San José *Herald-Mercury,* 379

Clark, Mrs. A. H., 319

Clem, Gen. J. M., 420

Coal strike in Pennsylvania, 129

Coffee House Movement (England), 328

Cohoes, N. Y., 31; in 1848, 30

Coleman, Edward, Lt. Col. of 49th Wisconsin, 204

Collins, Chief of Police Morgan, quoted, 360

Collins, Dr. William Russell, quoted, 350

Colman, Dr. Henry, 109, 111

Columbia University, 172ff, 228

Columbus, Wis., 90

Confederate representation at Grant Memorial, 417

Congregationalists, 153

Cook, Dr. Edward, President of Lawrence University, 109, 111

Coolidge, President Calvin C., 420

Cornell University, 227

Coughlin, Alderman John J. ("Bathhouse John"), 346ff; quoted, 347

Courant, The, quoted, 231

Cox, Gen. J. D., 288

Craig, A. J., State Superintendent of Public Instruction, 219, 222, 230

Cridge, Rev. Edward, consecrated bishop, 272

Cromwell, Oliver, 47

Crouch, Thomas, 235

Crowe, "Pat," 382

Cub who became editor, 345

Cummins, Bishop Geo. D., 441; assistant bishop of Kentucky, 241; organizes new church, 242; consecrates C. E. Cheney bishop, 242; death of, 272

Curley, Mr. William A., quoted, 343

Curtis, Dr. W. A., 443

"Daddy" Reed. *See* Clem Reed.

Dames of the Loyal Legion, 386, 419

Daniels, Prof. William W., 161

Dansville, N. Y., health resort, 281

Dante, quoted, 299

Darrow, Clarence, 405

Davies, Sister, 184

Dawes, Gen. Chas. G., 131, 427; quoted, 191; gives dinner for Pershing, 297

Dawes, Rufus C., quoted, 288ff, 297

Dawes, Gen. Rufus R., 288, 297

Day, Mrs. T. C. ("Kittie" Hunt-ington, sister-in-law), 137, 142, 158, 176, 177

Deach, Mrs. Inez R., 376, 424

Deansville, Wis., 119

Debs, Eugene, 224, 346

Declaration of Principles, Reformed Episcopal Church, 441ff, 443

Deneen, Senator Charles S., and parole law, 312

Devoll, Charley, 206; quoted, 198ff, 203

Diaz, Porfirio, President of Mexico, 346

Dill Pickles Club, 416

Dinsmore, Captain, 207; quoted, 208

Dixons, the George W., 359

Dodge, Gen. Greenville M., 416

Dow, Neal, 331

Drummond, Henry, 271, 277, 408

Dubois, Dr. Paul, 377

Du Page County, Ill., 398

Ecclesiastical Court, 432

Eckhart, Bernard A. ("Barney"), 217, 282, 346

Edens, William G., 348

Edinburgh, 277

Education: in Wisconsin in '40's, 65ff; cost of, in early Wisconsin, 77; and religion, 105ff; old system of education ending in '59 and new one beginning, 159; Galesville University, 161ff; salaries of teachers in '50's, 162; Harvard in 1861, 170ff; lack of graduate courses at American universities, 171ff; characteristics of old system and of new, 219ff; character of, in Wisconsin, 221; importance of Teachers Institutes, 222; pioneer experiment in University Extension, 249ff

Edward VI, 439

Eighteenth Amendment, 286, 328

Eleventh Illinois Infantry, 405

Eliot, Chas. William, President of Harvard, 228; Samuel Fallows meets (1871), estimate of, 228

Elmira Reformatory, 312

Elmore, R. P., 214; parrot of, 214

Emancipation Proclamation, 186

Emerson, Ralph Waldo, 224; quoted, 111

England, 363

English, Rev. Dr., quoted, 216ff

Erie Canal, 27ff

Ernst, William E., 338

Evangelical Alliance, 241, 440

Evangelical Party, Protestant Episcopal Church, 432

Evangelical Petitions, 440

Evans, Dr. W. A., 369

Evanston, Ill., 89

Evening Wisconsin, quoted, 213ff

FAIRCHILD, CHARLES, 228

Fairchild, Governor Lucius, of Wisconsin, 219, 227; offers Samuel Fallows military secretaryship, 231

Fairchild, Mrs. Lucius, 420

Fall Festival Committee, 348

Fallows, Anne (sister). *See* Mrs. William Knapton.

Fallows, Anne Ashworth (mother), 6, 7, 8, 9, 18, 22, 24, 27, 28, 38, 39ff, 42ff, 44, 50, 62, 63, 67ff, 69, 72, 73, 74ff, 81, 82ff, 85, 86, 93, 107, 110, 122, 124, 129, 137, 165ff, 239; reaction to American customs, 45ff; attends camp meeting, 51ff; changes the destinies of two, 78ff; death of, 194

Fallows, Annette Richards (granddaughter), 379, 419

Fallows, Charles Samuel (son), 293, 369, 376, 395; quoted, 422

Fallows, Mrs. Charles S., quoted, 421

Fallows, Daniel (brother), 9, 22, 69, 70, 73, 74, 84, 85, 88, 396; at sea, 23; stories of, 71ff; desires to go to gold fields, 75ff

Fallows, Mrs. Eda Bruna. *See* Mrs. Charles S. Fallows.

Fallows, Edward Huntington (son), 227, 228, 229, 244, 265, 268ff, 269, 380, 392, 395, 406, 419, 425

Fallows, Mrs. Edward H., 419

Fallows, Elizabeth Bruna ("Queen Bess," granddaughter), 422

Fallows, Fearon, astronomer, 19ff

Fallows, Helen (daughter). See Mrs. Edwin Sidney Williams.

Fallows, John (brother), 15, 22, 27, 48, 51ff, 63, 70, 81, 82, 85, 90, 99ff

Fallows, Lucy Bethia (wife), 139ff, 146, 158, 175, 176ff, 193, 194, 213, 224, 229, 239, 243, 244, 251, 253ff, 268ff, 270, 272ff, 276, 280, 281, 282, 283, 293, 299, 305ff, 311, 319, 337, 363, 382, 389; courted by Samuel Fallows, 141ff, teaches at Medina, 147; a Unitarian, 153; characteristics of, 156ff; struggle to become a Methodist, 157ff; becomes a Methodist, 159; preceptress of Galesville University, 161ff; in training as minister's wife, 182ff; first child born, 191; strongly Methodist, 239; helpmeet, 240ff; spiritual struggle of, 259ff; described, 264ff; letter to, 275; meets a crisis, 301ff; golden wedding anniversary, 379ff; last days, 386; death of, 388

Fallows, Mamie (daughter). See Mrs. Edwin Sidney Williams.

Fallows, Patricia Edwards ("Princess Pat", granddaughter), 422

Fallows, Samuel, childhood, 5ff; birth of, 7; schooldays, 11ff; in Warrington, England, 15; in Manchester, 18; ancestry, 19ff;

arrives in America, 26ff; excitements of canal travel, 28ff; family settles near Bird's Ruins, 38; first days in Wisconsin, 41ff; appeal of America to, 45; attends first camp meeting, 49ff; difficulties of early schooling, 62ff; caught by gold craze, 75ff; begins to earn his way, 86ff; attends Sun Prairie school, 89; teaches Gravel Church School, 91ff; attends University of Wisconsin, 99; joins the Athenæan Society, 102; attends Lawrence University, 108; espouses cause of woman suffrage, 110; LL.D. granted by Lawrence University, 112; makes first speech, 114; converted, 120ff; receives license to exhort, 122; the "Boy Preacher," 128; influence of Wm. P. Huntington, 133; early liberalism, 139; courts Lucy Huntington, 141ff; decides to enter the ministry, 148; tries out vice-presidency of Galesville University, 158; graduates, valedictorian of class, 159; vice-president at Galesville University, 161; seeks chaplaincy at first call, Civil War, 168; marriage of, to Lucy Hethia Huntington at Cedar Bluffs (Marshall), 168; goes to Harvard, 170; first parish at Oshkosh, 181; elected chaplain of the 32nd Wisconsin Infantry, 184ff; letters to his wife, 191ff; accepts parish at Appleton, 194ff; agent of Lawrence University, 194; appointed to professorship in Lawrence University, 194; recruits for 40th Wisconsin Regiment, 195; Lieutenant Colonel of 40th Wisconsin Infantry, 197ff; leads 40th Wisconsin Infantry in Forrest's

Raid, 201ff; recruits 49th Wisconsin Infantry, 204; commissioned colonel, 204ff; commander of post at Rolla, Mo., later St. Louis, and of first sub-district of Mo., 208; pastor at Summerfield Church, Milwaukee, 213; defends temperance, 215; pastor of Spring Street Church, Milwaukee, 215; supports woman suffrage, 216; State Superintendent of Public Instruction, 219ff; advocate of new system of education, 220ff; defends co-education in University of Wisconsin, 220; regent of University of Wisconsin, 220; letter to his wife, 227; meets President Chas. W. Eliot of Harvard, 228; completes plan for unifying state education, 231; helps secure free college education for Wisconsin students, 231, offered presidency of four colleges, 231; weighs changing denominations, 233ff, 240ff; accepts presidency of Illinois Wesleyan University, 243; pledges himself to Reformed Episcopal Church, 244; President of Illinois Wesleyan University, 249ff; introduces new departments at Illinois Wesleyan, 249; starts pioneer experiment in University Extension, 249; resigns from Illinois Wesleyan University and accepts call to St. Paul's Reformed Episcopal Church, Chicago, 251; pastor at St. Paul's, 253ff; editor of *The Appeal,* 257ff; philosophy of service in letter to his wife, 261; decides against Bible in schools, 267; elected and consecrated bishop, 272; appointed missionary bishop, 272; engages in church crusade, 274ff; letter to his wife,

275; Presiding Bishop of church, 276ff; visits England, 276; continues church crusade in United States, 277ff; chaplain for House of Representatives, 278; moves family to Brooklyn, 278; elected Presiding Bishop, 278; resumes rectorship of St. Paul's, 279ff; helps organize Christian Army, 284; chaplain of Veterans Union League, 286; speech at Army of Tennessee reunion, 288ff; pleads for acceptance of Martin offer, 291; lectures on Chautauqua circuit, 293; letters to his wife, 293ff; influence on young men, 296; pleads for ecclesiastical emancipation of women, 296; chaplain at Republican Convention, 297; chaplain of 2nd Regiment, 297; meets his vestry, 299ff; makes a choice, 301; founds American Society of Patriotic Knowledge and *Home, School and Nation*, 309; Presiding Bishop of church, also Bishop of Canada and the West, 309; compiles Webster's Encyclopædic Dictionary, 319; president Board of Trustees of Illinois State Reformatory, 311ff; on "Do Reformatories Reform?" 312; makes his first important speech on arbitration, 318; takes up cudgels for labor, 318ff; founds People's Institute, 231ff; preparing "Past Noon," 321; president Reformatory Board, 321ff; chaplain of 2nd Regiment, 321; participates in World's Fair, 323ff; chairman of General Committee on Education of World's Congress Auxiliary of World's Fair, also chairman of Special Committee on Public Instruction, 324ff; founds Home Salon and spon-

sors non-alcoholic beer, 327ff; as journalist, 336ff; methods of work, 336ff; founds University Association, 338ff; founds *World To-day,* 338ff; and Fall Festival, 347; chairman of Committee on Religious Services at Fall Festival, 347ff; officially investigates coal strike region, 351; vitality of, 353; at seventy, 357ff; illustrates his religion of optimism, 362; starts Christian Psychology movement (Health and happiness movement), 363; publishes "Science and Health," 364; publishes "Health and Happiness," 376ff; celebrates golden wedding anniversary, 379; makes trip to Philippines, 379ff; G.A.R. Department Commander of Illinois, 384; lectures on Chautauqua circuit, 384; presiding bishop; 384; at eighty, 386ff; in the World War, 391ff; town chaplain of Chicago, 394ff; advocates military training before United States Senate Committee, 396; shifts base, 400ff; celebrates peace, 403ff; takes up problems of peace, 405ff; letter in defense of Mercier, 407; at eighty-five, 411; his secret of happiness, 412; defends short skirts, 413ff; universality of Jewish opinion of Samuel Fallows, 415; president of the Army of the Tennessee, 416; presides at dedication of Grant Memorial, 420; chaplain at dedication of Lincoln Memorial, 420; attends his last Commencement at University of Wisconsin, 420; defends teaching of science in University of Wisconsin, 420; goes to California for vacation, 421; last days in Chicago, 423ff; death, and funeral services, 426ff;

tributes paid, 427; his Westminster, 428; appreciation of, by
Dr. Wm. A Freemantle, 443 ff
Fallows, Thomas (father), 8ff;
27, 31, 35, 42ff, 47, 49, 50, 63,
74, 85, 165ff; moves to Warrington, 15; suffers business
reverses, 21ff; moves to
America, 26ff; buys Wisconsin
farm, 38ff; attends camp meet-
ing, 51ff
Fallows, William (brother), 13ff,
15, 22, 24, 27, 28ff, 32, 35ff,
38ff, 41, 44, 46, 49, 51ff, 63,
69, 82, 83, 85, 88
Faris, Rev. Mr., 272
Farwell, Arthur Burrage, 359
"Father Tom," 285
Ferguson, Sgt. Leander, 183
Fifer, Governor Joseph W., 311
Fifth Ave. Presbyterian Church,
441
Finnegan, Richard J. ("Dick"),
editor of *Chicago Journal*,
quoted, 340, 344
Fisher, George, 331
Foch, Marshal Ferdinand, 400
Follansbee, Alanson, 214
Fond du Lac, Wis., 104, 129
Force, Gen. Manning F., 288
Forrest, Gen. Nathan B., 201
Forrest's Raid, 201ff, 204
Forsyth, Misses Jessie and Chris-
tina, 310
Fortieth annals of, 202
Fort Sheridan, Ill., 398
Fort Sumter, 274, 276
Fortieth Annals of, 202
Fortieth Wisconsin Infantry,
197ff; in Forrest's Raid, 201ff
Forty-ninth Wisconsin Infantry,
204ff
Foster, Geo. H., 214
Foster, Rev. John, 424
Foster, Dr. R. N., 224
Foster, Volney W., 349
Fountain Prairie, Wis., 90
Freemantle, Rev. Dr. William A.,
quoted, 336; gives history of

Reformed Episcopal Church, 439
Fribley, Mrs. Wilbur E., quoted,
361
Fuller, Melville W., Chief Justice,
235, 236
Fulton, J. L., 282, 283
Fulton, Mrs. J. L., story, quoted,
283; quoted, 302
Fundamentalists, 415

GALE, JUDGE GEORGE, 167, 169,
221; founds Galesville Uni-
versity, 162ff
Galesville, Wisconsin, 159, 167,
234
Galesville University, 161ff; cost
of course, 163
Gardner, H., 120ff; quoted, 122
Gardner, Commissioner Washing-
ton, 417
Garland, Benammi, 129
Geer, Prof. Curtis M., 326
Gettysburg, 288, 391
Gibbons, Cardinal James, 309
Gilman, Prof. Stephen, 230
Gladstone, interview with, 277
Glover, Joshua, fugitive slave, 129
Gold discovered in California, 74ff
Goldfield stories, 76
Good Templars, International
Order of, 267
Gough, John B., 267
Grand Army of the Republic, 315,
398; holds meeting in Boston,
227; influence in politics, 287;
reunions in '70's and '80's,
287ff; U. S. Grant Post,
Chicago, 287; reunion in Cin-
cinnati, 288; Samuel Fallows
Department Commander of
Illinois, 384; women of, 384
Grant, Col. Frederick D., funeral
of, 385
Grant, Mrs. Frederick D., 419;
quoted, 358

Grant, Gen. Ulysses S., 186; banquet to, 280

Grant Memorial, Washington, 416, 417, 418; dedication, 420ff; significance of, 420

Grant Post, U. S., Chicago, 287

Gray, Mr., 282

Green, Elder, 81, 83, 90, 94, 127

Gresham, Gen. Walter Q., 288

Gunsaulus, Dr. Frank W., 359

HADLEY, Mass., 174, 239

Hadley Congregational Church, 156

Hall, Azariah, 66, 77, 83, 84, 86, 94, 119, 120ff, 127, 134, 141, 148

Hall, Frank W., 84, 127; quoted, 358, 415ff

Hall, Dr. John, 241, 441

Hall, Mrs., 84

Hall, Robert, 139

Hamilton, Major-Gen. Schuyler, 189

Hamline, Bishop Leonidas L., 330

Hanchettville (Marshall), 38, 99

Hand, Elbert, 126

Happy Club, 368, 369, 373

Harding, President Warren G., 427; quoted, 417

Harper, President William R., of Chicago University, 346

Harris, U. S. Commissioner William T., 325

Harrison, Benjamin, nominated in Chicago, 298

Hart, Mrs. Harry, 359

Hart family, the 54

Harvard University, 138, 168ff, 176, 227ff; in the '60's, 170ff

Harvey, Mr., teacher, 89; influence of, 84; assists Samuel Fallows, 88ff; superintendent of schools at Beaver Dam, Wis., 89

Harvey, Mrs., Widow of Gov. Louis P. Harvey, 189

Hauser, Capt., quoted, 208

Hayes, President Rutherford B., 288

Haywood, William G., 343

H'Doubler, Alice Bemis (Mrs. Frank), 413

Health and Happiness movement, 363, 370

"Health and Happiness" published, 376ff

Healy, Col. Jas. J., president Veterans Union League, 286

Hendrick Hudson, 31

Hernando Road, 201

Hesperian Society, 113, 130, 222

Hickenlooper, Gen. Andrew, 288

High, James L., 128, 199; adjutant of the 49th Wisconsin Infantry, 204

Hinkle, Prof. Beatrice M., 378

Hirsch, Rabbi Emil G., 285, 364, 368

Historic Succession, 242, 443,

"History of Creeds and Confessions of Faith," 443

Holmes, Oliver Wendell, 223, 309

Holt, Dr. Luther E., 61

"Home Beyond, The," published, 293

Home Salon, temperance experiment, 328ff; success of, 335

Home, School and Nation, 337ff; founded by Samuel Fallows, 309

Homestead strike, 318

Hoover, Herbert C., 394

House of Bishops, Protestant Episcopal Church, 231, 233, 440

Howard City (Marshall), 38

Howe, Col. Jas. H., 183, 187, 189, 240, 253,

Hubbard, Rev. J. P., 440

Hudson River, described, 27

Hughes, Charles Evans, 214

Hugo, Victor, quoted, 303

Hull House, 295

Hundred and Thirty-second Illinois National Guard Reg. (formerly 2nd Reg.), 394

Hunt, Gen. Henry J., 288

Hunter, Rev. Mr., 272

Huntington, Bethia, 175ff; quoted, 176

Huntington, Dan, 175

Huntington, Mrs. Dan (grandmother of Mrs. Lucy Bethia Fallows), 156

Huntington, Elizabeth Whiting *See* Mrs. Dan Huntington.

Huntington, Ellery Channing (brother-in-law), 262ff

Huntington, Flora (sister-in-law), 137

Huntington, Bishop Frederic Dan, 157, 175, 228, 239ff, 260; visits Madison, 243; ordains brother, 243

Huntington, Frederick Sargent (brother-in-law), 158, 176, 260; death of, 310

Huntington, Helen. *See* Mrs. E. P. Brooks.

Huntington, "Kittie." *See* Mrs. T. C. Day.

Huntington, Lucy Bethia. *See* Mrs. Lucy Bethia Fallows.

Huntington, Lucy Edwards. *See* Mrs. Wm. P. Huntington.

Huntington, Dr. Wm. Edwards (brother-in-law), 134ff, 137ff, 141, 158, 199, 260, 379, 419, 420; first lieutenant 49th Wisconsin Infantry, 204

Huntington, William Pitkin, 141, 158, 167, 259ff, 264ff; shapes Samuel Fallows, 133ff; ordained deacon by Bishop F. D. Huntington, 243

Huntington, Mrs. William P., 136, 158, 177, 259, 263

Hyde, Prof. Charles Cheney, 339

"IF CHRIST CAME TO CHICAGO," by William T. Stead, 327

Illinois College of Dentistry, 414

Illinois Legislature and Temperance, 266

Illinois Senate and temperance, 266

Illinois State Reformatory, reformatory boys as borrowers, 309; Samuel Fallows appointed president of Board of Trustees, 311; growth of, 311ff; methods at, 311ff; indeterminate sentence, 312ff; parole system, 312ff.

Illinois Wesleyan University, 243, 249ff; music department, 249; law school started, 249; pioneer in granting degrees *in absentia*, 249

Insull, Samuel, 405

International Order of Good Templars, 267

Iowa, 325

Ireland, Archbishop John, 285

Iroquois Theatre fire, 361

Italian Commission, 398

JACKSONVILLE, FLA., 277

Janet, Prof. Pierre, 377

Japan, 363

Jaques, Prof., 262

Jastrow, Prof. Joseph, 377

Jenkins, Miss (Mrs. A. H. Clark), 379

Jewish opinion of Samuel Fallows, 415

Jewish ragman pays his tribute to Samuel Fallows, 427ff

"Joe" of the Pension Office, quoted, 417

Joffre, Marshal Joseph J. C., 393

"John, Prof." *See* John Sterling.

Johnston, Dr. Howard A., 359

Johnston, William, quoted, 360ff

Joinville, Prince de, 105

Jones, Judge and Mrs. Burr, 420

Junior Republic, 311

KEITH, D. W., 235

Keith, E. G., 235
Kellogg, Amherst W., 214
Kellogg, Anson P., 243
Kellogg, Dr. Louise Phelps, 214, 243
Kellogg, Prof. Romulus O., 109
Kenosha, Wisconsin, 398
Kenosha Monument, 287
Kent College of Law, 398
Kentucky, 433
Kilpatrick, Gen. Hugh J., 227
Knapton, William, 83
Knapton, Mrs. William (sister), 13, 22, 27, 41, 44, 51ff, 63, 82ff, 85
Knapton family, the, 51, 54
Ku Klux Klan, 416, 424
Kuh, Dr. Sidney, 370

LABOR and the Fall Festival, 346ff
La Crosse, Wisconsin, 162, 165
Lakin, George W., 214
Landis, Judge K. M., 359
Lang, Charley, 206; quoted, 207
Latané, Rev. James A., 272
Lathrop, Chancellor John H., 159
Laurier, Sir Wilfred, 346
Lawrence, Hon. Amos, 106, 221; founds Lawrence University, 103ff
Lawrence College, 398
Lawrence University, 89, 95, 99, 113, 123; founding of, 103ff; co-educational, 106; customs and studies, 108ff; women at, 109ff; Samuel Fallows agent of, 194; appoints Samuel Fallows professor, 194; Dr. Steele, president, 214; in '70's, 221
League of Nations, 406
League of Right Living, 377
Leonard, Lillian. See Lillian Russell.
Lepper, Rev. Howard A., quoted, 206, 286ff, 292, 394
Life Underwriters, 384
Lincoln, Abraham, 186, 194, 196

Lincoln Memorial, 420
Liverpool, England, 24, 26
Logan, Gen. John A., 285
Logan, Mrs. John A., 419
London University, 250
Lord, Daniel M., 346
Lost Dauphin (Eleazar Williams), 103, 104, 108; story of, 105ff.
Louise. See Mrs. Walter West.
Low, President Seth, of Columbia, 325
Lowden, Ex-Governor Frank O., 393, 405
Loyal Legion, 287
Luther, Martin, 254
Lutherans, 277

McCLAUGHRY, Major, Pontiac Superintendent, 314
McCloskey, Col. Manus, 414
McDowell, Mary E., 359; quoted, 320
McDowell, Bishop Wm. F., 339
McElroy, Col. John, 417
McKinley, William, 346, 347, 348; quoted, 349
McMahon, Mr., 387
McRoy, Samuel, 235
Madison, 49, 99, 107, 124, 132, 159, 165, 189, 196, 207, 228ff, 243, 398; first circus in, 21; first sermon at, 52; described, 100; lecture course in '50's, 117
Malines, Belgium, 407
Manchester, England, 9, 18, 23, 24, 30, 32, 36, 38, 69, 100; described, 5, 18ff; on Saturday night, 19
Manchester Free Grammar School, 18, 22, 100
Manchester Guardian, 23
Mann, Horace, 118
Markle, John, 353
Marriage of Samuel Fallows and Lucy B. Huntington at Cedar Bluff, (Marshall), 168

Marshall (Bird's Ruins), Wisconsin, 38
Martin, C. K., 214
Martin, Edward, 292; offers land to Reformed Episcopal Church, 290
Martin School of Theology (*see* also University of the West), 290
Mary Tudor, 292
Mathews, Dr. Shailer, 338
Maxwell, Chas., 235
Maxwell, Edward, 235, 251
Maymon, Richard ("Bow-legged Dicky"), 5, 6, 11ff, 16, 127
Meade, Gen. George, 227
Meister, Wilhelm, quoted, 33
Memphis, Tenn., 186, 197, 201
Men's Club, Trinity Reformed Episcopal Church, 398
Mercier, Cardinal Desiré J., 406ff
"Merry Vestrymen," the, 282ff
Metchnikoff, Elie, 374
Methodism, 259; in early '70's, 232ff.
Methodist Episcopal Church, 261, 263, 432; Samuel Fallows' estimate of, 154ff; attitude of, toward Samuel Fallows, 265ff
Methodists, 153, 258, 277; educational zeal, 104
Mexico, 363
Millennialists, 415
Miller, Prof. Dickinson S., 378
Milwaukee, Wisconsin, 35, 55, 75, 78, 139, 214, 216, 218, 228, 234, 253; in 1848, 32; Decoration Day, 225
Milwaukee Female College, 139
Milwaukee Sentinel, 216; first use of newspaper illustrations in United States, 215
Miners' Relief Committee of One Hundred, 351, 352, 353
Mitchell, John, 352
Modernists, 415
Montreal, 277
Moody, Dwight L., 270ff.

Morissey, Mrs. John (Bridget), 311, 313
Mormonism, 341
Morton High School, Cicero, Ill., 398
Moulton, Prof. Richard Green, 322
Moyer, Dr. Harold, 368, 370
Municipal Voters' League, 327
Murray, Father, 349
Muzzy Sardine, family, 54
Mystic Athletic Club, 398

Naperville, Ill., 398
National Army, 398
National Prison Association, 312
National Tribune, 417
National Women's Christian Temperance Union, 267
Nelson, Lord Horatio, 13, 19
New Brunswick, N. J., 440
Newman, F. L., 331
New York, 26, 234, 280, 315, 440 described, in 1848, 27
New York Tribune, 68
Newman, Cardinal John Henry, 432
Nicholson, Bishop Wm. R., 272
Nightingale, Rev. Thomas, 10
Nixon, Penn, 346
"Normalites" at University of Wisconsin, 220
Northampton, Mass., 174
Norton, Dr. Wm. B., quoted, 342
Noyes, Major David K., 204
Nyack, N. Y., 278

O'Brien, L. T., 331
Ocean Grove camp meeting, 278
Ochsner, Dr. A. J., 424
Oconomowoc, Wisconsin, 233
Oconomowoc camp meeting, 225; speech, 232
O'Donnell, Hugh, 318
O'Donnell, Patrick, quoted, 349

O'Hara, Ex- Lieutenant Governor Barrett, quoted, 359, 415
"Old Man Vilas." *See* Judge Vilas.
Older, Fremont, editor *San Francisco Call,* quoted 343ff
Olson, Judge Harry, 1
Oshkosh, Indian chief, 181
Oshkosh, Wisconsin, 104, 187, 207, 398; in '60's, 181
Oxford University, 18, 19, 22, 100, 101, 226, 233, 432

PALMER, S. W., 275
Parkhurst, Dr. Chas. H., 333
Parkinson, Prof. John B., 420
Parliament of Religions, 325
"Past Noon," 321
"Pat," of University of Wisconsin, 101
Patrick, Dr. Hugh, 370
Patton, Dr. Francis L., 255
Peck, Commissioner Ferdinand W. ("Ferd"), 297, 346
Pegler, A., quoted, 342, 358
Pendleton, England, 5, 7, 10, 15, 54, 239
Penology, Pontiac Reformatory, 311ff; reformatories justified, 312; Elmira Reformatory, 312; reform statistics, 312
People's Institute, 327; founded by Samuel Fallows, 321ff
Perham's Panorama, 27
Pershing, General John J., 427; quoted, 297, 417
Peterson, Dr. Frederick, 378
Philadelphia, 126, 234, 276, 278, 280, 291; Centennial Celebration, 273
Philippines, 297, 315, 425
Phillips, Wendell, 118, 133
Pierce, Franklin, 348
Pineville, S. C., 275
Pittsburgh, Penn., 318
Polk, James Knox, 46, 55, 74
Pontiac Reformatory, 312

Pope, Gen. John, 288
Porter, Philander, family, 54
Porter's Schoolhouse, 122
Potter, Bishop Henry C., 329
Powers, Thos. H., death of, 278
Presbyterians, 51, 153, 277
"Prof. John." *See* Prof. John Sterling.
Protestant Episcopal Church, 233, 242, 243, 244, 258, 439ff, 440 441ff; House of Bishops, 231, 233, 440; Evangelical Party, 440
Provoost, Dr. Samuel, 439
Psychology of early West, 60
Purdunn, C. A., member of Pontiac Board, 315
Pusey, Dr. Edward B., 440
Putnam, Dr. James J., 378

QUEEN VICTORIA, 8, 46, 122

RAILWAY TRAVEL in America contrasted with England, 29ff
Rainbow, 24
Rankin, Rev. J. E., 277
Read, Prof. Daniel, quoted, 364
"Red Barrett," 358
Red Cross, 398
Reed, Clem ("Daddy"), 315, 316ff; quoted, 313ff
Reed, Elizabeth Armstrong, Mrs. (mother of Myrtle Reed), 337
Reed, Myrtle, 337
Reed, Principal, 165
Reedsburg, Wis., 226
Reformed Episcopal Church, 249, 255, 261, 263, 398, 439ff; and Historic Succession, 242, 443; organized, 242, 441; possibilities of, 244; crusade of, 274ff; generosity of other denominations toward, 277ff; unique appeal of, 278ff; general council of '83 accepts Martin offer, 290; general council of '85 rejects Martin offer, 290; synod of Chicago and

Martin offer, 291 ; later value of Martin land, 292; early history of Anglican church in England, 439ff ; history in America, 439ff ; Cheney trials,440; early history, 440; Evangelical Party, 440; Evangelical Alliance meets in New York, 440ff ; Whitehouse-Cheney controversy, 441 ; Bishop G. D. Cummins resigns from Protestant Episcopal Church, 441; Declaration of Principles, 441ff, 443; description of church beliefs, 442ff ; appeal of, to Samuel Fallows, 443

Religion, early Methodist camp meeting, 49ff ; Wesleyan Methodists' opposition to camp meeting, 50; women preachers in England, 50; mission of circuit riders, 52ff; educational zeal of Methodists, 104ff; attitude toward Unitarians in '59, 153; characteristics of Congregationalists, 153; of Presbyterians, 153; of Methodists, 153; denominational exclusiveness in '59, 153ff ; appeal of Methodism, 157; characteristics of Methodism in early '70's, 232ff ; attitude toward skeptics in 1875, 254; passing of personal salvation ideal, 255ff ; unrest sign of progress, 260; camp meetings and revivals compared, 270

Religious Therapeutics (see also Christian Psychology), 365ff

Republican Convention, 297

Robertson, Dr. John Dill, 416

Robins, Raymond, 392

Rolla, Mo., 206

Rood, Hosea, 206

Roosevelt, Theodore, 343, 354; quoted, 392ff

Royce, Josiah, 378

Rudolph, Bishop Robert L., 419, 426

Russell, Lillian, 268

St. John, Everett, 282

St. Louis, 209, 280

St. Marks Reformed Episcopal Church, 398

St. Paul's Reformed Episcopal Church, 251, 253, 273, 279, 281, 282, 301, 309ff, 357, 368, 386, 388, 424; purchases American Reformed Church, 258; dedicated, 258; friendliness of, 283; sells Washington St. Church, 292ff; builds new one, 292ff; interior burned and rebuilt, 292ff; presents Samuel Fallows with flag, 415

St. Stephens, 275

St. Thomas Church, 11

Salaries of ministers in '60's, 217ff

Salvation Army, 284, 396

Sampson, William, 104

San Francisco, 315, 347, 422

San Francisco Call, 343

San Francisco Chronicle, 379

Sankey, Ira D., 270

Sartain's Magazine, 110

Saxe, John G., 117

Schurz, Carl, 159

"Science of Health," published by Samuel Fallows, 364

Seaborne, Mrs. Eliza, 387, 388, 397, 399

Seabury, Dr. Samuel, 439

Second Regiment Illinois N. G., 297, 301, 321, 388

Selfridge, Harry, 296

Semi-centennial of Negro Freedom, 341, 384

Serbia, 325

Seneca Falls, N. Y., 21

Seneca Falls Convention, 110

Sexton, Postmaster James A., 286

Shaftesbury, Earl of, 328

Shepherd, Jessie, 413

Sherman, Gen. William T., 288; quoted, 289

Sheridan, Gen. Philip H., 227 288

Sherrill, Col. C. O., quoted, 417

Shrimski, Israel, 425
Slaughter, Philip, 125
Slavery in Oregon, 55
Smith, A. S., 282
Smith, Bishop Benjamin Bosworth, 242, 441
Smith, Gerrit, 133
Smith, "Gipsy," 359
Smith, roommate, 124, 143
Smith Rev. Dr. R. Payne, 441
Smith, Rev. Silas, 56
Smith, Brig. Gen. T. C., quoted, 209
Smithfield Market, 19
Society of Psychical Research, 364
Somerset Club, speech of Samuel Fallows before, quoted, 329
Sonne, Rev. E. J., 421
Southard, Dr. E. E., 378
Southport, England, revisited, 277
Southport excursions, 14
Spiritualists, 415
Spooner, Sen. John C., 195, 200
Spring Street Church, Milwaukee, 218
Spurgeon, Chas. H., 277
Stanton, Elizabeth Cady, 216
Starr, Miss Ellen G., 309
Stead, William T., 327
Steele, Dr. George M., President of Lawrence University, 214
Sterling, Prof. John W., 101ff, 104, 115, 118, 126, 132; influence on Samuel Fallows, 101ff
Stevens, Bishop P. F., work among negroes, 274ff
Stoltz, Rabbi Joseph, 359
Stone, Dr. John Timothy, 359
Stone, Melville E., 282
Stone, Rev. S. M., 104
Storrs, Rev. Dr. Richard S., 309
"Story of the American Flag," by Samuel Fallows 396
Student Miscellany, 129
Summerfield Church, Milwaukee, 218, 241, 282
Sun Prairie, Wis., 55, 56, 89

"Supplemental Dictionary," Samuel Fallows prepares, 337
Sussex, Duke of, 20
Swing, Prof. David, 255, 285, 364
"Synonyms and Antonyms," published, 293

TAFT, LORADO, 347
Taft, William Howard, 288, 342, 395, 427; quoted, 403ff
Tallmadge, J. J., 214
Taylor, Bayard, 118
Taylor, Dr. Graham, 348, 359; quoted, 385, 401
Taylor, Rev. John, 128, 195, 200
Taylor, Zachary, 55
Teachers Institutes, 222, 223
Temperance, 45, 215; Sons of Temperance, 56; temperance movement in Illinois, 266ff; Eighteenth Amendment, 286; limitations of temperance movement, 328; opposition of liquor interests to Home Salon, 334ff
Thirteenth Missouri Cavalry, 207
Thirty-second Wisconsin Infantry Regiment, 183, 185ff, 186, 190, 194, 398
Thomas, Dr. H. W., 255, 285, 364; convicted of heresy, 256
Thomas, John W., quoted, 395
Tibbles, Mr., 148
Titus, E. H., 301, quoted, 296
Tolson, Prof. George T., 378
Touzalin, the Misses, 376
Tractarian Movement, 440
Training School for Home Nursing, 416
Travel, hardships of, in '70's, 226ff
Tuckey, Dr. Lloyd, 378
Tuthill, Judge Richard S., 359
Tyng, Rev. Stephen H., Jr., 440

UNDERWOOD, FREDERICK D., 354; quoted, 217ff

Unitarianism, 153ff, 259

University Association, founded by Samuel Fallows, 338ff; enrolls 60,000 people in 2,000 centers, 338

University Extension and community centers, Samuel Fallows makes pioneer demonstration of, 321

University of Aberdeen, 443

University of the West, 257, 262, 292; planned, 244; ideal for, 258; significance of, to Samuel Fallows, 290

University of Wisconsin, 297, 397, 398, 420; in 1854, 99ff; Athenæan Society, 102, 222; Hesperian Society, 113, 222; cost of living at, in '50's, 123ff; class of '59, 125; quality of students in '50's, 125ff; course of study, 126ff; devotion of professors, 126; Samuel Fallows editor of *Student Miscellany*, 129; early pranks at, 131ff; embryo athletics, 131; class of '64 graduates in field, 195; in war time, 195; "Normalites," 220; pioneer in new system of education, 220; in '70's, 221; women as "bachelors," 230; made head of Wisconsin educational system, 231; commencement, 1921, 413

Upham, Fred, B., 346

Van de Bogart, Mrs. Minnie, 375, 381ff

Veterans of Civil War, 285

Veterans Union League, 285ff 286, 287

Vienna, 325

Vilas, Judge Levi B. ("Old Man Vilas"), 113ff., 115

Vilas, U. S. Postmaster General William F., 113, 231

Vincent, Bishop John H., 295

Vittum, Harriet, 359

Viviani, Premier René, 393

Volstead, Andrew J., 266

Wacker, Charles H., 359

Wales, Prince of, 8

"Walker," 191; adopts the chaplain, 189; death of, 192

Walker, Annie J., quoted, 264ff

Walker, John, 282

Walworth County, 223, 224

Warner, Gen. Adoniram J., 288

Warner, Charles Dudley, quoted, 298

Warrington, England, 15ff, 18, 30, 47, 48, 54, 239

Washington, D. C., 277, 297, 419

Washington Park, Chicago, 398

Waterloo, Wis., 55, 56

Watertown, Wis., 55, 59, 164

Waukesha, Decoration Day, 225

Waukesha County Fair, 225

"Webster's Encyclopædic Dictionary," compiled by Samuel Fallows, 310

Weeks, Secretary of War John W., 417

Wesley, John and Charles, 45, 226, 233, 254

Wesleyan Chapel, Warrington, 47

Wesleyan Methodist Church, 10

West, Louise (Mrs. Walter), 418

Westerly, R. I., 432

West Side, Chicago, 299

Westminster, Duke of, 328

White, Bishop William, 439

White, Dr. William S., 374, 399

Whitehouse, Bishop Henry J., 241, 255, 440; made bishop of Illinois and sent to Chicago, 233ff; and Bishop Cheney, 235ff; builds cathedral, 238

Willard, Frances E., 267, 331

Willett, Dr. Herbert L., 359

Williams, Rev. Edwin Sidney, 387, 389; death, 404

Williams, Mrs. Edwin Sidney

("Mamie" and Helen), 214, 227, 228, 229, 264, 369, 376, 387 388ff, 404, 422, 426

Williams, Eleazar. *See* Lost Dauphin

Wilmarth, Mrs. Mary, 325

Wilson, George, 331

Wilson, Rev. Jos. D., 272

Wilson, Thomas, 340

Wilson, (Thomas) Woodrow, 388

Wisconsin, 74, 344; described, 22; population in '48, 31; alien law, 31; admitted to union, 32; contrasted with England, 35ff, 39ff; early history, 37; effect on Fallows family, 40ff; early trading in, 45; early religious services, 48; camp meeting in '48, 49; pioneer fare, 51; attitude of farmers toward education, 65ff; scarcity of reading matter, 68; debt to teachers, 85; lead mining, 128; attitude toward fugitive slave law, 129ff; the Forty Thieves, 130; religion in '59, 153ff; hardships of travel in, 226ff; Bible reading in schools, 267ff

Wisconsin State Historical Society, 197

Women, First Woman's Rights Convention, 21; Seneca Falls Convention, 110; Samuel Fallows espouses woman suffrage cause, 110; position at Lawrence University, 111; Samuel Fallows' support of woman suffrage, 216; Samuel Fallows pleads for ecclesiastical emancipation of women, 296; of the G.A.R., 384

Woodworth, Robert S., 378

Woolsey, Pres. Theodore D., of Yale, 228

World To-day, founded by Samuel Fallows, 338ff

World War, 390ff

World's Congress Auxiliary, 324ff

World's Fair, 315, 323ff, 338, 347; World's Congress Auxiliary of, 324; Parliament of Religions, 325

Worthington, Mass., 293

Wright, A. M., 282

Young, Ella Flagg, 359

Young, Rev. Joseph, 272

Young Ireland Rebellion, 21

Y. M. C. A., 296, 384, 396, 398

Y. W. C. A., 384